Also by Gordon G. Chang

The Coming Collapse of China

NUCLEAR
SHOWDOWN

Gordon G. Chang

NUCLEAR
SHOWDOWN

North Korea Takes On the World

RANDOM HOUSE / NEW YORK

Published in the United States by Random House,
an imprint of The Random House Publishing Group,
a division of Random House, Inc., New York.

RANDOM HOUSE and colophon are registered
trademarks of Random House, Inc.

Library of Congress Cataloging-in-Publication Data
Chang, Gordon G.
Nuclear showdown : North Korea takes on the world / Gordon G. Chang.
p. cm.
Includes bibliographical references and index.
ISBN 1-4000-6294-2
1. Nuclear weapons—Korea (North) 2. Korea (North)—Military policy. 3. World
politics—21st century. 4. Nuclear nonproliferation—Korea (North) I. Title.
UA853.K5C43 2005
355.02'17'095193—dc22   2005052067

Printed in the United States of America on acid-free paper

www.atrandom.com

1 2 3 4 5 6 7 8 9

FIRST EDITION

Book design by Dana Leigh Blanchette

To Lydia—

Maybe not always in the past,
but today and forever

History is the sum total of things that could have been avoided.
— Konrad Adenauer,
   first West German chancellor

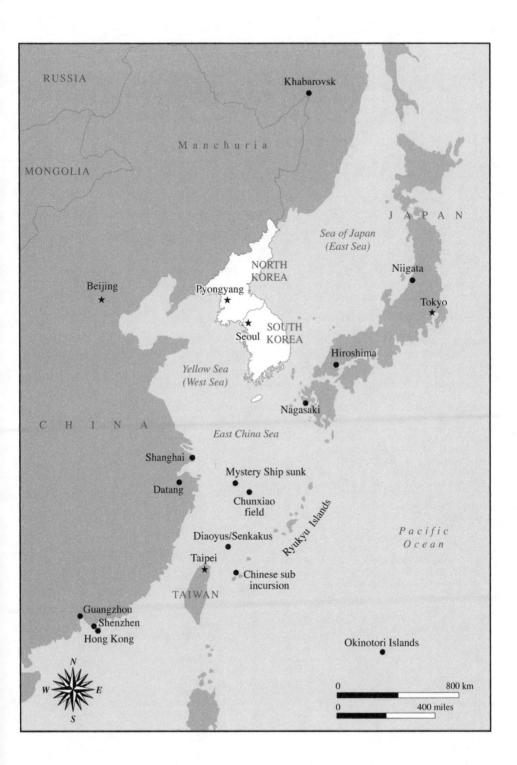

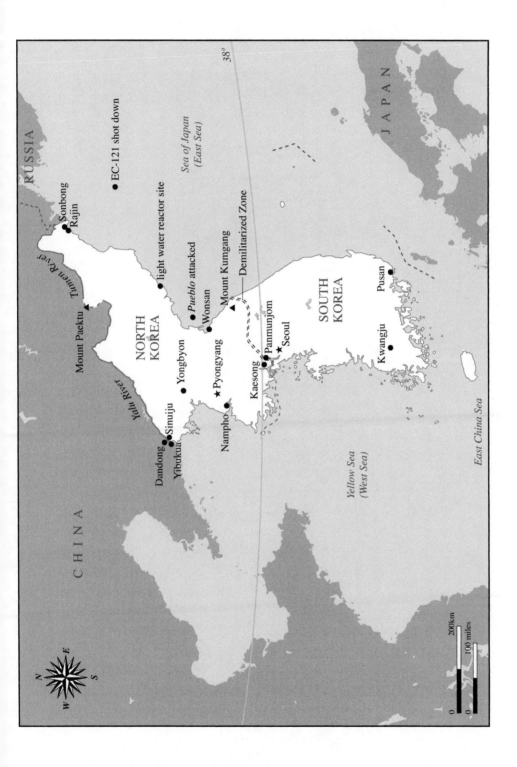

Contents

Note on Romanization of Korean Names

Koreans have their own alphabet, Hangul, which has twenty-four letters, ten of them vowels. Unfortunately, there is more than one way to romanize their widely praised language. In general, this book uses a simplified version of the McCune-Reischauer system. It also adopts the Korean practice of placing the surname first.

Nonetheless, there are many exceptions to these general practices in the pages that follow. First, on the belief that everyone has the right to romanize his or her own name, I have used such preferred romanizations whenever possible. Therefore, South Korea's first president is referred to as Syngman Rhee, its most famous autocrat as Park Chung Hee, and its most important dissident as Kim Dae Jung. Second, North Korean names are romanized in the manner used by Pyongyang's official Korean Central News Agency. Third, this book generally displays people's names as they are found in the sources I used when I did not know their preferred romanizations.

Foreword

North Korea Takes the World Backward

On the nuclear issue, it is five minutes to midnight.
—Lawrence Eagleburger, former secretary of state

"If we lose, I will destroy the world," said Kim Jong Il, supreme leader of North Korea. His renegade country publicly acknowledges that it possesses nuclear weapons, and he has repeatedly threatened to turn our planet into a battlefield. Will he change the course of human events with an act of unimaginable devastation?

The Democratic People's Republic of Korea, as North Koreans call their homeland, already has enough plutonium for between seven to ten nuclear devices. Analysts argue about the size of the DPRK's stockpile, but the exact number of weapons today is almost beside the point. It is one thing to have a handful of them, it's yet another to build the industrial capacity to accumulate an arsenal. North Korea, a country that cannot feed its people, is gearing up to make nuclear weapons on an assembly-line basis by reprocessing plutonium and, it appears, enriching uranium.

At the same time, the diminutive Kim Jong Il casts his shadow from his capital city of Pyongyang across the Pacific Ocean and onto the continental United States. The unbalanced autocrat already possesses long-range missiles that can reach the fringes of the American homeland. In a few years—probably as early as the beginning of the next decade—no city in North America will be safe from Kim's warheads of mass destruction.

Even today, all humanity is at risk. In 2003 a North Korean diplomat told an American envoy that his destitute country might "transfer" its weapons to others, thereby threatening to make itself the world's "nuclear Kmart." American intelligence believes Kim has already sold processed uranium to Pakistan, so the merchandising of completed weapons is all too possible. Who wants to live in a world where anyone with cash and a pickup truck can incinerate a city?

Yet the North Korean threat goes well beyond a single horrible detonation. Kim's Korea was the first—and so far only—nation to withdraw from the nuclear nonproliferation treaty. The DPRK, however, has paid no price for destabilizing world order. On the contrary, a frightened international community has rushed to provide material assistance to the North Korean regime as if small gifts would miraculously constrain Kim Jong Il's menacing behavior. Unfortunately, other leaders of rogue states have taken note of the ineffectual, if not feeble, reaction to Pyongyang's direct challenge. As a result, within a decade the world could see the creation of new—and hostile—nuclear powers as the global nonproliferation regime falls apart. The best period in human history could soon be followed by the worst. The stakes could not be larger.

Unfortunately, no one knows how to deal with North Korea. Neither friend nor foe has had much influence on the fanatical and militaristic state, not even the mightiest nation in history. The United States was able to defeat the Soviet Union in a worldwide struggle spanning decades, but for more than a half century Washington has been bedeviled and even humbled by Pyongyang. Kim, unlike anyone else in recent times, has shown Americans the limits of their power.

The United States had better figure this one out fast because geopolitical trends are working against its vital interests. China, Pyongyang's "blood" ally, is gaining strength and succeeding in reducing American influence in Asia and elsewhere. South Korea, nominally Washington's partner, is asserting itself and moving quickly into China's and North Korea's camp. Tokyo was headed in that direction as well but stopped short at just about the last moment due to ordinary citizens' outrage over Pyongyang's kidnapping of a thirteen-year-old Japanese schoolgirl. Russia, the other great power with an interest in the Korean peninsula, is adjusting to a China-centric world and beginning to acknowledge Beijing's primacy. Nowhere is the erosion of American influence so visible as the place it counts most: emerging Asia. If the United States cannot protect its vital interests against a small adversary—and so far it's not been able to do so— who will ally with Washington in the future?

North Korea was considered an "intractable" problem before, but now the challenges are even greater for the lone superpower. In an epoch it is supposed to dominate, America has been reduced to relying on China— *the other side's best friend*—to craft a solution critical to its future.

What kind of policy is that? Perhaps the only viable one. Diplomacy and engagement have not worked. Few Americans today would support a policy friendly toward a society that one former European official said is "beyond evil" and "exists in a parallel moral universe." Containment has no chance when North Korea's neighbors won't cooperate. War, the final option, could result in a million casualties by the end of the first day. The available choices, in the words of a senior official in the administration of President George W. Bush, "range from the deeply unsatisfying to the incredibly risky." Reliance on China, therefore, is the last remaining option in the minds of many analysts. The hope is that Beijing will decide to become a responsible power and impose the right solution on Pyongyang.

And do so in time. Ordinary North Koreans, oppressed for more than a half century, are beginning to remake their country from the bottom up. Economic stagnation and failure since the 1970s left their government without the means to feed and care for many peasants, workers, and even soldiers, so abandoned Koreans had to find ways to survive. As they did so, society changed in ways undermining the regime's mechanisms of control. Kim Jong Il's rule, therefore, is under pressure from the lowest rungs of the social order. He has reacted to this societal strain by undertaking increasingly reckless geopolitical behavior to obtain assistance and support from the international community. However effective his diplomacy may be, he has not been able to stop the forces of transformation inside his borders. That means, at a minimum, Kim will be continually forced into increasingly precipitous behavior as he seeks to buttress his rule in the years ahead.

If Washington finds it difficult to solve the ongoing nuclear crisis, it's because there are too many moving parts both inside North Korea and around Northeast Asia. The struggle with Kim Jong Il is complex. In this contest, where the currents are against Washington, the critical factor is not power but finesse. And time. As Joel Wit, a former State Department official, says, "It may be too late to stop what's going on in North Korea."

Washington, despite appearances, has not yet lost this critical test of will. But if the United States runs out of the world's most precious commodity as Wit suggests, there will not be much future for the American-led international order, which has brought peace and prosperity to the world.

This is now a crisis like no other, perhaps the moment of greatest consequence for the twenty-first century.

September 2005

NUCLEAR
SHOWDOWN

1

KU KLUX KOREA

America Creates a Renegade Nation

People that are really very weird can get into sensitive
positions and have a tremendous impact on history.
—Dan Quayle, former American vice president

North Korea insults us. Its very existence is an affront to our sense of de-
cency, perhaps even to the idea of human progress. At a fundamental level
it challenges our notions of politics, economics, and social theory. The
Democratic People's Republic of Korea—or DPRK as it calls itself—is not
only different, but abhorrent.

We abhor something we do not understand. The nation ruled from
Pyongyang is seemingly impenetrable; natural and artificial barriers wall it
off. Yet the biggest impediment to comprehending North Korea is its very
nature: the country defies conventional characterization. We call it communist—but it hardly resembles the other four nations sharing that label.

After all, communism, which claims to be the wave of the future, implies modernity. North Korea, on the other hand, is not just backward, it is essentially feudal, even medieval. Many say that the nation is Stalinist, but that's true only in the broadest sense of the term. Joseph Stalin himself would have been uncomfortable had he ever visited Pyongyang. The regime founded by Kim Il Sung is a cult possessing instruments of a nation-state, a militant clan with embassies and weapons of mass destruction. Kim, unrestrained by normal standards of conduct, created an aberrant society of almost unimaginable cruelty. North Korea is in a category by itself.

It is, from almost any perspective, the worst country in the world. The University of Chicago's Bruce Cumings, known for nuanced views, calls the nation "repellent," and American analyst Selig Harrison, always sympathetic toward Pyongyang, admits it's "Orwellian." Even leftist Noam Chomsky notes the country is "a pretty crazy place." How could any nation go so wrong?

The Unfortunate Peninsula

It took centuries of tragedy to produce today's Koreans, who have endured five major occupations and about nine hundred invasions during their history. Unfortunately for them, the Korean peninsula is where China, Japan, and Russia meet, and so their nation has historically been a prize for powerful neighbors. Yet as painful as its story has been, the last century and a half has been particularly harsh for "the shrimp among whales," as the people of Korea call their homeland. Perhaps it is no coincidence that this is also the period since the United States became involved in Korean affairs.

America's first contact with the Hermit Kingdom was a memorable occasion, at least for the hermits. In 1866 the *General Sherman*, a steam schooner, chugged up the Taedong River toward Pyongyang. After ignoring warnings to turn back from the locals, who were not interested in either American trade or Christian religion, the ship was torched and the crew killed and dismembered.

Despite the unpleasantness in the Taedong River, the Koreans eventually found some use for Americans. In 1882 they signed the Treaty of Amity and Commerce with Washington. This pact, their first with a Western nation, was intended as a defensive measure to ward off Korea's more immediately threatening neighbors.

The Korean king danced with joy on the arrival of the first American envoy, but that was premature: in a few years Washington would sell out their newfound Korean friends. The Japanese and the Russians were both interested in controlling Korea, and Tokyo proposed dividing the peninsula into spheres of influence along the 38th parallel. The tsar refused. These two powers could not peacefully reconcile their expansionist ambitions. The Japanese humiliated Moscow's forces in the Russo-Japanese War of 1904–05, the first defeat of a European power by an Asian one in modern history. President Theodore Roosevelt brokered the peace, which confirmed Japanese control over Korea. As part of the deal, Washington secretly obtained Tokyo's assurance that it would not challenge its control of the Philippines. Roosevelt received the Nobel Peace Prize for his efforts.

An American won the award, and Korea paid the price. As a result of Roosevelt's peace, Japan occupied Korea in 1905 and annexed the place outright five years later. In obliterating the Korean nation, the Japanese brought an end to one of the longest imperial reigns in Asian history, the Choson Dynasty, founded in 1392. Japan's occupation was especially cruel: the peninsula's new masters tried to kill off the concept of Korea. They forced their subjects to take Japanese names and tried to expunge the Korean language. Japan imported Shinto, its religion, and taught a new history to schoolchildren. Millions of Korean men and women were impressed into the Japanese war effort, many taken from their homeland. Koreans had to swear loyalty to the emperor in Tokyo.

It took Japan's defeat in World War II to end the occupation. Although Japanese troops went home, Korea, which technically did not exist during the fighting, was the Second World War's big loser. The Cairo Declaration of 1943 stated that "in due course, Korea shall become free and independent," but events—and the Allies themselves—conspired against the Korean people. America, concerned about the casualties resulting from a potential invasion of the Japanese homeland, persuaded the Soviet Union to declare war against Tokyo, which it finally did on August 8, 1945, just seven days before the emperor capitulated. Washington slammed the door on a Soviet occupation of Japan but permitted Moscow a slice of Korea. The Red Army, without firing a shot, invaded the northern part of the Korean peninsula on August 9.

Washington had given no thought in the closing days of the war about what to do with Korea. There were no American troops there, and to avoid a Soviet takeover of the whole peninsula the United States hastily proposed its division. As August 10 became the 11th in the American capital, two junior American Army officers, consulting a *National Geographic* map, picked the 38th parallel as the border for "temporary" occupation zones. By selecting a line with historical significance, Lieutenant Colonel Dean Rusk, later to become secretary of state, and his colleague inadvertently signaled to Moscow that the United States recognized the tsar's old claim to the northern portion of Korea. Whatever the Soviets thought, they accepted, and honored, the proposed dividing line. Korea, which had been unified for more than a millennium, was severed.

Korea's division was an afterthought. There was no justification for the act—if any country deserved dismemberment, it was Japan. In different times, there might have been no consequence to the last-minute decision to split the peninsula into two. In the global competition developing between Moscow and Washington, however, the stopgap measure took on significance. As every business consultant knows, there is nothing as permanent as a temporary solution, and Korea proved this proposition. National elections, to be sponsored by the United Nations, were never held. Eventually each side established its own client state. The American-backed Republic of Korea was officially proclaimed on August 15, 1948, and the Soviet-supported Democratic People's Republic of Korea was officially born less than a month later.

The new arrangement was in trouble from the beginning. Each of the two states claimed to be the sole representative of the Korean people, and both of them were raring for a fight. Neither big-power sponsor stayed around long to restrain its young ward. Soviet troops were off the Korean peninsula by late 1948, and the Americans decamped by June 1949. Two jealous children were left to settle their fate in zero-sum fashion. Both sides conducted guerrilla raids and battalion-size incursions across the 38th parallel.

On June 25, 1950, Kim Il Sung, the North's leader, initiated full-scale war by sending his tanks and troops south. President Harry Truman intervened immediately to stop what he perceived to be a Soviet test of Western resolve. The United Nations, prompted by Washington, showed remarkable resolve of its own: for the first time in history a world organization decided, in the words of historian David McCullough, "to use armed force to stop armed force."

Despite the unified response of the West, Kim's reunification policy almost succeeded. The North Koreans took Seoul in less than a week and had almost the entire peninsula under their control in a little over a month. Kim's forces were then beaten back almost to the Chinese border by troops from seventeen countries under the United Nations command led by General Douglas MacArthur. Chinese "volunteers" crossed the Yalu River into North Korea beginning in late October and pushed the American-led coalition south of Seoul by the end of 1950. During the remainder of the war the United Nations forces—primarily Americans—advanced only slightly northward during a period of essentially stalemated conflict.

The fighting during the "Great Fatherland Liberation War," as the North Koreans call it, lasted for three years and one month. Negotiations went on almost as long: they continued for two years and nineteen days. There were 158 plenary sessions before the parties could agree, and even then they only arrived at an interim arrangement, a cease-fire. To this day there has been no treaty formally ending the conflict, so the war technically continues.

Although South Korea ended up with slightly more territory than it started with, Seoul did not sign the armistice. Its leader, Syngman Rhee, wanted to keep marching northward. At the time, he looked like a warmonger. In retrospect, Rhee was right: America could have avoided more than a half century of suffering and turmoil caused by North Korea.

The failure to prevail in the early 1950s profoundly shapes Korean politics today. "Death solves all problems," Stalin once said, but in Korea it only exacerbated them. Blood spilled in war hardened differences, and a division that was seen as temporary has, with the passage of more than five decades, taken on an air of permanence. During the conflict China is thought to have lost somewhere between 900,000 and a million soldiers, including Mao Zedong's son. Almost 40,000 foreign troops fighting under the United Nations banner perished in Korea. And three million Korean civilians died along with over a half million soldiers from both halves of the peninsula.

For many Korean families the war is still a sharp memory. In the broader context of things, the conflict is another unhappy chapter in the country's turbulent history. But the conflict, as horrible as it was, became the defining moment of the Democratic People's Republic of Korea and for its founder, Kim Il Sung. Where we see stalemate, North Koreans perceive victory. The North Korean state is built on lies, distortions, and untruths of all sorts, but the most important of them says that Americans started the war and that Kim Il Sung beat back the aggression.

Americans, of course, do not subscribe to the DPRK's version of history, yet Kim's fabrication, like all good ones, was formed around a tidbit of truth. The Korean was correct in believing he had dealt a setback to the United States in the war. He had, after all, managed to do something that even Uncle Joe Stalin had not accomplished: at the height of the power of the United States he had dented, if not destroyed, the aura of American military superiority. After a magnificent show of determination in Europe during the Berlin Airlift of 1948 and 1949, American resolve failed in the mountains of Korea in 1950 to 1953. Stalin got it right when he noted that the Americans, armed with "stockings, cigarettes, and other merchandise," could not subdue "little Korea." "What kind of strength is that?" he asked.

Defeating Kim Il Sung and his Chinese allies would have been expensive, time-consuming, and bloody, but the United States, with the world's strongest military, could have prevailed. Washington believed that any American escalation of the fighting would have been matched by Moscow, but that was a misconception of the highest order. Contrary to American belief, the Korean War was not authored in the Soviet capital and Kim Il Sung was not Stalin's puppet. The war was Kim's idea, to bring about reunification of his peninsula. It is true that the Korean leader sought and obtained Moscow's and Beijing's approval to start hostilities, but it was his war nonetheless. China, which had the desire to fight, did not have the capacity to defeat the United States; the Soviet Union, which had a superb army, lacked the incentive. Washington simply underestimated its ability to win.

The West floundered many times during the Cold War, but, after the collapse of the Soviet Union, most of those mistakes no longer mattered. Yet it is still too early to predict that the Allies will escape the consequences of their misadventure in Korea five decades ago. The war has yet to be concluded by treaty, Pyongyang still poses a major threat to world security, and despite appearances of cooperation today, the contest between the two Koreas continues because Kim Jong Il has yet to give up his family's goal of ruling the entire peninsula.

It is too harsh to call the West's involvement in the Korean War a defeat, but it has many of defeat's trappings. Americans, for example, are embarrassed by the conflict and sometimes call it the Forgotten War. In 2003 *Time* picked eighty days that changed the world in its eighty years of publication. Not one event from the Korean War was considered worthy enough to be selected. The debut of *Star Wars* made the grade in *Time*'s list, but none of the moments of a real war. From the American perspective of the twenty-first century, more than four million people died for nothing.

Yet as much as Americans may want to forget, no person in North Korea does. By now, the people of the United States should have learned the value of listening to those who wish them harm. They neglected terrorist incidents until the morning of September 11; as pundits say, Islamic militants were at war with them but they were not at war with the militants. Perhaps Americans had an excuse for being out of touch with al-Qaeda then, but that is not the case with the DPRK now. Pyongyang publicly threatens to incinerate the United States every so often.

So what's North Korea's beef with America? Kim Il Sung, in his closed nation, was able to build a mythology upon the foundation of the Korean War, and it is hatred of the United States, the basis of that mythology, that sustains the regime today. The Kim family continues to call America the enemy, and America remains unaware.

God under Glass

At least we can't accuse David Letterman of forgetting about North Korea. "Are you familiar with Kim Jong Il?" he asked one night. "Maybe you remember his father, Men Ta Lee Il." The current ruler's father was born near Pyongyang to Christian and middle-class parents on the day the *Titanic* sank, April 15, 1912. Then, the little boy was known as Kim Song Ju—he later appropriated the name of a legendary Korean patriot, Kim Il Sung. His family moved to the Manchurian region of China when he was seven, and he stayed there during most of his formative years.

Kim got involved in revolutionary politics early. He joined the Chinese Communist Party in 1931 and in the following year organized a small band of guerrillas fighting the hated Japanese in what has been described as the longest engagement of the Second World War, the battle for control of Manchuria. Aided by a strong sense of destiny, he distinguished himself in various raids and skirmishes, becoming more than just a nuisance to the enemy. In late 1940 he retreated from Manchuria into the Soviet Union and was pressed into the Red Army, becoming a captain. Captain Kim spent the rest of World War II cooling his heels in Siberia: Moscow had not yet joined the war against Japan and did not want the Korean guerrillas on its soil to rile Tokyo.

In the heat of Cold War politics, Kim Il Sung was portrayed in the West as Stalin's stooge, but that is far from true. He was not part of Moscow's last-minute invasion of northern Korea at the end of the Second World War, and he even had trouble entering the Soviet zone of occupation after Japan's defeat a few days later. Kim had to worm his way into the country on a Soviet steamer, eventually arriving at the port of Wonsan on September 19, 1945, with his communist band of brothers, which by then numbered about sixty. He made up for lost time, however, outmaneuvering rivals and consolidating power within less than a year with some political support of the Soviets and the wholehearted devotion of his fellow guerrillas from the Manchurian campaign. Once in power Kim began to refer to himself as the Great Leader.

But Kim was greater than Great. Like a pharaoh, he was God. Christianity had strong roots in the northern portion of the peninsula, which meant Kim had competition. And so the North Korean leader, no stranger to the tale of Christ, simply deified himself. Kim even appropriated elements of emperor worship from the Japanese. In a few years after the end of the Second World War, Hirohito went from a god to a mortal in Japan and Kim made the reverse trip in Korea.

God in the human form of Kim Il Sung not only liberated Korea but also defeated the Japanese everywhere else in the Second World War—to this day North Koreans are stunned to learn that America had any role in stopping Japan. Then he beat back the American invasion that launched the Korean War. Kim also claimed to control the weather, arrange bountiful harvests, and, exposing a deficiency in Einstein's Theory of Relativity, transcend both time and space. "We were told that he crossed the river on a bridge of leaves and then he threw pine cones and they turned into grenades," says Ahn Hyeok, a North Korean and former political prisoner. "We heard this over and over, and we really believed that. So naturally we idolized him." By accepting Kim's claims, North Koreans disproved

Machiavelli's belief that it is better to be feared than loved and proved Hitler's notion that big lies are better than small ones.

Kim Il Sung didn't know much about Marx or Hegel, but he understood the psychology of the Korean people, who were more in tune to medieval times than modern ones. For an ignorant, traditional, and abused citizenry, he harnessed the powerful force of nationalism, retained elements of Korean feudal and Confucian society, and employed Leninist and Stalinist techniques of social mobilization and control. Like Hitler, he knew how to manipulate imagery and stir emotions. The society he created, while unfamiliar to the rest of us, made perfect sense to Koreans of that time because it fit in with their conception of the world. The charismatic Kim Il Sung exploited his people so well they did not feel oppressed.

But of course they were. Kim, with an obsessive thoroughness, built the most repressive totalitarian system in world history. Probably no one else ever had exercised such control over others, at least on a national scale. His overlapping security organizations were efficient, ubiquitous, and ruthless. The entire population was broken down into fifty-one categories and each person assigned a reliability rating. In Kim's system, every Korean, at least figuratively and often literally, was a soldier, an informer, and a part of the state. Lives were carefully scripted and people continually mobilized. There was no place for the individual in a mass society. The regime had, in the words of one Washington analyst, "an astonishing capacity for coercion." Parris Chang, now a legislator in newly democratized Taiwan, lived through the worst of his island's own dictatorship, so he knows something about oppressive societies. He first visited North Korea in 1985. "People asked me 'What's North Korea like?' I said, 'It's 1984.' "

It was always 1984 in Kim's Ku Klux Korea. He could hold his extremist society together only by keeping it apart from the rest of the world. That was possible because throughout the history of the Korean people, one foreign army or another marched through their fields. Moreover, it was not hard for Kim to convince the Koreans, who thought they were the origin of humanity anyway, that things were better at home than anywhere else. "I didn't know anything about the outside," says Lee Hye Lee, who eventually fled. "I thought North Korea was the best place in the whole world, a paradise." One of the Korean War's legacies for the North was the virtually impassable DMZ, the Demilitarized Zone, separating Kim's domain from the

South, the Brand X version of Korea. That barrier suited Kim's isolationist policies just fine.

The war also provided Kim Il Sung with what every autocrat needs: a foreign enemy to keep his own people in line. Pyongyang means "level ground," and that is exactly what the capital of North Korea was by the end of the conflict in 1953. In fact, Kim was left with few cities by the time of the armistice—North Koreans were living in caves. The United States dropped more than four times the tonnage of bombs on Korea than on Japan in World War II. In particularly regrettable acts, American planes destroyed massive irrigation dams holding water for three-quarters of the North's food production. Bruce Cumings, the academic, says that America bears primary responsibility for turning the DPRK into "a garrison state," a military-led nation, because of "our truly terrible destruction" of Kim's society during the war. Although that judgment sounds harsh—aggressors should not be relieved of responsibility for their own acts—Kim did solidify his rule after the cease-fire by demonizing the United States and by devoting excessive amounts of his nation's resources to the Korean People's Army. Perhaps no other nation in modern history has remained on a war footing as long as North Korea.

Kim remilitarized quickly because he was able to free his country from the constraints of gravity, at least in an economic sense: he managed to receive aid from both Moscow and Beijing, which competed for Pyongyang's affections in their tussle for leadership of the communist world. Kim was so successful in begging that he turned short-term tactical success into long-term strategic failure: North Korea became hooked on the heroin of outside assistance.

This dependency seems to run counter to Kim's own *Juche* philosophy, introduced within two years after the end of the Korean War. *Juche* literally means "master of one's self" or self-reliance, but the term was not intended to be fully understandable, at least by non-Koreans. In the world of *Juche* the state is an organism with the leader being the head and the people the body. Ordinary folk, therefore, have to follow their leader as the body follows the head. Nations without *Juche* were said to be colonies, so Washington, bent on world domination, was *Juche*'s enemy. One can peer deeply into its essence, but the concept is essentially nothing but nationalism. Kim Il Sung was the keeper of its meaning, and over time the term meant whatever he said it did. Even if foreigners could not fully comprehend *Juche*, it was Kim's gift to humanity.

By developing his own ideology, Kim, in both appearance and reality, staked an independent path, avoiding the close embrace of either major communist power. He may have made North Korea reliant on aid, but his country was never dependent on any single donor. When either communist giant spurned him, he merely took handouts from the other. In all cases, he ignored the wishes of his benefactors. Neither the Soviets nor the Chinese ever developed a satisfactory strategy for reining in Kim, Asia's Talleyrand.

Kim Il Sung's strategy worked well for a couple of decades as his North Korea outpaced the South in economic growth. Yet he could not outrun the inherent limitations of the system he adopted. As had occurred in both the Soviet Union and China, early gains from forced industrialization faded. The wily Kim could escape the clutches of Soviet and Chinese diplomats, but his country eventually fell victim to their socialism. Sometime during the middle to late 1970s Seoul overtook its northern rival and then left it in the dust. Kim, ignorant when it came to economic theory, tried various strategies, but despite great personal effort—he became famous for traveling around the country giving "on-the-spot guidance"—none of his remedies worked.

So the inevitable occurred. Moscow and Beijing, both eager to enhance ties with an economically vibrant South Korea, shifted sides. Karl Marx overstated the effect of economic factors on human events, but at least in this case money did buy love. The massive Soviet Union even obtained financial assistance from small South Korea for establishing diplomatic relations with it. The move by Moscow—effective September 30, 1990—was particularly bitter for Pyongyang: the USSR had been the first nation to recognize the North as the sole legitimate state on the Korean peninsula. In another defeat for Kim, China established ties with Seoul two years later. The Soviet Union ended aid to North Korea in January 1991, and China cut back assistance soon thereafter. A stunned Kim Il Sung could only watch his economy contract. He had become a relic, even an embarrassment, to his former big-power sponsors.

For many observers, Kim by then had already lost the peninsular contest with his mortal enemies below the DMZ. In the past, his arguments, if not always compelling to foreigners, at least resonated with Koreans, wherever they called home. Even as the South's economy overtook the North's, Kim could nonetheless be confident that he would ultimately prevail because, although he was an autocrat, he was a popular one and the autocrats in Seoul were definitely not.

As the South democratized in the late 1980s, however, the North Korean leader began to lose his audience. Kim had to stop his ghastly terrorist attacks—such as the bombing of the South Korean cabinet in Rangoon in 1983 and the downing of a South Korean airliner in 1987—simply because they became counterproductive. South Koreans viewed these assaults on their new democracy as especially abominable. A liberalizing political system created its own legitimacy, not only at home but abroad: the South began to garner world recognition and bask in approval, especially after the 1988 Summer Olympics in Seoul. As author Michael Breen points out, the leaders in the South had simply found "a better way to be Korean."

Kim, by contrast, found out what it meant to become irrelevant. He maintained the DPRK on a war alert, but there was no war he could fight. In comparison to booming South Korea, Kim's society looked decrepit and spent. Instead of appearing as the great Korean patriot, the proud Kim looked even more like a tyrant—he ran concentration camps the size of Houston—and a common criminal—he peddled narcotics through embassies and counterfeited large-denomination American currency. And so he lost support from the globe's geopolitical elite. Among world leaders, he could count only Joseph Mobutu of Zaire, Norodom Sihanouk of Cambodia, and "dictator groupie" Jimmy Carter as friends.

Bereft of friends, Kim Il Sung, the "Light of Human Genius" and the "North Star of the People," passed from this earth on July 8, 1994, after suffering a heart attack at the age of eighty-two. Animals wept, and so did mountains, rivers, plants, and trees. Reports of state media may have been exaggerated, but the authorities did not have to stage the outpouring of human hysteria—that mourning was genuine. North Koreans, within hours of the news, had heart attacks in sympathy. Millions came to Pyongyang to wail, beat the ground, and pay their last respects. Many dropped dead from excessive weeping. "Kim Il Sung was God to us," said Kim Goon Il, a former soldier. "When he died, people couldn't believe it. We all thought that he would live eternally. It was not conceivable."

"Because someone is dead doesn't mean they're gone," says the advertising slogan for a recent American horror movie, and that turned out to be true for the founder of the DPRK. Kim did not so much die as get kicked upstairs. Despite coronary complications, the old boy is still head of state with the title of "eternal president." He serves even though he is shot full of embalming fluid and lies under glass in a mausoleum that's been described as "bigger than Buckingham Palace." Officials even go through the pretense that he is still alive by having him sign the occasional document.

Alive or not, we have to admire Kim Il Sung's sense of timing. As Gore Vidal said of Truman Capote's passing, death can be a good career move. Kim, as it turned out, departed this world at a particularly opportune moment. Within months of his transition to a completely sedentary lifestyle, outsiders learned North Koreans were dying from malnutrition. Famine, which would kill so many, would rend the society that Kim worked so hard to build. The industrial economy continued its tailspin. North Koreans began fleeing the country in the tens of thousands, and the nation looked on the verge of collapse.

Was Kim Il Sung on the verge of a change before his death? He was trying to reform the North Korean economy, something that he alone had the power to do. Donald Gregg, former American ambassador to Seoul, has said that it was tragic that Kim did not live longer.

In reality, it's tragic that he had lived in the first place. For good or ill—and it's mostly ill—he was the one who grabbed power in northern Korea after the Second World War. As much as it may be unfashionable to say that individuals can change the course of global events, Kim Il Sung did so. He was the dominant figure on the Korean peninsula during five decades, and his legacy extended far beyond his homeland. Its effect on world politics has yet to be determined. Some argue whether Kim was a leader of great vision or folly, but we know that he was both.

Perhaps Ambassador Gregg is right in one sense. If life were fair—and we know that it is not—Kim Il Sung would have lived to see the end of the twentieth century's last decade. He caused the plight of the Korean people, and he should have either alleviated their suffering or at least shared it with them.

A Successful Miscreant

There is always hope for change after a despot dies. Kim Jong Il, however, disappointed. After his father's passing he did not attempt to rebuild the

North Korean state in a different image. The younger Kim evidently could not do so even though he was called a "contemporary god."

His divine status is evident from the miraculous circumstances of his birth. According to North Korean hagiography, he entered this world on February 16, 1942, in a log cabin on sacred Mount Paektu, the highest point in Korea and the mythical birthplace of the Korean people (and, therefore, in their eyes, humanity as well). The place of birth alone suggests that the younger Kim is a gift of the heavens to the people of the peninsula, and so does the simultaneous appearance of a bright star, a double rainbow, and a bird announcing the coming of a "general who will rule all the world." He's known as the last of the "three generals of Mt. Paektu"—the other two being his mother and father.

The unofficial version is he was born a year earlier, in a Soviet military camp near Khabarovsk, in Siberia, close to China. He was given the name of Yuri and was affectionately known as Yura until high school. Yuri Kim arrived in North Korea for the first time in November 1945 aboard a Soviet ship. He spent the Korean War in the safety of Manchuria.

Kim had the usual lifestyle for a North Korean tyrant in training. For example, the university he attended was named after his father. During his college days, he wrote more than 1,400 works. While taking classes and meeting his study obligations, the young Kim, according to North Korea's official news agency, performed "great ideological and theoretical exploits" and "made an immortal contribution to the development of revolutionary ideas of the working class as a great thinker and theoretician no one could match."

He was apparently good at everything he tried. While inspecting the country's finest marksmen, he picked up an old pistol on the spur of the moment and scored ten bull's-eyes in as many shots. Golfer Tiger Kim eagled the first hole he ever played. During the first round he shot eleven holes-in-one, although some reports said he merely had five. In any event, he ended up with an eighteen-hole total score of thirty-four, thirty-eight under par. The score was verified by the club pro and Kim's seventeen bodyguards. The PGA tour record for a round, by the way, is fifty-nine.

Dear Leader Kim Jong Il was so capable in all fields of endeavor that it was no surprise when North Koreans, suddenly finding themselves without a head of state in 1994, turned to him. After the end of a three-year period of mourning for Kim Il Sung, his son in October 1997 took over his position as general secretary of the Workers' Party of Korea, the one party in the North Korean one-party state.

In reality, the transition had been in the works since the early 1960s. In October 1980 Kim Jong Il was designated his father's successor at the Sixth Workers' Party Congress, when he was elevated to various high posts in the Presidium of the Politburo, the Secretariat of the Central Committee, and the Military Commission. Kim added important government (as opposed to party) titles along the way when he became supreme commander of the Korean People's Army in 1991 and chairman of the National Defense Commission two years later.

In retrospect, Kim Jong Il's elevation seems inevitable, but that was not always the case. Kim Il Sung had first designated his own younger brother, Kim Yong Ju, to succeed him. Yet more surprising is the notion that there should have been a transition from one family member to another. North Korea, after all, was nominally socialist. Kim Jong Il's elevation was the first—and still only—family transition in a communist society. "A totalitarian dynasty. Who has ever heard of such a thing?" asks one observer of the Kim family.

By selecting his son, Kim Il Sung solved the one problem that plagues every communist government: succession from one strong-willed leader to the next. North Korea's Confucian-inspired transfer of power from Great Leader to Dear Leader was as smooth as could be. Yet in that stroke Kim Il Sung burdened his country with the essential weakness of monarchy, the apparently unqualified heir.

North Korea no longer has the one element that every totalitarian society needs: the charismatic boss. Kim Il Sung was gregarious, and Mao, a contemporary, was mesmerizing. Castro is another charming communist. The Cuban can give eight-hour speeches, but Kim Jong Il can barely say six words. In fact, he has only ever said six words to the North Korean people in a public setting. During that occasion, Kim uttered "Glory to the people's heroic military!" He managed that in April 1992 during a celebration of the sixtieth anniversary of the army. Since his father died in 1994 Yuri has never said a single syllable to the 22 million people of the DPRK.

Kim Il Sung was outgoing, yet his son is shy to the point of being a recluse. It is often said that Kim Junior did not want to become head of state—a functionary named Kim Yong Nam fills that role—because he does not like seeing visitors. He will meet another world leader when he absolutely has to, but he almost always does so in Pyongyang so he doesn't have to travel. He often fails to attend state events and even celebrations in honor of his own birthday. He said nothing at the memorial service on the tenth anniversary of his father's death in 2004. He is the ultimate "behind-the-scenes operator," the global leader who most resembles the Wizard of Oz—or, perhaps more accurately, the Wizard of Odd.

Yuri Kim has been called North Korea's "least typical citizen," which must be true. He has a well-known taste for Swedish nymphets, NBA cheer-leaders, and "joy brigades" of naked Korean teenage girls. If you're looking for the perfect gift for the tyrant who has everything, a good choice would be S&M videos. Kim has had three wives, three sons, and three daughters, although there are reports that he has stashed seventy children in villas scattered throughout North Korea. These days his libido appears to be in serious decline, however. When not working on the destruction of the United States, he spends quiet time at home in his pajamas where he plays Super Mario and sits on the floor while he takes apart music boxes. He enjoys Daffy Duck cartoons from his personal collection, the world's largest.

The Devil may wear Prada, but when he appears in public it is usually in a tan leisure suit, which, in the words of Madeleine Albright, makes him look like a garage mechanic. He likes these clothes because he thinks they hide his physique, which he once compared to a "midget's turd." Kim also goes to great lengths to disguise his height. He wears rollers at home so that he can keep his hair in a bouffant that adds to his stature—and so do four-inch platform shoes. He's short, and so is his temper, which at times can be violent. Kim has ordered the killing of various officials and may have carried out one execution himself on the spot.

Monstrosity is the characteristic most frequently associated with the current leader of North Korea. Korea scholar Bruce Cumings argues that Koreans don't even have a notion of evil so it doesn't exist in their universe. Yet without resort to that concept it is hard to describe the younger Kim's extraordinary indifference to his people's suffering. For instance, he authorized the spending of something on the order of $900 million to convert his father's palace to a mausoleum for his preserved remains while hundreds of thousands, and perhaps millions, of North Koreans died from starvation.

"Is he insane or simply diabolical?" Fox's Greta Van Susteren has asked, and it's a good question. His malevolence may confound us, but what is even more astounding is that a man with all his deficiencies—and his are much more obvious than his father's—can succeed in governance, or at least succeed in maintaining his father's system.

Kim Junior successfully consolidated his power after his father's sudden death and, despite predictions to the contrary, kept the regime together. In the first few years of his rule he first scored a diplomatic triumph by getting the United States to sign an agreement preserving his nuclear program, then steered the DPRK through a famine that was its gravest crisis since the American advance to the Chinese border during the Korean War, and eventually engineered a slight recovery of the nation's beleaguered economy.

The fact that Kim is still around is an accomplishment in itself. As a person he may be a miscreant, but as a dictator "the Lodestar of the 21st Century" and "the Guardian of Our Planet" is absolutely brilliant. He has accumulated more than two thousand titles in all, but none is more important than "The Illustrious General of All Illustrious Generals." If there is one reason why Kim is still in power today, it is because of the Korean People's Army.

Kim Il Sung left his son a permanently mobilized nation; Kim Jong Il then increased the dominance of the armed forces still further. General Kim, the son, has never served in the military or appeared in uniform, yet he rules the country today as chairman of the National Defense Commission. This job was declared to be the highest post in North Korea in September 1998 by the country's head of state, so technically the DPRK is run by a military government. The commission, despite its name, now handles civilian affairs as well. Kim has let the Korean Workers' Party languish, which is highly unusual in a communist society, where the people's party is supposed to lead the charge to the perfect state of communism.

North Korea has never taken foreign ideology too seriously. In fact, Kim Jong Il had the country's constitution purged of references to Marxism in 1992. In its place he promotes his *Songun,* or "military first," politics. "Military first" means exactly what it says and maybe even a bit more. Kim's regime not only *begins* with the army, it *ends* with the army. The army may be the only tool that Kim has left to implement national, i.e., his, policy, yet for the meantime it is enough. When other Asian nations, even communist ones, are removing generals from civilian affairs, North Korea is giving them even more power over ordinary folk. For the personal fortunes of Kim Jong Il, that is the right move.

Aiding the Enemy

"From east to west, north to south, the Great General travels the country," says a North Korean TV announcer. "You warm us like the sun. Have you ever served a Great Leader like this?"

North Koreans are supposed to answer no. Even foreigners have not seen a despot to compare with Kim, except perhaps for his father. How did the Kims, father and son, build their "odiocracy"? Were they born bad? Even if they were, that characteristic doesn't fully answer why their nation went so horribly wrong, and historical and cultural factors, the favorite explanation of scholars, take us only so far.

The truth is the Kims have succeeded because outsiders have permitted them to do what they want. Moscow and Beijing, longtime sponsors, helped them along, of course, and, unfortunately, so did Pyongyang's historical nemesis, Washington.

The Great Fatherland Liberation War was not the last opportunity America had to kill off the darker version of Korea. In January 1968 North Korea captured the USS *Pueblo*, a reconnaissance vessel, in international waters in the Sea of Japan. It was the first time that a U.S. Navy ship had been taken on the high seas in peacetime in over 150 years. One crew member was killed and several wounded during the seizure. And during the next eleven months, the North Koreans beat *Pueblo* crew members with lumber, burned them against radiators, and kicked out their teeth. Some sailors were crippled and others almost blinded. The Johnson administration issued an apology to obtain their release. In April 1969 the North Koreans shot down an unarmed Navy EC-121 reconnaissance plane in international airspace over the Sea of Japan. All thirty-one crew members were killed, resulting in the largest loss of U.S. servicemen in a single incident during the Cold War.

President Lyndon Johnson did not retaliate against North Korea for the taking of the *Pueblo*. Richard Nixon criticized him for passivity yet did nothing after the loss of the EC-121 early on his watch. As Henry Kissinger wrote, an incoming administration "will suffer no penalty for prevailing with the methods of its predecessor; it will reap no plaudits for failing with a style all of its own." Doing nothing after the loss of the plane was the safe play and Nixon received praise for restraint, but Kissinger, national security adviser at the time, admitted that Washington's response to the shootdown was "weak, indecisive, and disorganized." As Kissinger wrote about the failure to respond, "I believe we paid for it in many intangible ways, in demoralized friends and emboldened adversaries."

Both the *Pueblo* and EC-121 incidents were barbaric. They were also acts of war. America was distracted by another war then, the one in Vietnam, so it didn't do anything about Pyongyang's blatant provocations. As it turned out, this conflict in Southeast Asia had no lasting geopolitical significance, but North Korea bedevils the world today. Each time Washington puts the DPRK on the back burner the cost of achieving lasting peace on the Korean peninsula goes up.

"I always had this philosophy of: 'It really doesn't matter,' " said Andy Warhol. This short sentence summarizes American policy toward North Korea over the past five decades. Now the DPRK really does matter, and America can only blame itself. The United States did not create the Kimist regime, but, through misjudgment and inattention from the Korean War to today, Americans have allowed it to become a grave threat.

AN ARSENAL OF AMBITIONS

Can North Korea Be Peacefully Disarmed?

Smith & Wesson beats four aces.
—Arthur Waldron, historian

On February 10, 2005, the Democratic People's Republic of Korea announced that it "manufactured nukes." If its boast was not a bluff, North
Korea joined the United States, Russia, Britain, France, China, India, Pakistan, and Israel as the world's nuclear powers.

So is North Korea to be believed? "The number of proven weapons is
zero," noted Charles Kartman when he was executive director of the Korean Peninsula Energy Development Organization. He spoke these words
before Pyongyang's dramatic announcement, but he is still correct today—
North Korea had not tested a weapon at the time of the February statement.

Donald Gregg, the former American ambassador and also a former CIA
station chief in Seoul, calls North Korea "the longest-running intelligence

failure in the world." Nuclear weapons are the deepest secret of a secretive regime, so it isn't surprising we don't know the precise amount of Kim Jong Il's fissile material—uranium and plutonium, the elements that give nuclear weapons their fizz—or the number of his bombs, if there are any in the first place.

The scarcity of real information gives ammunition, so to speak, to the skeptics. The Russians, who produced the first Potemkin village, and the South Koreans actually believe that the North Koreans have been fibbing all along. Pyongyang's claim to weapons is just hot air, said Sergey Antipov, the deputy head of Russia's Atomic Energy Agency, in 2005.

Just because there is no agreement on anything doesn't mean there is nothing. Most analysts take a commonsense approach and assume that, based on the amount of its fissile material, the DPRK probably has several nuclear devices. By now, the number could be as high as ten.

So does Kim have the ultimate weapon? And if he does, how did he manage to get it?

Reds Red-Handed

North Korea, despite recent assertions, did not begin its nuclear weapons program in the last couple of years. Kim Il Sung, the man with big ideas and outsized ambitions, was obsessed with building an atomic arsenal as early as the 1950s. Three years after the end of the Korean conflict the Soviet Union signed two agreements with Kim to transfer peaceful nuclear technology. North Korean scientists went to the Dubna Nuclear Research Institute, just outside Moscow, for training. At about the same time Pyongyang sent scientists to China for the same purpose.

In the middle of the 1960s the Soviets helped the North Koreans build a small research reactor, which was located at Yongbyon, about sixty miles north of Pyongyang. In 1977 the reactor was placed under safeguards—in other words, North Korea permitted international inspections—in return for uranium-mining assistance from the International Atomic Energy Agency, the U.N.'s nuclear watchdog.

It's unlikely that the Soviets were willing to help Kim build a bomb, but that's exactly what the North Korean leader had on his mind. In 1964, the year China successfully tested its first atomic device, he asked Mao Zedong to share bomb-building secrets. The Chinese leader declined to help. Mao turned Kim down again ten years later. The second refusal may have crystallized matters in Pyongyang—its nuclear arms program seems to have gone into high gear shortly thereafter, in the late 1970s.

Despite repeated Chinese refusals, Kim Il Sung did not give up seeking outside help to jump-start his program. As North Korean officials told their East German counterparts in May 1981, "We need the atom bomb." But as much as the Soviets wanted to court Kim at the time—they were in the midst of their struggle with the Chinese for control of the communist camp—they still didn't think it was a good idea to just hand him blueprints.

On the contrary, the Soviets tried to rein in Kim Il Sung. Moscow, at Washington's urging, convinced Pyongyang to join the Treaty on the Non-Proliferation of Nuclear Weapons in December 1985. Upholding their end of a bargain, the Soviet Union agreed to supply four light water reactors of the type operated in the Ukraine, specifically Chernobyl, for power generation purposes. That arrangement eventually fell through as relations between the two nations cooled. Kim, who may not have understood the consequences of being an NPT signatory, did not pull out of the treaty even after the deal with Moscow fell apart.

North Koreans had little reason to cause a stir—they were getting a free ride from an international community reluctant to deal with them. Initially, Pyongyang had eighteen months to negotiate a safeguards agreement with the International Atomic Energy Agency. IAEA bureaucrats, however, granted an extension for a like period because of their own mistake. They had initially sent the North Koreans, as a basis for negotiations, a model agreement covering the inspection of individual sites when they should have sent the form for inspections generally. Even with the extra time, which ran out in December 1988, the DPRK had not signed an agreement. They were apparently determined to stiff the international community. They had not allowed either their Chinese or Soviet benefactors to visit sensitive sites at Yongbyon—including a second and much larger reactor they started constructing around 1979—so they were especially reluctant to let IAEA inspectors in.

When North Korea's foot-dragging became public, Pyongyang said it would not allow international inspections as long as the United States based nuclear weapons in South Korea. It may have been just an excuse, but it was a darn good one. How could the world ask for a nuclear-free

North when the South was chock-a-block with bombs? American weapons were withdrawn by December 1991 as a part of President George H. W. Bush's worldwide removal of ground- and sea-based tactical nukes. Bush also gave a negative guarantee: the United States would not use nuclear weapons on nonnuclear states.

The withdrawal of American arms paved the way for fast progress on many fronts. On the last day of 1991 North Korea, shaken by the loss of its Soviet patron, initialed a landmark agreement with the South. Both halves of the peninsula pledged not to possess, develop, or use nuclear weapons and agreed to conduct reciprocal inspections. Furthermore, Pyongyang, showing uncharacteristic flexibility and accommodation, signed the IAEA safeguards agreement in January 1992.

Kim Il Sung signed because he said he had nothing to hide. In December 1991 the North Korean leader told a visiting American congressman, "We have no nuclear reprocessing facilities!" That was a fib of major proportions. Beginning in March 1986 American reconnaissance satellites over Yongbyon monitored the construction of a large oblong building. The structure—about six stories tall and two football fields long—contained features common to facilities that reprocess plutonium, a step whereby that element is separated from spent uranium fuel to create cores for bombs. The North Koreans, however, called it a "radiochemical laboratory." Although nearby reactors could have been used to generate electricity, other images showed that the Yongbyon complex, containing over a hundred buildings, had military applications. Satellites in 1983 had photographed patterns of cylindrical craters in sand on a riverbank close to Yongbyon. In 1986, when similar patterns appeared nearby, it was clear that the North Koreans were testing explosives used to trigger nuclear weapons.

IAEA inspections, which began in May 1992, caught the North Koreans in numerous untruths. For instance, the Koreans, who obviously underestimated the sleuthing capabilities of the agency, had claimed they had separated plutonium only once, in 1990. Isotope analysis proved they had done so three times, once in 1990 but also in the years immediately before and after. Tests also indicated the North Korean plutonium was coming from one or more undeclared sources. The inevitable conclusion was that they were hiding plutonium.

As IAEA inspectors found more and more discrepancies, Pyongyang refused further cooperation. Hans Blix, then head of the IAEA, presented to his Board of Governors in February 1993 satellite imagery and other evidence demonstrating that the North Koreans had not told the truth about Yongbyon. As they listened to the presentation, the DPRK delegates first sat with their mouths wide open, then denounced the satellite photos as doctored, and finally walked out. Based on overwhelming evidence, the IAEA board voted to demand "special inspections" of two Yongbyon sites that North Korea had earlier declared off-limits. Caught red-handed and left with no other options, Pyongyang, on March 12, 1993, announced its withdrawal from the NPT to take effect after the required three-month waiting period. The Democratic People's Republic of Korea is the only nation to have ever announced its withdrawal from the NPT.

The possibility of a nuclear-armed North Korea was not just a matter of politics; it was, in the words of former South Korean national security adviser Kim Chong Whi, "a question of civilization." Unfortunately, civilization, at least as it existed in the United States, was unprepared for a crisis with Kim Il Sung. The new administration of Bill Clinton did not want war, did not want to negotiate, and did not pursue any other option. With just a month to go before Pyongyang's withdrawal would take effect on June 12, the North Koreans got the ball rolling by picking up the phone and calling Kenneth Quinones, then the State Department's DPRK desk officer. On June 11, 1993, the Americans and North Koreans, after three days of negotiations in a coffee shop on 42nd Street in New York and talks at other locales, hammered out a joint statement by which Pyongyang suspended its withdrawal from the NPT and the United States, by signing on, implicitly recognized the legitimacy of North Korea.

From this point, however, talks went downhill. It's unlikely that Kim intended to use nukes as bargaining chips in the initial stages of his arms program, but somewhere along the line, possibly in 1990 or early in the following year, he began playing his best card, hoping to win both aid and diplomatic recognition from Washington. With an economy that was faltering, he had little choice. Mostly as a result of hard-line North Korean tactics, the promise of the first years of the 1990s, when Kim Il Sung signed agreements at a fast clip, gave way to the disappointment of the second half of 1993 and the superheated threats of 1994.

In early May 1994 the North Koreans began unloading fuel rods in apparent preparation for reprocessing. In the middle of June they announced they were pulling out of the IAEA, creating a confrontation that could not be ignored. If the IAEA could not conduct inspections at Yongbyon—and Pyongyang was blocking them at almost every turn—then the international agency essentially had no purpose. Unfortunately for Kim Il Sung, North Korea was the test case of the organization's credibility after its failure to uncover Saddam Hussein's nuclear weapons program before the Gulf War of 1991.

Washington, not left with many options, was ready to move for sanctions, a step that North Korea said was tantamount to war. In one of those rare moments of unity, most of the world was ready for tougher measures against the North. Even China, the DPRK's staunch ally, had warned Kim Il Sung that it might permit the United Nations to impose penalties. Because Pyongyang was saying that sanctions meant war, the United States began preparing for just that. Its air force had been making contingency plans for air strikes on Yongbyon since at least the beginning of the decade, but military preparations took on urgency as the Pentagon began marshaling its worldwide assets for conflict. Pyongyang was probably just letting its word wizards work when they said "there is no mercy in war" and that they would turn Seoul into a "sea of fire," but American policymakers had to take them seriously nonetheless.

It is, of course, possible that Kim Il Sung was willing to engage in an act of sure self-destruction—initiating military conflict with a vastly superior foe in the form of the United States and South Korea—yet we will never know. Just as America was within days of finally taking decisive action against the North Korean regime, in walked an itinerant peacemaker. Jimmy Carter, who was looking for ways to improve his legacy, told Bill Clinton, then president, that he was going to Pyongyang to meet Kim Il Sung to smooth out the apparent disagreement. His attempts to travel to the North Korean capital in 1991, 1992, and 1993 had been rebuffed by the State Department, but his insistence on going at the height of the crisis in 1994 overwhelmed both a White House still in disarray over the crisis and a South Korean government that did not quite know how to tell him no.

Carter, who put the Arabs and Israelis on the road to peace with the Camp David Accords of 1978, saw an opportunity for a similar personal triumph on the Korean peninsula. In talks with Kim in Pyongyang in mid-June he worked out a tentative deal that echoed Korea analyst Selig Harrison's suggestion to the Great Leader of a week before: a freeze of North Korea's reprocessing in exchange for "proliferation-resistant" light water reactors (ones that do not produce easily harvested fissile material). Then to make sure that his personal diplomacy would not be undone by Washington or Pyongyang, Carter, still in the North Korean capital, gave his now famous live interview to Wolf Blitzer of CNN during which, among other things, he praised Kim's flexibility.

Carter termed his work in Pyongyang, with some justification, "a miracle." Overnight, he defused the first nuclear proliferation crisis after the end of the Cold War and probably prevented conflict. The outlines of his deal with Kim, who died three weeks later from a heart attack, survived to be incorporated into the Agreed Framework, a deal signed in Geneva on October 21, 1994.

Pursuant to this arrangement—the Clinton administration refused to call it a treaty to avoid the necessity of Senate ratification—North Korea froze its nuclear reactors in Yongbyon and "related facilities" and agreed to dismantle them when they were replaced by light water reactors with a total capacity of two thousand megawatts. The United States did not agree to provide the reactors itself—it merely committed to leading an "international consortium" that would do so. South Korea and Japan ended up footing most of the bill for the Korean Peninsula Energy Development Organization, which was created to procure the reactors and build the generating facilities. Before completion of the reactor project, the United States agreed to provide 500,000 tons of heavy fuel oil annually. The North's fuel rods from the old reactors would be disposed "in a safe manner that does not involve reprocessing in the DPRK."

The North Koreans committed to remain a part of the NPT. They also agreed to permit IAEA monitoring of frozen facilities, international inspection of facilities not subject to the freeze, and full implementation of their existing safeguards agreement "before delivery of key nuclear components" of the light water reactors.

Both sides agreed to reduce barriers to trade and investment, open liaison offices in each other's capital, and "move toward full normalization of political and economic relations." Washington agreed to provide "formal assurances" to Pyongyang "against the threat or use of nuclear weapons by the U.S." North Korea, for its part, said it would implement its 1991 nuclear agreement with South Korea and engage in "dialogue" with Seoul. Both parties also committed to reaching an arrangement on the "peaceful uses of nuclear energy."

The crisis had passed, and Washington largely ignored North Korea until the middle of George W. Bush's first term. In October 2002 American envoy James Kelly, while on a trip to Pyongyang, accused the North Koreans of carrying on a secret nuclear arms program based on uranium. To his surprise, the North Koreans admitted—"boasted" is a better word—that they were doing so. Washington had assumed that Pyongyang would, as it had in the past, deny the existence of the uranium program. America was completely unprepared to hear the truth.

Kelly's confrontation with Pyongyang started an unanticipated—and terrifying—downward spiral in relations. After the United States stopped shipments of heavy fuel oil that December in response to DPRK belligerence, Pyongyang immediately disconnected IAEA monitoring devices at Yongbyon, ejected international weapons inspectors, announced its withdrawal from the NPT the following January, fired up the Yongbyon reactor shortly thereafter, resumed construction on two other reactors, and removed eight thousand fuel rods from Yongbyon's cooling pond for the purposes of reprocessing. In short, the Agreed Framework died rather suddenly.

Pyongyang blames the death of the deal on the Clinton administration for failing to honor its end of the bargain. It's true that America's record of compliance with the 1994 arrangement was a bit spotty. The no-nuclear-attack pledge, for instance, was not formally given, and there is absolutely no excuse for this failure. Moreover, there is no good explanation why the United States did not lift some sanctions and ended other ones years late.

The promised reactors were woefully behind schedule, which was primarily an American failing, yet North Korean red tape and intransigence contributed to construction delays. Moreover, Pyongyang can hardly complain: the United States supplied the heavy fuel oil that was intended to tide the DPRK over until the new reactors came online, and, in any event, Pyongyang was not ready to connect the reactors to a power grid. It is hard to see what difference the unfortunate delays made.

America was also slow on its commitments to establish relations. The Agreed Framework was particularly unpopular in Washington, and the Republican sweep in the congressional elections of 1994 forced the administration to shelve its promises to Pyongyang. Everyone thought that North Korea was going to collapse, so Clinton believed America did not have to keep its word. The failure was regrettable and sent a bad message about American reliability as a treaty partner. Yet despite the American failure to act, Pyongyang was also slow in normalizing relations. And Pyongyang did not restart talks with the South.

"There is blame on both sides," said Jimmy Carter in December 2002 as he defended his 1994 nuclear deal with Kim Il Sung. Carter was correct to find fault everywhere. Yet what the former president did not mention was that Washington had committed misdemeanors while North Korea was guilty of high crimes. It is one thing to be negligent, and it's another to completely renege. The 1994 Agreed Framework, based on Carter's handshake arrangement with Kim Il Sung, specifically refers to the North's plutonium program because that was the only one known in the West at the time. Pyongyang's uranium program, however, was still a violation of the Agreed Framework because in that document North Korea agreed to abide by two comprehensive treaties: the global NPT and the 1991 denuclearization agreement with South Korea.

The North Koreans, in short, were negotiating in bad faith the whole time and violated the Agreed Framework before the ink was dry in Geneva. Pyongyang propagandists can blame Clinton lapses or Bush hostility for their country's own failures of compliance, but such protestations ring hollow. The secret uranium program was one of the most brazen betrayals of an international agreement in the last half century.

The DPRK probably began its uranium-based program in the 1980s, but it had certainly gone beyond the planning stage by the beginning of the following decade. Dr. Abdul Qadeer Khan, the father of Pakistan's atomic bomb and the ringleader of a global black market in nukes, says he began working with North Korea around 1991. Among other things, Khan supplied equipment for centrifuges—supersonic-speed machines that separate uranium into its different isotopes and upgrade the potent stuff to weapons-grade purity—until as late as the middle of 2002, shortly before Khan came under suspicion for black market activities. In return for the favor, Pyongyang helped Islamabad with its missile program. North Korea calls reports of the missiles-for-nukes barter and the uranium program a "whopping lie" fabricated by the United States, but evidence, such as Khan's confession, numerous sightings of him in the DPRK, and satellite photos of North Korean missiles being loaded onto Pakistani planes, confirm the allegation. North Korean agents have also been caught buying items that are useful only in a uranium bomb program, such as aluminum tubes suitable for

Khan-type centrifuges. Pakistan's help may have continued until as recently as 2003.

Number of Nukes

The CIA for a long time maintained that North Korea had enough plutonium for one or two weapons but had no capability of producing more because, even though the Agreed Framework did not require the DPRK to give up its plutonium, the material was nonetheless locked down under IAEA seal.

In September 2004 Pyongyang boasted it had reprocessed and "weaponized" all the Yongbyon fuel rods. If the claim is true, the North has enough plutonium for another six to eight bombs. China, which knows North Korea the best and is trying to keep peace in the region, doubts the weaponization boast. The State Department, which also tries to avoid overheated assessments, merely says "we take all their claims seriously." Given the stakes involved, that's a sound approach. Worst-case arithmetic says Kim can put his hands on enough plutonium to make ten weapons today. That figure, however, does not include plutonium that North Korea has produced after restarting Yongbyon in 2003. Future plutonium production might yield enough material for another thirty bombs a year, according to Georgetown University's Robert Gallucci, who negotiated and signed the Agreed Framework on behalf of the United States. Moreover, there is always the possibility that North Korea has also surreptitiously bought plutonium from Russian sources.

So North Korea has the fissile material. Has it actually constructed a weapon? That's not clear. In 2003 American intelligence spotted in North Korea a crater in a shape indicating a test of explosives used for plutonium weapons. The characteristic mark usually indicates the last step before the testing of a nuclear device itself. In that year the CIA revealed that the North had probably mastered the techniques to build a plutonium weapon and had the technology to test it without detonation. Pakistan taught North Korea how to conduct a "cold test"—a simulated nuclear explosion—but these experiments cannot provide complete assurance that a complicated plutonium device will work.

North Korea reportedly told China in the middle of 2005 that it knew how to build all the components of a bomb but had not actually assembled one. Pyongyang's statement, a direct contradiction of its February 2005 declaration that it had already built nukes, was probably just an attempt to hide its weapons capabilities. It was much more probable that, having gained all the technology and know-how, North Korea has actually constructed a weapon, as one recent defector claimed in a debriefing conducted by South Korea's National Intelligence Service.

Pakistan's Dr. Khan says that sometime at the end of the 1990s he actually saw three North Korean nukes in an underground facility an hour outside Pyongyang. Many say it's unlikely the DPRK would have let a foreigner see its stockpile, and Khan, a metallurgist and not a weapons designer, might not have known enough to distinguish a dummy device from the real thing. Nonetheless, Washington generally believes that the Pakistani was telling the truth. His report would be especially credible if Pakistan in fact tested a North Korean plutonium bomb when it detonated its own uranium weapons in 1998, as some suspect.

It is possible, although unlikely, that North Korea has already produced bombs based on uranium. Khan's operation delivered most everything needed for a uranium weapon, including complete centrifuges and tens of thousands of parts ordered from a shopping list. Yet parts are one thing, putting them together to make a bomb is another. Khan's nuclear black market also sold parts and plans to Libya's Mohammar Qaddafi, who left many of his purchases in packing crates for years.

From all we know, however, the Koreans were more industrious. Yet there is wide disagreement as to how far advanced the North Koreans are. Some say Pyongyang's program graduated from research and development to full-scale uranium production in 2000. Others disagree. In June 2002 some parts of the American intelligence community thought that the DPRK was at least three years from assembling centrifuges in a small test cascade—hundreds or even thousands of centrifuges strung together to shorten the enrichment process. In September 2002 the United States believed that a "production-scale" centrifuge facility was almost complete. In 2004 the Pentagon's Defense Intelligence Agency estimated that the uranium program would be operational by the end of that year, but the highly respected intelligence unit of the State Department and others were skeptical of that assessment. Toward the end of 2004 John Bolton, the State Department's senior arms control official at the time, said North Korea was on the threshold of essentially "unlimited" bomb production, an assessment that might have been based on South Korean intelligence. The soundest view is that the North Koreans will be producing uranium sufficient for between two and six bombs a year by the end of 2007.

Once North Korea has the uranium it undoubtedly has a weapon. Uranium devices are simple to design and not that hard for a government to build. The scientists at Los Alamos did not even bother testing their first uranium bomb before unloading it over Hiroshima. With the passage of time building a weapon is no longer a matter of science but one of engineering. In any event, Khan may even have sold Pyongyang a set of designs or even a ready-to-use device.

We can argue about the numbers of Kim Jong Il's weapons, says Gallucci, but not about the direction of his arms program. The trend is not our friend—the opposite of what stock analysts say. When both plutonium and uranium programs are running in tandem, as they will by 2007 at the latest, Kim will be producing weapons of mass destruction on a mass-production scale. "It's one thing to make one or two," said a Bush administration official speaking anonymously in 2003. "It's another thing to have a process in place to make hundreds. They're on their way to be able to make hundreds within the next couple of years."

Hiroshima in Honolulu

Kim Jong Il's scientists will continue to reprocess plutonium, enrich uranium, and manufacture atomic bombs. But to make himself a real threat, he must do much more. "It's one thing to be able to make nuclear weapons," says Robert Alvarez of the Institute for Policy Studies. "It's another thing to deliver them, and if you are going to be taken seriously as a military power, you have to have a capability to put these nuclear weapons on missiles that will go great distances and hit their targets."

North Korea, unfortunately for everyone but North Koreans, is becoming one of the world's masters of intercontinental delivery systems. As U.S. Air Force General Paul Hester remarked, the DPRK is capable of "remarkable breakthroughs" in missile technology at any time. Even now, Kim Jong Il poses a threat to nations far from Pyongyang. "North Korean missiles can reach any part of the United States of America," says Kim Myong Chol, a DPRK commentator who is often referred to as the country's "unofficial spokesman." "There is no shelter for Bush."

The current president, at least for the moment, can rest easy. Today, the longest-range missile actually deployed by North Korea, the one-stage Rodong, can put a 1,500-pound payload approximately eight hundred miles downrange. Launched from the DPRK toward Washington or Crawford, Texas, a Rodong would fall a bit short. When North Koreans say American warnings about their ballistic missiles are "a whopping lie"—there's that phrase again—they are telling the truth.

But perhaps not the whole truth. To borrow a Bushism, we seem to always "misunderestimate" Pyongyang. In 1995 a National Intelligence Estimate, containing the consensus of the American intel community, downplayed the notion of a North Korean ballistic missile threat for at least fifteen years. In 1998, Donald Rumsfeld disagreed. The then former and future secretary of defense suggested that Washington not be so complacent about the North Koreans. The commission that bore his name in July of that year issued its report warning that Pyongyang would soon be able to hit cities in an arc from Phoenix, Arizona, to Madison, Wisconsin.

Rumsfeld's timing couldn't have been better: within two months the North Koreans, without warning, fired off a three-stage Taepodong from the eastern part of their country. Its trajectory arced over Japan's main island of Honshu and out to the Pacific Ocean. It looked like a ballistic missile test at the time but was actually a failed attempt to put a satellite—a radio playing patriotic music—into orbit. The third stage either misfired or failed to ignite, and debris landed in a place called Alaska.

American analysts were stunned. They knew the North Koreans were preparing to launch but were expecting something completely different—and much less sophisticated. The DPRK went from a one-stage missile to a three-stage one in one great leap. "If you're going to try to hit the continental United States, you need a multistage missile with lots of integration," says Scott Conwell, who worked in the Defense Department's Ballistic Missile Defense Organization when the Taepodong was launched. "The fact is, they did it on the very first try, and they did it with a lot of successful integration."

Kim's technological success highlighted America's intelligence failure. Americans test and build and then test some more. Their approach is slow and methodical—and it incidentally lets adversaries monitor their progress, thereby ensuring at least a degree of transparency. The Russians go at weapons development much the same way. The American intelligence community, therefore, assumed North Korea would also adopt the "test, build, test, build" model. Any other approach would, they believed, fail. Rumsfeld, however, had warned that Pyongyang might not follow that path and thereby take Washington by surprise.

That is, in fact, what happened. North Koreans amazed the world— they simply skipped two-stage missiles in their effort to develop an intercontinental one. "We don't know what's happening there," says Conwell. "There's a lot of things that they could be doing that we don't know about."

This we do know: if the DPRK could scorch snow in Alaska in 1998, it has the lifting power to deliver a nuclear warhead there as well. How much farther can it airmail a payload today? The North may be in the process of deploying a land-based missile that has a range of 2,500 miles. That means they will soon have the power to put plutonium in the paradise of Hawaii.

In 2003 George Tenet, then director of Central Intelligence, said North Korea could also strike the American mainland with a ballistic missile. Analysts think a new version of the Taepodong can hurl several hundred pounds up to 9,300 miles, enough to hit the West Coast with a warhead and possibly even the rest of North America. Without testing, the missile is not reliably accurate, but when it's carrying a nuclear payload, who cares if it misses by a few miles?

And who needs great range when you can position your missiles just off the American coast? North Korea is also building intermediate-range missiles that can be fired from merchant ships and submarines. The DPRK does not yet have a sub that can launch the missile, but there have been troubling rumors that it has been trying to buy a Soviet one and it certainly has cargo ships galore.

So far, it's not known whether North Korea has miniaturized its nukes so that they can fit atop their missiles or developed the shielding necessary to protect warheads on reentry into the atmosphere. Pyongyang implies that its technicians have mastered these tasks, but that is unlikely. Nonetheless, their record of past achievement suggests they cannot be too far from success. We may not know precisely how advanced Kim's weapons are and how many he has, but we do know it is just a matter of years before he can deliver a warhead to any place on earth.

Therefore, the world has the incentive to solve the North Korean problem soon. As Ari Fleischer, then President Bush's spokesman, said, "Technology and time mean that regimes like North Korea will increasingly have the ability to strike at the United States." Pyongyang says its missile program "is of purely peaceful nature and does not pose a threat to anyone." Even if its capabilities are intended for deterrence and not attack, everyone remains at risk as long as there is a crisis on the Korean peninsula.

Selig's Solution

"Why are Americans so afraid of North Korea?" asks Song Young Gil, a member of South Korea's national legislature. "I don't understand." Many echo this view. "I have always believed that the United States has overreacted to North Korean threats in the nuclear and missile area," says Donald Gregg, the former American diplomat and spy. "I say this because we successfully deterred the Soviet Union for decades with its thousands of nuclear weapons on accurate missiles." North Korea, he points out, is a much less powerful foe. Today, the Kim regime has at most a handful of bombs and only primitive ways of delivering them. If Gregg is right, then what is all the fuss about?

The historical record supports Gregg, now head of the Korea Society in New York. Although the DPRK may be run by an evil and odious regime, Pyongyang has not waged war—against a militarily inferior South Korea or any other nation—since 1953. The Kimist state may be headed by a reckless rogue, but we need to know only two words when it comes to keeping him in check: "deterrence works." Although America's North Korea policy has been one misstep after another for over five decades, Washington has been able to contain a militant and seemingly irrational regime with the threat of massive retaliation. The caution of Kim Jong Il—"the little madman with the passion for plutonium"—shows that deterrence, which helped prevent nuclear war in the era of intense U.S.-Soviet rivalry, also dampens conflict in the post–Cold War period.

Despite the success of deterrence, America nonetheless believes that North Korea must give up its nuclear arsenal. As the world knows, Washington's policies to disarm the regime have been varied. The United States has threatened war as a means of ending the Kim family nuclear weapons program and has also tried neglect and negotiation, but all of its approaches have so far failed. Today, the DPRK has more fissile material than ever before: it has never had more plutonium and may now have enriched uranium as well. As the only superpower, America should be humbled and embarrassed by the results of its North Korean diplomacy.

For many, it is time to try a new way to deal with the younger Kim. For instance, the analyst Selig Harrison thinks American hostility has been the essence of the problem. Where others see the DPRK as an intractable situation, he sees a simple solution. Decades of Washington's bellicosity have made them belligerent, he maintains. Therefore, the United States should sign a treaty to finally end the Korean War, lift sanctions, establish diplomatic relations, and forge lasting economic ties. "Unless we become friends, they will continue to develop nuclear weapons," Harrison says.

When they feel secure, he believes, North Korean leaders will reveal the extent of their program and give up their arsenal. "The only reason we are developing nuclear weapons is to deter an American pre-emptive attack," Kim Yong Nam, North Korea's number two leader, told Harrison, who is known for his good contacts in Pyongyang. "We don't want to suffer the fate of Iraq." "Why would we need nuclear weapons if we no longer feel threatened?" an unnamed official said to the American. "Why would we give up our right to have them if you keep talking about regime change? It's as simple as that."

Actually, it's not. Fundamental to Selig Harrison's position is the notion that American belligerence is responsible for the North Korean nuclear arms program. The United States, however, has had sound reasons for being out of sorts with the DPRK, dating back to 1950. Washington withdrew its troops from the Korean peninsula a full year before Kim Il Sung attacked the South in that year. Kim, nevertheless, blamed the conflict on an American invasion.

It's true that in 1953 President Dwight Eisenhower hinted he was willing to drop the bomb to end the Korean War, but that was a conflict Kim Il Sung started. Ike's comments may have been ill-advised when we consider their longer term implications on nuclear proliferation, but an aggressor can hardly use the words of a victim as an excuse for nuclear armament.

The United States, in fact, had little contact with the DPRK after the unpleasantness of the Korean War. Once the armistice was signed, Washington restrained Seoul and urged limited reconciliation with Pyongyang.

In the encounters that did in fact occur during this period, America usually came off second best and hardly looked threatening. If anything, the United States was far too restrained in dealing with serial provocations. At least two horrible acts—the taking of the *Pueblo* in 1968 and the downing of the EC-121 reconnaissance plane the following year—showed that Pyongyang was asking for war and Washington was declining its invitations.

Moreover, the claim of American belligerence does not fit easily with the trend of events. From the end of the 1960s America was in general retreat in Asia. President Nixon's 1969 remarks in Guam, where he announced the doctrine that bears his name, made it clear that American allies in Asia would have to rely on themselves for their own defense. North Korea's nuclear weapons program, according to many accounts, began after the fall of Saigon. The loss of all of Indochina may not have meant Washington's permanent withdrawal from the region as many at the time thought, but that development certainly made America look impotent. The United States hardly constituted a threat to North Korea at that time.

On the contrary, Ronald Reagan tried to reach out to the DPRK with his "Modest Initiative." The diplomatic overture, unfortunately, got caught up in the first nuclear crisis, which was started by Pyongyang during the presidency of George Bush Senior. U.S. policy of the second George Bush may sound hostile, but it is far from belligerent in substance, especially considering the historical context. Recent American comments about the desire for regime change hardly account for North Korean bomb-building efforts that occurred decades before. Moreover, Washington today is one of the biggest supporters of the regime, continually donating tons of food.

Some analysts argue that the North initiated its nuclear arms program primarily in response to the American nuclear presence in South Korea. The United States, after all, based tactical nuclear weapons—gravity bombs, artillery shells, and land mines—in the South until 1991. Nonetheless, these arms were part of a force structure that was purely defensive in nature. Neither the Americans nor the South Koreans were configured for attacking the DPRK—and Kim Il Sung, despite all his ranting, had to know this.

Moreover, even if America were audacious and aggressive, Kim Il Sung and his nation were protected by the Soviet "nuclear umbrella": Moscow's massive arsenal sheltered North Korea every minute of every day. Kim had all the security he ever needed—and it was provided without cost. Soviet protection was in addition to his conventional deterrent, which was, in all likelihood, sufficient on its own.

Protected by the seemingly invincible Soviets and facing less than fearsome Americans, Kim did not need nuclear weapons of his own unless he had plans to use them in some fashion. The first Great Leader was, among other things, an unrepentant aggressor. At least through the mid-1970s he still harbored notions of unifying the Korean peninsula by a second war. Kim devoted an inordinate proportion of his resources to building a first-class military for a fifth-rate nation. So the genesis of the DPRK bomb program is most likely found in the martial nature of the regime he founded. It is only natural for the world's most militarized state to desire the world's most destructive weaponry.

The historical record, in short, doesn't provide much support for blaming the United States for the DPRK's bomb building, which goes back to at least the late 1970s and possibly before. Selig Harrison, who has unrivaled access to the North Korean leadership for a private citizen, is just too accepting of whatever his hosts happen to say at the moment. As a nation America should accept responsibility for many unfortunate developments since the end of World War II, but Pyongyang's nuclear weapons program is not one of them.

Moving Backward

"When the American President today is faced with a military threat, his first question is not 'What strategy will work to fundamentally put an end to this threat?' Rather, his first question is 'How much do I have to pay to get this show off CNN so I can forget about it?' " writes *New York Times* columnist Thomas Friedman. "Everything gets contained, but nothing gets solved." In June 1994 Jimmy Carter told us the Korean nuclear crisis was over. In a limited sense he was correct, yet Clinton's Washington just contained matters. "We both implemented phase one," said one Clinton administration official referring to American and North Korean compliance with the Agreed Framework. "In truth, neither of us wanted to do the rest of it. It was easier to declare victory and say we solved the nuclear problem."

Containing, as opposed to solving, is an acceptable strategy when time works to one's favor. The Agreed Framework, for all its faults, bought time.

With time, Washington could figure out what to do with the North Korean regime. In the event, however, it just ignored the problem, throwing away the most important benefit it had obtained.

The world has signed agreements with the Kims, father and son, about their arms programs. Every one of the documents solved the moment's crisis, yet none of them provided a lasting solution. Each of them was sensible in its time yet damaging in the overall context, postponing the resolution of critical issues to a future when North Korea would be better armed and stronger. If there is one thing that all parties to the dispute agree, it is that time now favors a North Korea that is expanding its arsenal as the years pass.

Bill Clinton's indifference to a stronger North Korea was followed by . . . the indifference of George W. Bush. Kim Dae Jung, then South Korea's president, insisted on making a hastily planned trip to Washington in March 2001, when he became the newly installed administration's first foreign visitor with serious diplomacy on his mind. Colin Powell thought it was a splendid idea to work with Pyongyang, as the South Korean president so earnestly urged, and the new secretary of state said so publicly. Bush, however, took a tough line, in the process rebuking his chief diplomat and humiliating Kim.

Bush wisely decided to conduct a thorough review of policy toward Pyongyang and in June 2001 declared that he was willing to talk to the North Koreans at any time and at any place. Yet after September 11 he understandably forgot about the Korean peninsula. Along the way he managed to include you-know-who in the axis of you-know-what, thereby provoking the always sensitive North Korean Kim, Kim Jong Il. The "evil" Kim took his revenge against the otherwise preoccupied Bush by manufacturing another crisis just as the American president was gearing up for war in Iraq.

The frightening spiral of events beginning at the end of 2002, which was marked by the removal of IAEA inspectors and the DPRK's withdrawal from the nonproliferation treaty, bore more than a passing resemblance to the emergency in 1994. As *The Wall Street Journal*'s Hugo Restall pointed out, both crises appeared "grim" because that is how the Kim family wanted them to look.

The Bush administration did not want to negotiate with Pyongyang, but, left without a military option — the bulk of American forces were then committed to the grand adventure in Iraq—it had no choice. The Bushies insisted that there was no crisis in North Korea even though its program was much further advanced than Saddam Hussein's. The Iraqi nuclear program—largely in the form of papers, notes, and plans—was buried in the garden of a scientist in Baghdad while the North Korean one had, in all probability, produced enough fissile material to kill millions.

Pyongyang demanded one-on-one dialogue with Washington, which for its part insisted on discussions in a multilateral setting. The North Koreans would not admit they had a uranium bomb program while the Americans said that was the reason for talks in the first place. Kim Jong Il wanted aid for merely freezing his plutonium program. Bush declared he would not pay the DPRK for adhering to its existing obligations. "We're not going to be threatened," he also proclaimed in April 2003, but of course Kim Jong Il had already done that long ago.

Threatened by North Korea, the Bush administration agreed to negotiate. The Chinese hosted three-party talks in April 2003 in Beijing. Although the gathering looked like multilateral discussions among the United States, North Korea, and China, the smiling hosts acted as if their only responsibilities were to provide tea and make sure the North Koreans arrived on time. China wanted the parties to engage directly with each other, which is exactly what they did—but only for a brief moment. During informal pre-dinner chitchat North Korea's Li Gun said his country had nuclear weapons and would test, export, or use them, depending on what the Americans did. Predictably, when Bush was told about this, he did not react well.

The three-party talks were merely a prelude to those involving six nations—Russia, Japan, and South Korea joined. The first round including the expanded group took place the following August, also in Beijing. For the first time all of North Korea's neighbors, the three with actual land borders and two others that resided in geopolitical proximity, were sitting in the same room at the same time.

China, Japan, Russia, South Korea, and the United States all say they want the DPRK to disarm. So the six-party talks, at least at first glance, don't look like a fair fight. On one side sit five powerful nations. There is the solar system's undisputed heavyweight champion, the sole superpower. There are also two other nuclear-armed nations, one of which is the world's most populous state and the other is its largest as measured by geographical area.

The planet's second largest economy sits at the table as does Asia's fourth biggest. These five nations account for 31 percent of global population and 47 percent of its economic output. North Korea, by contrast, represents about one-third of one percent of humanity and an even smaller percentage of its economy.

In numbers there is strength, especially when the strong gang up on the weak—or as the University of Pennsylvania's Arthur Waldron once put it, "Smith & Wesson beats four aces." The fact that so many gathered together was a feat of sorts for George W. Bush, who wanted to show Kim Jong Il that his nuclear weapons program was distinctly unpopular in the region. In fact, the strategy was initially successful in isolating Pyongyang. The North Koreans were "rather shocked" that they found themselves so unloved during the first six-party round.

By corraling all the principal parties, Washington hoped to forge a consensus—"a common understanding and approach"—that would stop Pyongyang from playing off one nation against the others. "No longer can the North tell Beijing one thing, Tokyo another, and Washington yet another," says former State Department official Mitchell Reiss. "No longer can it harbor any illusions that its nuclear weapons program is—as it so often claims—a purely 'American' concern."

That's the theory. "The trouble with allies is that they sometimes have ideas of their own," said Winston Churchill, who was also a bit headstrong at times. Unfortunately for the Bush team, not all the parties in Beijing—there are upward of 120 people in the room during six-party sessions—shared American views. Three of them—China, Russia, and South Korea—essentially sided with North Korea, and Japan, the sole reliable ally for the United States, carried little weight and remained an outcast. What was supposed to be an ambush of Kim Jong Il turned out, on many occasions, to be a mugging of the Americans. Washington's diplomats increasingly found themselves alone in a very big room in a very foreign country.

The United States, slow to realize its isolation, staked out an uncompromising position that failed to attract support from the other parties to the talks. Early in the negotiating process it insisted that Pyongyang accept a formula reduced to the acronym CVID: complete, verifiable, irreversible disarmament. The Bush administration, however, adopted a seemingly fatalistic approach of "no carrots and no sticks" and was unwilling to do anything to persuade the North Koreans to accept its terms. The president, who said he was unwilling to run the risk of inaction on Iraq, did exactly that with a far more dangerous DPRK. CVID, in Washington circles, became known as "Confusion, Vacillation, Indecision, Delay."

According to Bill Richardson, sometimes called the "U.S. ambassador to rogue states," the North Koreans were outraged by being neglected by Bush. So they upped the stakes by engaging in increasingly menacing behavior—harvesting more of Yongbyon's plutonium for bombs, for instance. Pyongyang had always sought to create a sense of impending doom. In the past, the Kims invariably used threats and got what they wanted, so they were emboldened to become even more aggressive. The result is that the North Koreans were able to institutionalize brinkmanship. For the first time in decades, however, Washington was not buying their act.

Yet ignoring Pyongyang's escalating threats also meant courting disaster, and the prospect of turmoil in North Asia made many in Washington—and elsewhere—uneasy. As a result, Bush's get-tough tactics lost support, and they did not survive the arrival of Condoleezza Rice as secretary of state in early 2005. Her noticeably softer approach limited some of the extraordinary risk inherent in the high-wire strategy of the first Bush term.

The new American posture paved the way for an agreement of sorts. In what was described as a "breakthrough," all six parties to the Beijing deliberations issued a statement of principles in September 2005. North Korea committed itself to giving up "all nuclear weapons and existing nuclear programs" and pledged "at an early date" to rejoin the nuclear nonproliferation treaty and submit to IAEA safeguards. South Korea said it would not deploy nukes and confirmed that it currently possessed none. Both Koreas reaffirmed their 1991 denuclearization agreement, which had by then become a dead letter. Pyongyang and Washington agreed to respect each other's sovereignty and normalize their relations while Pyongyang and Tokyo made a similar pledge. The parties promised "energy assistance" to the DPRK, and South Korea specifically referred to its earlier proposal of providing two million kilowatts of electric power. There was a reference to creating "a permanent peace regime" for the Korean peninsula. Washington confirmed that it had "no intention to attack or invade" the DPRK. All six parties to the talks agreed "to promote economic cooperation."

The most controversial aspect of the joint statement is its implicit acceptance of a North Korean nuclear energy program. In the document

Pyongyang asserted its right to one, and the five other parties expressed their "respect" for the DPRK's position and promised "to discuss at an appropriate time" providing a light water reactor. The statement suggests that the "appropriate time" is after the completion of North Korea's disarmament, but Pyongyang, just one day after the deal was announced, reminded everyone just how hard it would be to reach a final agreement. In harsh language that cast doubt on Kim Jong Il's commitment to disarm, his Foreign Ministry told North Korea's five negotiating partners that they should give it reactors even before it surrendered a single weapon. Then the following day Pyongyang's Korean Central News Agency issued a statement that threatened nuclear war with the United States.

The Bush administration had continually derided 1994's Agreed Framework, but the joint statement looked a lot like that arrangement—one wag dubbed the 2005 document "Framework Two"—because, among other reasons, they both contemplated buying off North Korea with a civilian nuclear energy program. We shouldn't be too surprised by the similarity between the two deals, even though they were separated by more than a decade. After all, George W. Bush was not writing on a blank slate.

In 1994 Bill Clinton chose to bless, rather than bludgeon, the North Koreans by adopting the Agreed Framework. That agreement, we often forget, strengthened North Korea at a critical moment. It provided an economic lifeline and signaled to Pyongyang's elite American acceptance of the regime's existence. When the United States signed in Geneva, it instantly enhanced the DPRK and made it viable. From that moment on, Washington had no peaceful alternative but to continue to engage it. Not to do so by dishonoring its obligations, which was America's eventual course of action, only bolstered an adversary and weakened its own standing in the world. As a result, Washington was friendly enough to strengthen Kim Jong Il's economy, hostile enough to increase the dictator's standing at home among his people, and not threatening enough to actually endanger his regime.

Subsequent events suggest that Clinton took the wrong path in 1994—and he certainly didn't bargain as hard as he could have—but the fact is that he committed his country to more than just a particular agreement with North Korea. He settled on a general approach that would set the stage for all other dealings between the two countries, perhaps for decades. Now, the question for Washington is how, in the context of the past, can it disarm the regime?

The joint statement of 2005 contemplates the disarmament of the DPRK, but the document is not as useful as it could have been because at a critical moment America flinched. "We cannot create ambiguities at this stage that would cause confusion in the future," proclaimed Assistant Secretary of State Christopher Hill, the chief American representative at the Beijing negotiations, a couple of days before the announcement of the 2005 statement. "We're not going to get there by papering over these differences and kicking the can down the road."

But that is exactly what Washington did. The joint statement is imprecise, even for a document of its type. There is no mention in the statement of the existence of the DPRK's uranium weapons program—the primary subject of the talks—and only a passing reference to the verification of Pyongyang's disarmament pledge. There are no details explaining the nature or extent of the various promises of the parties and only the vaguest references to when they must perform their obligations. Soon after the announcement of the statement, each of the six parties issued its own interpretation of the document, and it became apparent that there was little agreement among them. When the world needed a definite road map to an enduring solution, America accepted an arrangement that permitted even more North Korean delaying tactics and bad-faith negotiation.

At this moment, there is not even the appearance of progress. Nothing is being contained, much less solved.

Risk-Free Diplomacy?

As six-party talks in Beijing go on—this installment of the Korean crisis has now lasted far longer than the one last decade—the United States clings to the CVID formula. "We will not tolerate nuclear weapons in North Korea," says President Bush, summarizing the American position. "We will not give in to blackmail. We will not settle for anything less than the complete, verifiable, and irreversible elimination of North Korea's nuclear weapons program."

And we should not believe this, at least the part about blackmail. Although Bush will not publicly say so, it is now evident that he is willing to buy North Korea's bomb program. The underlying rationale of CVID, however, is that Washington will do so only one more time. Kim Jong Il wants to both receive aid and keep his arsenal—who wouldn't?—but it is now up to George W. Bush to force the North Koreans to make a choice.

Acceptance of strict inspections—which Pyongyang calls "taking off one's pants"—is the true test of North Korean intentions. If Kim cannot agree to disrobing, then it's unlikely he is truly willing to disarm. North Korea has violated too many of its nuclear obligations—the nonproliferation treaty, its safeguards agreement, the 1991 denuclearization pact with South Korea, 1994's Agreed Framework, and the Pyongyang Declaration, issued in 2002 after a summit with Japan—to be trusted to honor any future pledges on its own. Selig Harrison does not believe the DPRK's leaders can accept Washington's formula. "They absolutely simply will not agree to CVID," he has said.

Harrison's assessment, from all we can tell, appears correct. Kim Jong Il's nuclear arms program is the source of his power. It makes him geopolitically relevant, ensures aid from foreign nations, destabilizes South Korea. It also provides an "aura of invulnerability." Without unconventional weapons, he would be just another ignored leader of one more failing state. With them, he can get what he wants. Kim may also enjoy looking fearsome—power, as Henry Kissinger said, is a good aphrodisiac.

Power is also an excellent deterrent. Kim Jong Il has all the deterrence he needs with his massive conventional forces, but the bomb is his "ultimate weapon of survival." Boris Yeltsin, in an unheralded act of history, withdrew the Soviet nuclear umbrella from the unloved Korean state. Kim and his cohorts are still protected by a mutual defense treaty with China—Beijing's only formal alliance—but the strength of the Chinese commitment may be waning. Although the two communist states are bonded by battlefield blood, their interests are diverging in important ways and their friendship is strained. North Korean leaders, deserted before, feel they might be abandoned again. It's no wonder the Koreans now want their own buttons to push. That, after all, is what their *Juche* demands.

It's hard to see how a country based on *Juche*, an unmistakable assertion of national independence, can ever agree to surrender the ultimate symbol of self-reliance. Worse, how can Korea ever give in to its archenemy, the United States? As powerful as he may be, Kim Junior is nonetheless constrained by his own ideology and, therefore, domestic political opinion.

He is handcuffed by elite politics as well. He may have the power and authority to trade away his powerful arsenal, but he has to consider the hard-line views of his base of power, the army, which thinks he made a poor bargain with the Americans in 1994. Another diplomatic deal, therefore, poses a grave risk for Kim. He has to wonder about the generals' loyalty if he ever gave the order to completely disarm. The nuclear weapons program is the only unqualified success that Kim can claim during his troubled tenure, so it would be especially hard for him to give it up. And there's one more consideration relating to the military elite: How can Kim abandon a weapon so fervently pursued by his father, who is still popular among senior military folk?

As his father knew before him, peace does not suit the purposes of North Korea's ruling family. Now, the younger Kim—the "radioactive lunatic"—realizes that his nuclear arms are useful for creating continual crisis, which distracts attention from domestic difficulties. North Korea historically has thrived on confrontation, and genuine peace would fundamentally transform it. It's improbable that Kim Jong Il is interested in change of that sort. Why should he be? Atop the political system, he has more to lose than gain from a reordering of a society that is already in transition and increasingly unstable.

Some nonetheless argue that Kim Jong Il is merely trying to get the best price for his arms program and that, if he really wanted to go nuclear, he would have just done so long ago with a test or something else dramatic. Although few in the Bush administration share this optimistic view, Washington has been talking with Pyongyang, even if only as a prelude to tougher action. The prevailing opinion in the American capital is that China, Japan, Russia, and South Korea will sign on to sanctions or stronger measures only if they are convinced that America has exhausted diplomacy.

So many consider diplomacy to be risk free. Yet the recent past shows that is not exactly true. As negotiations continued, the North Koreans increased their arsenal. The Bush administration, however, did not appear to care. "They have had these couple of nuclear weapons for many years, and if they have a few more, they have a few more, and they could have them for many years," said an apparently blasé Colin Powell.

Powell's argument was simply untenable. "If you have only one or two bombs you don't have a military strategy," says Robert Einhorn, a Clinton-era State Department official involved in talks with North Korea. "But when you have six or seven you can develop a strategy of threatening or even using some weapons while holding some in reserve. You can do more than simply fire off a single weapon in desperation or in revenge." The DPRK can, for example, sell some. There is simply no denying the fact that, as time passed, a nuclear North Korea became even more dangerous.

So the confrontation with Pyongyang is not just a true zero-sum contest, the fiercest game of chicken on the planet. It's an encounter in which time is the decisive—and forgotten—factor.

THE PYGMALION OF PYONGYANG

North Korea Tries Reform and Creates Geopolitical Crisis

Without deviation progress is not possible.
—Frank Zappa, dead musician

In a tightly scripted totalitarian society, can there be such a thing as coincidence? In July 2002 Pyongyang implemented sweeping wage and price reforms. Two months later Kim Jong Il confessed to visiting Japanese prime minister Junichiro Koizumi that his country had previously abducted some of Japan's citizens to North Korea. Then, Pyongyang made an even more stunning admission: in October of that year the regime acknowledged to the United States that it had a uranium weapons program.

There is not much room for the random act in a government controlled by one man—as Madeleine Albright witnessed, Kim Jong Il can make a hundred thousand people in Pyongyang "dance in step." And as she also observed during her tenure as secretary of state, he can force powerful countries to step on each other's toes.

Events have taken a few strange turns since Kim Jong Il introduced his economic plan in 2002. He is raising the stakes and threatening to plunge the world into the next Dark Ages at this moment because he needs money to keep his reforms on track. If there were ever a tail-wags-dog tale in the history of humankind, this is it.

The nuclearization of North Korea is first and foremost an international crisis that can bring down the world's arms control structure. Yet the timing of recent events is best understood as an outgrowth of domestic crisis inside the DPRK.

Communist Cocoon

In the programmed reality of Korea, Kim Il Sung, the father of the current leader, and his allies thought they could determine almost every last detail of their new domain. At first, it looked as if they might succeed. Like China's Mao Zedong, North Korea's revolutionaries started their transformation of society in the countryside by implementing land reform. Beginning in the spring of 1946—soon after the division of the Korean peninsula and more than two years before the formal establishment of the DPRK—Pyongyang redistributed about 99 percent of tenanted land to more than half the population in an essentially bloodless program. Toward the end of the summer of that year the government started to nationalize industry, taking possession from Japanese owners and the defunct colonial state. The plan did not meet resistance—no Korean, communist or not, would think of inviting the Japanese to resume ownership after the war. In two quick—and popular—strokes the provisional government in Pyongyang had transformed society in less than a year.

What Kim Il Sung giveth, Kim Il Sung would soon taketh away. Like Mao, the North Korean leader decided to do away with small farming after completing land reform. In 1954 Kim began the collectivization of land into cooperative farms, which were thought to be the best way to rebuild agriculture. Private land ownership was totally abolished a half decade later. The collectivization process was completed without the famine or hardship evident in the other communist states of China, Mongolia, and Vietnam.

Communism in the countryside was matched by communism in the city. First Kim and then Mao opted for Stalin's centrally directed development of heavy industry. In China, one five-year plan methodically followed another beginning in 1953. Across the border in North Korea, however, Kim began earlier—in 1947—and he did it with a bit more flexibility. There were two one-year plans, one two-year plan, a three-year plan, a five-year plan, a six-year plan, and three seven-year plans known, of course, as the First Seven-Year Plan, the Second Seven-Year Plan, and the Third Seven-Year Plan.

The North Koreans also launched numerous economic campaigns and movements, many with a martial flavor. If you were fortunate enough to attend the Sixth Congress of the Korean Workers' Party, you would have learned about the Ten Major Goals, which followed the Four Major Military Roads. There were two Flying Horse movements, the first of which in 1958 was Korea's first mass mobilization of people and resources. And in 1975 Pyongyang announced the Three Revolutions—the ideological revolution, the technical revolution, and the cultural revolution.

North Korea's revolutions, including its cultural one, were not as abnormal as China's. Mao Zedong also applied Stalin's formula for rapid industrial growth, but he lost his way with the zany Great Leap Forward, which began in the late 1950s, and the hugely destructive Cultural Revolution, which essentially lasted a decade until his death in 1976. Kim Il Sung, on the other hand, kept his focus and forged straight ahead. From the end of the Korean War to the middle of the 1960s, North Korea, as a result of government plans and campaigns, produced some of the highest rates of economic growth in the world.

The Chinese people noticed. They fled the instability caused by Mao's mistakes for the relative prosperity of Kim's Korea. And people in the South watched as well. In the race for control of the peninsula, the North definitely pulled ahead. It is true that Kim Il Sung had superpower assistance, but so did the South Korean leaders, who enjoyed aid from America. Yet help from outside was not the decisive factor. The DPRK outperformed its southern rival because Kim was more ruthless than any of his counterparts in Seoul. The Soviet model of forced economic mobilization through dictatorial control actually proved to be the winning formula.

But only at first. "The concept of dictatorship being good for development is flawed," argues Jean-Pierre Lehmann of the Evian Group, a think tank in Lausanne. "The only countries that have been able to maintain prosperity over the long term, say, fifty years, are democracies, not a single exception."

Not even North Korea: Kim's run of good times lasted just two decades, not five. His economy may have doubled in size from 1965 to 1976—but that was the last gasp of rapid growth. Signs of serious dislocations first appeared during the earlier part of this period as shortages began to plague the country. The First Seven-Year Plan, which was supposed to be completed in 1967, essentially became a ten-year plan when it was extended to 1970, and every subsequent plan also failed to meet its targets on time. During the 1960s the North stopped publishing comprehensive economic statistics, another sign that goals were not being met. Kim, as capable and energetic as he was, eventually took socialism as far as it could go, which means he ultimately exhausted the altruism of the North Korean population.

While Kim's economy slowed, South Korea's accelerated. Seoul's system also relied on planning and coercion, yet it left much more room for individual initiative. Economic output in the South more than tripled from the middle of the 1960s to the middle of the 1970s, and soon Kim Il Sung found himself in second place on the peninsula. By the end of the 1970s per capita output in the South exceeded that in the North.

Kim should have abandoned the more rigid aspects of socialism at the first signs of the exhaustion of his system, but he was reluctant. Early triumph is often the enemy of later success: the memory of the DPRK's rapid growth immediately after the war discouraged fundamental change later on. China, in contrast, was not burdened by past glory and long-serving leaders—the death of Mao and the almost complete failure of his economy forced the country to rethink its approach. As a result, Deng Xiaoping, who took power at the end of 1978, was able to introduce a dose of free market thinking, what he called "socialism with Chinese characteristics." There would be no such reevaluation in Kim Il Sung's North Korea.

Instead, Kim borrowed a Chinese phrase with an unfortunate history and inaugurated his "Great Leap Outward" in the early 1970s. This initiative, which marked a partial move away from his isolationism, consisted of purchasing foreign production lines and whole factories—including ones for such consumer-pleasers as panty hose—from Japan and Western Europe. Pyongyang also bought fleets of Mercedeses and Volvos and the latest in Siemens medical equipment. Like all good socialists, he had a penchant for projects with low economic returns and even those with no return at all—the North Korean leader loved oversized monuments with computer-controlled heating and air-conditioning.

Kim's great foreign shopping spree was essentially an attempt to avoid reform by creating growth. The adventure, which cost the country billions of dollars, was largely financed by debt. Unfortunately, his timing was terrible: the Arab oil embargo and the subsequent global recession of the early 1970s made it difficult for North Korea to repay mounting foreign obligations. So Kim just reneged, making his country the first communist state to do so. He stopped paying in late 1974, but he was largely able to keep creditors at bay until 1986, when Western banks formally declared North Korea to be in default.

By refusing to pay back the debt, Kim shut North Korea off from the West again and thereby made his country even more beholden to the Soviet Union, hardly a model for economic reform, and China, which was still stumbling in the dark at that point. For the most part, he reverted to isolationist policies founded on *Juche* and resumed his competition with the Albanians to create the most closed nation in the world.

Yet Kim, to his credit, did not close off the world entirely. In 1984 he tried one more series of experiments with foreigners, this time seeing if he could attract investment by offering them the opportunity to participate in joint ventures. Although this business program offered surprisingly generous provisions, the initiative failed because the government did not implement the broader changes necessary for successful commerce.

Kim also tried to establish a special development zone. Unlike Deng Xiaoping's zones in coastal China, Kim's experiment didn't work. Rajin-Sonbong, the first North Korean zone, was tucked in the northeastern part of the country and ringed by barbed wire. It was too isolated from the rest of society to succeed. Hardy foreign pioneers lost bundles of cash. Again, Kim Il Sung was prepared for change but not fundamental change.

Closer to Kim's heart were his efforts to make socialism work better. Like Soviet and Chinese Marxists, he tried economic rejuvenation through science and technology, specifically concentrating on automation, computerization, and robotization in the middle of the 1980s. Kim even experimented with minor structural reform. Pyongyang retreated from the worst aspects of central planning by pushing down responsibility to production units, which were allowed to keep earnings after quotas were met. This adjustment was tried in most other communist nations, but in North Korea it produced even more dismal results due to Pyongyang's ambivalence toward decentralization—and backtracking.

Kim's attempts to remake an overly bureaucratized system were far too timid. Liberalization, as Western economists know it, was not in the cards. Kim was not about to adopt market mechanisms or even incentives for individuals because he would not permit power to shift away from the state. As a result of this halfheartedness, the economy remained grossly inefficient. For most of the 1980s it looked as if Kim Il Sung was merely devising more modern ways to achieve failure.

From the perspective of 1989, however, Kim looked like a genius, or at least a lot smarter than he did before. In that year Tiananmen Square in Beijing and city centers throughout China were filled with ordinary citizens singing, praying, chanting, striking, and fasting. Demonstrators almost ditched the dictatorship of the Chinese proletariat although that was not their intention. Bolder protesters in Eastern Europe—and weaker leaders there—actually brought down governments. Events abroad convinced the members of the North Korean ruling elite that their communist cousins had not quite mastered the dynamic relationship between economic and political change. In the face of calamitous developments elsewhere, Kim Il Sung became even more intransigent about reform.

Mikhail Gorbachev, on the other hand, became bolder, and Kim soon lost his primary benefactor in another unexpected upheaval. In the space of a few years the world was left with just a quintet of communist nations—China, Vietnam, Laos, and Cuba were the others—and North Korea was in many ways the most vulnerable of them. Although it was never a Soviet satellite, it had nonetheless grown heavily dependent on Moscow's largesse.

As Kim, the *Juche* Master, should have known, dependency can lead to disaster. The North Korean economy first started to contract in 1990, but the crunch didn't occur until the following year when Soviet concessional trade arrangements ended. Up until then, more than half of North Korea's total foreign commerce was with the USSR, and China did not pick up the slack. By the beginning of 1992, the falloff was so dramatic that trade was negligible. The result of the sudden decline was that North Korea did not have enough energy to keep factories running. Oil was so scarce that the country ultimately had to convert vehicles so that they ran on charcoal—or not use them at all.

The slide was unprecedented for Korea. North Korea's gross domestic product fell each year from 1990 through 1998 according to the Bank of Korea, South Korea's central bank. During this period the economy shrank by about half. In December 1993 the Korean Workers' Party made the unprecedented announcement that an economic plan had failed to achieve its goals. At the end of the Third Seven-Year Plan, which was extended two years until 1995, the DPRK gave up its multiyear blueprints, thereby becoming, in the words of economist Mitsuhiko Kimura, "a planned economy without planning."

The extent of the failure was worse than a missed deadline, however. One of Kim's early successes had been to put a floor on poverty, but that floor—a system of comprehensive social services and guaranteed distribution of food—was giving way. He had built an economy that was "controlled, centralized, collectivized," but now it was also crumbling.

Other countries have experienced failures of this magnitude, but North Korea was, as usual, different: the fall of the DPRK economy was not caused by either political or economic restructuring. It was, as American analyst Nicholas Eberstadt wrote, the virtually inevitable result of "relentless enforcement of economic policies that range from the manifestly wasteful to the positively injurious."

Of course, the breakdown of North Korea was more than the work of just one man. In order to ensure an orderly succession to his eldest son, the Great Leader had given wider latitude to the Dear Leader in the handling of governmental affairs. As Kim Jong Il appeared to have events under control, Dad in his declining years retreated to the life of an elder statesman and country gentleman. Junior was even more orthodox than his father and emphasized ideology at the expense of real solutions, which was the sensible approach for an insecure heir. Playing safe, however, was bad governance in view of the obvious need for radical restructuring.

Kim Il Sung partially reengaged when he realized the severity of the problems. He knew there had to be change and made some effort to adjust to circumstances, but his actions were largely gestures. When he took real action, he pushed the country in the wrong direction. He tried, for example, to emphasize agriculture by bringing new areas under cultivation, but that ultimately caused deforestation and erosion. Famine would soon result.

Yet the biggest blot on Kim's final years is his failure to put a dent into military spending. This was by far the most important reform, and it was something that only he could accomplish. A mere 22 million people continued to support the world's fifth largest armed forces. Approximately a quarter of the nation's output had been devoted to the military for several decades, and the army's share of the economy was probably *growing* in the mid-1990s. No economy, no matter how efficient or productive, can bear such a burden. Under Kim Senior, North Korea was always on a war footing.

By failing to curb military expenses Kim proved once again that it is easier to build than to reform. So we shouldn't be surprised that at the end of his life he could not fix the DPRK. For all his considerable talents, Kim Il Sung's vision was limited. His life, regrettably, was lived almost entirely inside a communist cocoon. He had never met a sitting leader of a major Western country and, apart from trips to Algeria and Indonesia, spent every moment of his life in Marxist nations once he returned to Korea in 1945. He could wear a Western business suit, as he did in his later years, but sartorial preferences said little about his world outlook.

Perhaps it is unfair to judge such a leader by today's standards. Kim came of age in the midst of anti-colonial struggle in Asia. Communism at that time promised modernity, equality, and even a measure of freedom, at least freedom from one's powerful neighbors. It is no accident that the world's three Sinic cultures—Chinese, Vietnamese, and Korean—all chose Marxist theories and Leninist tactics as a way out of their predicaments. Communism and anti-colonialism were seen, if not as twins, at least as cousins. If we criticize Kim Il Sung's early views on economics, what we are really saying is that he did not have the foresight to look beyond his time and place and see what was evident at the end of the twentieth century.

But let's not be too easy on Kim. Even if we choose to look at him in the context of contemporaries like Mao and Ho Chi Minh, Kim, unlike them, lived to see the global fall of communism. So a comparison with Fidel Castro is probably fair, at least as fair as cross-country and cross-cultural comparisons get. Gorbachev's severing of aid devastated both the DPRK and Cuba, which became the only remaining branches in the heavily pruned family tree of "old system" communist states. Castro, who shared Kim Il Sung's reluctance for reform, eventually adapted to the withdrawal of assistance while the North Korean could not. As a result of Kim's rigidity, his people suffered more than the Cubans. The first Great Leader could have, and should have, done more.

Because he could not embrace real change, the best thing Kim could have done in the last decade of the twentieth century was to get out of the way. At least he accomplished that, on July 8, 1994. Kim Il Sung is one problem that death ultimately solved.

Enter "the Sun of the 21st Century"

The Great Leader's passing, however, created another problem, for it led to the eventual elevation of his son. In the opaque world of Pyongyang's politics, we don't know why it took Kim Jong Il more than three years to formalize his role as his father's successor, as he eventually did in October 1997. Most observers say he needed time to obtain the support of the old guard, and perhaps that is true. In any event, the junior Kim's timing was just about flawless. He assumed the mantle of leadership months before the North Korean economy hit bottom, thereby permitting him to claim that the recovery was his doing. According to most observers, 1999 was the first year of economic expansion since the beginning of that decade.

So should Kim Junior get the credit for the recovery of the economy soon after his elevation? Yes, he should, but only for excellent stage management. When it comes to his mastery of economics, it is still unclear how we should judge "the Sun of the 21st Century," as he is called by Pyongyang's propagandists.

Few leaders in history have been able to do much when both an economy and a society are in free fall. Kim Jong Il's inhumane approach was to perform triage, which came naturally to a man who is said to lack empathy. The solution was also logical, at least in one sense. Gaul was divided into three parts, and so is the North Korean economy. Korean analyst Kongdan Oh identifies a "palace economy," a "military economy," and a "civilian" one. It is only the third one that took the big hit last decade because Kim Jong Il concentrated his dwindling resources on the first two. So neither Kim Jong Il and his small circle of cadres nor the armed forces suffered nearly as much as ordinary citizens.

For this last group Kim did little except to exhort the common folk to rely on "inner reserves." He even announced that the way to the future was to return to the past, specifically an increased reliance on mass mobilization and intensified ideological indoctrination. Kim literally asked workers to do the impossible and perform miracles, which really was outside their job descriptions. After all, he, not them, was the deity. God—the one resident in Pyongyang—was also fond of "speed battles," both short-term and decade-long campaigns targeted to hike production. Unlike harmless harangues, these drives actually damaged the economy because temporary gains in production in one area were more than offset by distortions caused by the shifting of resources from others to meet artificial targets.

Kim's goals were as wrongheaded as his tactics. What was his development strategy for the economy? As late as 1998 he said North Korea should concentrate on heavy industry. That statement bordered on the ludicrous: his solution was to build steel plants and petrochemical complexes while the country could not keep bicycle factories open—and while North Koreans were starving to death in extremely large numbers.

Yet for every nonsensical statement from Kim Jong Il there was a perfectly reasonable explanation. The first Kim so dominated society that structural reform was not possible for at least a decade after his departure. Kim Il Sung was the system, and the system remained Kim Il Sung's. Even if the younger Kim had different ideas or wanted to build his own legacy— and it is not clear what he thought or wanted to do—he had little room for maneuver. His father's advisers, for one thing, retained their positions of influence and control. Frank Zappa may well have been right that deviation is the parent of progress, but in "the Kim Il Sung nation" where the dead Kim Il Sung still presided as president, Kim Jong Il could not deviate from his father's course. Therefore, failure, at least for ordinary North Koreans, was the only option.

So Kim Junior was really not able to help the common folk, except to provide thoughts on self-reliance. *Juche*, the guiding philosophy of the nation as a whole, became applicable to the smallest unit of society, the family. Kim abandoned his people because, by the time he took over, the civilian economy had fallen into a "poverty trap"—it did not earn enough to replace building, machinery, and other productive assets as they wore out. By the middle of the 1990s North Korea had lost the ability to mend itself and was headed for a postindustrial—actually preindustrial—existence.

Whole factories, sold for scrap, were dismantled and carted across the border to China.

The *Juche* nation eventually began to recover, but not because of internal reform or even local efforts. North Korea was put back on its feet largely because South Korea, the erstwhile mortal enemy, was under new management. Kim Dae Jung, the former dissident who made his reputation challenging military governments in Seoul, started to provide aid to the North in 1998 when he took office as the president of the newly democratized nation. South Korea's assistance, which was large in relation to the North Korean economy, jump-started economic growth.

China also stepped up aid. Unlike Seoul's assistance, Beijing's help came at a price. Chinese leaders demanded some measure of reform, presumably because they did not want South Korea to absorb the North, which for them was a buffer state. In May 2000 they summoned Kim Jong Il to the Chinese capital, his first trip outside the DPRK in seventeen years. Then Beijing pulled the string again in January of the following year, resulting in Kim's visit to the bustling Shanghai metropolis for a show-and-tell session on economic development.

Kim Jong Il was not only constrained by Pyongyang politics—"Expect no change from me," he famously said in 1996—but there were international politics at work on him as well. Pulled in two different directions, he was about to prove that his pa was right—nations dependent on others lacked *Juche* and were little more than subjects. The Chinese, on the other hand, had loads of *Juche* and were trying to call the tune on a North Korean *domestic* matter, economic reform. In July 2002 it looked as if they had succeeded in getting the stubborn Kim Jong Il to undertake the first step away from the Kim Il Sung system.

A Tale of Two Confessions

In post-Mao China, everyone was in on the secret. Even poor proletarians in far-flung provinces sensed economic change was coming well before Deng Xiaoping had replaced Hua Guofeng, Mao Zedong's chosen successor, in December 1978.

In North Korea, however, few had a clue. Brian Bridges, a British academic known for his connections to Pyongyang's bureaucracy, spent June 2002 in the capital and traveling throughout the rest of the DPRK. He reports that even senior officials had no inkling of impending events.

Yet on the first day of the following month North Korea announced its package of economic measures, called the first real attempt in the history of the DPRK to implement sweeping change. Official commodity prices were raised for the first time in more than two decades. Rice, the staple, went up 550 times, for instance. Wages, last adjusted some twenty years before, skyrocketed by as much as sixty-fold. Rationing—formally known as the Public Distribution System—was cut way back. The so-called farmers' markets, where peasants and entrepreneurs came together to sell both produce and consumer products, were brought one step closer to legitimacy. And for the first time, North Koreans had to start paying for housing and utilities.

As a part of the package of reforms, the official price of the won, the currency, was repegged much closer to prevailing exchange rates. In August 2002 the won was devalued from 2.16 to the American dollar—Kim Jong Il's official birthday is February 16—to 150 when the black market price was around 200.

Other changes echoed prior reforms. North Korea took another stab at decentralization, pushing even more authority down to local governments and even business enterprises. Pyongyang curtailed subsidies to the businesses, which were also made responsible for their own costs. The government significantly increased the size of farmers' "private plots."

Workers were happy—at first. Wage hikes meant they could splurge for the first time in memory. Then, of course, the inevitable occurred. Even in a centrally controlled economy, when there's too much money to spend and not enough goods to buy only one thing can happen: inflation. Inflation in North Korea took back all the gains almost immediately. Some workers then lost their livelihoods because business enterprises, cut loose from the state, could not afford to pay their staff. Even whole factories shut down. The end result of the July 2002 changes was a severe downturn that has yet to reverse itself. Rising prices have more than canceled out small increases in output reported by Pyongyang. The resulting economic dislocation created a whole new underclass of urban poor. Many factory hands headed to the countryside to sweep dirt from the roads or work as manual labor on farms.

And others fled north. Severe economic failure brought back memories of the great famine of the previous decade and triggered a new flood of refugees across the Yalu and Tumen Rivers to China. North Korean officials told people it was better to die at home than flee, but few listened. The refugee tide, which was highly embarrassing to Pyongyang, made it apparent that the country was going to need even more time—at least a half decade—and additional outside aid to keep the economy going in a period of economic dislocation. To bridge the transition the government needed to provide additional food until farmers could ramp up production and come up with extra cash to pay workers in struggling enterprises.

To obtain assistance, Pyongyang made its foreign policy serve domestic needs for the first time in its history. By 2002 the DPRK was also coming off a flurry of diplomatic activity that began with the historic "two Kims" summit in 2000 between Kim Jong Il and South Korea's Kim Dae Jung. That meeting in Pyongyang was followed by four agreements on economic cooperation between the two Koreas and the establishment of ties with countries around the world, including those in the European Union. So 2002 looked propitious. Kim, having laid the groundwork, believed the international community was then ready to support a new North Korea.

The major initiative of 2002's coordinated campaign involved an easy mark. Japan's prime minister, Junichiro Koizumi, wanted a diplomatic triumph, even if it meant distancing himself from traditional ally America. Kim Jong Il had his Japanese counterpart come to Pyongyang in September 2002 so that they could settle matters left over from World War II and normalize diplomatic relations. Kim expected a big transfusion of assistance from the taxpayers of Japan, perhaps as much as the equivalent of $10 billion, as a form of disguised reparations.

Kim and Koizumi both thought they could come to agreement in a short period. Yet the North Korean knew that he had to remove a longstanding stumbling block before he could get his hands on the dough. During this crucial summit in Pyongyang, Kim acknowledged his country in the 1970s and 1980s had abducted thirteen Japanese nationals, who were nabbed so that they could train North Korean spies. Having for years angrily denied any responsibility, he now blamed the series of kidnappings on rogue elements working for some dead Korean named Kim Il Sung. Kim Jong Il said only five of the original thirteen abductees were alive and that the remains of the other eight had been washed away by floods or were otherwise lost.

That explanation was good enough for the eager Koizumi. Japanese citizens, however, were outraged and in no mood to let the matter drop. The public in Japan sensed what senior politicians in Tokyo could not: the kidnappings were unforgivable, the North Korean leader was insincere, and the admission was phony on several counts. Ordinary Japanese were not about to pay reparations to the North Koreans—on the contrary, they wanted Pyongyang to pay reparations to Japan for the abductions. Kim at that point had no choice—he had to release the five surviving abductees, who immediately returned to Japan. He still held their children born in North Korea, but by then the outraged Japanese prevented their government from ransoming the kids left behind. Kim, taken aback by the reaction of Japan's public, had to strike Koizumi from his list of possible new donors.

The failure of the Japanese to make big payments left only one source of quick cash, but it was the mother lode. The following month, visiting American assistant secretary of state James Kelly accused Pyongyang of starting a secret uranium-based nuclear weapons program. To the American's surprise, Kang Sok Ju, Kim Jong Il's right-hand man, admitted it had. The following April during talks sponsored by China, North Korean diplomat Li Gun told James Kelly in Beijing that his country possessed a nuclear weapon. He then asked the American, "Now what are you going to do about it?"

Kim expected the Americans to do what they had done in the past: panic and then come to terms. This time, however, Washington would try a different tack.

Missing a Historic Moment?

"Kim expected big investments from the U.S., Japan and South Korea after the reforms, but they didn't come," says a Chinese official in frequent contact with the North Korean government. It's quite evident to us why the world failed to help. But the North Korean leader, who had seen his father easily manipulate the Chinese and the Soviets, misjudged the Japanese and the Americans. With Washington, he had overplayed his hand and triggered a crisis over the most important thing he had to sell—his nuclear arsenal. George W. Bush, to the surprise of Pyongyang, reduced the flow of material assistance to North Korea instead of increasing it, thereby setting the stage for an especially nasty spat. The July 2002 reforms pointed the DPRK in the direction the world wanted that nation to take. The United States, however, turned its back on Pyongyang in a moment of need. By denying aid, some argue, America helped preserve the country as a communist state. So did Washington miss a historic opportunity to help change North Korean society for the better? Only if Kim Jong Il was serious about changing his country.

So does the leader of the Democratic People's Republic of Korea really want to reform his economy? When there's not much to go on, the simplest explanation is often the best. The least complicated theory is that the North Korean capital is inhabited by the ignorant and the timid. For example, Marcus Noland, an economist with the Institute for International Economics in Washington, D.C., sees all the hardship that Pyongyang's policies have caused and raises the possibility that reform is being implemented by people who do not understand basic economic principles or are at least afraid to speak out. If true, this theory lends support to the notion that Kim is genuinely trying to modernize his economy. The fact that he is not succeeding may be due to faulty implementation rather than bad intentions.

Yet the simplest explanation is not always the most prudent one to make. It's generally risky, after all, to believe that one's adversaries are making mistakes. Despite all the hardship caused by recent reforms, we have to consider the possibility that Kim Jong Il is doing exactly what he set out to do.

The most important evidence about his intentions is found in the July 2002 reforms themselves. In that package of changes Kim did three things right: he essentially eliminated price controls, he lifted wages, and he devalued the currency. He also did one thing horribly wrong: he continued to suppress private enterprise, potentially the most productive part of the economy. Inflation would not have been so bad had private parties been freed to produce as much as they could. The fact they were not says a lot about Kim's intentions, or at least his fears. If he had given nonstate producers the green light, he would have encouraged considerably more economic and social change in North Korean society.

Apparently, Kim did not want to lose control of the economy to ordinary citizens. Yet he already had, and that was partly what July 2002 was all about: maintaining power. The changes announced that month were dramatic, and on their face they were more substantive than anything the Chinese, for instance, ever did at any one time. Yet many parts of the package merely ratified what had already occurred, and others represented attempts to get ahead of expected change. In short, the North Korean people were already reforming on their own.

To catch up to his followers, Kim largely structured the reform package to bring the economy back under state supervision. For instance, runaway inflation, considered by most analysts an unintentional result of the changes, substantially devalued currency held by black market operators. Crippling them helped Pyongyang regain control. Farmers' markets were already operating freely throughout the country; it was pointless to consider them illegal and better to bring them under official regulation. By offering near-market prices for goods, Kim Jong Il was trying to attract money back into the official economy. Moreover, Kim's floating prices allowed state enterprises to better fix their own charges for goods—by seeing what the limited free market was doing—thereby making socialism work better. Rationing had already broken down outside Pyongyang anyway. Farmers had long ago appropriated large tracts of state land for private plots. The government could not afford continued subsidies, so it was better to make the cutoff look like conscious policy.

Balbina Hwang of the Heritage Foundation goes so far as to argue that the July 2002 initiatives do not necessarily represent "reform." The economy had failed, she argues, so there had to be changes of some sort. It's more precise to say they were "desperate measures." Perhaps we call them reforms because that's something we desperately want to hear. Events since July 2002 show that there was in fact no breakthrough in Pyongyang's mentality. First, in December 2002 the government tried to stop the circulation of American dollars, the preferred currency of the North Korean people. Hard currencies, and especially the dollar, were powering the black economy. Forcing people to use the North Korean won would go a long way to bringing the economy back under state control. People were ordered to exchange their dollars at state banks for euros, the then-new currency for much of the European Union. The banks, of course, did not have European money, so people got won back instead. The decree, therefore, was essentially an expropriation of hard currency.

Next, in March 2003 North Korea issued its first bonds since 1950. The People's Life Bonds, which resemble raffle tickets more than debt instruments, are perhaps the worst bargain in the history of modern finance.

They don't pay interest during the first five years of their existence. Holders of the bonds are, however, eligible for the return of principal and prizes in periodic lotteries. Although purchase of the bonds was technically "voluntary," many workers were forced to contribute at least a third of their salaries by payroll deduction or compelled to take them in lieu of wages.

The bonds at least showed that the government was not resorting to the printing of money to avoid a liquidity crunch. Yet that was the extent of the good news. By essentially appropriating a large portion of people's salaries, the government made common folk use hidden savings and thereby squeezed money from out of their mattresses. The bonds, which are akin to expropriation in several respects, are not the typical act of a government committed to reform.

Moreover, reforming governments always cut back military spending. At least since the end of the Second World War, no country has created self-sustaining economic growth while giving its armed forces the first claim on national resources. North Korea is moving in the wrong direction: the military's economy has taken turf from the civilian one after Kim Il Sung's death and now accounts for perhaps 30 to 50 percent of GDP. Until Kim Jong Il breaks the grip of the army—and there is no indication that he is trying to do that—real reform will never take place.

Uncontrollable Change

Kenneth Quinones, who says he is the first U.S. diplomat to have visited North Korea, argues that Pyongyang suspended the July 2002 economic reforms in the spring of 2004 because it considers them failures.

Quinones's announcement, which raised eyebrows, suggests a fundamental question: Does it really matter what the DPRK government does, or does not do, about its economy? At least in the long run, the answer is no. In China, government-sponsored reforms led to informal change, but in North Korea, the situation was reversed. In July 2002 we saw evidence that the North Korean people could push their government around. The DPRK is now on a trajectory of its own—North Koreans, often called the most oppressed people on earth, have set their own direction.

In fact, they were setting it by the mid-1990s. Kim Jong Il coped with the great famine by cutting people loose from the totalitarian state—a state that no longer provided food and essential social services for many civilians outside Pyongyang. Moreover, social controls broke down as people roamed the country—and crossed back and forth across the border with China—looking for food and water. Many died; those who survived did so by thinking for themselves. For the first time in their lives, people acted without state direction or even state sanction. State failure, even though temporary, made North Korea a freer society.

After the end of the "Arduous March"—Pyongyang's code for the famine—the state was able to reassert a measure of control over people's lives. Yet it never recovered all the ground it had lost. In the space of a few years, the mentality of the North Korean population had changed—completely.

And irrevocably. Political scientists talk about the relentlessness of reform, but that was not what North Koreans experienced during the last decade. People lived through something even more dramatic: the almost complete failure of society. In the 1990s ordinary citizens on their own figured out how free economies work, and there's no going back once people learn what is possible. Governments can reverse a particular change by fiat—China has done so many times in the last quarter century, for instance—but the *process* of transformation over time is inexorable. Change, unfortunately for autocrats, always continues under the surface. It is unstoppable because it happens inside people's minds.

In their minds the common folk of North Korea no longer define themselves in relation to the state—they now do so in relation to the market. For more than a decade ordinary citizens have learned to survive without government support in what is an informal and primitive market situation. It's a black market, which means it is free. Today, even after all the "reforms" intended to corral change, the fastest-growing part of the "world's last truly command economy" is the private sector. About twice as much money circulates in the unofficial economy as in the ailing state one.

These days, money circulates fast. There wasn't much need for cash when the state provided everything. Now, when it offers little, people earn and spend at a rapid pace. As a result, people developed their own "money culture." The obsession with cash has made people coarse: wealthy entrepreneurs have replaced soldiers as the most eligible husbands and wedding guests are served different grades of food depending on the size of their presents, for instance. But, as aid worker Kathi Zellweger points out, their new outlook has also permitted them to dream—and dreaming is something they have never done before. In the new North Korea, where the power of the state is not so evident, citizens have found that with money almost everything is possible. As Zellweger notes, North Koreans for the first time say, "I can do things now."

In a society of possibilities, people explore what they can achieve. In a culture obsessed with the group, people now are acting on their own. At the beginning of the 1990s there were almost no small businesses in North Korea. Today, people sell trinkets by the roadside, markets have spread across the country, and entrepreneurs develop their own products.

And tomorrow? "One change leaves the way open for the introduction of others," Machiavelli told us. In North Korea, the famine and economic failure of the last decade led to the tentative reform of this one. Tentative reform is now creating its own momentum. The July 2002 measures, which were essentially designed to slow and even halt change, have nonetheless ended up creating it. Even if Kenneth Quinones's claim that they have been repealed is correct, the reforms have nevertheless spread faster and further than almost anyone had anticipated and are now beyond the control of the bureaucrats in Pyongyang. It's not so much their specific provisions; it's the signal that people read. Change, in their view, has now been legitimized.

Kim Jong Il, however, has gone to extraordinary lengths to rein in the process of transformation. By necessity, he has had to open up parts of his economy—the Chinese, his main benefactors, require economic change and the South Koreans nudge him to show progress. Kim's clever solution is a throwback to his father's time: to limit real change to restricted zones. In addition to the failed Rajin-Sonbong zone established in 1991, there is a new tourist project at Mount Kumgang—Diamond Mountain—and an industrial park in Kaesong, both run by hopeful South Koreans. The Mount Kumgang zone is hermetically sealed from the rest of North Korea and is, by all accounts, a calamity. Kaesong, which is under construction, has a chance of sparking industrial rejuvenation in the North, yet it is too early to tell. The United Nations Development Programme has sponsored a zone-like project for the Tumen River delta, which is supposed to be the "future Rotterdam" for Northeast Asia. Although the Chinese are supportive because they want an outlet onto the Sea of Japan, the concept has languished for years because North Korea has not been interested in opening that area to the outside.

That leaves Kim Jong Il's brainchild, the Sinuiju Special Administrative Region, across the Yalu River from China's Dandong City on the DPRK's northwest border. The zone, once labeled "the delivery room of hope," will essentially be an independent country of around fifty square miles. The enclave will have it own flag, passports, and a European chief justice. Every currency in the world will be accepted. Citizens of all countries will be able to enter visa-free. North Korea's people, however, will be kept out by a wall. In fact, two-thirds of the city's current 600,000 residents will be moved out of the territory to be occupied by the zone.

The plan suffered a setback in 2002 when China arrested the man Kim picked to become Sinuiju's chief. Yang Bin, at the time China's second richest person, was detained the day he was to leave the Middle Kingdom to take up his post in the Hermit Kingdom. Beijing was miffed at not being consulted about the plan and was probably concerned that it would turn into a haven for fugitives from Chinese justice. Since that time, Kim has looked at potential replacements and in 2004 decided on a woman from California's Orange County.

Zones might be a good idea for North Korea, but only if they serve as laboratories for reforms that are eventually applied to the country as a whole. China has used its zones in that way, mostly with success. Yet apparently Kim sees his only as sources of cash. As one North Korean official said, "Let's consider the Najin-Sonbong area as a pigsty. Build a fence around it, put in karaoke, and capitalists will invest. We need only to collect earnings from the pigs." The Mount Kumgang area is structured the same way: self-contained as if it were not part of North Korea. From all accounts, Sinuiju, if it ever gets off the ground, will be based on the same concept.

The zone approach can be called part of the "Chinese model" of economic change. Yet Kim Jong Il told Madeleine Albright that he is not interested in Beijing's style of market reforms. The North Korean leader is a keen student of the disturbances in Tiananmen Square as well as the collapse of the Eastern European satellites and the failure of the Soviet Union. It's no wonder he tells visitors that he's more interested in the "Swedish model" and the "Thai model" (presumably referring to national development strategies and not something else).

While he amuses visiting dignitaries with his theories on economic restructuring, his government does little to change the economy. With the failure of his diplomatic initiatives toward Japan and the United States, he has tried to slow down what passes for reform in North Korea. North Koreans, however, are getting on with their lives. That means Kim Jong Il doesn't have forever to shore up his rule over a people in motion. If he is to stay on top, Kim needs to force more assistance from the world to support the transformation of his faltering economy. That means the world will hear from him again—and probably soon.

4

COLLAPSE PERHAPS?

"Oppressed" North Koreans Are Remaking Their Society

I believe that the ideals of socialism, which
are so generous and appeal so much to solidarity
and fraternity, will one day disappear.
—Fidel Castro

"The half-life of Plutonium-239 is 24,400 years," says Harvard's Ashton Carter. "What is the half-life of the North Korean regime?"

Not long ago observers thought the DPRK had only months to live. Yet the government in Pyongyang did not fall when Kim Il Sung died or even during the devastating famine. Because analysts were so wrong a few years back, they have now swung to the opposite conclusion about regime change. "Don't wait," advises Charles "Jack" Pritchard, a former State Department official. "It's not going to happen."

It won't? The experts were mistaken before, and of course they could be mistaken now. It's hard for outsiders to understand the Kimist system, even after continued contact with it. For one thing, the normal rules of social stability do not seem to apply to the DPRK, and the country's family dictatorship has a hidden resilience. Its apparent internal strength defies our hopes for the North Korean people.

And for ourselves. The stability of nuclear North Korea is now a matter of global significance. Our future depends on knowing whether we are dealing with a fundamentally strong regime or a weak one. So how long can Kim Jong Il continue his clan's peculiar form of despotism?

The Struggle to Obey

As much as we like to think that people don't put up with atrocious leaders and bad forms of governance, history proves otherwise. The plight of the North Koreans, for example, illustrates how a people's past and culture can conspire to make them passive. Kim Il Sung, as tyrannical as he turned out to be, could oppress his fellow Koreans largely because he did not look bad in comparison to his immediate predecessors, the brutish Japanese during the harsh colonial period and the rapacious Soviets of the subsequent occupation. Moreover, the Great Leader could mask his great crimes by speaking the same language as his victims and glorifying their common heritage.

Because Kim Il Sung was one of them, he knew how to make Koreans accept oppression. He understood, for instance, his people's ability to endure hardship—to "eat bitterness," as the Chinese say—and how far he could push them. And through a series of bad decisions he unintentionally acclimatized the Korean people to continuing economic failure. When famine came shortly after his death, they were ready to cope with hunger or at least to die quietly. The long starvation of the 1990s even worked to the benefit of the regime as it made many North Koreans weak. Ordinary folk simply did not have the strength to complain about their patently incapable leaders.

Even if they had the stamina, they did not possess the imagination. There is, unfortunately, something passive in the traditional Korean character. "Western history, you could say, is a history of disobedience," says

Paik Sang-chang of the Korea Social Pathology Institute. "But our history is one of the struggle to obey." "Korean heroes," author Michael Breen notes, "are the loyal subject and the filial son, whose exemplary virtue is their suppression of self in the course of obedience."

In the last six hundred years Koreans have largely succeeded in the struggle to stay in line. Yi Song Gye successfully upset the established political order through force in 1392 when he founded the Choson Dynasty. Then the Korean people went quiet and regime change on their peninsula occurred only at the initiation of outsiders. The Japanese got rid of the Choson rulers in 1910, the Allies ditched the Japanese at the end of the Second World War, and the Americans and Soviets left the peninsula of their own accord after establishing two separate governments to take their place. The South Koreans, however, began to reverse a half millennium of meekness in the late 1980s as they changed the nature of their government. The same, sadly, cannot yet be said of their brothers and sisters in the northern half of the peninsula.

We can credit the Kims, father and son, for making sure that the DPRK reflected the old values of obedience. Their all-inclusive political system surrounded the North Koreans from birth to death, and strict isolation left them ignorant of most everything. And there was the regime's trademark repression. Kim family rule, always brutal and mostly unforgiving, was exceedingly effective, depriving people of the means to topple the existing system. "If you know your family will be taken away, who would dare demonstrate?" asks Kang Chol-hwan, who escaped from the DPRK and now lives in the South. No wonder the North didn't have strong opposition groups or celebrated leaders waiting to stage a revolt.

Moreover, it was not only their history and culture that helped strengthen the regime against its people. Foreigners helped too. During the Cold War, Kim Il Sung enjoyed international support, at least enough to sustain his rule. He received sufficient aid from Beijing and Moscow to keep the elite members of the regime fed, and that's what mattered. Today, none of the three countries sharing a land border with the DPRK—China, Russia, and South Korea—wishes to see his son go, so not one of them provides comfort to scattered dissidents.

The people are repressed, and the government, although weakened, has been able to survive. The prospects for political upheaval, therefore, appear negligible. Kim Jong Il, however, is leaving nothing to chance, even going so far as to rewrite the book on communism, the ultimate one-party system. Fidel Castro said, "we only need one party," but the North Korean leader gets along without any. Since his father's death, he has let the Workers' Party decline. In many places it has almost stopped operating. In its place the armed forces and a multitude of security services now go about administering, in the words of Donald Gregg, "the most successful totalitarian regime ever constructed."

Kim's boast—"My power comes from the military"—accurately identifies the source of his current strength. In a country of a little over 20 million souls, he is defended by 1.2 million active-duty soldiers and at least 5 million reservists. Kim handpicked about a thousand of the nation's 1,200 generals, lavishes senior officers with luxury cars and dachas, and makes sure they get all the resources his country has. He may remain aloof from the citizenry, but he keeps close tabs on the base of his power, retaining command-and-control authority over officers in the DMZ, for instance. There is only one constituency that counts in North Korea, and he makes sure he can count on it.

Kim is also rewriting theories of political science. Totalitarianism, most believe, is not viable in the twenty-first century. We also think that countries moving *down* the ladder of economic development are inherently unstable. Mr. Kim, however, seems to be proving us wrong. His emerging no-party state looks sturdy and suggests that an isolated premodern society can exist in an increasingly globalized and interdependent world. A government, we are learning to our dismay, can be stable at any level, and perhaps an economically stagnant and odious regime is in the most solid state of all. As Homer noted, "There is strength in the union of very sorry men."

Since the end of the First World War no nation has matched the DPRK's record of all-around underperformance and regime longevity. North Korea has experienced decades-long hardship, yet there is relatively little internal dissent. Poverty, barbarity, incompetence, and death: North Korea has them all. Yet the nation and its government manage to survive. The Democratic People's Republic of Korea has now spanned seven decades. It is surprising that it lasted that long, but there are remarkably few instances in history when desperation alone has sparked revolution, and it has never happened in a totalitarian society.

Middle-Class Struggle

The North Korean regime has demonstrated that it can cope with continued failure. But can Kim Jong Il survive success? There is one important
sign that he will not: he and his father have managed to create the greatest
potential enemy of all totalitarians, an emerging middle class.

A middle class in destitute North Korea? Industrialization in the early
years of Kim Il Sung's regime helped form a new social grouping composed
mainly of office workers. The class grew quickly as the nation enjoyed its
own boom after the Korean War. People took up specialized tasks at work,
and that process resulted in the loosening of social controls.

Good years for the DPRK's bourgeoisie were followed by bad ones. The
famine and economic failure of the 1990s hit white-collar workers outside
Pyongyang especially hard because they generally had no ties to the land—
and, therefore, no access to food apart from severely depleted state channels. Even middle-class members of the Korean Workers' Party were cut off
from staples, and many either died or fled. In fact, middle-class North Koreans appear to comprise a large portion of those who left the country—and
are still leaving.

Yet those who remained started a renaissance outside the capital. While
husbands stayed at their posts at offices or in dormant factories—on the assumption that hard times of the 1990s were only temporary—wives began
small businesses. In many households women became the sole source of
sustenance when state enterprises stopped paying wages and the rations
ended. Today many of these homegrown—and illegal—businesses are
flourishing. Husbands are now leaving official jobs to tend to household
chores while their wives build capitalism in the northern half of Korea.
Some middle-class Koreans are even getting prosperous by DPRK standards, as are formerly lower-class ones. Now, most middle-class North Koreans outside Pyongyang no longer depend on the state for their livelihood.

Capitalist transformation is not so evident in the DPRK's capital, however. The regime, concerned about political stability, looked after middle-
class Pyongyangites, who always received food and other necessities from
the state. Moreover, they were under stricter government supervision and
had fewer opportunities to go into business for themselves. Yet there is newfound prosperity for the middle class in the capital as they benefit from the

country's economic uptick, which was especially evident after the start of the millennium. Fortunate folk in Pyongyang even have money to burn these days. Foreign analysts don't know where all the cash is coming from — it could be the result of the diversion of foreign aid and misuse of government resources — but people are spending it nonetheless. In newly established markets there are, besides North Korean produce, agricultural products and consumer goods from China, Thailand, and Japan. Pyongyang now has four revolving restaurants, enough eateries to have its own foodie guide, and a new club scene where the young Moonwalk. And if you're ever in the busy Beijing airport and need to find your way to the Air Koryo flight to Pyongyang, almost any bystander will tell you to follow the men clutching the Gucci bags.

There are now guys in Gucci and dolls in Dior. Middle-class North Koreans are trading in drab duds for more flattering attire just as the Chinese began to do at the end of the 1980s. Beginning at the end of the 1990s North Koreans began to shed their clothes of synthetic vinalon, the "fiber of self-reliance" supposedly invented in the DPRK, in favor of Disney-branded merchandise and colorful gear imported from China. Baseball caps, the quintessential American headwear, are fashionable too. Today, the Kim Il Sung badges are attached to the new symbol of youth rebellion, the black leather jacket.

Sartorial flair does not necessarily translate into political restlessness, but Pyongyang's leaders must nonetheless be concerned about the social changes taking place around them. After all, they believe it was the new middle classes that pushed change in Eastern European states and the Soviet Union. And they can see their own middle class following trends once evident in those countries and now apparent in neighboring China.

Analysts believe that the middle class, big winners during the last quarter century of Chinese reform, generally support the Communist Party. Yet prosperity has made China's citizens complainers. The most interesting trend in the world's most populous nation is that middle-class Chinese are taking matters into their own hands by demonstrating in the streets and engaging in even less acceptable forms of protest. In China today the well-to-do act like rabble-rousing peasants if that's what it takes to defend their rights. Ownership, everyone knows, "breeds a sense of entitlement." Entitlement, in turn, often leads to conflict with a state still uncomfortable with the concept of private property and hence reluctant to protect it.

Beijing scores points for surviving the Soviet collapse and gets extra credit for restructuring its economy and achieving extraordinary growth. Yet senior Chinese officials now face the dilemma of all reforming authoritarians: sustained modernization endangers their continued control. Reform, notes Samuel Huntington of Harvard, often becomes a catalyst for revolution rather than a substitute for it. Upheavals occur under many conditions, but especially when political institutions do not keep up with the social forces unleashed by economic change. That's the story of Tiananmen Square in 1989 and the increasing unrest across China since 2002.

Today, the world wants to see change in North Korea and constantly urges its leaders to imitate China. No wonder Kim Jong Il, who believes in being in full control, is not enthusiastic about Chinese-style reform. His country already has a "Chinese problem" — economic and social change in North Korea has not been matched with political reform — and he apparently doesn't want to make this contradiction worse. Beijing's leaders caused their predicament by sponsoring more than a quarter century of spectacular economic growth, perhaps the fastest in human history. The DPRK, on the other hand, experienced much less prosperity and is still a long way behind China when it comes to economic or social development. So Kim Jong Il still has plenty of time to figure out what to do to remain in control.

Maybe. Apart from the general notion that support for the regime has thinned since the death of Kim Il Sung, we know little of current attitudes of the DPRK's middle class, whether inside or outside Pyongyang. The fundamental problem is that in a totalitarian society subversive views are always suppressed, so no one, especially an absolute ruler, knows what people really think. Yet anyone can see what has happened to other hard-line regimes as citizens became prosperous, independent, and ultimately defiant.

And that's why no despot sleeps soundly when trying to rule an emerging middle class.

Transforming Totalitarianism

The existence of a middle class in North Korea indicates that the country, despite vociferous claims of uniqueness, is traveling the same road as its communist cousins, both dead and alive. If social changes are not as evident as they are elsewhere, it is only because the DPRK is bringing up the rear when it comes to the transformation of totalitarianism.

The central challenge for totalitarian states has been the reform of their centralized command economies. Socialism, at least as practiced so far, is not particularly efficient or productive, and, for better or worse, most people in the world have chosen the reality of material prosperity over promises of equality. As Fidel Castro said in a rare moment of candor, "I believe that the ideals of socialism, which are so generous and appeal so much to solidarity and fraternity, will one day disappear."

Will the Kimist state disappear as its socialism crumbles? From any economic criteria we choose, North Korea is the weakest of the five remaining communist nations. Its institutions are so uniquely odd that it's almost misleading to include the DPRK with the other four, although it was clearly part of the communist bloc during the Cold War. It survived the fall of its major patron, the Soviet Union, in part because it managed to distinguish itself from Moscow's regime. "In North Korea it's all Kim Il Sung, Kim Il Sung, Kim Il Sung, and it's not socialism or communism, it's *Juche*," explains Ruediger Frank, a German academic.

Soon after its introduction in the 1950s, the malleable concept of *Juche* was used to differentiate the DPRK from the Soviet Union and China so North Koreans were probably not surprised by Kim Senior's attempts to distance himself from communist comrade Mikhail Gorbachev. "If rain falls in Moscow, East European nations put up umbrellas," the North Korean said in 1991. "It is natural that socialism has disappeared in nations without independence."

Nonetheless, Kim Il Sung was all wet. He spoke of "socialism of our style" to suggest the North had a future on its own, which it did. His words implied he had figured out how to make that ideology work, which he hadn't. That feat would have been a real contribution to humankind, but, unfortunately, he was no better a magician than any other Marxist of the twentieth century.

Today, the DPRK still suffers from Kim Il Sung's utterly human failure to change course during his last years. Pyongyang now talks about "practical socialism" just as Beijing speaks of "socialism with Chinese characteristics." The trouble with these concepts is that, whatever else they may be, they are still socialism. Because China and North Korea fail to acknowledge that their common ideology doesn't work, both nations have ended up developing bifurcated economies with vibrant private sectors—and stagnant state ones. As much as they have tried, neither country has reformed communism in general or socialism in particular. To varying degrees and in different ways, they have merely permitted, or watched, the replacement of old economies by new ones.

Transformation is at work in both people's republics, but the Chinese during the past quarter century have been better at keeping the process moving in the proper direction. In all fairness to the Koreans, officials in Beijing possessed one enormous advantage: U.N. forces killed Mao Zedong's first son during the Korean War. That accident of history ended the possibility of dynastic succession in China, so its new leaders have had a freer hand in repairing damage caused by their republic's founder. They reinterpreted or ignored Mao as the circumstances dictated and thereby pushed the Chinese state in a new direction.

Kim Jong Il, on the other hand, was stored in Manchuria during the war and emerged unscathed, at least physically. Having the material to work with, Kim Il Sung created his own form of monarchical government. In that monarchy Kim Jong Il succeeded his father, but he has yet to escape him. As the son and successor in a Confucian society, he cannot help but carry his father everywhere he goes. And so the new ruler is constrained by the policies of the old one—as well as by the old ruler's advisers. The aging Manchurian guerrilla fighters who surrounded Kim Senior now keep the legacy alive as do younger officials who benefit from the old man's system. Time will solve this problem, but the issue is whether it will do so in time.

In Pyongyang, like Beijing, ideology slows the rate of transformation. A set of ideals gives strength to governments, but totalitarian ideology, which is supposed to govern all pursuits from "from poetry to potato farming," can make regimes brittle. Kim Senior aggravated the problem for North Korea by providing guidance on everything and everywhere during his lifetime of meddling—ignoring even his picayune instructions is still a task of some delicacy. State media, a decade after his death, still calls for implementing Kim Il Sung's instructions to the letter.

If Kim Il Sung was unerring in the past—and it is this belief that gives the regime its legitimacy and strength—how can Pyongyang's leaders change anything today? The trouble with supposedly infallible regimes is that they must always appear perfect. One mistake—perhaps any mistake—is a crack that, with time, can lead to the fall of the state.

One unintended consequence of Gorbachev's refreshing candor was the ultimate loss of his job: people could more openly talk about the shortcomings of their system and thereby develop a consensus that the communists had to go. That's not a mistake the Chinese are going to make: even after more than a quarter century of market reforms, Hu Jintao, China's current supremo, still exalts socialism, although most people reject that concept in his country.

By contrast, North Korea is still in the initial stage of internal ideological struggle. So far, its method of implementing change is to insist that it has not been doing so. Pyongyang has only begun using the word "reform"; the government much prefers the more neutral "modernization." Senior officials like to label the sweeping July 2002 changes, which essentially recognized the existence of capitalist market mechanisms, as the "perfection" of communism.

How does the DPRK make necessary adjustments to a system already called perfect? Like the Chinese, the North Koreans generally begin their process of change with a long period—often years—of reformulating ideology so that any movement in a new direction does not jeopardize the integrity of their creed or the stability of the state. Fortunately for Kim Jong Il, his father gets the credit for inventing *Juche* so he can adjust it as the need arises—*Juche* is assumed to be correct because of its source, the Kim family. Yet the younger Kim, an otherwise absolute leader, can only make changes that respond to changing circumstances: just as questioning ideology is considered an attack on him and his authority, his manipulation of *Juche* must not be seen as an assault on Dad. So *Juche* is both a weapon and a prison for Kim Jong Il. *Juche* bolstered the regime at a critical time in the 1990s as the nation weathered the fall of Soviet communism, but in the first decade of this century it is impeding change.

As change is deferred in the North Korean capital, reform—or "modernization" if you prefer—occurs nonetheless. Kim, not surprisingly, isolated himself and the Pyongyang elite from hardship. The consequence of doing so, however, is the loss of initiative, which means that his power is beginning to slip outside the capital. Outside Pyongyang the country is being transformed by its own officials, who do not always wait for Kim to act. The farther away from the capital, the more reform is implemented by stealth. In recent years central officials have formally transferred more power to the provinces, but that is mostly recognition of a process that was already under way as first the people and then local officials reacted to hardship and famine in the 1990s. Local initiative is also the natural consequence of the July 2002 economic measures. Some bureaucrats, reacting to the economic shocks they caused, are no longer following orders from the center. Kim can still make decrees and get his own way in his hometown, but if developments are left unchecked, people in the provinces will eventually forget how fearful they have been and create their own version of Korea, a more chaotic, colorful, and freer society than the official one run from Pyongyang.

In the emerging people's Korea almost anything goes. Perhaps the single most important aspect of the ongoing migration of refugees from the DPRK is not that conditions are harsh or that people are desperate. The crucial point is that the poorest elements in society—those citizens who are the least able to get what they want—can roam the supposedly totalitarian country and cross its international border at will. In almost any foreign survey the nation is ranked as the world's most repressive, yet the mechanisms of state control are apparently losing strength. Kim, unlike Castro, has never encouraged migration, so the steady flow of refugees must mean there has been a breakdown of the institutions of government.

Even a pauper can bypass the government. A bit of cash or even a pack of good cigarettes will get a potential refugee past military guards and to North Korea's border with China. Kim must preside over one of the most commercialized societies on earth. "As a matter of practice, bribery makes everything possible," writes Kang Chol-hwan, who bought almost everything he wanted in North Korea, including his way out of the country. "The regime that never tires of denouncing capitalism has birthed a society where money is king—more so than any capitalist society I have visited."

North Korea's "money culture" has accelerated that country's almost complete breakdown of law and a partial breakdown of order. State officials set the tone for society by looting property not only from the government but also from state companies. Kang, now a journalist in Seoul, reports that one of his friends ran over "a group of soldiers" while speeding at seventy miles an hour. He was sentenced to death and served three months in prison before his case was *dismissed.* The price for his release was refrigerators, color televisions, and "bulging envelopes." Even political crimes are forgiven with the right amount of cash. North Koreans who want to listen to stations in the South need pay just a little "hush money" to avoid registering a radio with the state. From the bottom to the top, the North Korean government can be bought—and that includes its security apparatus. As one senior North Korean official said recently, "We'll do anything to make money."

And so will North Korea's less fortunate citizens. The DPRK, like neighboring China, experimented with private plots, but its peasants did not wait for the state to expand upon initial reforms. In the 1990s they began to appropriate land from collective farms and other tracts available for the taking. The state was vehemently opposed to the land grabs, but there was little bureaucrats could do: the peasant movement was too strong. The state eventually had to give ground in more sense than one. As a result, the North's agriculture is making the transition from communism to capitalism—and peasants are going from poverty to something much better. We can call it privatization if we care to use euphemisms, but a better term is wide-scale theft. The totalitarian state outside the boundaries of its capital has disintegrated more than adapted.

North Koreans, for the first time ever, seem to have taken the initiative, and Pyongyang has largely failed to respond. Ordinary folks, the sort we usually call "oppressed," carved out their own tracts for farming, sold the state's industrial property to foreigners, started their own markets, and became middlemen, all in defiance of local and central authorities. They may not be free, but the North Korean people seem to be making their own way. So where did they learn to do that?

The Socialization of Socialism

North Korean society is already in the midst of the relentless process of transformation partly because there has been a "failure in socialization" in their socialist country. In the early 1960s Kim Il Sung noticed that the zeal of revolution did not burn so brightly in the hearts of younger North Koreans. They may not have been hippies, yippies, or flower children, but they had not suffered the Japanese occupation, felt the exhilaration of liberation, or fought fanatically against Americans during the war. What they had experienced was the relative prosperity of the postbellum period. "Our younger generation do not know very well what landlords are like, what capitalists are like and how malicious the imperialists are," Kim said in

1963. The problem is that kids, who were "emerging as masters of our society," were soft and did not quite get the hang of revolutionary struggle or sacrifice.

The failure of Kim, the real master of society, to inculcate his views in the next generation eventually had consequences. Educational institutions, and especially the university that bore his name, became centers of dissent. Students and intellectuals began to form underground cells that connected to disaffected military and party elements in the 1980s. At least two such organizations were discovered late in the decade. It appears that all known members of the cells were executed. Dissidents continued to organize during the early 1990s. Students returning from the Soviet Union and Eastern Europe—at the insistence of Pyongyang—were especially susceptible to joining anti-government organizations. To stamp out any possibility of unrest, almost all who studied in the USSR in the 1980s were executed after coming back to North Korea.

There were also scattered student protests against the regime at that time, but in Kim Il Sung's Korea there was nothing like the Beijing Spring of 1989. Young North Koreans, unlike their Chinese counterparts, did not have much of an audience outside their campuses. They surreptitiously passed out leaflets and hung wall posters but without much effect. They hardly posed a serious challenge to the government during Kim's life, yet the underlying message of discontent was a symptom of a degenerative malady afflicting the state. As in other communist societies, the concept of revolution was the DPRK's primary tool to mobilize the population. Kim Il Sung spoke of "continuous revolution," but that was no more possible in his North Korea than was Mao Zedong's "permanent revolution" in China.

Kim, the revolutionary, had become old, fat, and establishmentarian. His decline was matched by that of the North Korean state, which in the 1980s exhibited all the classic symptoms of age. Although Kim was still personally popular, he could only watch his movement slowly—but irretrievably—lose its appeal. Worse, his system began to lose its ability to provide for the North Korean people. As food shortages became chronic, citizens of the self-proclaimed greatest nation on earth realized that socialism was failing and that they had to feed themselves. And they attempted to do so spiritually as well as materially. Christianity, in the form of the underground "catacomb church," began to make a comeback in the early 1990s. At the end of his life Great Leader Kim was left with the unpalatable choice of revolutionaries successful enough to age: either change the nature of the regime or rely on co-option and coercion.

Other communist societies have also faced this choice after being diminished by widespread disenchantment and the rejection of socialism. The Soviet Communist Party, for instance, met the challenge by trying to free communism from ideology. In 1961 it declared itself to be "a party of the whole people." It was Gorbachev, however, who actually abandoned the notion of class struggle. Yet his attempt to accomplish two conflicting goals—strengthening communism and reforming it—resulted in his losing everyone's support.

This same risk is faced by China. The Chinese Communist Party, in a bid to revitalize itself, adopted the Three Represents, which holds that it should represent the foremost productive forces in society, the most advanced culture, and the fundamental interests of the people, in other words, just about everything and everybody. Written into the nation's constitution in 2004, this doctrine implicitly replaces Marxism with utilitarianism and makes the Communist Party a ruling organization rather than a revolutionary one.

Kim Jong Il, albeit hesitantly, seems to be thinking of putting North Korea on the same path as the Soviet Union and China. His government, through subtle pronouncements, is beginning to admit that entrepreneurs—exploiters in the socialist world—have a place in the DPRK, which is supposed to be dedicated only to workers, peasants, and intellectuals.

Formally acknowledging the contributions of entrepreneurs should eventually lead to the revitalization of the North Korean economy, yet to do so is to switch the base of the regime's support and to alter its fundamental principles. That's always a risky undertaking, especially in a country that has prided itself on ideological purity. There are many explanations for why the Soviet Union fell, but one that is gaining currency in Beijing is that Moscow's elite just gave up after losing faith in socialism.

As Kim thinks about accommodating new ways of thinking and tries to represent every group in society, he faces the same dilemma as Cher: How can you reinvent yourself and draw new fans without alienating the old ones? Kim did not have to answer the question in 2002 when he refused to accommodate entrepreneurs, but if he accepts them now he will have to figure out how to do so without tossing out the old supporters of the regime. One man, even one as omnipotent as Kim Jong Il, cannot speak for both the exploited and the exploiters. "I don't know the key to success," come-dian Bill Cosby once said, "but the key to failure is trying to please every-body."

When Perceptions Shift

Kim Jong Il is now pleasing enough people to stay in power, and the safe bet is to say he will continue to do so. The Kimist state is now more than fifty-five years old, and longevity is both a result and predictor of success. The historical record is a tough opponent for those who foresee collapse.

Regime collapse, as we know, is a low-probability event. Governments fall only when a series of rare mishaps occur at about the same time and in the right sequence. No wonder bad systems last so long: it's not easy to get historical forces to converge on cue. Political scientists, who like to bring order to the inexplicable, tell us that a host of factors are required for regime change. There must exist, for example, general discontent or even anger, solidarity among the aggrieved, the ability to resist official action, strong leadership of the challengers, demands with mass appeal, a broad coalition, and a divided government.

Almost none of the listed requirements can be found in North Korea today—or at least they can't be found in sufficient quantities. The DPRK, it would then seem, must be a long way from a change of government. Whatever one may think of political science, it's hard to argue with this list, which is, after all, a compilation of the lessons of the past. As Marx said, the past has a tendency to repeat itself.

One repeating pattern of recent times is that autocratic systems collapse without much notice and in defiance of the predictions of political scien-tists. They, along with futurists and analysts, have a terrible record in pre-dicting the turning points in the course of human events. That's because nobody in history has ever been fired for extrapolating or agreeing with everyone else. Although the meek may inherit the earth, they're not very good in predicting the events that defy existing trends.

Yet who can blame the timid? Revolution is almost by definition the re-sult of the unexpected. "Many great things in history started out as crazy acts," says one of the survivors of Castro's ill-fated raid that launched his grab for power. Irrationality is often the motor of violent political change. No wonder we rarely have a clue as to when it will make itself felt.

"Revolution is a trivial shift in the emphasis of suffering," noted Tom Stoppard. The playwright obviously read his Tocqueville, who explained why a period of reform is the most dangerous moment for a bad government. "Patiently endured so long as it seemed beyond redress, a grievance comes to appear intolerable once the possibility of removing it crosses men's minds," wrote the Frenchman. "For the mere fact that certain abuses have been remedied draws attention to the others and they now appear more galling; people may suffer less, but their sensibility is exacerbated." Nobody likes the combination of reform and repression.

At some point, a society gets to the "tipping point." Writer Malcolm Gladwell likens social change to epidemics, which begin with the smallest of events. "Things can happen all at once, and little changes can make a huge difference," he writes. So change rarely occurs gradually; usually it takes place in one critical moment. At that point, some trends overwhelm others and societies take sharp turns. That critical moment occurs when enough people think the same way.

Unfortunately, there is often little visible evidence of this most important change in society. "I recall that my friends and I for decades were asked by people visiting from democratic Western counties, 'How can you, a mere handful of powerless individuals, change the regime, when the regime has at hand all the tools of power: the army, the police and the media, when it can convene gigantic rallies to reflect its people's "support" to the world, when pictures of the leaders are everywhere and any effort to resist seems hopeless and quixotic?' " wrote Vaclav Havel, who knows something about how people under communist governments think. "My answer was that it was impossible to see the inside clearly, to witness the true spirit of the society and its potential—impossible because everything was forged. In such circumstances, no one can perceive the internal, underground movements and processes that are occurring. No one can determine the size of the snowball needed to initiate the avalanche leading to the disintegration of the regime." Even after the loss of the Eastern European satellites, Soviet citizens despaired of changing their government. They felt that change would not happen because there was no opposition.

Will North Korea be the next Leninist society to "tip"? "The fall of the

North Korean leadership is inevitable, and the leaders know this," says a well-known American academic who does not wish to be quoted by name. One reason the Kim government will fail in the near future is that, in a society in an unplanned transition, too few people have a stake in the continued existence of the system. The DPRK, among other things, suffers from an extreme concentration of power at the top.

North Korean society has an elite of perhaps three hundred citizens, most of whom reside in one place, Pyongyang. For a society of some 22 million, that's an awfully small crew. Yet the group of the really powerful is even smaller than that: it numbers just one. There is, as they say, only one fat man in North Korean society.

In a country where everyone except Kim Jong Il is thin, there are bound to be some hungry for power. One-man dictatorships are the simplest forms of governments, but they are generally the least stable. In the Kim Il Sung generation, loyalty to the dead dictator is probably sufficient to prevent attempts to ditch his son, but younger officials are not restrained by shared ties. A few years ago, for instance, a junior Foreign Ministry official attached to the powerful Flood Damage Rehabilitation Committee was speaking to a delegation of German politicians in Pyongyang. "As we all know, there's only one natural disaster in North Korea," said the official, who then looked over his shoulder at two portraits of Kim Il Sung and Kim Jong Il. "And this natural disaster is still ongoing."

As this particular disaster continues, North Korean society can tip at any time. "My guess is that something precipitous will happen that will accelerate the chain of events quickly even though we seem to be in this slow-motion situation for the last two or three decades," says Tim Peters, a refugee activist in Seoul. Because many North Koreans share the same thoughts, they can react together. "Ten years ago North Koreans would talk to no one. Five years ago they would talk to their sons. Three years ago they would talk to their wives. A year ago they would talk to strangers," said Erica Kang, an aid worker, in 2004. When people realize they're not alone, governments crumble. Citizens lose fear, gain hope, and then let little stand in their way. In just one moment everything we know about the North Korean people—their passivity, their fear, their respect for authority—can be rendered obsolete. As Karl Marx said, "Slaves create history."

When perceptions shift, almost anything can happen. And North Korea is in the middle of one grand transition. The country may be changing because it's reforming or reforming because it's changing. In a sense it doesn't really matter. The July 2002 measures are moving North Korea from elite to mass politics. People are developing their own stake in the private economy, which means they are becoming stakeholders in society. When South Korean president Roh Moo-hyun says that the DPRK "cannot reverse" its acceptance of "market economics," he is correct insofar as he refers to the North's common folk. Now Kim Jong Il confronts the challenge of trying to rein them in.

So how is Kim going to keep tabs on millions of Koreans in motion? The successful tyrants of history have stayed in power through the consistent application of coercion. The Kims have been masters of repression, but Jong Il had to relax his grip during the calamitous famine and now has trouble keeping up with all the rumors of plots and protests, especially those involving the military. These days, every month brings new reports suggesting trouble inside the DPRK. Kim family members are shooting each other, public executions are becoming common, and high officials are shipping out belongings to China.

The Kimist system of multiple and overlapping security organizations weakened as the economy failed during the 1990s. Now, Kim Jong Il has tightened some political controls because he fears the social and political consequences of economic reforms. Yet the added costs may be a bigger burden than his nation can bear. In 2004 Pyongyang required North Koreans to turn in their cell phones—the cost of monitoring every conversation was simply too high. Kim requires substantial resources to maintain his infrastructure of fear. Yet to keep his economy going he needs an open society. In an open society, the cost of repression goes up. There is supposed to be about one informer for every fifty citizens in the DPRK. In a more dynamic country, how many more will Kim Jong Il need? So coercion is not a long-term solution for him. That is especially true because the state is losing the ability to reward the obedient or punish offenders.

Kim Il Sung was able to maintain his hold on North Koreans because most of them had no basis to compare their society to others. Yet it's obvious that his son cannot maintain isolation in the long run, and openness has enormous political ramifications for isolated and atomized societies. Kim Jong Il puts the children of returning diplomats, students sent overseas, and loggers in Siberia into reeducation camps to remove the taint of living abroad, but does he really think they will forget what they have seen?

Yet Koreans do not have to leave their homeland to learn the truth. And even the smallest truth can change them. One North Korean decided to defect after he saw a discarded wrapper that had blown across the DMZ— he simply wanted to live in a country prosperous enough to package noodles. Today, North Koreans talk to relatives in the South with smuggled cell phones, listen to foreign radio programs, watch smuggled videocassettes and DVDs of South Korean soap operas, and even converse with the occasional outlander they come across in their country. They hear about the outside world in multiple ways and find it alluring. And, increasingly, they understand Kim's version of life outside North Korea is simply not true.

Moreover, the members of the elite don't have to step outside to see the world. They have access to foreign media and are shaped by outsiders' opinions of their bizarre country. A high-ranking general's daughter, who has access to CNN and English-language newspapers and listens to Japanese pop, refuses to have portraits of the two Kims in her home in Pyongyang, a requirement for all living quarters and workplaces in the country. "I don't like them," she told a European visitor in 2000. Those who have benefited the most from Kim Jong Il's policies—this young woman flaunts her Gucci accessories as well as her politics—are often the most critical of the current leader. Most tellingly, some of Kim Jong Il's own children now live abroad.

Kim, who appears to be well aware of the consequences, is trying his best to keep his country cut off from the outside while he rearranges its economy. There's a lesson he should learn from the Soviet Union. Although Gorbachev's name is associated with shock therapy, he initially believed that reform could be imposed from the top in limited doses and controlled. He was wrong, because it exploded from the bottom up. Change, at least over the long run, cannot be planned, ordered, or contained.

And history cannot be managed. Most of the time it just happens. None of the great reformers of the past was able to foresee—much less control— what followed. How can we say that the North Korean regime is here to stay when the country is in the midst of a transition more wrenching than any other nation's in the last half century? Experts argue that Kim Jong Il can hold on to power indefinitely, but his North Korea is changing and change is the one precondition for government collapse. History, paradoxically, is just not kind to despots when they have to reform.

HOUSEWIVES FOR NUCLEAR TERROR

Seoul Becomes Pyongyang's Ally

If the United States left, I wouldn't mind. If North Korea wants
nuclear weapons, I think they should have them. The U.S. and so
many other countries have them. There's no way North Korea
will attack us with their nuclear weapons. I don't think so.
We're the same country. You don't bomb and kill your family.
We share the same blood.
—Kim Young Ran, South Korean citizen

It takes a Korean to understand a Korean, at least according to Koreans. So
should the world just let Seoul settle the proliferation puzzle posed by
Pyongyang? That is apparently what South Korea's president, Roh Moo-
hyun, would like. "Don't worry too much about North Korea," he advises
Americans. If the DPRK's nuclear weapons present a problem—and many
South Koreans don't think they do—it is something they can solve on their
own.

"Koreans are very cocky at the moment," says South Korean Usung Chung, the commentator behind the provocative EyesonKorea blog. "They think they can do anything." South Korean politicians, for instance, believe they can find a solution that has so far eluded the Americans, Chinese, Japanese, and Russians, who are also participating in the six-party talks in Beijing. President Roh, pronounced "No," explained it this way at the end of 2004: "The North Korean nuclear issue depends on whether we will assure their security and give them a chance to recover from their difficulties through reform and opening their country. The other points of negotiation are only technical matters."

For South Korea, which considers itself a "shrimp," the solution appears to be simple. For superpower America, on the other hand, the problem is intractable. Something, therefore, is out of kilter. The gulf between Seoul and Washington is wide, and unless bridged, the odds for a peaceful resolution for North Korea are long. Unfortunately, the divide between the two capitals is growing, not narrowing.

So perhaps it is time to pose a question that America is afraid to ask: Is its ally South Korea still on its side?

The Rise of the Shrimp

During the final stages of the Korean War, Seoul's leaders were disagreeable but easy to control. Although President Syngman Rhee had wanted to continue the fighting, Washington had the means to stop his plans for military advance. By the end of the conflict Rhee's republic, defiant and proud, was also destitute and ruined.

The inconclusive conflict elevated the importance of the American commitment to Seoul. What is now viewed in Korea as the "Korean Civil War" was seen in Washington as the first battlefield in the global struggle against communism. America did not intend to create an ugly police state, but that is in fact what happened. Rhee, who in exile had collected degrees from enlightened institutions such as Harvard and Princeton, turned out to be a repressive and particularly intolerant leader. But he was a virulent anticommunist, and Washington supported him to the hilt as it went about building a bulwark against the man perceived as Moscow's puppet in

Pyongyang, Kim Il Sung. Aid from the United States accounted for perhaps half of the South's governmental expenditures in the years after the conflict.

Rhee, who made himself rather unpopular in his time in office, got considerably worse with age. Massive student demonstrations, one of which ended in more than a hundred deaths after guards at the presidential palace opened fire, destabilized his regime. Washington eased his way out of a tight spot in April 1960, permitting the octogenarian ruler and his Austrian wife to go to exile in Hawaii. South Korean crowds cheered Americans for arranging the transfer of power.

Rhee's regime was followed by the Second Republic, Korea's first democratic government. The South during this time was part of the free world, but it was hardly free of Washington, which essentially ran Seoul in the absence of strong local leadership. Neither the Americans nor the South Koreans could make the Second Republic a showcase, however. Among other failings, Seoul could not get free market capitalism to work, even with generous support from American taxpayers. The South could not even feed itself: peasants in the spring of 1961 had run out of food and were foraging in the mountains. Kim Il Sung's republic started to look attractive to South Koreans, who could be excused for associating democracy with economic failure, dependency on the United States, and political instability during moments not marked by repression.

The Second Republic didn't get a second chance. In the first hours of May 16, 1961, just a little more than a year after Rhee headed for Honolulu, a group of army officers launched a bloodless coup that installed one of the more unlikely leaders of the twentieth century. In a society that hated the Japanese and was dominated by anti-communists, a former communist and one-time Japanese collaborator grabbed power and held on to it for almost two decades. History knows him as Park Chung Hee, but he once went by the name of Lieutenant Masao Takagi and was later called "Parkov" for his Red associations.

Park Chung Hee scared Washington at first. The Kennedy administration was concerned that he was still a communist—Park had, after all, survived to lead the 1961 rebellion only because Rhee commuted a death sentence for his role in a failed communist revolt. Kim Il Sung, for the same reason, was initially delighted by Park's coup and immediately sent an emissary to Seoul. The new South Korean leader quickly ended Pyong-yang's hope for early reconciliation: he ordered the detention and execution of Kim's representative.

Park may not have wanted much to do with Communist Kim, yet he liberally followed his counterpart's organized approach to national development. One of the South Korean's very first acts was to establish the Economic Planning Council, which heralded a departure from the haphazard ways of his predecessors. In the year after grabbing power Park adopted the first of his five-year plans, those notorious hallmarks of socialist regimentation. His general approach applied communist-style planning to a Japanese-inspired model relying on the nation's largest business groups, the *chaebols*.

But what made Park's system really hum was Park. Personally meticulous, he constantly kept watch over details of the economy's progress, attending to delays in the tunneling for a new expressway one day and monitoring the business plans of a *chaebol* the next. He scrutinized every government project and most of the private ones as well. Park Chung Hee, like Kim Il Sung, was an on-the-spot meddler. Few places in South Korea, which is about the size of Indiana, were out of reach of his helicopter.

Park's government-led growth was wasteful, but his "guided capitalism" worked. He tripled the size of the economy during each of his two decades, thereby compressing a century's worth of progress during his tenure. Per capita income increased more than tenfold during that period.

Park and Kim were alike in many ways, but the former's vision of Korea was demonstrably better. Despite Kim's head start of more than a decade on his rival, the South's economy surpassed that of the North during Park's second decade. The South Korean not only outpaced his northern rival, he left a mark that few in his time equaled. There were better-known nation-builders in a century marked by economic advance, but in the long run only one of them—Singapore's Lee Kuan Yew—was as successful as Park Chung Hee.

There was a price for all the progress of the Park years. If younger South Koreans do not look back fondly on the father of modern Korea, it is because Park the nation-builder was also Park the autocrat. From the beginning American policy tried to nudge the South Korean leader, who disdained the inefficiency of democracy, to relax the worst aspects of his authoritarian political system. Yet the pattern was set when Washington did not move to stop Park from taking power—and maybe even before when it acquiesced to Rhee's repressive rule. Despite the obvious imbalance in power, Park usually came out on top in his tussles with Washington.

After the 1961 coup the Kennedy administration leaned on General Park to return the country to civilian rule. The former collaborator and communist ran successfully for president in 1963 and 1967. After sponsoring a change to the constitution to permit a third term, he beat Kim Dae Jung in a close race in 1971, but only after promising not to ask South Koreans to vote for him ever again. As analyst Don Oberdorfer points out, Park was as good as his word. He abolished direct elections in 1972 when he imposed his so-called *yushin*—"revitalizing reforms"—system. For the remainder of his life Park won additional terms from a compliant national convention.

American diplomats in 1972 did not object to Park's "Korean-style democracy." Richard Nixon's Washington, adopting "a policy of disassociation," let Park impose martial law, scrap the constitution, and do away with the National Assembly just as it had meekly acquiesced to Ferdinand Marcos's junking of democracy in the Philippines three weeks earlier. If America's defense of representative government in Asia was weak, it was the product of Nixon's general perception of the limits of Washington's influence.

Of course, America could not so easily disclaim responsibility for Korea's "internal affairs." When it came to roasting dissidents over an open fire—known as a "Korean barbecue"—or administering pain in less medieval fashion, Washington, the ultimate guarantor and supporter of Seoul, was complicit. Nixon's team may have thought that they could escape responsibility for the actions of the increasingly hard-line regime, but that's not how ordinary South Koreans, whether they liked Park or not, viewed the situation.

Jimmy Carter, global human rights advocate and American political leader, unintentionally proved just how much pull Washington in fact possessed. The new president, to his lasting credit, brought a much needed emphasis on democracy to America's Korea policy. As a result of his fresh perspective, Washington publicly rebuked Park for his heavy-handed tactics and thereby diminished his stature among South Koreans. Carter also managed to win freedom for a large number of dissidents during his frosty mid-1979 meeting with Park in Seoul. This release of political prisoners emboldened opposition leader Kim Young Sam to take on the regime even more aggressively, thereby contributing to Park's growing woes. Moreover, Carter's ill-advised plan to withdraw American troops from Korea—why he thought this would be a good idea in view of the continuing North Korean threat remains one of the great mysteries of the twentieth century— provided even more evidence to South Koreans that Washington was turning its back on a weakened President Park. Carter, more than he intended, delegitimized an already shaky government.

And, it appears, he inadvertently contributed to the deed that ended Park's long reign. Kim Jae Kyu, the head of the Korean Central Intelligence Agency, shot and killed the South Korean president during a private dinner a few months after Carter's 1979 visit. Kim was privy to the uncomplimentary communications whizzing between Washington and Seoul during that time and evidently came to believe that the United States would welcome Park's assassination. He was reading too much in the messages he saw, but the incident shows the immense power that Washington wielded, whether intentionally or not, over the workings of the South Korean government.

Carter hesitated immediately after Park's death. Opting for stability, Washington at first publicly refused to support a transition back to democracy in South Korea. Behind the scenes, however, it began to encourage the interim government to dismantle Park's *yushin* system. Liberalization proved popular with the populace but not with the military. So the inevitable occurred. In December of that year another general, Chun Doo Hwan, staged a coup with the help of his close associate, General Roh Tae Woo. Taking a page from Park's playbook, they used South Korean forces nominally under American military control, including those stationed near the DMZ. Again, Washington said that it was "at a loss" as to what to do.

Chun, on the other hand, did not suffer from bewilderment—or indecision. He politely listened to American protests over his power grab and then ignored them. The American-educated general knew that the United States was too preoccupied by the ongoing Iranian hostage crisis to do much about him. Besides, this confident young general already controlled the country.

Chun could brush off high-ranking Americans, but ordinary South Koreans were another matter. In May 1980 he declared full martial law— supplementing the partial martial law that had been in effect—to counter massive student riots that followed a relaxation of repressive political measures. He closed universities, shut the National Assembly, imposed even stricter censorship, and jailed many. Caught up in the nationwide dragnet, along with a multitude of students and dissidents, were two famous Kims, Kim Young Sam and Kim Dae Jung.

Throwing Kim Dae Jung into the slammer turned out to be a monumental mistake. Although Seoul remained mostly sullen during Chun's latest assault on the country's political institutions, the incarceration of Korea's leading dissident sparked riots in Kwangju, the capital of Kim's home province in the southwestern part of the country. Soldiers, backing up police, used indiscriminate force and further inflamed an already volatile situation. Riots became pitched battles, and pitched battles grew to an insurrection. The insurrection appeared to be the beginning of civil war.

"Democracy requires blood," says Song Young Gil, a current member of the National Assembly. And blood was the price the South Korean people paid for their representative government of today. The military first withdrew from the center of Kwangju and then sealed off the city. After a brief lull, South Korea's 20th Infantry Division, along with the reviled special forces, stormed the city center. After days of fighting, hundreds, perhaps thousands, of civilians lay dead, certainly many more than the official toll of 240.

Kwangju, a name now evoking an event more than a place, was a juncture, akin to China's Tiananmen Square. From that point forward military government in Korea was in retreat. General Chun weathered the immediate crisis, but South Koreans would inevitably have their "democratic moment." That point occurred in 1987, when widespread street protests forced a direct presidential election that took place in December. Roh Tae Woo, Chun's co-conspirator in the 1979 coup, emerged victorious in the 1987 poll because dissidents Kim Dae Jung and Kim Young Sam almost evenly split the opposition vote. Yet although a former military officer won, democracy, paid for in lives at Kwangju, had finally prevailed.

So Chun and his military were long-term losers after Kwangju, but they were not the only ones. South Koreans may generally be grateful for American assistance since the founding of their republic, yet many feel resentment, anger, and disappointment for the events of May 1980. For some, perhaps most, Koreans under the age of fifty, a week of American miscalculation overshadows Washington's support and sacrifice spanning seven decades. Why such an apparently harsh judgment?

The slaughter in Kwangju could not have happened—and would not have happened—without the tacit consent of the United States. If Washington had been dead set against the use of the South Korean military in Kwangju, the military would not have been used. American generals tightly controlled the movement of Korea's armed forces: since the days of Syngman Rhee, who had wanted to forcibly take all of the DPRK, the joint command was structured to restrain South Korea's army from attacking northward.

It's true that the young General Chun had at an early moment assumed command of the troops that invaded Kwangju: America did not have operational authority over South Korea's special forces and Chun had withdrawn elements of another unit, the 20th Division, from the Combined Forces Command prior to the imposition of full-strength martial law. Yet the technical exculpatory arguments sound unconvincing. America, to its lasting shame, simply failed to say no when it had at least two opportunities to do so in the earlier stages of the crisis.

Moreover, the United States was asked to intervene to halt further killing. The beleaguered residents of Kwangju appealed to America for help against their brutish government in the wake of the first bloody round of fighting. From the surrounding circumstances, if nothing else, it was clear that lives would be lost when troops set out to retake the city. "The Americans knew that the South Korean army would kill people in Kwangju," says Jung Sunghwan, a South Korean born the year before the massacre. Washington, however, did nothing.

In fact, the White House was not opposed to Chun's anticipated use of military force. Jimmy Carter's cherished emphasis on human rights came out second best when the stability of the South Korean state appeared to be at stake. As Zbigniew Brzezinski, the national security adviser at the time, said, the short-term goal was to support Seoul and only in the long term should the United States apply pressure for political liberalization.

In retrospect, it is hard to see what Washington could have done by the later stages of the Kwangju crisis without endangering South Korea's security. By then, Chun was intent on implementing a short-term military solution to essentially a long-term political problem. To many South Koreans a silent Washington looked complicit. And perhaps a bit cynical as well. After Chun dealt with Kwangju in his own way, Carter's Washington maintained a "cool and aloof" posture toward him as a means of expressing disapproval of his methods. Postponing visits or delaying loans may mean something to diplomats schooled in nuance, but South Korean citizens missed the subtlety.

What they remember today was Ronald Reagan's quick and public embrace of the reviled regime after America's presidential election in 1980. On the day after the Gipper's first inauguration, the White House announced that Chun, who himself had become president the preceding September, would come to Washington. The visit, in early February 1981, was the first for a head of state in Reagan's administration and conferred legitimacy on the government in Seoul—as well as engendering Korean anger against the United States. Unbeknownst to people at the time, Chun's invitation to Washington was the price America paid for the life of Kim Dae Jung. Kim was tried, convicted, and sentenced to death for instigating the events in Kwangju. He may have committed many sins up until then, but the dissident was definitely not guilty of the crime charged: he was, after all, imprisoned at the time of the uprising. We may never know whether Chun Doo Hwan was bluffing when he said that Kim had to die, but Reagan's foreign policy team was not about to take any chances. Yet, as we know by now, no good deed goes unpunished, especially when Americans do them. South Koreans today still bear a grudge against the United States for accepting Chun.

Associating with Chun was probably the right thing to do at the time. Reagan, despite his fondness for right-wing dictators, ultimately did more for democracy in Korea than Carter. Even before he met his South Korean counterpart, the Republican began working on Chun to ensure an eventual transition to democracy. It is said that Chun, as part of a complex deal to spare dissident Kim's life, also agreed to step down at the end of his seven-year term. Moments before seeing Reagan in 1981, the story goes, Chun was handed a slip of paper documenting that understanding in Korean. After nodding his assent, the South Korean was led into the meeting he had worked so hard to arrange with the American president.

And when in 1987 it looked as if Chun was about to renege on his promise of an on-time departure, Reagan personally intervened with his counterpart, just as he had in the previous year when he helped ease Marcos out of Manila in the face of "People Power" protests. In one of those happy moments in history, Chun decided not to declare martial law hours after receiving a letter from Reagan. Enticed by an offer of another visit to Washington after he retired, Chun, the most reviled political figure in

South Korea's history, became the first of the country's leaders to leave at the end of his constitutional term.

Chun could have toughed his way out of the 1987 crisis, but he must have realized then that his grip on power was coming to an end. Like the massive 1986 demonstrations in the Philippines, the protests in South Korea in the following year were fueled, and ultimately sustained, by wide middle-class support. It was not the students who ushered Chun out of power, it was their mothers and fathers and grandparents. More or less uninterrupted prosperity in South Korea had taken its inevitable toll on authoritarianism. By the late 1980s stability of the government in Seoul, America's overriding concern since the end of the Korean War, was threatened more by the aspirations of ordinary South Koreans than by the tanks of a declining Kim Il Sung. The United States, perhaps for the wrong reason, finally did the right thing.

If South Koreans do not appreciate Washington's contribution to their vibrant democracy of today, it is partly because too many compromises were made along the way and the good work was performed mostly out of sight. What people saw, and remember, is a beaming Chun Doo Hwan standing next to Ronald Reagan. In 1988, shortly after Chun left office, South Koreans booed American athletes at the Olympics in Seoul. At the time Americans were shocked, and befuddled, by their ally's public displays of disaffection.

"Anti-Americanism emerged as a necessary part of the Koreans' raging against their past," writes Michael Breen, who perhaps understands Korea's people as well as any foreigner. "They were throwing off their own historical habit of dependency, rather than making valid comments about any particular American offenses." Perhaps he is right, but Americans must admit that their country gave angry South Koreans plenty of ammunition nonetheless. So South Korean resentment of America, born during the tumultuous times of the democracy movement, troubles relations today.

The Strong Absorbing the Weak

If anti-Americanism is the reaction to Korea's yesterday, then reunification is the nation's hope for tomorrow. We should stand united, Koreans say, as we are people of "one blood."

One blood or not, most of the people who have it are divided into two competing countries. There is the ROK or Republic of Korea, which is in fact democratic, and the Democratic People's Republic of Korea, which is not. Nonetheless, it is inevitable that the Korean nation will be reunited, everyone agrees. Is not Germany, once partitioned into two, a single state now?

So why isn't Korea? The twentieth century was a "deliberate plot" against the Koreans, some of them say, and in light of the way things worked out, it's hard to disagree. As great powers—and bad fortune— worked to keep them apart, the Koreans, at least in their version of the past, have struggled to put themselves back together.

Kim Il Sung favored a single state almost from the beginning of the division of the peninsula. The Korean War, after all, was a unification policy employing extreme means. And for a brief moment, when his enemy was driven back to a perimeter around the southeastern city of Pusan in the early days of the fighting, it looked as if he would prevail by force of arms. Then General Douglas MacArthur advanced United Nations forces to China's doorstep along the banks of the Yalu River, but Mao Zedong's intervention pushed him back south. Neither side could make its military solution stick—the conflict has been dubbed the "accordion war"—and since the temporary armistice Korea has remained divided for over a half century.

Kim, despite the setback of the war, did not give up trying to unify the peninsula. In 1960 he proposed a confederal republic that contemplated one Korean nation with two separate governments. He returned to the idea in the 1970s and 1980s and never abandoned the concept. A fundamental aspect of his plans was the exclusion of foreign troops from the unified Korea, which would be neutral in the Cold War. If Kim's ideas were unworkable in the context of the times, they at least had great appeal, even among South Koreans.

In fact, *especially* among South Koreans. For all his faults, Kim Il Sung had always appeared as the great Korean nationalist of his time and, therefore, the peninsular leader with greater political legitimacy. He believed in self-reliance when the South Korean presidents put their trust in international commerce and, worse, depended on a foreign power, the United States, for "self" defense. Kim was the great fighter against the Japanese while the South Korean state was infested with collaborators, most notably the president who once served the Japanese as Lieutenant Masao Takagi. Kim's *Juche*, it is sad to say, is very Korean. It doesn't matter whether the concept is utterly impractical and has failed the DPRK over the course of decades; it nonetheless survives because it speaks to long-held aspirations of the Korean people to be independent. *Juche* paints their picture as they wish themselves to be.

And they all wish, in one way or another, to be part of a single Korean nation. So Seoul's leaders have championed the cause too. Syngman Rhee's concept of unifying the nation was to "march north" and vanquish Kim, who still harbored ambitions of advancing in the opposite direction. After Rhee was vanquished by his own people in student-led riots, unification—and neutralization—fever swept the Second Republic. Park staged his 1961 coup just days before students were to meet their North Korean counterparts at the Panmunjom truce village in the DMZ. The timing of the military takeover was not coincidental.

Park, the former Japanese army officer, was on the defensive when it came to nationalism and so recognized its power. As a masterful politician he sought to harness the force for his own ends. On July 4, 1972—the day and month were chosen with care—his emissary and Kim Il Sung's issued a joint statement that committed both Koreas to seek peaceful unification. The declaration surprised both halves of the peninsula and, for that matter, the rest of the world because it seemed to signal the end of inter-Korean hostility. Unfortunately, the statement did not herald a breakthrough. Both regimes found the appearance of peace useful, both internally and externally. Pyongyang, for example, wanted to decrease peninsular tensions to facilitate the removal of American troops from South Korean soil. When the aura of cordiality outlived its usefulness, both sides went back to their established ways of being disagreeable.

The 1972 declaration was ultimately a failure, but it at least paved the way for future progress. Almost two decades later the two Koreas took a giant step forward with the announcement of two agreements in 1991. In addition to the denuclearization pact described earlier, the North and South signed the Agreement on Reconciliation, Nonaggression and Exchanges and Cooperation. In the latter accord each side essentially recognized the other as legitimate and the two sides declared themselves to be in "a special interim relationship stemming from the process toward unification."

If such a process existed, it was a long one. In the early 1990s the two

Koreas were more serious about building a relationship than before, but they were still not ready to join together as one. South Korea's president at the time, Roh Tae Woo, had proposed a "Korean Commonwealth" or "Korean National Community." Although in broad outline the concept resembled Kim Il Sung's 1980 proposal for a "Confederal Republic of Koryo," the plans were different in important respects. Generally, Kim favored a centralized and integrated government. Roh's idea was to have a much looser arrangement.

The problem, of course, is that Seoul and Pyongyang govern conceptually incompatible societies that are unequal in every respect. Therefore, it is impossible to have a marriage of equals. The South has a population about double that of the North, and the southern state is stronger in almost every respect except military power. At one time Kim Il Sung thought he could eventually take over Seoul through the confederation process, but now his son is the one worried about being absorbed.

Yet Kim Jong Il should not lose too much sleep. The anomalous outcome of the confederation saga is that, as the two societies have headed in opposite directions, the differences in their unification proposals have narrowed. The ailing North has had to give ground, but the magnanimous South is making even more concessions. South Koreans, for example, are talking about abolishing their anti-communist National Security Law, removing American troops from their soil, and unifying free of "foreign interference."

The transformation of Seoul's relations with Pyongyang is nothing short of stunning. For a half century the South's policy was designed, in one way or another, to defeat its rival to the north. Rhee, Park, and Chun had little time for Kim Il Sung and essentially engaged in zero-sum contests, often involving fatalities, with the North Korean leader. Roh Tae Woo and his successor, former dissident Kim Young Sam, adopted more accommodating positions but did not substantially alter course.

Then came D.J., as Kim Dae Jung is known. The longtime opponent of Seoul's military regimes took office in 1998 and immediately promoted his Sunshine Policy, named after the Aesop fable in which the Sun is able to persuade a man to take off his coat after the North Wind fails to do so. In his inaugural address in early 1998 Kim laid down three principles. "First, we will never tolerate armed provocation of any kind," he said. "Second, we do not have any intention to undermine or absorb North Korea. Third, we will actively push reconciliation and cooperation between the South and North beginning with those areas which can be most easily agreed upon."

Agreement with Pyongyang did not come easy in any area. Conditioned by a half century of South Korean antagonism in those moments not punctuated by violence—but whose fault was that?—the North did not react well at first to Kim Dae Jung's new direction. The DPRK, in its moment of greatest economic stress in early 1998, had asked Kim's administration for 200,000 tons of fertilizer, but Seoul wanted Pyongyang to agree, as a measure of goodwill, to reunions for families living on both sides of the DMZ. Even though it desperately needed assistance, the North demanded that the aid be received free of conditions and refused to commit to reunions. Pyongyang, apparently, was concerned that poor North Koreans would learn just how prosperous their southern family members were. South Korea responded by not providing the aid.

Pyongyang, starring in the role of supplicant, objected to Seoul's bargaining, which it termed "horse trading." Largely in response to the brotherly criticism, the South Korean Kim soon began adopting the Chinese approach, no longer insisting on immediate reciprocity but instead according Pyongyang one-way favors. Critics called the president's new policy asymmetrical, nonsimultaneous, and unbalanced.

And worse. Sunshine, *The Wall Street Journal* thundered, was "appeasement" masquerading under "an appropriately naive name." The soft South Korean approach, many noted, did not decrease military tensions; indeed, the DPRK even increased infiltrations and incursions. Kim's Pollyannaish diplomacy with the North weakened ties with the South's protector, Washington. As we now know, Pyongyang just took Seoul's cash and continued making ballistic missiles and nuclear weapons. Sunshine, from all appearances, stopped being a policy and became an end in itself. Too much sunshine, activist Norbert Vollertsen maintained, created a desert. We became "sun burnt," says Park Jin, a prominent opposition figure in South Korea's national legislature.

The unfavorable reviews resonated with some at home but many abroad. So Roh Moo-hyun, Kim's successor, sought to fix the problem—by changing the policy's moniker. Seoul, these days, talks about a Peace and Prosperity Policy when, in reality, it has continued, virtually unchanged, the old Sunshine approach.

The consistency of approach is a testament to its popularity in a democratic polity. As much appeal as the general notion of reunification has, most South Koreans are not in favor of combining with the North at either this time or any moment in the foreseeable future. Although America is often held responsible for standing in the way of union—who better to blame?—the fact that it has not occurred more than a decade after the end of the Cold War indicates it is the Koreans themselves who are the obstacle. The Sunshine Policy may be considered a prelude to unification with the DPRK, but it is also a means to defer that event.

The Koreans watched the reintegration of Germany and learned that national union can be a complex and grossly expensive exercise. Since the beginning of the 1990s, analysts have estimated the cost of Korea's unification from about $600 billion to $1.8 trillion, but in any event the price tag has always been judged too high. When President Roh Tae Woo said in 1991 that "our people do not want accelerated unification," he was telling the truth. Absorption of the DPRK—the cherished goal of a long line of South Korean leaders—was simply abandoned. We should remember that Kim Dae Jung's second principle is that Seoul no longer sought to take over the North.

The North, of course, was skeptical of the good intentions of its erstwhile foe. Indeed, the best argument for the much criticized Sunshine Policy is that Pyongyang fears it as fundamentally threatening. As North Korea watcher Selig Harrison has noted, D.J.'s strategy, in the eyes of the DPRK's leaders, was "more dangerous" than previous attempts at subversion "precisely because it was more subtle." By making the North dependent on the South's generous assistance and one-way concessions, Kim Dae Jung, as Pyongyang saw it, was enticing Kim Jong Il into a trap, making him beholden to Seoul—and thereby paving the way for the ultimate elimination of the Kim Il Sung nation. North Korea, the state founded on *Juche*, is deeply anxious about its dependence on others but especially archenemy South Korea.

So the DPRK, despite its reliance on South Korean aid, has not responded positively to Seoul's initiatives. That alone is proof of the correctness of the Sunshine Policy. Pyongyang's reluctance to open North Korean society to the outside demonstrates its concern about the viability of the regime in a peaceful era. If Kim Jong Il needs enemies to maintain power, as does most every totalitarian, then D.J.'s ostensibly friendly concept cannot be as spineless as it looks at first glance.

Just who, we could ask, is getting sunburned now?

The Weak Absorbing the Strong

Although the DPRK may fear Sunshine, the policy has actually undermined the South more than the North, at least in its initial phase. The most important shortcoming of Kim Dae Jung's approach is that it convinced South Koreans that the life-and-death competition between the two Koreas was over when in fact it was not. The Korean struggle has merely entered a less transparent phase.

Cocky South Koreans, however, overflow with overconfidence. If the Sunshine Policy is based on any assumption, it is that the South has already won the battle of ideology and the struggle for control of the peninsula. Seoul plays the role of the richer and older brother, says Tim Peters. The refugee activist and longtime resident of the South sees his neighbors sympathizing with their northern brethren and saying, "We're simply going to help you along the way until the inevitable happens and your system just kinda falls apart."

We can hardly blame South Koreans for thinking the peninsular contest was over when well-known experts were producing books with titles such as *The End of North Korea*. The DPRK, Nicholas Eberstadt wrote in that work in 1999, "is *systemically incapable* of accomplishing the very objectives that justify its existence. The failure of North Korea's unification quest and the failure of the North Korean economic formula mark the end of any positive purpose for the North Korean state."

If the DPRK had indeed lost the decades-long peninsular struggle, there was no harm in Kim Dae Jung volunteering to go to Pyongyang for the first-ever summit between Korean leaders. The meeting took place in June 2000 and was marked by surprisingly little of lasting substance. The parley was notable, however, because it radically changed perceptions of the DPRK in the South. "For South Koreans it was just a startling experience to actually see Kim Jong Il meeting and shaking hands with Kim Dae Jung on TV," says Seoul aid worker Erica Kang. "It's like 'Oh my God, it's a human being after all.'" "It was like a cartoon shaking hands with a person," noted Hansol Seo, a young South Korean journalist.

If Kim Jong Il was not really a cartoon, then what other images of North Korea were inaccurate? For decades, authoritarian governments in Seoul had presented almost surreal pictures of the DPRK and its leaders. For

President Kim Dae Jung, the former dissident who repeatedly suffered at the hands of his predecessors, almost none of the propaganda ever had any currency, but his summit, if it had any lasting effect, discredited the previous governments' views of the North in the eyes of his fellow South Koreans. In the euphoria of the historic meeting in Pyongyang, many people in the South could only see that their brothers and sisters in the North were starving. They did not ask why that was happening. Kim Jong Il, for them, was no longer a perpetrator or even an autocrat. He was simply the leader of the other Korea.

And to the extent South Koreans wanted an explanation for Pyongyang's predicament, they viewed North Korea as the victim of a large and thoroughly despicable power, the United States of America. The outpouring of sentiment in favor of the North after the June 2000 summit was matched by a torrent of anti-Americanism. An acquittal by a military tribunal of a pair of American soldiers for the accidental deaths of two schoolgirls sparked daily protests in late 2002 by tens of thousands in Seoul and by multitudes in other cities. Their unfortunate deaths—the girls were run over by an armored vehicle on training maneuvers—were considered deliberate by many South Koreans. Yet when five of Seoul's sailors were actually gunned down by a DPRK vessel in southern territorial waters in the same month as the schoolgirl fatalities, there were no large-scale expressions of outrage. South Korea is a society that has seemingly lost its bearings. When nuns there wear "Fucking USA" badges in public, something has gone terribly wrong.

"Anti-Americanism is getting intense," says one Korean academic. "It used to be widespread and not so deep. Now it's getting widespread and deep." That change is the result of many factors, but especially the inevitable passing of generations. Older Koreans remember the wartime sacrifice of America and are generally wary of the North. Yet their place in society is being taken by the population group named after a computer chip, the so-called 386ers—those in their thirties, who came of age in the 1980s, and were born in the 1960s. This generation, now moving into its forties and positions of power, was shaped by the Kwangju massacre and its struggle against authoritarianism. The 386ers have no particular love of the United States, which is perceived to be the ally of the old military governments. As they displace more conservative elements in the electorate, society has swerved sharply left.

With South Korean society changing so much, is it only a matter of time before the government, and even the nature of the state, changes too? Kim Dae Jung had long advocated a "confederation of Korean republics," which contemplated a long period before the two Koreas would join, either in name or substance, to form one nation. He even said that unification would take "several decades." Kim may not have advocated the South's absorption of the North, but his working assumption was that, over time, the northern state would become just like the southern one, thereby making national integration painless. Kim Il Sung had originally proposed a federated state, but his son later suggested a looser concept of confederation to protect his weakened society in a unified Korea.

The declaration issued shortly after the June 2000 summit "acknowledged that the different formulas that the North and South favor for reunification have common factors." That statement glossed over important differences in the "confederation" proposals of each side, yet it was nonetheless a reaffirmation that both Pyongyang and Seoul were working toward union. Moreover, South Korea, by agreeing to pursue confederation, adopted a road map to unification that was first proposed by Kim Il Sung and that had become part of the "progressive," or leftist, agenda in the South.

The June 2000 statement could have become just another forgotten declaration on unification, but Roh Moo-hyun, Kim Dae Jung's successor as president, is working to implement it. Roh has vigorously promoted his version of the Sunshine Policy, which is, after all, a prelude to a union of two equals.

More important, Roh is pushing political changes that harmonize Southern politics with those of the North. His most important initiative is to abolish the South's draconian National Security Law, which dates back to 1948 and was used by authoritarian governments to stifle dissent. Even more controversial is his announced desire to legalize communist parties.

Both of these proposals are consistent with an agenda of democracy and human rights, but, judging from other acts, Roh's intentions may not be so benign. He also sponsored two laws, both effective in the middle of 2005, that were apparently designed to cripple newspapers, or, more precisely, the most popular of them. The legislation essentially caps the circulation of the country's most widely followed dailies. Any paper with more than 30 percent of the market is subject to onerous restrictions, as are the three biggest papers if they hold a combined readership of over 60 percent. If South Korea had no media but its top newspapers, the president's general notion of stimulating competition would make some sense. Yet the mass-circulation dailies compete against television, radio, and the nation's lively Internet and therefore have no monopoly on the dissemination of information. It just so happens that all of the target newspapers take a conservative line and do not support Roh Moo-hyun's policies on North Korea. The legislation also requires papers to provide to the authorities sensitive internal information, effectively permits government regulation of editorial content, and permits Roh to use public money to subsidize papers that support his programs. The new laws, which probably violate South Korea's constitutional guarantees of press freedom, have been called incompatible with democracy by international observers.

Moreover, Roh Moo-hyun's public embrace of Song Du-yul, an admitted member of Kim Jong Il's Korean Workers' Party and undoubtedly a North Korean agent, has little to do with furthering democracy. Taking everything together, there is a basis for assuming the worst about the president's plans. His recent steps indicate that, whatever his motives, he is not attempting to democratize South Korea but trying to move it leftward instead. As Roh has said, "Permitting a communist party will complete democracy in Korea." Yet it's also true that such a step could help extinguish it. Kim Jong Il does not need military force to bring South Korea under his rule; he can accomplish the same goal through the ballot box. Thanks to Kim Dae Jung, there is already momentum for a peninsula-wide confederation of some sort, and elections to determine the structure of a new government could open the door to any system. "The only thing left is to change the constitution," says Lee Do-hyung, editor of *Korea Forum*, a magazine devoted to politics.

Could South Koreans freely choose, in the words of South Korean legislator Song Young Gil, "unification under the red flag"? A peninsula-wide state run by Pyongyang is inconceivable to Americans, but that's not how a substantial group of South Koreans feel. More than three out of ten of them polled in the middle of 2004 wanted unification *regardless of the conditions*. That figure was more than three times larger than the corresponding percentage in 2002. If this trend continues, Kim Jong Il's allies in the South could fashion a majority in favor of his type of Korea within a decade or two, especially if he is allowed to intimidate voters in the South as well as the North. Political blogger Usung Chung predicts that the DPRK leader will employ both a North Vietnamese–type "peace offensive" with North Korean–style coercive tactics. "Basically we expect Vietcongs," he says. In this still unresolved contest the weak are not meek and could inherit the earth, or at least South Korea's portion of it.

"This is not a country where logic prevails," Chung noted. "You have to appeal to the emotion. And that emotion changes so wildly." As a result, no democratic nation with the possible exception of Taiwan—another young democracy facing a communist threat—has had more interesting politics in recent years than South Korea. Virtually nobody gave human rights lawyer Roh Moo-hyun a chance in the days preceding the presidential contest in 2002—he was thought to be losing by the middle of election day and prevailed only because young supporters mounted a noontime Internet campaign that resulted in a late-day surge of voting. After his stunning win with the help of the "2030 Generation," twenty-somethings, he fell from grace with the voters within months of taking office. His own political party launched his impeachment in the National Assembly in 2004 after a fistfight, and the progressive Uri Party won a legislative majority in April of that year, less than six months after it was formed. The 2004 victory of the progressives ended more than four decades of conservative rule in the legislature. Politics in Seoul, once stable, are now highly personal, volatile, and inherently unpredictable. South Koreans, in short, are in the middle of a grand experiment.

Which means nearly anything can happen, so we should not assume the Republic of Korea will survive in recognizable form. As the Sunshine Policy continues to soften Southern perceptions of the North and as current voting trends continue, the DPRK could take over the rest of the peninsula through constitutional means. Where Kim Il Sung's hard-line tactics failed, those of Kim Jong Il, his supposedly underachieving son, may actually work.

Fortunately, extrapolation is the last tool to use when making predictions about South Korea. As we know by now, little has traveled in a straight line during the past few years in that country, which is lost in transition and has yet to find equilibrium. If change itself is the only constant—it is said that in South Korea a "generation" is only three years—then the derailed train of politics could jump back onto the tracks in the next half decade.

"We have hope," says Park Jin. The well-known national assemblyman is referring to his conservative Grand National Party, or GNP, which ruled the legislature from the time the party was formed in 1997 until early 2004. The GNP's hopes now center on the next race for the Blue House, Seoul's White House, which is, incidentally, within Park's legislative district.

The next presidential elections are scheduled for December 2007. Roh Moo-hyun—also known as "Roh the idiot" and "Captain Roh"—is barred from seeking a second term, and the GNP has a leader who could actually win despite the general leftward drift of the electorate. Park Geun Hye is the popular daughter of Park Chung Hee, whom many fondly remember for creating national prosperity. She is determined to wipe out corruption, which has plagued politics in South Korea since her father's day. The elder Park had forged close links between the government and the *chaebol* conglomerates, and that tight relationship inevitably had a corrosive effect on the political system. To remain viable, the GNP must convince the voters that it has freed itself from corrupt ties and has revitalized itself. Moreover, it is also moving left to take ground away from the Uri Party, the first in South Korea to refuse to have an English name. "Uri," appropriately enough for a nationalist organization, means "our" in Korean.

Park Jin, once Kim Young Sam's presidential spokesman, talks about "patiently" waiting for the country to swing back to conservative politics, but the 2007 presidential elections could be that party's last realistic chance in decades to set the direction for South Korean society. The GNP's conservative base is slightly less than half the electorate, as recent elections show. But its older supporters are literally dying off while the Uri Party, its primary antagonist, is consolidating power after its dramatic rise. Uri leaders say they can hold on to power for decades, which sounds boastful but may also be true. They caught "the momentum of generational change" to grab control of the national government and are now moving to the center to create a new "political core." It can't drift too much to the right, however, because the ultra-leftist Democratic Labor Party came from nowhere to grab about 13 percent of the electorate in 2004. The Uri Party, therefore, has to protect its critical left flank. If it can do so while holding back the GNP challenge for the center, the Uri progressive agenda will dominate for "generations"—at least as they are defined in South Korean terms.

But the Uri Party had better keep its eye on an ever-changing society. The younger half of 2030 Generation, the newest subgroup in the South Korean electorate, has sided with progressive forces—but not by a wide margin. Furthermore, there is a rapidly growing "New Right" movement, which is mainly composed of disillusioned 386ers. If these batches of voters signal a trend, South Korea could develop a new equilibrium with a political system finely balanced between progressive and conservative elements. And in the normal course of events, a maturing democracy will, in the long run, produce institutionalized political parties and stability.

Unfortunately, there might not be a long term for the increasingly volatile South Korean state. Democracies, like other governments, can tear themselves apart when internal strains are too great—especially when they are also being undermined from the outside. The general move toward confederation in conjunction with current national trends—the increasingly favorable perceptions of North Korea, growing antagonism against the United States, a push to dismantle internal security mechanisms, and generally volcanic politics, to name just the most prominent of them— could lead to the DPRK's triumph over the South Korean state in relatively short order.

The problem for South Koreans is that their current political leadership misperceives the danger. Confederation, as contemplated by the June 2000 declaration, will result in a melding of the two rival states in a synthesis. Yet as they exist today, the societies in the South and the North are antithetical. In all likelihood, any blending won't work and one system will eventually prevail. It may seem inconceivable in this enlightened age that a failing totalitarian regime could absorb a vibrant and prosperous democracy, but that is exactly what could happen when Seoul's leaders no longer believe that their society must win.

Appeasing Appeasers

What must win, in the view of Koreans, is Korea. The most important force on the peninsula today is nationalism. After four decades of colonization and six more of division, a people considered "too noisy, too spicy, too proud, too nationalistic" want their country back.

The rest of the world, on the other hand, wants the DPRK to disarm. Yet for many South Koreans that goal is not overly important. Or not important at all. In "a land of extremes," extremist views are often heard. "I want

North Koreans to develop nuclear weapons," says Park Soon Jae, a housewife in Seoul. "After all, we are one nation." Kim Jong Il's nuclear device is not the DPRK's weapon; it is a "Korean bomb."

If the North's bomb belongs to South Koreans, will South Koreans help to disarm the North? Although ordinary citizens are going on a nationalist bender, Seoul is still on record as wanting to denuclearize Pyongyang. As President Roh Moo-hyun has said, South Korea will "never accept" North Korea's nukes.

Yet there is a noticeable "panic gap." The perception of danger increases with geographical distance from Pyongyang, so, paradoxically, a Washington far beyond the range of Kim Jong Il is almost apoplectic while Seoul, which can be incinerated in minutes, is nonchalant.

There are powerful incentives for South Korean leaders to not care too much about Kim Jong Il's nuclear arms. For one thing, almost half of their constituents live within the range of North Korean artillery and so are hostages already. Moreover, many voters—perhaps as many as a fifth of them—want their country to side with the North against the United States, and many others are sympathetic to Pyongyang. Some South Koreans wouldn't mind inheriting the arsenal if the Kim regime fails. Finally, most politicians have, along with the voters, become desensitized to danger after more than a half century of border incursions, assassinations, and assorted violence.

But more than anything else, the South's leaders are scared. "I believe the danger of war on the Korean peninsula is slight—in fact, nonexistent," said Kim Dae Jung shortly before leaving the Blue House. If Seoul's leaders always hope for the best in the face of Pyongyang's hostility—D.J. made this comment after North Korea threatened to pull out of the armistice and thereby resume the Korean War—it is because the alternatives for them are too horrifying to contemplate. "We will lose everything if there is another war on the Korean peninsula," said Roh Moo-hyun, quantifying the stakes as soon as he succeeded Kim.

The risks, as Roh weighs them, lead him to only one policy choice: "It is my firm determination that there shall be no war under any circumstances." No one can blame him for sharing the goal of almost all his predecessors or reflecting the strain of pacifism evident since the Korean War. Yet Roh's extreme position has led him not only to tolerate the DPRK—an acceptable moral choice—but to actively support it—which isn't. As he said, his policy is to "guarantee the security and survival of the North." "Koreans," he declares, "should stand together."

Showing solidarity, South Korea provides aid to the DPRK and refuses to criticize its leaders for either unforgivable abuse of the citizenry or flagrant conduct abroad. Seoul's officials hinder dissidents seeking change in the North and hamper North Korean refugees from entering the South. But most shamefully, Seoul ignores the plight of about 540 South Korean soldiers held as prisoners of war by Pyongyang for more than a half century in violation of the armistice and does nothing for at least 486 South Koreans kidnapped by North Korean agents. The South's government has turned its back on its most basic obligation as a state—protecting its own nationals—so that it will not offend the neighboring despot.

It is, however, willing to offend, and sometimes obstruct, the only guarantor of its own security. President Roh, playing to his young constituency, once offered to "mediate" between Washington and Pyongyang as if his nation were a neutral bystander and had no stake in the outcome. Then he said that South Korea should play a "balancing role," switching sides on an issue-by-issue basis between the "northern alliance" of Beijing, Moscow, and Pyongyang and the "southern alliance" of Washington and Tokyo. "The power equation in Northeast Asia will change depending on the choices we make," he said.

Moreover, at the six-party talks in Beijing, South Korea is the country that most consistently sides with North Korea against the United States. In particular, Seoul questions whether the DPRK even has a uranium weapons program and does not support the American formula of complete and verifiable disarmament. By opposing American initiatives, Seoul gives Beijing and Moscow the cover to do the same. Moreover, Kim Jong Il is not likely to make concessions when he knows he can rely on support from the other Korea.

"Success or failure of a U.S. policy toward North Korea isn't too big a deal to the American people, but it is a life-or-death matter for South Koreans," explains President Roh. "Therefore, any U.S. move should fully consider South Korea's opinion." In effect, Seoul sees Pyongyang's development of nuclear arms and intercontinental missiles as a bilateral matter between the two halves of the peninsula. Unfortunately, it is not. And unfortunately Roh's belief that it is makes a multilateral solution to a regional—and global—problem especially difficult to achieve.

If Roh is oblivious to the wider implications of Pyongyang's activities, he is only exhibiting an insularity that has continued to characterize Koreans, even in the twenty-first century. "South Korea is not a nation with a strong vision of the world beyond its frontiers," writes David Scofield, an academic. The country exported its way to prosperity and depends on others for national security, but it has gone its own way—disregarding the wishes of its longtime supporters—when it comes to dealings with the North.

Perhaps Koreans have adopted a particularly parochial view because they think they can handle things on their own. The stunning economic development of the South now gives its leaders the means to shape events for the first time since the division of the peninsula, and they are demanding a rebalancing of their alliance with America to recognize their newfound strength. "I think in some respects our recent problems are similar to those encountered by married couples," says Roh Moo-hyun, who should have used the parent-child analogy instead. "People are often hurt when a close friend or partner appears to ignore their feelings or emotions."

To avoid a separation, analysts say Washington will soon have to bend to Seoul. Americans are, unfortunately, almost as out of favor in the South as they are in the North. The military alliance may not be "defunct," as one Asia expert recently wrote, but it is shaky nonetheless. Roh has said on various occasions that it is not "reasonable," "honorable," or "good" to rely on foreign soldiers. Planned American troop withdrawals are forcing the modernization of the South's already formidable army, and someday Seoul will actually make good on its pledge to become militarily self-reliant.

When that happens, the alliance will undoubtedly end because Washington and Seoul do not agree on the important issues of the day and, beyond generalities, do not even share a common vision of the future. If anything, Seoul is closer to Beijing than to Washington these days. Korea was a minor asteroid in the Chinese solar system before and could enter Beijing's orbit again.

As long as the American military alliance remains in place, South Korean leaders can afford to do as they please. Whether Americans agree or disagree with his approach, they have given Roh Moo-hyun a free hand. With that freedom he has chosen to placate the North and cozy up to

China. "Appeasement of tyrants is fine for backwater nations that plan to ultimately rely on modern powers to fix the damage," writes Mary Anastasia O'Grady of *The Wall Street Journal*. She is correct of course, but Roh is making it especially hard for Washington to attend to the repair.

Will Americans continue to tolerate policies incompatible with their own? Today, they are patient and permit Roh to bedevil them to keep the alliance intact. The U.S. government is, perhaps for good reason, appeasing an appeaser. It complains about Roh's brand of engagement—or is it neutrality?—but has not required him to choose. Yet if Washington believes the DPRK poses a critical threat to global security, at some time it must force South Koreans to make a historic decision.

Do they stand with America or with the other Korea? At some point, America—and the West—will have to know.

6

SYMPATHY FROM THE DEVIL

China Stands Behind Kim's Korea

Chinese officials can find three people practicing
Falun Gong in some dirt pot in Xinjiang, but they
don't know about a 5,000-ring-magnet sale to Pakistan.
—James Swanson, American defense analyst

If it takes a thief to catch a thief, do we need communists with nuclear weapons to rein in Kim Jong Il? The Chinese know how the North Koreans feel today—they were, after all, in their position just a couple of decades ago. If any nation has influence over the People's Republic of Pyongyang, it is its next of kin, the People's Republic of Beijing.

With its clout Beijing can either solve the Korean nuclear crisis or let it fester. The mighty United States, therefore, is now looking to China to fix a problem it cannot handle on its own. Will the Chinese pressure their only formal ally, the DPRK, in order to help America, the nation they admire but also revile?

And how could Washington ever find itself in such a position of dependence? There are many reasons, but the most fundamental of them is that the grand sweep of events is conspiring against America. China, not the United States, looks like the world's sole superpower a few decades from now. The periods of European and American ascendancy may be just minor interruptions in the natural state of Chinese domination of world affairs. Even today, Eliot Cohen of Johns Hopkins calls China "the most important power in the world."

Although the transition to a China-centric geopolitical order has not yet occurred, such a shift appears all but inevitable. As powerful as America is, it cannot forever withstand the grand global tide in favor of the rising Chinese state. So perhaps in the beginning of the "Century of the Pacific," or more to the point, "China's Century," Americans should be getting accustomed to going to Beijing to ask for favors.

Big, Bad, and Bellicose Beijing

It's a shame everyone's not Chinese, for their country is a wonder to behold. China is the world's biggest producer of, among other things, steel, cameras, toys, sex toys, sporting goods, shoes, garments, textiles, televisions, cell phones, pens, and mobile phone batteries—one enterprise, Shenzhen-based BYD Company Ltd., has more than 50 percent of the global market. One city in China, Datang, weaves more than a third of the world's socks: about a pair and a half for each person on the planet each year. The country produces eight out of ten of the world's microwaves and nine out of ten of its DVD players. The Chinese file the most trademark applications. The nation makes about 70 percent of all counterfeit goods.

Half the world's pigs oink in a Chinese dialect. The Middle Kingdom is the solar system's champion rice grower and beer brewer. That's good because the People's Republic has just replaced the United States as the world's top consumer. The Chinese shovel down more rice and puff more cigarettes than any other national group, of course, but they also use more coal, tin, zinc, platinum, and iron ore. The country, in fact, uses about half of the world's cement, one-third of its steel, one-quarter of its copper, one-fifth of its aluminum.

The Chinese have built the largest dam, shopping center, power grid, and golf club. Soon the nation will have the tallest TV tower and biggest garbage treatment facility, both to be built in the southern city of Guangzhou, and the largest shipyard, now under construction in Shanghai. Of course, we shouldn't forget the Chinese are assembling the world's biggest Ferris wheel.

No other country has more mobile phone or cable television subscribers. In 2004 there were over 218 billion text messages—more even than my daughter sends and more than the rest of the world combined. Over half the world's stamp collectors are Chinese.

The nation contains human beings by the bushel load. The largest city in the world is China's Chongqing, which boasts 32 million souls and occupies an area roughly three times the size of Belgium. There are 166 cities with a population over 1 million in China. The United States has nine. The number of Chinese undercounted in their census is about equal to the total combined population of Germany, France, and the United Kingdom. The People's Liberation Army is the world's biggest military. There are only seventeen countries that have more residents than China's Communist Party has comrades. With nearly 70 million card carriers, it is the largest membership organization on the face of the earth. If "demography is destiny," then the West is doomed. China's population is about 1.5 billion, more than five times that of the United States. Only India comes close to having as many people—and it is about a half billion folks behind.

China, in a word, is big. Yet it is bigger than that—as Singapore's Lee Kuan Yew said, that nation "is the biggest player in the history of man." And it is growing faster than any other major state. Investment bank Goldman Sachs says the Chinese People's Republic could have the world's largest economy by 2039. Many others believe China will overtake America long before then.

People may debate the date of Beijing's takeover of the top spot, but the general trend is no longer in dispute. The Chinese, in short, appear to be riding a tidal wave of awesome proportions. Some say the country's rise is an event that happens only once every century or two, but others think it is of even greater historical significance. "I believe that we are in a process which doesn't happen every fifty years, it is only once every three or four hundred years when something this big, this all embracing, happens," proclaims Kenneth Courtis of Goldman Sachs. It's possible that Beijing's rise is even rarer than that. Says Columbia University's Jeffrey Sachs, "China is the most successful development story in world history."

If Sachs is right, the Chinese state will be a geopolitical wonder soon. America ultimately attained political and military dominance as well as cultural influence due to the strength of its economy. Power seeped across the Atlantic from the quarreling states of Europe to the United States of America, and now it is flowing across the Pacific to the People's Republic of China. As development spreads around the globe because of trade and investment, a China five times more populous than the United States should end up five times as powerful. "The sleeping dragon is awake, dude," the *Far Eastern Economic Review* told us.

In the future, the Chinese state will probably dominate the United States across the board. In the long run, America's fate is to become a second-ranked power residing in an unimportant part of the planet. Norway is a wonderful country, superior to the superpower in many respects. So are Sweden and Switzerland, as any tourist can attest. None of them pose an overall challenge to America, however, because they are, in the final analysis, too small. America too is small compared to China.

This trend, it's safe to say, is as clear as they get. The timeline, however, is not. Despite all the predictions of the impending geopolitical marginalization of the United States, at this point we have no idea when Beijing's rulers will relegate America to second place.

To figure out the future, we need to consider the past. The increasingly accepted view that we are living in China's era is based, for the most part, on the straight-line analysis that tomorrow will just be more of today. Yet history rarely cooperates with the extrapolators, at least in the medium term. In recent memory, oil-pumping Arabs, loaded down with petrodollars, were set to dominate the planet. I finished college in 1973—around the time of the oil embargo—with the certainty that I was going to be working for some Bedouin or sheik for the rest of my life. Next came the Japanese, who accumulated great amounts of cash by marketing consumer goods around the globe. At the end of the 1980s—the height of their glory—most everyone talked about the "Japanese Century." Now the Chinese look like the next group poised to exercise planetary control. They too will stumble someday—the country is, after all, in the grips of a turbulent makeover—

but in the meantime Beijing poses a challenge of immense proportions to the West and especially Washington.

In the early days of New China, as the People's Republic likes to call itself, that challenge was direct and unmistakable. When Mao Zedong wasn't confronting the "imperialist" United States, "the paper tiger," or quarreling with the "revisionist" Soviet Union, he was fomenting trouble somewhere on the planet or instigating the occasional border incursion. "All is chaos under Heaven, and the situation is excellent," he characteristically noted during the decade-long Great Proletarian Cultural Revolution.

Yet for all his verbal assaults on America and its running dogs, China was not an effective challenger in large part because it had no diplomacy to speak of. From 1967 to 1969, for instance, Beijing had only one ambassador abroad—and even he was almost recalled.

After the border skirmishes with Moscow's troops in 1969, Mao began to see the benefits of contact with foreigners. China, for example, joined the United Nations in 1971 by taking Taiwan's seat and began cooperating with Richard Nixon's Washington. China's leader even got the American president to stop by Beijing for a chat in 1972. Nonetheless, Chinese foreign policy could hardly be called effective. The nation, even with its slightly more open outlook, remained behind the "Bamboo Curtain."

Deng Xiaoping, Mao's successor, reoriented the country's foreign relations as he went about undoing much of his predecessor's work. The diminutive Chinese leader staked the survival of the Communist Party on trade-induced prosperity and inward foreign investment, and despite some regrettable incidents, like the failed 1979 invasion of Vietnam, Deng generally sought to "bide time" and "keep a low profile" in external affairs. Beijing established relations with other nations, such as the United States in 1979 and South Korea in 1992, and began to join multilateral institutions like the World Bank and International Monetary Fund. Deng's outreach to global and regional organizations, however, was only tentative: he feared they would restrain a growing China. Moreover, he did not change the antagonistic posture of the People's Republic toward international norms, and the Chinese government still carried its sense of grievance against the West and Japan for events, some of which took place in the distant past.

Yet because of all the material progress in the last quarter century, Beijing's diplomats are beginning to see themselves as representatives of history's next great power instead of its most undeserving victim. Fortunately, a more confident China is a more moderate one, at least in tone. Its leaders say they will never seek hegemony or superpower status and, to their credit, talk peace and harmony. Officials still speak of the Five Principles of Peaceful Coexistence—mutual respect for sovereignty and territorial integrity, mutual nonaggression, noninterference in others' internal affairs, equality and mutual benefit, and peaceful coexistence—as the bedrock of their foreign policy. If they mention their emergence at all—and many in Beijing are uncomfortable doing so—they use terms like "peaceful rise" or "peaceful development" to allay concerns about their growing clout. "We are trying to make as many friends as possible," said Li Zhaoxing, China's foreign minister. "The more friends China has, the better."

Today, China has more than just friends, it has active supporters across the globe. The emergence of great powers is always a time of geopolitical discomfort, and America, for reasons both altruistic and selfish, has tried to ease China's transition from Marxist economics and Maoist political institutions.

Washington's policy, the grandest wager in history, looks like a good bet so far. Inside the existing geopolitical order China has prospered. In the past quarter century the people who have benefited the most from the American-led system are not the Americans but the Chinese. In a peaceful world they are manufacturing and trading their way up through the ranks of nations and, as a consequence, are transforming their country for the better. As they have done so, their leaders began to accept the world as it is, developing relations with other states, signing global treaties and conventions—including at least twenty-one international human rights covenants—and joining a host of multilateral and regional institutions and groups. The People's Republic, for the first time in its six decades of existence, is working inside the international system. And as it assimilates into that global order, the country, although it is beginning to think like a great power, speaks in pleasing tones. Once shrill and ideological, Chinese diplomacy is now deft, subtle, and patient. It is, says Marvin Ott of the National Defense University, "a thing of beauty."

As well as a threat. China is still trying to change the global system for good—but not for the better. Beijing's leaders constantly campaign for a "multipolar" world, which means they want a global order where America is cut down to size as only one of many powers. "China is not America's ally and never will be," notes a prominent Beijing academic. Says American analyst Robert Sutter, "China is the only large power in the world preparing to shoot Americans." And sometimes it does more than just prepare. It has aggressively challenged American patrols in international airspace and waters off its coast, as the notorious EP-3 reconnaissance plane and *Bowditch* incidents show.

Americans can't blame China for trying to increase its influence, but its effort to generally push them aside makes that nation a "strategic competitor." Washington is full of analysts who say that the United States shouldn't call China an enemy because that will make it one—there is more than a measure of common sense in that general proposition—but Beijing has by its own words branded itself an adversary. Although the challenge may be "discreet," it is nonetheless real. Chinese diplomats try to maintain cordial relations with their Washington counterparts and cooperate when it is in their interests to do so, but *People's Daily*, the Communist Party's flagship publication, daily condemns America and tells it to step out of the way of China's preferred international system.

Unfortunately, Beijing's idea of a replacement for the current global order is still a bit fuzzy. The best that its leaders can say is that all countries, large and small, are equal. The logical consequence of this egalitarian proposition is that Zimbabwe, Sudan, and North Korea should have as much say in world affairs as Britain, Australia, and the United States. Although the Chinese may not actually believe this doctrine, they have helped legitimize the concept by making it a cornerstone of their policy. It is ironic that a nation that fights so hard against democracy at home speaks of the "democratization of international relations."

As the Chinese denounce American "unilateralism," they actively work to reduce Washington's influence. China talks of an Asia seeking a "common cultural identity," which is really a polite way of saying that Americans are outsiders and should leave. Beijing is still angry at Singapore, despite that island's friendly posture toward China, because the country permits the U.S. Navy to dock at its port.

Moreover, Beijing continually advocates the formation of Asian political and economic organizations that exclude the United States—and which the Chinese can dominate. These days, China complains of American involvement in Asia by talking obliquely of "strangulation" and "encirclement." The new code words, if anything, betray a rising anti-

Americanism of a foreign policy establishment that is hesitant to use "imperialist" in public.

To defeat the unnamed imperialist Beijing is setting up the East Asian Community. In November 2004 China took a big step toward implementing an "unprecedented grand endeavor" by agreeing with ten other Asian nations to establish the world's largest free trade area by the end of this decade. The new grouping, representing more than two billion people, could soon outstrip the European Union.

Until it can surpass Europe, the Chinese are trying to drive a wedge through the Atlantic Alliance by wooing France, always a thorn for America, and other EU members into its orbit. At present, it is making progress toward this goal by chipping away at the EU's arms embargo on China. The Chinese portray the sanction as a "relic of the Cold War," but it was in fact imposed because of what the world calls the Tiananmen massacre and Beijing delicately refers to as "that 1989 affair."

Tiananmen is the ball at the end of the chain attached to the ankle of the modern Chinese state. That event poisons Sino-American relations to this day and serves as a reminder that China is not just a bigger version of France. In fact, the autocratic nature of the Chinese government puts real limits on how far the nation's diplomacy can progress. "A liberal internationalist foreign policy is incompatible with China's illiberal domestic order," writes Minxin Pei, an analyst at the Carnegie Endowment for International Peace in Washington. "Although an illiberal regime can occasionally demonstrate tactical brilliance in diplomacy, its execution of a constructive, long-term foreign policy will be undermined by the character flaws inherent in autocracies: insecurity, secrecy, intolerance and unpredictability."

The optimistic say that an insecure, secretive, intolerant, and unpredictable China can continue to evolve its foreign policy for the better. That is, of course, possible, but the best indication of how a powerful China will treat its small neighbors in the future is how its repressive state deals with its own people today. How can a country that plays so rough at home now be so benign abroad tomorrow?

Another good predictor of Chinese foreign policy is its current one. Even at this moment China acts highhandedly with its neighbors when it has the power to do so. For instance, the downstream countries of the Mekong River complain bitterly about Beijing's extremely selfish use of that vital artery's water, and the Japanese are upset by incursions by Chinese vessels, both above and below the sea's surface. Beijing supports almost every rogue state in the region plus many others elsewhere. The Philippines cannot forget that as late as 1995 China fortified a reef just off its western shores. Although Beijing in recent years has shown a commendable desire to settle border disputes with its fourteen land neighbors, it nonetheless maintains expansive claims to the continental shelves of Brunei, Indonesia, Malaysia, and Vietnam in addition to that of the Philippines. Beijing also retains outsized claims to the entire South China Sea itself, thereby impinging on generally accepted notions of free passage on and over international waters.

Beijing's treatment of neighboring countries betrays more than a trace of imperial attitude, which survives despite the passage of a hundred years and the occurrence of two great revolutions. Although China is not trying to replicate the formal relations of the imperial tributary system by having foreigners publicly acknowledge the Middle Kingdom's primacy, there is a sense of entitlement evident in the Chinese capital these days and an assumption that others, especially the Koreans, should see things Beijing's way. By its mere presence the country deserves, in its own view, to receive the respect, goodwill, and cooperation of its neighbors.

As its neighbors fall in behind China, American influence in Asia is declining. Recent Washington lectures to the region's leaders on terrorism fall flat while Chinese messages of common prosperity resonate. "It is an irreversible trend that the world wants peace, people want cooperation, nations want development, and society wants advancement," Comrade Hu Jintao, China's current leader, said in his New Year's message for 2004. That's a line everyone wants to hear. Beijing's effective advocate, American businessman Laurence Brahm, notes that developing nations are now happy to see China "once again standing up for something."

But what does China stand for? As wrongheaded as it was, Maoism at least served as a beacon to much of the developing world. After Deng Xiaoping dismantled Mao's economic system, China represented no idea, unless economic growth qualified as a principle or a concept. Unfortunately, the country's leaders cannot talk about liberal values, because they're not yet accepted by the Communist Party at home.

The United States, on the other hand, has loads of lofty ideas. In the

most important region in the world the nation that stands for noble principles is in danger of being overrun by an authoritarian one that has none.
America is in retreat where it really counts.

Pandora's Passport

China has had lots of experience in outmaneuvering America in Asia in
the past few years. For more than four decades Beijing has posed a critical
challenge to Washington and the global order.

Chinese leaders say that their nation "has always adopted a serious
and responsible attitude towards preventing the proliferation of nuclear
weapons." That claim, however, reflects a China they now want the world
to see. In an earlier time, Maoists in Beijing viewed things differently. As
good students of history, they applied Marxist analysis. Nukes in the hands
of imperialists were detrimental to world peace, they said, and socialist
weapons advanced it. And to bolster its effort to lead the Third World,
China even said it was all right for "other peace-loving countries," the non-
aligned states, to possess them.

Some think Beijing's pro-proliferation policy was the result of a sincere
belief that the communist camp needed extra firepower, and others say it
was just tactical maneuvering to justify their own bomb building. Whatever
the case, shortly after their first detonation of an atomic device in 1964 Chinese leaders changed tunes. Said one Beijing official the following year,
"The just struggle of Afro-Asian countries against imperialism and colonial-
ism is the best atom bomb." The other argument was that all the oppressed
were "elated" because, as a result of China's detonation, "they, too, have
nuclear weapons." By 1983, its pro-proliferation rhetoric was a thing of the
past.

So Chinese leaders, despite big talk, ended up looking like responsible
custodians of nuclear weaponry. Their abrupt post-detonation switch in announced policy seems to validate the theory of Kenneth Waltz of Columbia
University that nuclear powers act carefully when it comes to their arsenals.
China, the one nation that might have dispersed nuclear weapons widely,
acceded to the Treaty on the Non-Proliferation of Nuclear Weapons in
1992 and signed the Additional Protocol to the NPT in 1998 and the Com-

prehensive Nuclear Test Ban Treaty in 1996. Beijing has, as it is so proud of saying, enacted comprehensive nuclear export control legislation and established stringent licensing for nuclear material, dual-use items, and related technology. Since 1984 it has been a member of the International Atomic Energy Agency. China stopped testing nuclear weapons in 1996.

Moreover, the Chinese state—unlike a superpower we shall not name—has exercised admirable restraint by adopting a policy of "minimum deterrence," thereby keeping its nuclear arsenal small. And Beijing's public position is avowedly anti–nuclear terror: "China consistently advocates a complete prohibition and thorough destruction of nuclear weapons," says Hu Xiaodi, a senior Chinese diplomat, speaking on behalf of his government.

China, resolute and responsible, looks like the planet's model nuclear citizen. And it has every reason to be. "China is really located in a very, very difficult position," says Yan Xuetong of Tsinghua University in Beijing. "China is almost surrounded by many nuclear countries, not like the U.S. or like the U.K. and France. And so China is most sensitive to the nuclear situation."

China has more nuclear neighbors than any other nation. Russia, India, Pakistan, and North Korea all share a land border with China, and all have the ultimate weapon. Chinese leaders had no hand in Moscow's nuclear program, which predated Beijing's. Yet despite what Professor Yan implies, China has little right to complain about nuclear encirclement. Beijing did not help rival India develop its weapon, but New Delhi started its nuclear program in response to China's—the Indian effort was a foreseeable consequence of Mao's 1964 detonation. Moreover, Beijing has been directly responsible for the Pakistani and North Korean programs—and just about every other ongoing bomb-building project in the world today. "There is a circle of countries that want nuclear weapons," says Richard Fisher, a leading analyst of the Chinese military, "and in the center of that circle of evil is China."

If Pandora carries any passport these days, it is, as Fisher suggests, Chinese. Starting during the reign of the "reckless" Mao Zedong and continuing through the rule of the "pragmatic" Deng Xiaoping, the "modern" Jiang Zemin, and the "populist" Hu Jintao, Beijing's leaders have shared a box of nuclear secrets with other nations. They did not dispense weapons technology indiscriminately as they had threatened in the Maoist years. On the contrary, China's proliferation has been structured to advance national, as opposed to ideological, goals.

One of China's primary strategic objectives has been to assist one of its more troublesome neighbors, the Islamic state of Pakistan. Beijing began helping the fundamentally unstable nation build a bomb in 1974, the year of detonation of India's "peaceful nuclear explosive," by training Pakistani nuclear technicians. The initial aid may have only been in the form of "crude technology," but it got the ball rolling. In the early 1980s, just when China began to say the right things about proliferation, Beijing transferred to Islamabad plans for a nuclear warhead and enough enriched uranium for two weapons. In 1994 and 1995 the Chinese sold five thousand ring magnets, used in gas centrifuges for enriching uranium, to the laboratory of the now infamous Dr. Abdul Qadeer Khan, the Pakistani nuclear black marketer. The sale was in violation of China's newly undertaken NPT obligations and U.S. law. Beijing also appears to have provided nuclear test data, more modern warhead designs, and plutonium technology for which there are no peaceful uses. China may even have tested a Pakistani device on its soil. Chinese help has been crucial, extensive, and continuous.

But is it also ongoing? The State Department maintains that China's assistance to Pakistan "is much diminished if not eliminated," and that assessment might be correct. Beijing's help these days may be limited to answering the phone—such as when Dr. Mohammed calls Mr. Zhou to find out how to fit two pieces together without incinerating Islamabad—but the damage has already been done. By now Beijing has had three decades to deliver all Islamabad needs for a splendid nuclear device. "If you subtract China's help from Pakistan's nuclear program, there is no nuclear program," said Gary Milhollin of the Wisconsin Project on Nuclear Arms Control.

The Pakistanis are delighted by their one-way relationship with the Chinese, from whom all blessings flow. Blessings flow because Beijing, despite its talk about disarmament, apparently believes the spread of nuclear weapons is inevitable and so is trying to take maximum advantage of the process. If there is such a thing as "managed proliferation," the Chinese are its masters.

And Pakistan is the surrogate, the strategic proxy, for distributing nuclear technology across the Asian landmass from the Middle East to East

Asia. John Loftus, an American commentator on intelligence matters, says that China traded technology for the "Islamic bomb," as Pakistan's atomic weapon is known, for Middle Eastern oil and that the trade was made through Dr. Khan's smuggling ring. The arrangement may not have been as formal as that sounds, but Beijing has been active in proliferating nuclear technology to the Middle East, has persistently sought access to oil in that region, and has used Pakistan as its front for many of these activities.

Islamabad, in short, has been the tip of China's spear. Khan confessed to nuclear sales to Libya and Iran, but there are suspicions he had other customers in that general part of the world. The biggest black marketer in history peddled Chinese technology or at least technology developed with substantial assistance from Beijing. He even sold Libya blueprints—adorned with Chinese characters—for one of China's older warheads. After Libya abandoned its nuclear program, Tripoli surrendered the Chinese warhead plans in 2003. The blueprints are now in American custody—and duplicates may also be in the hands of Iran, thanks to Khan.

The depth of Chinese involvement in the Pakistani program was revealed when Islamabad ended the Khan ring in the early part of this decade. China pressured Pakistan's leaders to conduct their inquiry quickly to avoid exposing his network's China connection. A hurried probe, followed by Khan's confession and immediate pardon in 2004, is in fact what happened. Beijing supported Pakistani General Pervez Musharraf's controversial decision to end the inquiry prematurely.

The apparent breakup of Khan's network and Libya's nuclear about-face have been setbacks for Chinese ambitions. Nonetheless, China's general plan to use Pakistan to nuclearize the Middle East, the world's most volatile region, and adjoining North Africa has been a success. Beijing proliferated nuclear technology to build relationships with Tehran, Riyadh, Cairo, Algiers, Damascus, Saddam's Baghdad, and the Chinese continue the wily stratagem to this day. We do not know the final consequence of this bit of geopolitical mischief, whether it will be temporary disorder or horrible grief.

We do know, however, that China is coming to grief over the second part of its Pakistani maneuver. One of its primary strategic objectives has been to contain that other large Asian state, India, so Beijing's nuclear assistance to Islamabad, New Delhi's mortal enemy, made sense from a Chinese perspective. By giving the Pakistanis the means to kill Indians by the millions, however, Beijing has pushed New Delhi into a closer relationship with Washington. President Bush's agreement in July 2005 to cooperate with India across the board—including sharing nuclear technologies that have weapons applications—signals the creation of a partnership that is obviously directed against the Chinese state.

America's alliance with India, even if it remains informal, is a disaster of immense proportions for China. Unfortunately for the Chinese, they and their Pakistani allies will be hard-pressed to counter the combined geopolitical weight of the world's largest democracy and its most powerful one. China is strong, but its friend Pakistan is not. Islamabad, for one thing, has proven to be uncompetitive in the matchup with India: despite being led by military governments, Pakistan has not been able to win wars against its gargantuan rival to the south. So China violated Oscar Wilde's first rule of successful international relations—"A man cannot be too careful in the choice of his enemies," he told us—and is now racing to patch up relations with an aggrieved and peeved New Delhi.

As China used Pakistan's weapons program to annoy India, it is employing North Korea's to preoccupy its other Asian adversary, Japan—as well as the United States. Although Mao ruled out handing over an atomic device on a platter, Beijing nonetheless provided crucial technical assistance to North Korean scientists from more or less the beginning of their efforts. China's help is the best explanation for how destitute DPRK, which can barely master the processes needed to manufacture bicycles, maintains an active nuclear weapons program.

Most Chinese aid, however, was not extended directly. Instead, Beijing's support was channeled through surrogate Pakistan. As noted, the infamous Dr. Khan had been assisting North Korea since the early 1990s, until at least the middle of 2002. In the later stages of their cooperation the Pakistanis traded their uranium-enrichment expertise, in the form of centrifuges, for DPRK missiles. Pakistan's air force planes that carried the missiles flew through Chinese airspace and refueled on Chinese soil. Beijing had to have known what was happening and, in all probability, arranged the trade between the two nations. It's possible China orchestrated the North Korean uranium-enrichment program in the first place. Beijing may have even developed a long-term master plan that contemplated Pyongyang eventually surrendering the visible plutonium effort and continuing the covert uranium one.

There is some circumstantial evidence supporting this theory. China, for instance, reportedly ordered the North Koreans to retract their October 2002 confession to James Kelly of the existence of the uranium program. Moreover, China steadfastly—and mystifyingly—supports the current North Korean denial of the program's existence. Then President Jiang Zemin told George W. Bush at his Crawford ranch in October 2002 that China was "completely in the dark" about the uranium effort, and Beijing has publicly maintained that position until today. The astounding denial is, as John Loftus notes, "a real signal of partnership."

And so are China's diplomatic efforts to provide political cover for the DPRK. Beijing denounced American unilateralism for bypassing the Security Council and invading Iraq in 2003, yet at the same time it blocked Washington's efforts to have the Council censure or sanction North Korea. The Chinese have, at crucial junctures, stepped in to shield Pyongyang's nuclear program from the world community. They continually make the case that America's tough tactics are premature and in any event counterproductive, and they may be right from time to time. Yet they are always the ones arguing that the moment is not ripe for effective action. China has also wielded the threat of a Security Council veto to protect its other nuclear client, Iran.

The pattern suggests, despite what Beijing says, that China has not stopped playing "the proliferation card," its most powerful tool for accomplishing its most important strategic objectives. As much as we would like to think otherwise, the Chinese are willing to risk nuclear winter to get their own way in the world. From Mao's day to the present, they have been less worried about the danger of nuclear weapons than other nations' leaders have been, more confident about controlling the consequences, and utterly ruthless.

As well as perfectly pragmatic. How can Americans blame the Chinese for proliferating when they have not really tried to stop them? Washington policymakers, from one administration to the next, seem incapable of acting against Beijing's initiatives to spread nuclear weapons technology. American inaction is inexcusable by now because there is a known cycle that China employs. First come the categorical denials of wrongdoing and protestations of innocence. When these become untenable, there are denials of *state* sponsorship, the shifting of responsibility to "rogues," token actions against the few, the issuance of new policy guidelines, perhaps the attribution of responsibility to previous leaders, and new assurances to foreigners.

This sequence is predictable, oft-repeated—and always effective. President Clinton, for instance, could not bring himself to sanction China for selling the ring magnets. How could Beijing leaders not have been responsible for that blatant transaction? "Chinese officials can find three people practicing Falun Gong in some dirt pot in Xinjiang, but they don't know about a 5,000-ring-magnet sale to Pakistan," Washington defense analyst James Swanson points out.

From time to time Clinton and his successor have slapped temporary sanctions on China's state-owned enterprises for particularly egregious conduct, but the effect has always been negligible. Because sanctions have been so ineffective, we can only conclude that they were intended to be so. Whatever the merits of restraint may be, the point is that America has never made Beijing pay a price for activities that threaten its existence. The pattern of regularly occurring transgressions shows that Washington's policies have completely failed. American diplomats say that China's proliferation is "unacceptable," but then do not act as if it is. Why should the Chinese ever stop proliferating in these circumstances?

And what could be worse than failing to halt Beijing? Americans have acted so meekly with the Chinese that they are giving the Russians the idea that they can get away with it too. Despite its best efforts, Washington has not been able to prevent Moscow from selling reactors to the Iranians for their Bushehr project, even though it is probable that Tehran is maintaining a covert bomb program. Moscow's motives may be more monetary than malevolent, but the effect is just as bad from the world's point of view.

Beijing, to borrow a Chinese metaphor, is "killing with a borrowed knife." It's actually more complicated than that: China is using two daggers, Pakistan and North Korea, at the same time.

The Lips Talk to the Teeth

Does North Korea even have a nuclear weapons program? Don't ask China's foreign minister. "If there is one, it has nothing to do with us," said Li Zhaoxing in 2003. George Bush, refusing to take "nothing" for an answer, decided on the opposite tack, insisting that the DPRK program had everything to do with China. In his view, the solution to Pyongyang's nukes runs through Beijing.

Bush's premise is that the Chinese, who helped arm Kim Il Sung, should—and will—strip away weapons from his son, Kim Jong Il. If the American president has his way, North Korea's only ally will be the force that puts an end to the nuclear program of the Pyongyang regime.

The plan is Bush at his best—or perhaps at his worst. At first glance, the policy looks optimistic in the extreme. Why should the world's arch-proliferator become a force for disarmament? Nonetheless, China is in the beginning of a once-in-a-lifetime realignment of its foreign policy and its leadership is completing the process of generational transition. That means Chinese foreign policy toward North Korea will undoubtedly change, and the new thinking in Beijing favors greater distancing. Younger Chinese are beginning to accept nonproliferation norms and believe their country no longer benefits from spreading nuclear weapons. And there is apprehension about what America might do to stop Kim Jong Il should diplomacy fail.

It is conventional wisdom that China will do nothing to cause North Korea to completely fail, yet even this bedrock proposition is under assault. Shi Yinhong, a Beijing international relations expert, argues that North Korea's collapse would be good for Beijing: a newly unified Korea would gravitate toward China, once again becoming its satellite. Moreover, Korea would naturally distance itself from Japan and have no need for American troops. Some say that, should North Korea fail, China's military could march south, establish order, and either annex the DPRK or leave behind a compliant government. Korea would, once again, fall into China's lap, substantially strengthening Beijing's position in Asia.

There is even talk that, despite treaty obligations, the People's Liberation Army would not come to Pyongyang's aid in the event of American military attack. James Lilley, former American ambassador to Beijing and Seoul, even believes Kim Jong Il "knows the Chinese are getting ready to sell him out as a loser." In any event, the North Korean is losing support in the Chinese capital. No one, it seems, likes the erratic little troublemaker.

America's generous policy of integrating China into the world community has set the stage for a realignment of Chinese foreign policy, and Washington's relationship with Beijing is perhaps the best it has been in thirty years. At this propitious moment, the United States has appealed to the better instincts of the Chinese—and to their well-known sense of pride. As Chinese military expert Tai Ming Cheung says, Washington told Beijing, "If you want to be a world player, you will have to step up to the plate." China is now doing so, says Cheung, "perhaps in contradiction to its traditional interests."

Whether or not acting in self-interest, the Chinese have brought their North Korean counterparts to the bargaining table, literally and figuratively. Moreover, they have pressured them to stay there. China, it is reported, even plunked down cold hard cash to keep Pyongyang at the six-party talks in the Chinese capital. "China will never allow a nuclear weapon in North Korea," declares Shi Yinhong, the foreign policy analyst. Referring to disarming North Korea, Kong Quan, chief spokesman for the Chinese Foreign Ministry, says, "I believe you can never push too hard for a good purpose."

So decades of patience with the Chinese leadership could now be paying off. The stars are beginning to fall into alignment for a fundamental change in Chinese proliferation policy. The current leaders in Beijing, for one thing, are beginning to see the limitations of their pro-proliferation stance. North Korea's increasingly threatening posture is already pushing Tokyo to rearm, thereby undermining Chinese dominance in the region. A nuclear Japan, once an impossibility, would be a stunning setback for Chinese foreign policy. Proliferation has scored big benefits for Beijing so far by keeping its adversaries off balance, but now, because of "blowback" in East Asia, it looks as if China will end up in a worse position than it was in when it started.

Pyongyang, in short, has put Beijing into a tight spot. The tie-up between the two capitals is perhaps the world's oddest bilateral relationship. Mao said that his China and the DPRK were "as close as lips and teeth," and that description was mostly accurate for a while. Kim Il Sung sent Korean fighters to aid the Chinese revolution, and Mao returned the favor with his own "volunteers" during the "War to Resist US Aggression and Aid Korea," Beijing's term for the conflict we know by a more succinct name.

Kim Il Sung and Mao Zedong may not have been the best of buds after the Korean War, but they shared much in common, especially on a personal level. The charismatic communist comrades were Chinese-speaking, Confucian, and chubby. No wonder diplomacy between the two countries was conducted on a personal basis. Relations have not been the same since younger generations on both sides of the Yalu River took over. Jiang Zemin, the recently retired supremo, still felt an emotional attachment for his

North Korean counterpart, but he did not know him very well. In early 2004 the two of them were wrapped in a tight hug and looked as if they were about to kiss on the lips, but the real relationship was not actually that close.

These days, it seems the "lips" and "teeth" barely talk to each other. Hu Jintao and Wen Jiabao, the current Chinese leaders, have no warm feelings for Kim Jong Il. For the two of them, the Korean is just a tool. They reportedly make Kim nervous. The North Korean, for his part, is also supposed to feel more affinity with Russians, like dour Vladimir Putin, than with the Chinese.

Strained personal relations at the top are matched by communications problems at lower levels. Neither capital retains strong institutional links with the other even though they are each other's only formal ally. Kim Jong Il started purposely removing officials who had good relationships with China in the 1980s in a bid to shore up his position as his father's successor. Since the middle of the last decade Beijing's relations with Pyongyang have been handled by people who know much less about the North than their predecessors. For example, the 2003 retirement of Defense Minister Chi Haotian marked the formal passing of China's generals who fought in the Korean War. The influential Chi is still in the background, but ongoing institutionalization of the military has diminished the influence of elders like him.

The changing of generations, however, cannot alter one fact: the two nations are locked in a permanent embrace of location. A common border both separates and unites the partners in communism. Their boundary is arbitrary, drawn after conquest, and has a single ethnic group living on both sides. It has proved impossible to patrol without extraordinary effort. In winter one can walk across the ice to China and in the summer wade. At one point—at Yibukua, which means "one step across"—the Yalu River is so narrow that people cross without wetting their feet.

From the northern side of this imaginary line the Chinese, for hundreds of years, viewed the Koreans as inferiors, vassals to their grander kingdom and followers of their more magnificent culture. Beijing leaders, although they may not say so publicly, see the Korean peninsula as a part of their natural sphere of influence. The DPRK also serves as a buffer against a true capitalist society, South Korea, host to over thirty thousand American troops and foreign ideas. From the south side of that same line, the North

Koreans bitterly resent their condescending overlords, as subjects tend to do. They are also contemptuous of the communists who abandoned Marxism, upset at the allies who diplomatically recognized the enemy in Seoul, and suspicious of the friends who sided with America in recent years. Pyongyang's cadres despise the Chinese, but worst of all they feel betrayed.

The North Koreans, as a result, chew on the hand that feeds them. The Chinese are by far the DPRK's largest source of foreign food and energy, donating at least hundreds of millions of dollars in yearly assistance. The help sustains the Korean People's Army, which "could neither bark nor bite" without Beijing, and aid from China may be the only reason Kim Jong Il is still ruling today. Although his regime is particularly opaque, common sense, if nothing else, tells us that the North's coldly rational leader knows that he should not risk the loss of Chinese material and diplomatic support. And yet the North Koreans do not show gratitude to their benefactors in Beijing.

Why should they? Beijing, the Koreans shrewdly reason, provides all the support for its own benefit and has no choice but to keep its knife, the DPRK, sharp. China, after all, is not a charity. The constant flow of Chinese aid, whatever the Kimist regime does or doesn't do, is one indication that Pyongyang has correctly assessed the current situation. Weakness, in the right circumstances, confers strength.

That's why Kim Jong Il can afford to annoy his benefactor most of the time. "We have some influence, but we don't have the kind of relationship where we can tell Kim what to do," says one Chinese expert on Korea. "If we tell him to do something, he doesn't listen. If we threaten him, he listens even less." Since the earliest days of the Kim Il Sung regime, Pyongyang has been famous for going its own way. Beijing leaders, therefore, have been telling visiting foreigners, and especially anxious Americans, they cannot control Kim's wily son.

Yet the Chinese doth protest too much, methinks. If Kim Jong Il doesn't appear to listen to China's officials, it's partly because they don't expect reciprocity each and every time. Beijing pursues its plan of supporting the Koreans, whether or not they express gratitude at any particular moment, because the Chinese believe in the longer run their allies will realize their debts. The Chinese know they have influence and can use it at any moment, notes Chung Jae Ho, a Beijing watcher at Seoul National University, but they prefer not to do so all the time. It's good enough for the Chinese that the Koreans know their obligations and will pay back when asked.

Or at least do as they're told after being particularly stubborn. In June 1994 the Chinese apparently had to resort to public means to get Pyongyang in line. *Ta Kung Pao*, a Hong Kong newspaper that often voices Beijing's positions, suggested that China might adhere to any embargo imposed on North Korea and stop food and oil supplies. Pyongyang took the hint and immediately softened its position on starting talks over its production of plutonium. During this decade's installment of the nuclear crisis, Beijing, anxious to start negotiations, cut off oil for three days in February 2003 as a warning. Pyongyang agreed to sit down for multilateral talks shortly thereafter.

Whether or not one believes all this maneuvering is kabuki staged for the benefit of foreigners—author Bill Triplett, for instance, maintains "Pyongyang and Beijing have operated one of the most successful denial and deception operations ever mounted"—it's clear that China can force Kim Jong Il to act when it sees the need. "The truth is, they have the power to bring him down," argues the Heritage Foundation's John Tkacik. "They just don't want to use it." For example, China does not want strict inspections because that would expose its role in North Korea's nuclear program.

By cutting off all aid, by welcoming every North Korean refugee, or by sending in the People's Liberation Army, Beijing can put an end to Kimist rule. China, however, will not do any of these things now. Hu Jintao, for one thing, finds Kim useful for complicating the life of George W. Bush. In any event, Chinese foreign policy has not evolved to the point where Beijing is disposed, by itself, to openly interfere in the affairs of a neighbor in such a drastic manner. Most important, there is no consensus in the Chinese capital that it's in the nation's interest to destroy an ally, the DPRK, as a favor to an adversary, the United States.

For Bush's audacious concept to work, China must do more than just *begin* a fundamental shift in its foreign policy—it must *complete* the process of shedding the self-image of an outsider and ending its traditional role as an adversary of the existing global order. Such a change inevitably occurs when a rising power matures, but it only happens after internal perceptions have shifted over time. In short, the Chinese still calculate their interests in a way different than Americans do. President Bush may say that the DPRK nuclear problem "binds" the United States and China "in a common purpose," but it does not compel them to favor the same solution.

At this time Beijing is only willing to offer Washington something that is completely unacceptable from geopolitical and moral points of view: a "package deal" whereby Washington abandons democratic Taiwan in return for help on North Korea. Chinese leaders have even threatened to halt cooperation altogether, such as it has been, if Washington does not come around on the island republic that China claims as its own. "But what we are saying is this: The United States cannot expect us to continually give unless it gives us something, too," says a Chinese government adviser. "That's how the real world works."

In the world as it actually is, China has been "free riding" for the past three decades, enjoying the benefits of the international system and contributing little in return. Although Chinese attitudes are moving in the right direction, they are not evolving fast enough. The DPRK, unfortunately, poses a challenge that must be met now. Kim Jong Il can bring down the global nonproliferation regime or spark conflict in North Asia years before Beijing becomes a positive force.

The United States is generously—some say too generously—offering China a leading role in world affairs by making it the focus of efforts to denuclearize North Korea. The problem is not that America's policy is too philanthropic toward Beijing—although that is a concern. The fundamental fault with Washington's policy is that China is just not ready to accept its historic role as a great power.

TOKYO, TARGET FOR TERMINATION

Japan's Relations with Asia Complicate the Nuclear Talks

Of course, both South and North Korea would smile
if a nuclear weapon went off in Japan by accident.
—Tony Michell, Seoul-based business consultant

On the street that ends at the water, Megumi Yokota fell victim to "an act beyond comprehension," a crime that continues to this day. At twilight on November 15, 1977, at least one man, and probably two, forced the thirteen-year-old schoolgirl into a car just a couple of short blocks from her home in Niigata and within sight of the Sea of Japan. A neighbor heard a cry at the time she disappeared, yet no one witnessed the actual abduction and no one in Japan has seen her since.

Megumi, apparently, was not the kidnappers' first choice that day. They had previously driven up to one of her neighbors and motioned her to come near with the wave of a hand, but the neighbor could not see a face behind the tinted window and did not like the look of the black car. Toward evening, two men approached another schoolgirl, who was frightened and ran home. Megumi had left school after badminton practice with two friends, but they had gone their separate ways by the time she reached the spot where she was taken.

The authorities in Niigata conducted a massive investigation and initially came to the conclusion that Megumi was snatched in a copycat kidnapping based on *High and Low*, a film by the legendary Akira Kurosawa. Yet the Yokota family never received a ransom demand as depicted in the movie. There were so few clues at the time that police ended up unsure as to what had happened. Megumi's mother, Sakie, never gave up hope, however. Her little girl kept coming back to her in vivid dreams after the disappearance, and so she thought Megumi might still be alive.

Megumi was indeed alive and even safe, in a manner of speaking, in the Democratic People's Republic of Korea. The schoolgirl was probably put in a body bag at the point of abduction. She was then driven a few short blocks to the beach, where she was loaded onto a rubber raft and taken out to a waiting spy ship. On the voyage over the Sea of Japan a North Korean agent tied her up, knocked her unconscious, and left her in a storage room. When she recovered, Megumi cried for her mother and almost pulled her nails out scratching the walls and the door. Upon arrival in North Korea, she was covered in blood, as was the room. Her urine and the contents of her stomach were over the floor.

Almost twenty years passed before Megumi's parents got wind of her whereabouts. In January 1997 her father, Shigeru, first heard that a North Korean defector had said a girl was abducted to Pyongyang because she happened to see its spies on the verge of leaving from a beach in Japan. She learned Korean in the DPRK on the promise that she would be sent back to her mother. When the girl was about eighteen and realized that was a lie, she suffered a mental breakdown. The defector's description almost perfectly matched Megumi.

Exhilarated to hear that she might be alive, her parents mounted a nationwide campaign, which soon took on the attributes of a crusade. Her mother wrote a successful book, *My Daughter, Mother Will Come and Find You*, and she meant every word of that touching title. The Yokotas, and especially the Mrs., were relentless, turning up the heat so much that even Kim Jong Il had to take notice.

In September 2002 Kim confirmed to Japanese prime minister Junichiro Koizumi that rogue North Korean agents—are there any other kind?—had abducted young Megumi Yokota along with twelve other Japanese from 1977 to 1983. Five of the abductees were still alive, Kidnapper Kim said. Megumi, however, was not among them. She had, according to the North Korean leader, taken her own life in 1993. The government said it could not locate her remains. The five living abductees were later returned to Japan.

"I know that everything in that country is a lie," says a frail-looking Sakie Yokota, referring to Kim's Korea. In a nation of prevarication, invention, and fabrication, the most perverse untruth is the heartrending story of Megumi's suicide. Pyongyang kidnapped the thirteen-year-old and other Japanese to obtain language and culture instruction for its undercover agents.

Mrs. Yokota's daughter has been spotted in the DPRK after she supposedly took her life and is probably still alive. Pyongyang won't release her and the seven others because, it appears, they know too much about Kim Jong Il's responsibility for clandestine activities and terrorist acts.

The tale of Megumi's death allowed Kim to acknowledge the incident yet provide a cover for his direct responsibility. As such, the fib was an integral part of a step-by-step plan to improve relations with Tokyo, agree on reparations for Japan's long occupation, and get on with the business of making the world safe for Kimism and the Kims.

Mrs. Yokota, on the other hand, is only trying to save one poor soul. She has no clever plan for getting Megumi back and does not command the resources of a nation-state, but she nonetheless refuses to yield to the DPRK. With her husband she has turned the plight of their daughter into an international custody battle framed as a struggle of innocence versus evil. As a result, the Japanese, who inflicted so much pain during much of the last century, today are more bothered by the suffering of one young girl. Megumi, alone among the eight unreturned abductees, has become a symbol of a nation's indignation. More important, her parents symbolize the transformation of ordinary Japanese citizens from the meek and mild to the assured and assertive.

No one is safe when the Yokotas are on the march. Like the other relatives of abductees, they criticize Kim as heartless and despicable, but they also target their own leader, Koizumi, as weak and ineffectual. Evil North

Koreans are expected to commit dastardly deeds, but new-style Japanese politicians are supposed to try to stop them. Junichiro Koizumi, who took office in 2001, has unfortunately proven to be a great disappointment.

The first question is why the Japanese prime minister was so supine from the get-go. Perhaps it was because he was eager for a foreign policy success. Risking a split with Washington, Koizumi got Beijing to broker the September 2002 meeting with Kim Jong Il so that he could be the first Japanese leader to summit with a DPRK supremo. Like former South Korean president Kim Dae Jung, Koizumi was prepared to accept whatever slop Kim Jong Il was prepared to dish out in Pyongyang. Upon arrival in the North Korean capital, he suspended the operation of his critical faculties by accepting the actuarially improbable notion that almost two-thirds of the young abductees had croaked and the medically incredible claim that both a twenty-four-year-old male and a twenty-seven-year-old female had died of heart disease. The Japanese prime minister didn't even blink when Kim blamed the abduction of the unlucky thirteen on the "blindly motivated patriotism" of a few of Dad's runaway employees.

We can excuse the North Korean honcho for thinking that any improbable explanation would do because that is what the Japanese leader believed as well. Apparently, it had not occurred to either Kim or Koizumi that Japan's public could get so worked up over so few people. If there was a rush on both sides to force closure on this issue, it is not hard to see why.

North Korea, after all, was not the only nation with something to hide. Tokyo had long suspected that North Koreans were nabbing its unsuspecting citizens on Japanese soil and abroad. Nonetheless, Japan's police and political leaders did virtually nothing about it, thereby permitting Pyongyang's agents to continue their highly inappropriate activities. If the number of abductees is actually in the hundreds as some claim, then the government's lack of response looks reprehensible rather than cautious.

Megumi's father, it should be noted, did not hear about her extended stay in the DPRK from Japanese authorities acting in the course of their duties. He learned about the abduction through the personal efforts of Tatsukichi Hyomoto, the secretary of a Japanese Communist Party member serving in the Diet, the national legislature. Hyomoto ran across an old magazine article about Megumi and thought her parents should see it. In the Yokota episode, the government in charge of protecting thirteen-year-olds and the other citizens of the great nation of Japan was simply derelict.

"The primary duty of a nation is to safeguard its people's properties and lives," says Shintaro Ishihara, former novelist, playwright, and pundit and current governor of Tokyo. "The Japanese government has not been able to fulfill this mandate. It hasn't even tried." If Prime Minister Koizumi has not made an effort on behalf of kidnapped countrymen—and there have been far too many occasions when he has not been firm—it's because he has not had many options. Ishihara would like Japan to "stop dilly-dallying around" and go to the DPRK to rescue the abductees, for instance, but we can't blame Koizumi for not attempting that because Japan's men and women under arms, the Self-Defense Forces, are not capable of staging an Entebbe-style raid. Moreover, the prime minister is constrained by a half-century-old political system that favors deliberation over decision.

Nonetheless, Governor Ishihara, Japan's most popular politician, is on to something that has somehow eluded Koizumi, the country's most powerful one: the Japanese, after a half century of stupor, have had enough. The public would undoubtedly forgive their prime minister for failing to extract the abductees by force—that would be a difficult task even for a superpower—but they are impatient with Tokyo's old habit of setting out to fail.

The prime minister, continuing to chart an unambitious course, has waffled, mumbled, and made himself look less than resolute. In the wake of the September 2002 summit, for example, Koizumi got around to calling North Korea an "unpardonable country" for abducting and killing Japanese citizens. That was a good start. Yet the prime minister soon reverted to his original plan of trying to establish diplomatic ties with Pyongyang. "We must normalize this abnormal relationship," he said in May 2004 at the time of his second summit meeting with Kim Jong Il, as if that were possible or even the right thing to do under the circumstances.

At that second meeting Koizumi, to his credit, secured the release of five children of the abductees. Yet his accomplishment came at a personal cost. The prime minister reduced himself to the role of "hostage negotiator" by agreeing to pay ransom, in the form of aid. Japan, he pledged, would donate $10 million of medical and other humanitarian supplies and a quarter million tons of rice. Japan, he insisted, was being nice. It was not "collateral," Koizumi firmly stated. "It's the responsibility of the international community to aid North Korea."

Responsibility or no responsibility, Koizumi did not deliver all the promised assistance. He cut off aid deliveries in December 2004 when it became evident that North Korea was backsliding on commitments to resolve the abductee matter. In 2002 the DPRK handed over remains said to be those of Kaoru Matsuki, one of the young male abductees, but testing later showed they were those of an elderly woman. Ever patient, Japan gave North Korea another opportunity, and Pyongyang in late 2004 released seven container loads of "evidence" relating to the fate of the supposedly dead abductees plus what it claimed were the ashes of two of them, Matsuki and Megumi. This time the North Koreans told Japan to forget about the story that they had lost Megumi's remains—the previous explanation—because her "husband," one Kim Chol Jun, had fortuitously dug up her ashes two and a half years before and kept them in an urn. DNA testing in Japan, however, revealed that the two piles of dust were not Matsuki and Megumi. "This case clearly shows how inhumane and heartless North Korea is," said Sakie Yokota, who was otherwise relieved not to receive confirmation of her daughter's demise.

"When I think of Ms. Yokota, I am so angry I'm at a loss for words," said Tsutomu Takebe, secretary-general of the Liberal Democratic Party, which has dominated Japanese politics since the 1950s. "I think Koizumi is the angriest of all." The prime minister, upset as he may have been, was pleading for more time as he tried to head off calls for sanctions from an infuriated public. "We will have to see how North Korea responds to demands for the truth," Koizumi said in December 2004 after the DNA testing showed that Pyongyang had fibbed on both sets of remains.

The North Koreans, if anything, have shown that further discussion is pointless, yet Junichiro Koizumi keeps on trying to give them additional chances. What, after all, is the point of providing Pyongyang a third opportunity to supply misidentified ashes or the forty-seventh time to change its story?

So what has the Japanese prime minister learned so far? Obviously not much, but the citizens of his nation have begun to catch on. Prompted by the plight of one schoolgirl, Japan began addressing a problem with North Korea. Yet as we know by now, they were really addressing the problem with Japan.

The Two Kings of Tokyo

Pity Sakie and Shigeru Yokota. "They have learned that all the Japanese government can do is to betray them," writes Yuichi Yamamoto, the merciless TokyoFreePress blogger. Pity Koizumi too. The never-ending abductee crisis has made the prime minister, called the "Lion King" for his mane of flowing gray hair, look weak and indecisive when not appearing cynical and hypocritical.

Koizumi, unfortunately for him, leads a country that even its people think is strange. Japan, a nation of islands, has never been like its continental neighbors, and its recent history has not helped it fit in. Its citizens did not live through a "twentieth century" like the rest of us. They had, more precisely, two half centuries divided by 1945, the year of their unconditional surrender in World War II.

At the end of that conflict Japan lay prostrate after the firebombing of Tokyo, the obliteration of Hiroshima—the Yokotas' old hometown—and Nagasaki, and the devastation of other cities. What America destroyed it had the obligation to rebuild: God made the world in six days, but it took General Douglas MacArthur six years to lay the foundations for a modern Japan. The American, who acted like a deity most of the time, kept Emperor Hirohito on the throne, generally retained the prewar elite and civil bureaucracy, and created democracy from the top down.

MacArthur, the "second emperor," also came up with the "Peace Constitution," which was adopted—actually imposed—in 1946. By Article 9 of that document the Japanese people "forever" renounced both "war" and "the threat or use of force as a means of settling international disputes." They also promised "never" to maintain "land, sea, and air forces, as well as other war potential."

The stringent Article 9 worked well for Japan in the years after the war. The nation relied on the American military, "the honorable Mr. Watchdog" in the words of a Japanese foreign minister in the 1960s, and lived under its nuclear umbrella. Without having to think about its own defense or pay much for it, Japan prospered. Displaying the same fanatical drive and absolute devotion evident throughout its modern history, salarymen, guided by bureaucrats, created a miracle of awesome proportions. Like the South Koreans and Chinese who would follow in their footsteps, the

Japanese created economic growth by supplying the exuberant American consumer first with trinkets and then with televisions. By the end of the 1960s Japan had zoomed past West Germany to claim the title of world's second largest economy.

Then came a moment like no other. Toward the end of the 1980s Tokyo was on the verge of writing a new chapter in human history. Hordes of Japanese businessmen, bankers, investors, and tourists were engulfing the world. And buying it up as well. Fueled by an abundance of artificially cheap money at home, Japan binged on speculation. Banks, securities houses, and even manufacturing companies simply lost any sense of proportion when it came to money. That led to unparalleled asset inflation and even more investment.

The emperor's Imperial Palace, not even three hundred acres, was valued at more than all the real estate in California. Land in Japan in 1990 was worth 50 percent more than the remainder of the planet. The value of stocks listed in Tokyo exceeded the *combined* value of those on the New York, Frankfurt, London, Paris, and Toronto exchanges. All of the world's ten largest banks were Japanese, as were its four largest securities companies. Japan's achievements were astounding, the generation of wealth unprecedented. Then the Japanese people, who had denied themselves for so long in order to create prosperity, went wild, importing ice cubes from Antarctica and buying others' icons like Rockefeller Center and Pebble Beach. They were giddy; the rest of us were terrified, if not a little dazed.

The extraordinary boom—a bubble really—couldn't go on for long. So it didn't. The "Japanese Century," famously predicted by futurologist Herman Kahn, was the quickest hundred years in world history. In fact, it was over before it was supposed to begin at the birth of the new millennium. A grossly distorted economy, managed by a few technocrats in the Ministry of Finance in Tokyo, simply fell apart. After the government tried to dampen runaway speculation, the stock market crashed in the beginning of the 1990s, losing two-thirds of its value over the course of a couple of years. In 1993 land values collapsed in the largest asset deflation in modern history. Banks and brokerages, sitting on about $6 trillion of bad loans secured by grossly overvalued real estate, became insolvent and failed as defaults tsunamied through the economy. The Godzilla nation looked a lot less terrifying after the crash.

The Japanese endured the so-called Lost Decade as they struggled to re-cover from the excesses of previous years. The standing joke was that a slid-ing Japan would become the world's next developing nation. The country was said to be mired in never-ending recession in the 1990s, but that was not technically true. Successive prime ministers, their names essentially unimportant, were able to eke out minimal economic growth by excessive government pump priming—it seems that every riverbank in the country has been paved over at least once in Tokyo's relentless quest to spend money, for instance. As they struggled with a limping economy, the na-tion's politicians looked out of touch and decidedly inadequate.

The country's befuddled leaders led a bewildered country. The stock and real estate crashes led to shared disorientation (the Japanese seem to do everything together, including getting lost). There was, unfortunately, nothing to take the place of failing banks, companies, and other institu-tions in a society noted for its groupism, the glue for an already homoge-nous people. In the economic downturn, a nation that did not stand for any enduring principle not only misplaced its sense of direction but also its self-worth. Japanese commentators across the political spectrum noted something was "missing."

What was missing, Japan's neighbors said, was a sense of responsibility for its aggression in the first half of the twentieth century. Japanese prime ministers and political figures have bowed and apologized on innumerable occasions—by now they're getting very good at it—but nearby Asians still think more contrition is in order. As Tokyo is often reminded, none of its leaders has fallen to his knees as German chancellor Willy Brandt did in 1970 at the Warsaw Ghetto memorial. On the contrary, the Japanese aggra-vate the situation by performing acts—like visiting Tokyo's Yasukuni Shrine, dedicated to the nation's soldiers, including World War II war crim-inals—that inevitably inflame regional opinion against them.

The Japanese should make a better show of remorse, but Asian self-righteousness gets a bit thick at times. "As you know, in our five-thousand-year history we've never invaded another country," says the earnest South Korean legislator Song Young Gil. "We were more powerful than the Japanese in ancient times. If we wanted to invade Japan, we could have, but our ancestors didn't because we liked peace and were very cultured."

Koreans certainly have a wonderful culture, but they also possess bad historical memory. They joined Mongol attempts in 1274 and 1281 to invade Japan. If today's Japanese don't bear a grudge for the thirteenth-century transgressions, it's partly because they won. A "Divine Wind," or *kamikaze* as it is now called, came out of nowhere and swamped the navies of the would-be aggressors on both occasions.

The Japanese, who have bought into pacifism for more than a half century—surely a more sincere sign of remorse than kneeling—have not managed to avoid trouble. Nearby aggressors interpreted Japan's newfound peacefulness as weakness, and that perception just brought out the villains' worst instincts. The North Korean kidnappers of Megumi Yokota, for instance, obviously figured the meek Japanese to be easy pickings and in any event judged them to be deserving of their fate. "Speaking of kidnappings, during the Japanese colonization they kidnapped 200,000 women or girls, virgins, for their comfort girl," sputters Sohn Jangnai, a retired South Korean major general who now has close ties to Pyongyang and disseminates its views. "Compare the seriousness and numbers. They drafted a half million Korean youth to the Japanese army. And they got most of these Korean people killed during the Second World War."

Although Japan can never make up for its wartime atrocities and hideous acts, there is also no excuse for brutalizing a schoolgirl like Megumi. Kim Dae Jung during his presidency wisely accepted Japan's apology to Korea for its occupation and then moved on, but his successor, Roh Moo-hyun, has given voice to pan-Korean anger and has taken Pyongyang's side in the abduction issue. He recently declared "tough diplomatic war" against Japan, leading his country into the past.

Which is where the Chinese currently live. Pursuing territorial claims based on history, Chinese leaders believe their nation should be larger than it is today. While fixing boundaries with others—even historical adversaries Russia and Vietnam—they've chosen to act irresponsibly toward Japan. Beijing claims the barren islands that it calls the Diaoyus and Japan names the Senkakus. The islands, off the northeastern tip of Taiwan, are between China's coast and Japan's Ryukyu island chain and are generally recognized as Japan's. Washington returned them to Tokyo in 1972, Japan in fact controls them, aviation maps show them as Japanese, and Mao Zedong wisely chose to ignore China's claims when he reestablished diplomatic relations with Tokyo in 1972. Since that time, Chinese activists periodically sail out to the islands to occupy them for the Motherland, and the Japanese turn them back, usually without loss of life.

The other dispute between the two nations involves the boundary between their Exclusive Economic Zones in the East China Sea north of the Diaoyus/Senkakus. Beijing has taken matters into its own hands, granting drilling concessions for gas in the disputed Chunxiao field. Three of the concessions are entirely in Japan's claimed EEZ and one concession is partly in it. The point is not so much which country's position is eventually upheld—the matter could go either way—but that China has tried to solve the problem through unilateral action, thereby risking conflict and raising the stakes.

To buttress its claims to the East China Sea, China has repeatedly intruded into Japan. In one of the most blatant incidents, a Chinese *Han*-class nuclear submarine in November 2004 entered Japan's territorial waters and passed between two islands in the Ryukyu chain without surfacing. The crew, running at a deep level, seemed familiar with the undersea terrain, indicating that the Chinese navy had already surreptitiously surveyed Japan's seabed. Beijing, by repeatedly refusing to promise that there will be no future incursions, is essentially saying that it retains the right to infringe Japanese territory.

Relations between Beijing and Tokyo should be getting better rather than worse—economic ties are making the two giants mutually dependent and the World War II generation is rapidly departing from the scene. Yet just as totalitarian Korea needs an enemy, so does authoritarian China. Most days Chinese state media reports Japan's World War II atrocities as if they were news and warns that Japan is a present-day menace. Beijing, in short, defines Chinese identity as being anti-Japanese, and years of tirades have made anything but complete humiliation of Tokyo politically unacceptable for the Communist Party. So China's leaders, after inflaming public opinion, now have trouble giving up an inch. And that spells trouble. "We should teach the Japanese a good lesson and let them know how tough the Chinese people are," says Li Jin, a freelance writer in his late twenties. "Maybe we should nuke them once and for all."

Why do bad things happen to peaceful people? If the neighbors kidnap their children or secretly send vessels of war into their waters, it is because the Japanese have made themselves vulnerable. The challenge for the current leadership is to start showing strength without embroiling the region in turmoil. For decades the Japanese were content to be weak by subcontracting their security to Americans. The arrangement not only pleased Japan but also comforted East Asians, who realized that Washington's alliance restrained Tokyo as well as protected it.

Yet the Japanese now find themselves needing to break free. They have to deal with an aggressive neighbor that America, for its own reasons, has accommodated more than confronted. During the Clinton years Washington even looked as if it might ditch a declining Tokyo for a rising China. And although George W. Bush obviously does not care for the leaders in Beijing, he nonetheless needs their diplomatic support for his grand geopolitical projects.

In reaction to Chinese and North Korean assertiveness and American ambivalence, the Japanese are arriving at a new consensus about protection of their homeland. "Unless we have the will to defend ourselves, no one will lend us a helping hand in earnest," says Ishihara. He sensibly argues that Japan should have the means to fend off Chinese incursions with force if necessary, but his plan is broader than that. The Tokyo governor believes Japan should get rid of its American-imposed constitution and start "from scratch." Less radical proposals from others would at least remove one offending provision. As scholar John Nathan points out, pacifist or warmonger, no person in Japan takes pride in Article 9.

Perhaps that is why no Japanese government after 1954 has honored it either. Tokyo maintains approximately 240,000 soldiers, sailors, and pilots supported by the world's fourth largest military budget. Even though it is labeled a force for self-defense, it is unconstitutional nonetheless. The wording of Article 9 does not permit the use of arms for *any* purpose, even protecting Japan against attack.

That legal difficulty, however, has not been much of an obstacle, the Japanese being adept at interpreting, ignoring, and flouting the disliked provision. It has been stretched so far that it has become virtually meaningless as a practical matter and important only as a symbol. Today Article 9 is interpreted as a ban on participation in "collective self-defense," but even that prohibition has been eroded as Japan sent minesweepers to the Persian Gulf in 1991, an Aegis destroyer to the Indian Ocean in 2002 to support U.S. operations, and, most notably, a contingent of troops to Iraq in 2004. Although Tokyo's troops are mere decorations—Australian, Dutch, and

British soldiers have been assigned to guard the Japanese, who are not even allowed to come to the aid of their protectors or other Coalition forces— the important thing is that they are there. The Iraq deployment is considered the first time Japan sent troops to a war zone since the end of World War II. And, unlike its 1992 mission in Cambodia and later peacekeeping efforts, the Iraq deployment was the first time that soldiers were sent abroad outside the United Nations framework.

Japan, despite all the progress, is still not a "normal country," especially when it comes to matters of defense. What restrains the Japanese is more a fear of themselves than anything else. "We follow too easily, question authority too little," says Masamichi Misawa. "We cannot allow ourselves to go abroad again with guns. I do not trust our society enough to hold back." The World War II veteran, held by the Soviets for four years after capture in 1945, echos the nearly universal judgment of Asians old enough to remember. As former Singapore prime minister Lee Kuan Yew said, permitting the Japanese to carry arms abroad, even in peacekeeping missions, is like "giving liqueur chocolates to an alcoholic."

Yet Lee, Asia's meddler in chief, is living in the past. Only 40 percent of Japan's current population was alive in 1945. Governor Ishihara was twelve when Japanese officials, looking ridiculous in top hats and formal Western attire, signed surrender documents on board the *Missouri*; Prime Minister Koizumi was only three. The bottom line is that Japan, as dangerous as it once was, is by no means a threat to regional stability now. Who, after all, should be terrified of a nation that is still influenced by a pacifist mentality, that possesses no nuclear weapons, that tries to appease its neighbors, and that is cutting its defense budget? As much as the Japanese are afraid of the demon dwelling inside, they are rightly more frightened by the devils lurking nearby. Tokyo has had little choice but to confront a most unpleasant reality: in a world that should be peaceful, militant adversaries exist.

To protect themselves from those antagonists, the people of Japan are beginning to embrace Shintaro Ishihara, who is setting the direction for national politics and becoming the country's leading political figure. His words from time to time sound purplish—he has, for instance, said, "I feel that the state would be extinguished if I died, as if Japan were inside my body and I was perfectly identified"—yet he reaches a broad range of the public because he promotes an alternative to despondency and national malaise. Most people do not subscribe to all his ideas—and some of them are better left unimplemented—but they nonetheless like the idea that he doesn't like being put upon by overbearing neighbors. For many Japanese, what happened six decades ago is finally in the past. For Ishihara, nick-named the "Sun King," national strength means never again having to say they're sorry.

The Powell Doctrine

Some countries, however, want even more apologies from Tokyo. Japan sits at the six-party talks with two of them, its principal tormentors, China and North Korea. More victims than participants, the Japanese look out of place at the bargaining table. It's clear Japan has a stake in what happens at the contentious negotiations, but its presence, like Russia's, seems an after-thought. Unlike Russia, however, Japan is not an inert presence at the talks.

Tokyo won a seat at the negotiations due to Washington's backing. Every state with an interest in North Asia had said it was in favor of a nu-clear-free North Korea, even North Korea. There was, however, no consen-sus as to how to disarm Pyongyang, which meant there was really no agreement at all. Today, Washington's move to include Japan looks pre-scient: the Chinese have disappointed Washington at the talks so the super-power needs a helping hand. Tokyo is not America's only ally at the table—Seoul is nominally one too—but it is the participant closest to the Americans.

For Tokyo the victory is the invitation. In the 1994 version of the crisis, Japan had no voice in the Geneva talks but was saddled with much of the cost of the Agreed Framework. The Japanese agreed to fork out about $1 billion toward the two light water reactors promised in the deal. Multilat-eral talks this time ensure they will have a say as to how others spend their money.

From Japan's perspective, that is progress. For all the cash they spread around the world, the Japanese get little influence in return. Now, how-ever, Asia's largest economy has a platform in its own region where it has generally been sidelined—or, more often, sidelined itself.

So far, Tokyo has generally followed Washington's lead in the Beijing talks. That's not surprising, as the unwelcome events of the last few years have convinced the Japanese that they need America's military protection more than before. Yet the closeness of the American and Japanese positions may be more apparent than real. As Prime Minister Koizumi has said, Tokyo's circumstances are different from Washington's, so it's natural that they have different positions.

The Japanese, for instance, are less insistent on making the North Koreans disarm before receiving rewards from the international community. And Japan, like South Korea, is nervous about taking tough action against the North. Koizumi even got Bush to engage in a bit of "alliance management" in June 2004 by backing a Japanese and South Korean approach to ending the standoff. George Bush, trying to placate both Koizumi and Roh Moo-hyun, backed off his unyielding position and proposed benefits for Pyongyang as part of a package arrangement. Japan, like South Korea, has also opposed Washington's plans to kill off the Korean Peninsula Energy Development Organization, which is responsible for providing the two promised reactors. Keeping the organization in place preserves a framework for building a relationship with the DPRK in the future. Tokyo's negotiating positions should be of no surprise: Japan reflexively tries to use money to make problems go away.

There are, however, some disputes that cash cannot solve. Koizumi, as noted, promised humanitarian aid as a means of rescuing the abductees and their children. That plan was unrealistic and subsequently flopped. Now Japan is trying to use the Beijing talks to extract its kidnapped citizens. Washington, usually accommodating to the Japanese, has initially gone along with Tokyo's strategy.

Japan's Foreign Ministry has always insisted that Pyongyang's arms program is more important than the abductee matter, but that is not how Japan's ordinary citizens see it. For them, the plight of those held hostage in the DPRK has always been more immediate than any other matter involving Kim's Korea. The Japanese, understandably, want Megumi back.

And they want their government to do something about it. Koizumi has tried to play for more time but is running out of it. Kim Jong Il has skillfully held the abductees for ransom and dribbled them out in small doses. Now he is down to the remaining few whom he cannot return without undermining his own standing. So Japan and North Korea, two countries that are stubborn in their own ways, find themselves in a standoff. "There is not a

shred of sincerity in North Korea's attitude," says Shinzo Abe, a leading figure in Japan's ruling Liberal Democratic Party. "It now seems meaningless
to discuss this issue with them."

When there's no point in talking, is it time for tougher measures? Imposing sanctions on the DPRK is the overwhelming choice of Japan's increasingly fed-up populace. Forced by public opinion, Tokyo in 2005
imposed maritime insurance regulations that are intended to severely re-
strict trade with Pyongyang. American and South Korean diplomats, however, are leery of any actions that could derail the six-party talks over what
they consider a side issue.

Side issue or not, the abductee matter is complicating the already pre-
carious nuclear negotiations in Beijing. Pyongyang has been enraged by
Tokyo's charges that it supplied misidentified remains and has threatened
to pull out of the six-party talks and demanded that the Japanese leave instead. China will not walk out on the negotiations it hosts, but its frosty relations with Tokyo put them at risk. Unlike the DPRK's abduction of
Japanese citizens—which, although tragic, is really only a geopolitical annoyance—Beijing's aggressive posture toward Tokyo endangers regional
stability and even global order. China has either directly or indirectly used
the DPRK to keep the Japanese off balance. So unless Beijing and Tokyo
come to terms on their overall relationship, it's extremely unlikely that
China will help solve the North Korean nuclear crisis.

As the disagreements between Beijing and Tokyo grow, the prospect for
a settlement of the crisis diminishes. Problems in Northeast Asia are now
layered, one atop the other, making the solution to any of them even more
difficult. The risk is that one incident could trigger others because China,
the two Koreas, and Japan all feel aggrieved over so many matters. And
Washington has, to varying degrees and for many reasons, let problems
fester.

Problems can smolder forever unless something changes. What is
changing is Japan. In the past, neighboring adversaries could always count
on Japan backing down—its diplomats and prime ministers practiced
"kowtow diplomacy" and sought to soothe by submission. Now the Japanese public won't let them resort to the old way of doing things.

As a result, Tokyo's foreign policy is no longer predictable. Kim Jong Il
was taken aback by the reaction of the Japanese public to his admission
about kidnapping young Japanese. Even seasoned observers were aston-

ished by Tokyo's 2003 assertion of a right of preemption against the North Koreans. And Japan amazed everyone when it sank an unflagged "mystery ship" at the end of 2001, the first time since the end of the Second World War that Japan had sent a foreign vessel—which turned out to be North Korean—to the bottom.

What happens when Tokyo sinks or captures the next Chinese sub lurking in its waters? As the Japanese electorate moves to the right, what was once considered extreme is now viewed as moderate. If regional conflagration occurs, it will probably be because Tokyo's tormentors, Beijing and Pyongyang, do not correctly perceive where the volatile Japanese public draws the line.

"History is littered with wars that everyone knew would never happen," observed Enoch Powell, the English politician who rose to prominence in the 1950s. To many Japanese, conflict in Northeast Asia seems remote. "The chances of North Korea launching an atomic weapon at us are probably one in ten thousand," said Japanese citizen Kazuo Morimoto, who was born just after Hiroshima and was commemorating the event on its fifty-eighth anniversary in 2003. Maybe so, but Koreans have a different perspective. Many in the South, especially those who see Japan as the main threat, fantasize about the incineration of Tokyo.

And those in the North might actually be planning it. Kim Jong Il has a history of using unexpected violence to change an unfavorable status quo. In the past, he had to settle for inflicting deaths in small quantities when he was trying to make a point. Now he has the means to slaughter hundreds of thousands at a time. It's unlikely he would initiate conflict with a truly horrendous act, but given the volatility of Northeast Asia the next minor incident he starts could spiral out of control.

What happens when events escalate? Mr. Kim's primary launch vehicle of today, the highly inaccurate Rodong missile, is militarily useful only for ferrying nuclear warheads, and it has sufficient range for reaching Japan, which would have about ten minutes' warning. Targeting Tokyo would make sense for Kim because Beijing's leaders, for geopolitical and cultural reasons, would be less likely to take sides against him for an attack on Japan than one on South Korea. Moreover, Seoul is more asset than adversary for Pyongyang because, as Roh Moo-hyun has said, it might remain neutral in any conflict. North Korea's rationale for attacking Japan has been clearly stated over time: it is America's "advance base" against the DPRK. More important, it is, in Pyongyang's words, "the sworn enemy of the Korean nation."

That's why North Korean diplomats privately say that their country needs only four nukes—one for each of Japan's main islands. Whether they are joking or not, they reveal that Pyongyang's nuclear weapons doctrine contemplates the destruction of the Japanese homeland. Hwang Jang Yop, after he defected from the DPRK, confirmed that North Korean strategy in any conflict is to take the Japanese hostage. That, after all, is the pan-Korean dream, to avenge transgressions going back to the sixteenth century. "Of course, both South and North Korea would smile if a nuclear weapon went off in Japan by accident," notes Tony Michell, a Seoul-based business consultant with close ties to Pyongyang. Or as former U.N. weapons inspector Scott Ritter says, North Korea "won't be satisfied till Tokyo is reduced to a slab of radioactive waste."

Japanese leaders desperately want peace, but their neighbors are increasingly hostile. If anything, today is beginning to feel like the period between the two great wars of last century except that China is now the aggressor. Asia has never experienced a time when both Asian powers were strong. Now, we are approaching an era when they both will be.

The world has not been so dangerous for the Japanese since the last days of the last world war. In that conflict, Tokyo "used its men as if they were mere ammunition." Since then, no member of the Self-Defense Forces has been killed in combat. Young folks signed up for the SDF, "a pacifist military," because it was safer than joining the police. Those peaceful days, however, are nearing an end.

In an ever-changing environment, it's no surprise that Japan sometimes looks like "a bewildered giant." Yet there is a new consensus forming in Japanese society, and once it solidifies, the country could again move with a terrifying sense of purpose and speed.

And perhaps in time to rescue Megumi Yokota.

AID CHARADE

How the World Helps North Korea Build Nuclear Weapons

If the military is actually starving,
let's feed the military as well.
—Erica Kang, South Korean aid worker

"I can still hear the cry of the people in my heart," says "Eunju," a defector, referring to the moment when Kim Jong Il came to power and the government stopped distributing staples in her hometown. Food had already been in short supply for more than a decade, and soon people began to starve. "I couldn't open my eyes to see it," she says of the deaths around her. But then her younger brother and sister perished, and so did her sister's children. Eunju had heard that China and South Korea were giving aid but saw none of it. She was a member of the ruling Korean Workers' Party in her city located in the northern part of North Korea, but she and her family were nonetheless denied food. At the time, few received rations from the government. People died in fields eating unripened crops, young soldiers begged for food, parents abandoned their children.

With her son, she walked northward to the Tumen River and then swam to China, where she began using her assumed name. Eunju was fortunate to escape the gangs that prey upon North Koreans and found safety in an underground church. Her refuge was only temporary, however. Her small Christian community was raided by the police. She hid from the authorities in fields for days in the rain and eventually made her way to Beijing. There, with other desperate North Koreans, Eunju and her son broke into the German embassy to seek asylum in the South.

"Anyone who has stood as I have beside a person slowly dying of hunger—who has seen this horror with his own eyes—will never linger to debate the pros and cons of food aid," writes Kang Chol-hwan, who also fled his homeland for the more prosperous, freer, and better Korea. Kang need not worry: almost every nation says it is in favor of feeding hungry North Koreans.

Kim Jong Il, however, puts the rationale for humanitarian aid to the test. He runs a hideous regime, brutalizes Koreans, kidnaps foreigners, and threatens to sell plutonium and even completed warheads. America is locked in a standoff with him that he is winning. His government fails to meet its most basic obligation of feeding its people but survives because of outside help, even Washington's. Isn't it time for the world to stop providing assistance to North Korea?

Leave No Despot Behind

"You cannot make the children, the ill people, the old people victims of a political crisis which they have nothing to do with," said the U.N.'s Maurice Strong, when he was Kofi Annan's special emissary in connection with North Korea. Yet the Kims have done precisely that. They not only adhered to a fanatical ideology for decades—a monumental problem in and of itself—but also allocated a disproportionally large chunk of national resources to the military, including its bomb-building programs. As Ronald Reagan famously said, "a hungry child knows no politics," but North Korean children had better learn fast because it is politics that has made them hungry.

And it is politics that keeps them hungry. North Koreans of all ages had been undernourished since the 1980s, but an overfed Kim Il Sung was kept in the dark about food shortages during the last years of his life by his overweight son. In the early part of the 1990s Pyongyang asked Seoul for 500,000 tons of rice but only if the donation was kept secret. The South, however, would not make surreptitious shipments.

Pyongyang delayed openly asking for assistance until Kim Il Sung had passed from the scene. It issued its first public appeal in the summer of 1995 after devastating floods hit. The international community, led by the United States, quickly responded by shipping rice and other staples through the World Food Programme of the United Nations, the planet's largest humanitarian agency.

North Korea responded to the outpouring of global generosity with undisguised hostility. Pyongyang gouged nongovernmental organizations for exorbitant rents for offices in Pyongyang. The government's Flood Damage Rehabilitation Committee, which oversees foreign assistance, severely restricted the movement of aid workers. Whole sections of the country were declared off-limits. In other areas, interactions between foreigners and ordinary folk, when they were permitted, were strictly controlled. North Korean officials would not allow into the country any aid worker or monitor who understood Korean. Random checks were forbidden, as were surveys on food needs. As the initial crisis subsided, the FDRC became even more intransigent and adversarial. Pyongyang, donors soon learned, was more concerned about monitoring monitors than feeding Koreans.

So NGOs began pulling out. Doctors Without Borders, CARE, and Oxfam left, as did a host of smaller groups. Donor countries got fed up too. The United States, for instance, cut off food aid in December 2002, soon after the revelations of the North's uranium weapons program. The U.N.'s Maurice Strong complained that Washington was playing politics with the lives of young, ill, and old North Koreans, but Andrew Natsios, the head of the U.S. Agency for International Development, noted America had stopped aid only because North Korea had repeatedly refused monitoring safeguards accepted everywhere else. Washington had threatened to stop assistance the previous June, months before the nuclear imbroglio erupted. "We want to be generous," Natsios said. "There are a lot of hungry people in North Korea."

Few of them, however, lived in Pyongyang. The regime directed aid to favored citizens, especially those living in the capital and militarily sensitive areas. The other big beneficiary of foreign assistance was the Korean People's Army. China's food aid is thought to have fed the armed forces, which also took the first cut of the home harvest. Therefore, some argue that there was little or no need for the army to divert other aid, especially that channeled through the World Food Programme.

Nonetheless, the evidence of diversion was troubling, as there was both motive and opportunity. Despite Beijing's assistance, soldiers still starved to death during the great famine, and some of them were malnourished even after the crisis was officially declared over. So there was motive.

And there was plenty of opportunity. The World Food Programme accepted limits on monitoring that it did not tolerate elsewhere. The Flood Damage Rehabilitation Committee was almost entirely composed of former military personnel. That made sense because the Korean People's Army distributed foreign aid. It was the only group in society with the vehicles and fuel to do so. A North Korean soldier who defected says his unit put on casual clothes and switched to civilian license plates whenever food inspectors came around.

In fact, non-Chinese food wound up in the hands of the armed forces. Senior commanders appropriated the rice from South Korea because it was the best. "North Korea is based on military-first politics," the defector explained. "There is no need to pay attention to the residents." The Korean People's Army once snatched almost five thousand tons of American food aid at gunpoint in front of World Food Programme officials at the port of Nampho. Canned food from America was even found in a North Korean submarine that had run aground in the South.

"We don't want to feed any militaries anywhere," says Andrew Natsios. The sentiment is understandable, but in a militarized society the distinction between soldiers and civilians may not be so important. As Kang Chol-hwan points out, Pyongyang's military "is not a professional army cut off from the rest of the population." Erica Kang, the aid worker in Seoul, argues that soldiers are people too, and if they're hungry, we should feed them. "When you have two-thirds of your youth in the military, the target group that you're trying to feed is actually in the military," she notes.

As a practical matter, the world already feeds North Korean soldiers. Aid is fungible. Every dollar of food assistance means Kim Jong Il can devote one fewer buck to lowland agriculture and one more to plutonium production. Donors can say they're earmarking food for the needy, but that's just a charade: the world's donations allow Mr. Kim to shift his resources elsewhere. Colin Powell when he was secretary of state said, "No North Korean child can eat enriched uranium." Yet they don't have to because the international community provides chow.

"If India builds the bomb, we will eat grass or leaves, even go hungry," Zulfikar Ali Bhutto said when he was Pakistan's foreign minister. "But we will get one of our own." Bhutto was speaking figuratively, of course, but North Koreans did in fact eat grass and leaves and some did not eat at all as their nation used its resources to develop nuclear weapons. "The best way to stop the nuclear program is to stop the aid," says North Korean defector Ma Young Ae, once a counterintelligence agent. "We will not use food as a weapon," declares Natsios. "But we want to make sure they don't use it as a weapon either." Yet we know that the North Koreans have done that already.

It's easy to understand what Kim Jong Il has to gain by engaging in "mendicant diplomacy," or "the tactics of tears" as he calls it. But why does the world play along? For Kathi Zellweger, who exudes Christian goodness, the issue is a moral one. As a part of Caritas, the Catholic relief agency, she finds the reason to help in the teachings of the Church—and in the faces of needy North Korean children. "If I'm very frustrated I look at these kids and then I know what I'm here for," she says.

Aid workers speak for those left out of grand geopolitical debates. Because they focus on saving the world one soul at a time, they don't dwell on the long-term consequences of their acts. By and large, humanitarians say those considerations are above their pay grade or simply not relevant. Somebody has to take on that unpleasant task, however. Kim Jong Il maliciously plays politics with his people, so, despite what the U.N. says, the rest of the world has an obligation to think about political issues too.

First of all, someone needs to take into account the welfare of future generations of North Koreans because no one—not even aid workers— speaks for them. By relieving today's regime of its most basic obligation, those who provide aid help support it. By supporting it, they help condemn tomorrow's Koreans to a grim life under the Kimist state.

Kim Jong Il uses aid to keep his old system in place. He channels donated food to the Pyongyang elite and the military, thereby keeping their loyalty. Without outside help, he would have to implement structural economic reform to stay afloat, just as the Chinese did. As it turns out, international assistance allows Kim to make the minimum changes possible in the circumstances—his July 2002 reforms essentially recognized change that had already occurred and did not mark a turning point. At a time when the world wants to see a transformation in the DPRK, it hands Kim the means to prevent it.

"Marxist economies require constant inputs," says Dennis Hays of the Cuban American National Foundation. Even more than Cuba's, the North Korean economy proves the truth of Hays's proposition. It almost collapsed when the Soviets cut off assistance and the Chinese reduced aid in the early 1990s, and it picked up when the South Koreans and others began to help during the latter part of the decade. Today, despite—or thanks to—more than a half century of outside assistance, the economy is still not self-sustaining.

The nation's agriculture is also limping. After more than a decade of food relief—no other country receives more—the DPRK still cannot feed itself. People may no longer be starving to death in great numbers, yet malnourishment is chronic. The World Food Programme does not know when North Korean agriculture will be able to meet the country's nutritional needs on its own. And that's no surprise. As American analyst Marcus Noland asks, why should Kim Jong Il improve agriculture or import food when he receives so much for free?

At any moment, there are humanitarian crises all over the globe. Unfortunately, we cannot feed all the world's hungry, so we have to make choices. In 1921 the United States provided famine relief to the Soviet Union and probably saved that regime. Now Americans give cereals to Kim Jong Il, a serial abuser of aid who torments them.

What sense does that make?

Sum for the Summit

Sometimes there are no sensible options. We must, unfortunately, deal with the world as we find it. With the Democratic People's Republic of Korea, the world's responsibility is to select the least atrocious choice.

But America has only itself to blame for its poor choice of options today. In the middle of the 1990s South Korean president Kim Young Sam publicly warned America not to provide aid to Pyongyang while the North Koreans concentrated their few resources on their People's Army. Washington ignored his commonsense advice, however, and saved the DPRK during its moment of great need. During this dire period at the peak of the famine, Pyongyang did not open its military storehouses, did not buy food for the dying, and did not, as far as we know, cut spending on its armed forces. Yet America provided assistance nonetheless. And by providing aid, Washington made it acceptable for others—especially Kim Young Sam's successor, Kim Dae Jung—to give crucial assistance just when the North Korean regime came closest to losing power.

By the middle of the 1990s the DPRK economy was close to certain collapse. It had fallen into a cycle of accelerating disintegration from which there was no escape without external assistance. Although the regime proved surprisingly resilient, it is unlikely that Kim Jong Il could have survived complete and simultaneous failures of both agriculture and the civilian economy.

South Korea, however, started shipping aid in 1998 and thereby stabilized the DPRK. At a time when the total economic output of the North's civilian economy was minuscule, Seoul provided $200 million in assistance. A little cash went a long way. North Korea's gross domestic product immediately started to show increases. Starting in 1999, when the country began its recovery, and continuing through the present, economic output has grown every year. Kim Jong Il is living large in Pyongyang these days because Seoul bailed him out at just the right time.

As well as every year since then. It is evident that aid has generally gone up over time. Seoul, however, does not publicly disclose all of its government-to-government assistance to Pyongyang. In fact, it's impossible to determine the full extent of the South's help because much of it has been disguised.

Seoul has channeled aid through Hyundai Asan, for instance. The South Korean company agreed to pay Pyongyang $942 million over six years to operate the Mount Kumgang resort just north of the DMZ. This figure is a ludicrous amount for a purely commercial transaction of that sort. Hyundai Asan's former chairman, Chung Mong Hun, admitted to transferring $400 million to North Korea to facilitate the groundbreaking

June 2000 meeting between Kim Dae Jung and Kim Jong Il. The sum for the summit, or at least a portion of it, is thought to have been included as a part of the Mount Kumgang payments. In any event, Hyundai Asan eventually scaled back its financial obligations to Pyongyang—a sure sign that the original $942 million figure was not dictated by commercial considerations. Another indication that the payments were partially intended as aid is that the South Korean government provided cash subsidies to Hyundai Asan to continue the money-losing Mount Kumgang venture.

Even if Washington could get Seoul to terminate aid—and that would be an extremely difficult task—Beijing would just take up the slack. Under no circumstances will China let North Korea go under. To keep its North Korean ally above water Beijing supplies 90 percent or more of the North's requirements for crude oil as well as almost half its food. The amount of annual aid ranges from several hundred million dollars to a couple billion. The best estimates put the total figure somewhere between $600 and $700 million a year. This assistance includes outright aid and discounts on the purchase prices of goods, and on the value of goods purchased on credit. North Korea runs a trade deficit with China, and technically the DPRK is obligated to pay the Chinese back. No one, however, expects the North Koreans to actually do it—after all, they stiffed the Soviets, with whom they had a similar arrangement.

Beijing has increased economic support recently. And so has South Korea. They both feel they must avoid the collapse of the North Korean state. One approach for the international community is to let Beijing and Seoul do all the heavy lifting from here on out. Why should Americans, Japanese, and others use their resources to accomplish Chinese and South Korean goals? Foreigners get little goodwill in return for their aid.

In a world of bad options, there are good reasons for the world to continue assistance, however. First and foremost, there is the plight of helpless North Koreans. Beijing's and Seoul's government-to-government aid largely does not reach them. Kim Jong Il has shown an inhuman disregard for their welfare, so he lets them fend for themselves even when the consequences are severe. "If those people die, they die," explained a North Korean official, referring to his country's more unfortunate citizens.

If poor citizens perish, the world would blame Americans, for instance, rather than Kim if they did not help the starving. "It is morally wrong to let people suffer and die on the grounds that humanitarian assistance might be used to support an unpopular government, the elite or army," declares Kathi Zellweger. Her statement is far too broad—would it have been right, for instance, to feed the guards at Treblinka?—but her words resonate around the planet.

The world, in short, will not stomach empty stomachs. People do not think about the grand issues when they see others perish. In a contest of wills, will a destitute devil always prevail over a wealthy superpower?

Piling It On at Panmunjom

Political activist Norbert Vollertsen thinks it doesn't have to be that way. Don't cut off aid, he argues. On the contrary, flood the North Korean regime with food. "Food, medicine, whatever you like, millions and billions of dollars in a huge convoy of trucks, a whole train, in Panmunjom," says the German doctor, practicing what he would say to the authorities in Pyongyang. "Here, you can get it. Right now. Take it. Nobody has to starve anymore in your country."

There would be only one catch. In his zany plan, CBS journalists would accompany the aid into every kindergarten, nursery, and hospital. That's one way to end the regime, but of course the North Korean leadership will never allow reporters to run free. Nonetheless, Vollertsen adopts the correct approach as he tries to take the spotlight off rich donors and put it where it belongs—on Kim Jong Il.

Kim gets away with all his aid shenanigans because the West has never challenged him—at least challenged him effectively. But suppose the international community piled up millions of tons of food in the DMZ's truce village in Panmunjom and told the North Koreans they could have it as long as they allowed real monitoring? North Koreans fed by foreigners would undoubtedly think of outsiders in a more favorable light.

So the world would win if Kim takes it. And it would win if he doesn't: as CBS—and the BBC and CNN—broadcast images from the DMZ of rice rotting in the rain, it would become evident—perhaps even to the U.N.—just who is responsible for the widespread suffering.

Suffering has always been widespread in the northern part of Korea. In 1946—two years before the formal establishment of the DPRK—the authorities in Pyongyang started rationing. Since then they have striven to make food available only through the Public Distribution System, the nation's rationing mechanism. By the late 1960s they had succeeded: the system had a virtual monopoly on food. During the famine of the 1990s, however, the government ended rationing to those, like Eunju, considered expendable. Driven by necessity, disfavored North Koreans found food outside PDS channels. In the process, the regime lost an important measure of control over large portions of society.

Today, Pyongyang is trying to reassert its authority by making international aid agencies, such as the U.N.'s World Food Programme, use the PDS as the primary means of distributing international assistance. In a real sense, therefore, the U.N. props up the Kim regime. "The purpose of humanitarian aid is to save lives, but by channeling it through the regime responsible for perpetuating the suffering, it has become part of the system of oppression," writes Fiona Terry of Doctors Without Borders. That is, in the words of *The Washington Post*, "morally repugnant."

And where there's oppression there is silence. In April 2002 journalist Lynne O'Donnell, with a group of aid workers based in North Korea, went to a local restaurant in a lane opposite the Pyongyang Hotel. "As we entered, a young woman emerged from a backroom dragging a sack of corn that clearly had 'USA' printed on it," O'Donnell noted. "There were others stacked near the cashier's desk. None of the aid workers blinked an eye." In every country where there's food assistance, there's diversion from hungry recipients to corrupt officials—and ultimately private entrepreneurs—to some degree. The difference in North Korea, as O'Donnell's friends indicated by their lack of reaction, is that the misuse of aid is open and pervasive. Yet you don't have to go to the North Korean capital if you want to find evidence of diversion of assistance: you can, if you like, *buy* American agricultural aid in farmers' markets across the country. But don't ask the World Food Programme if you want to know what's going on. Today, aid agencies, such as the WFP, keep quiet because they're afraid that nations would stop sending food if they knew the full extent of the misuse.

Washington is not blameless either. Because donors channel their aid through the WFP, they strengthen the government that threatens them, one canned sardine at a time. But it doesn't have to be this way. Aid, distributed under the right circumstances, can undermine a heartless regime—and, incidentally, feed its most unfortunate subjects.

"Anybody, a twelve-year-old, can improve on that system of distribution," says Tim Peters, the Seoul-based refugee activist. The WFP sends food in enormous quantities, tens of thousands of tons at a shot. Large shipments, however, are easily manipulated by the top dogs in Pyongyang. Peters, who also glows with Christian generosity, has a much better idea: "shotgun" aid through small NGOs, five, ten, fifteen tons at a time. North Korea's big cheeses don't care about such small amounts and so leave them alone.

Moreover, the smallish organizations, especially the Asia-based ones, are much better at monitoring than the gargantuan WFP. For instance, Taiwan's "Mother Teresa," Master Cheng Yen, a Buddhist devotee, began distributing aid directly to North Korean recipients during the 1990s famine through her own organization. If she can, then why can't the much larger and infinitely more powerful United Nations? Because she insisted. As a practical matter, the smaller NGOs have good records of establishing aid interventions and checking their progress. North Koreans say that monitoring hurts their feelings, but they have accepted it nonetheless from groups that have established good relationships at the local level. In any event, the largest organization, the World Food Programme, is among the least effective in making sure that food is reaching the hungry instead of, for instance, being traded for arms or reshipped to Africa as aid from Pyongyang.

Working with small NGOs also confers another advantage: the presence of so many foreigners from so many groups limits the regime's ability to maintain isolation. Kathi Zellweger, for instance, has made almost fifty trips to the DPRK. She is the first foreigner many North Koreans have ever met. Recently, in a remote area a gaggle of children thought she was Chinese because they knew she wasn't Korean. Their next guess was Russian, which was also wrong (she's Swiss). As the encounter suggests, she is opening Korea as she helps it, one small group at a time.

The Flood Damage Rehabilitation Committee, as large as it is, has had trouble keeping track of Kathi and all the other aid workers inside the DPRK. Foreigners, by virtue of their presence and nothing else, test the limits of the state's surveillance system. There are simply not enough local minders for the foreign workers, doctors, and monitors. Not surprisingly, there has been unsupervised contact between foreigners and Koreans as minders have made mistakes or let down their guard. Perhaps the most subversive consequence of the foreign presence is that government officials have now traveled inside their own country and seen, many for the first time, the failures of the Kimist state. Foreigners inside the DPRK tent present an unintentional challenge that Kim cannot win, at least in the long run.

Maybe that is why in August 2004 the "beggar state" told the United Nations that it didn't want humanitarian assistance for the following year. The decision stunned and baffled the aid community because North Korea needed food for more than six million people, a little under a third of its population. If Kim truly doesn't want international aid, then maybe we should be trying to provide it. The beauty of Vollertsen's proposal of unlimited assistance is that Kim Jong Il will be in trouble however he decides to respond.

If food aid is subversive, development aid is a menace. Pyongyang needs development assistance so that it can eventually become self-sufficient. Ask the Taiwan government's Lin Chiou-Shan. On one of his many official trips to the DPRK he visited a farm with chickens that refused to eat. Lin's expert could see the reason right away. The hens were not sick, as the local farmers thought. The birds simply did not have enough air. All the North Koreans had to do was open the windows.

In more ways than one. "I have said publicly in North Korea that if you listen to me and accept my advice I can feed the people in three years," Lin remarked. Kim Jong Il chose to ignore him, however. Letting foreigners into his country would be, in Lin's words, too "political." Development assistance requires a long-term foreign presence that is almost impossible to control. This type of aid would eventually strengthen Kim's government by improving food production, but not before it so undermined the DPRK that it failed completely. At least that is what North Korea's leader apparently thinks.

Becoming Complicit

"We want to find out from the DPRK how they think we can best help to avoid a humanitarian crisis," said the U.N.'s Maurice Strong on one of his various trips to Pyongyang to assess the North's food situation. If there is a "crisis," it is taking on the appearance of a permanent condition. After more than a decade of large-scale food aid from the international community and years of offers of development assistance, North Korea is no nearer attaining the ability to feed itself. On the contrary, it appears the country is headed to another famine. Kim Jong Il's July 2002 reform program has made food either too expensive or unavailable, so people are again scavenging for grass, leaves, and seaweed.

Up to now, the U.N. and donor nations have doled out food as if Kim Jong Il's domain were just another struggling society with a temporary problem. By doing so, they have played into the hands of the very autocrat who blundered into a humanitarian emergency and now uses it for personal benefit. If the United Nations wants to put an end to the continual suffering of the North Korean people, the organization should think about how to loosen the grip of the Kimist regime—or how to get rid of it altogether.

Whatever path it takes, the community of nations has an obligation to change the way it provides food assistance to the DPRK. Donors have permitted the North Korean regime to use their aid to fortify its power over the Korean people. By now we know—or at least should—what Kim Jong Il is doing with the donations we make. At a minimum, we have an obligation not to assist Pyongyang's leader, who is perpetuating misfortune on a national scale. By continuing the old ways of donating food to him, we are not helping the Korean people—and we are becoming complicit in his rule.

9

FLIRTING WITH UNSPEAKABLE EVIL

Should the World Engage Pyongyang to End a Planetary Showdown?

I believe we are on an irreversible trend toward
more freedom and democracy—but that could change.
—Dan Quayle

Can the world help the DPRK change for the better?

"No one has found a way to persuade North Korea to move in sensible directions," says Stapleton Roy, a former American diplomat. The country refuses to conform to standards of international conduct, and for decades neither friend nor foe has had much influence on Pyongyang.

Nothing has worked: the tactics of both generosity and hostility have failed. There has been no political liberalization, no embrace of economic restructuring, no relief for oppressed citizenry, no normalization of relations with Seoul, no demobilization, no reduction of threat. North Korea remains a horrible blot on humanity.

So how do we get rid of this damned spot? The country is the most miserable remnant of the greatest mistake in history, the communist tide of the twentieth century. The West overcame more powerful foes but cannot find the right formula for this adversary. Could it be possible that North Korea is so intransigent that there is nothing the world can do?

Perhaps the world need do nothing. "We go forward with complete confidence in the eventual triumph of freedom," President George W. Bush declared in his second inaugural address. If he's correct that the course of human events has a direction, then the impersonal forces of history will take care of the Kim family for the rest of humanity. The DPRK leader, the confident Texan would say, is a goner.

But what about those of us who don't buy into Bush's thoughts on inevitability? "I believe we are on an irreversible trend toward more freedom and democracy—but that could change," said Dan Quayle, the hapless former vice president. If, as he suggests, the flow of events can go into reverse, then Americans can't count on historical forces to do in Kim Jong Il for them. That means they had better get their policies toward Pyongyang right. As the last half century shows, bad decision-making in Washington can indefinitely prolong the existence of miserable leaders in Pyongyang.

Few people like America's current North Korea policy. Those who criticize Washington usually urge engagement of the unlikable regime led by Kim Jong Il. Americans see their calling as the creation of the conditions under which oppressed peoples can build their own liberal institutions. Engagement—working with bad regimes to improve them—appeals to everyone's better instincts. So should Washington change course now and embrace a policy of peaceful change of the DPRK?

The Geometry of Geopolitics

"Why are we afraid of dealing with the North?" asks David Kang of Dartmouth College as he questions Washington's attempted containment of Pyongyang. "If we really want capitalism and American values to influence the North, let's start exporting them as soon as possible."

Implicit in Kang's words is that Americans can eventually turn the vilest and most destitute state into a prosperous democracy. There is "constructive engagement," "cooperative engagement," "preventive engagement," and dozens of other varieties, but they all assume the United States will prevail over despots like Kim Jong Il due to the overwhelming attractiveness and strength of the American system.

Are democracy and capitalism really that powerful? The universality of American values is now accepted by most Americans. Any doubts on that score were surely dispelled by the sight of East Berliners first squeezing and then surging through cracks in a wall that once looked impregnable. Another supremely confident people, the South Koreans, look across a barrier of a different sort. Many of them believe they've already won the contest of legitimacy against the system on the other side of the Demilitarized Zone. Like Bush, they see the future as a confirmation of their victory. North Korean tanks would never reach Seoul, its residents like to say, because they couldn't get through the traffic jams. According to South Korean president Roh Moo-hyun, Pyongyang knows "red unification" is now beyond its grasp.

With the assumption that the South has already prevailed, engagement of the North is the obvious policy choice. Why rub Kim Jong Il's nose into the dirt? That's just dangerous. As a South Korean foreign minister once said, a mouse, when cornered, will even bite a cat.

The feline's task, therefore, is to manage reconciliation with the rodent. South Korea will create an environment in which the northern regime can choose on its own to change itself and open to the world. How does the South do that? "First we need contact points," said Jeong Se-hyun, when he was minister of unification. "Such contact points grow into a line. Connecting lines form an outline, which in turn expands to create space."

As Seoul seeks to increase the geometry of interaction, Pyongyang limits it. So far, the northerners, who know what their counterparts are up to, have succeeded in containing the forces of engagement. South Koreans visiting the DPRK have been confined to small spaces. The Mount Kumgang resort, Hyundai's investment, has the feel of a well-appointed internment camp, the reunions for families divided by the DMZ are held in one center just inside the DPRK, and Pyongyang's economic zones are at the periphery of the country and cut off from the rest of society. South Korean officials brag about the new relationships they have established, but, for all the money they have spent and time that has passed, they have yet to move beyond the contact point stage and establish even one line.

Seoul's initiatives have not reduced the threat along the DMZ, not changed the Kimist regime, not opened up North Korea beyond border areas. They have, however, strengthened the DPRK with infusions of cash and split the South's alliance with America, the only nation that has pledged to protect the South Korean people. It's hard to identify even one benefit Seoul has obtained apart from low-cost kitchenware purchased from a DPRK economic zone. By any measure, the Sunshine Policy has been a dud.

But only so far. "It's easy to prove that the grass doesn't grow," says Stapleton Roy. "You take your chair and sit down in your yard and watch the grass. And three or four hours later you've seen conclusively that nothing has changed." Kim Dae Jung initiated his Sunshine Policy when he took office in 1998, and Roh Moo-hyun has continued the same approach during his term. If they have yet to achieve results, perhaps it's because not enough time has elapsed—or maybe because we've been watching the wrong things in the yard known as North Korea.

If Seoul's goal is to reform the one man in the one-man regime in Pyongyang, it will never be successful. Kim Jong Il, for as long as he darkens the DPRK, will remain a perverse villain. Of course, he is capable of dramatically changing his country's policies—he is, after all, an autocrat. Yet we don't have much evidence that *he* can be effectively *engaged*. Engagement didn't have much effect on Stalin, Hitler, or Mao. As historian John Patrick Diggins notes, Ronald Reagan engaged the Kremlin as his final tactic, but Gorbachev was already a reformer before Reagan considerably softened his line. Sadly, history records that no one had lasting influence on Kim Il Sung, the tutor of the current leader in Pyongyang. Put another way, North Korea is, as analyst Nicholas Eberstadt suggests, "an unappeasable state."

But if South Korea's goal is to use engagement to *undermine* Kim Jong Il's rule and change the system, however, it has an excellent opportunity to succeed because North Korea is based on fibs of monumental proportions. Kim Il Sung created an abnormal society so he had to protect it with high and strong walls. The DPRK has been resilient mostly because his subjects were separated from everyone else. Kept apart from the rest of the world, North Koreans naturally accepted the alternate reality he crafted for them.

This isolation, however, is ending as Kim's successor has had to retreat from the most illogical elements of his system. And as Kim Jong Il does so, all the forces that apply around the world—political, economic, and social—are inevitably beginning to influence the people of North Korea. It may take some time for the DPRK to come to terms with the rest of humanity, but at some point the country will take on the look, and even some of the feel, of the modern world. Engagement accelerates a process that by now is irreversible.

"If they try to change it's good for us whether they succeed or fail," says Eric Heginbotham of the Council on Foreign Relations, referring to the DPRK's leaders. "If we don't try to change North Korea, we know what it looks like. It's the worst possible state." In the immediate future, engagement can strengthen the one-man system, especially if Americans cannot stop Seoul from shoveling even more cash directly to the regime, yet they have little to lose by opening that bizarre society. They win if Kim Jong Il commits to transformation. Totalitarian societies can deal with most everything but internal bottom-up change.

So a sensible engagement policy seeks to separate ordinary North Koreans from their leader by fomenting this type of transformation. At first glance, that would appear impossible in a society with an unchanging "theology" and an unyielding "culture of hatred." "The single-hearted unity of the party and the people around Kim Jong Il is much stronger than a nuclear weapon," Pyongyang's propagandists tell us. Moreover, the DPRK is a society featuring spectacles where tens of thousands move as one. And where the heart of one belongs to the leader. Emily Zhang, a tourist to the North, noticed there were no souvenir stands during her trip in 1998. She saw some kids with Kim badges pinned to their shirts and asked the tour guide to buy a few of the symbols. The children refused to part with them, however. "These buttons are our hearts," they replied. "We cannot give you our hearts."

"I was so taken aback," Zhang recalled. "I was just like that during the Cultural Revolution." North Korea's young may be loyal today, but so were the children of the People's Republic of China three decades ago. Emily Zhang, so devoted to Mao Zedong back then, later fled her homeland for Flushing, New York. Although the Democratic People's Republic of Korea appears all too unique, all totalitarian societies are essentially the same. "The leader puts his statues everywhere and gets 100 percent of the vote—and you know life must be living hell in that country," said one Chinese citizen observing the fall of Baghdad in 2003. Engagement changed the larger people's republic, so it can obviously remake the smaller one too.

North Korea, despite initial appearances, might not be such a tough target for engagers. For one thing, there are so few in the ruling group. The rest of North Koreans are "all talented and good people," in the words of Shin Sang-ok, who was once kidnapped on the orders of Kim Jong Il so that he could direct movies for the North Korean state (his then wife, an actress, had been nabbed by Kim earlier). Even among the elite there has been a long-standing desire for change. "Not everyone here wants to be closed off," a Pyongyang academic confided to David Zweig, a political scientist from Canada, as long ago as 1989.

Connected to the world, North Koreans will hasten the ongoing transformation, which is already occurring at a quick pace. Peasants are starting to act like owners, and trinket sellers see themselves as entrepreneurs. The real story in North Korea is not so much the breadth of economic change but the change in people's thinking. With even just a small stake in their own future, North Koreans are more independent and demanding and sometimes defiant. For the regime, that's a challenge of the highest order.

Foreigners can best foster economic modernization and a change in the North Korean people by inserting themselves into their society. "There is no greater subversive in a Communist country than an American factory manager," writes Nicholas Kristof of *The New York Times*. Why? Factory managers may not talk about politics during their stays in totalitarian societies, but they bring fresh notions of how to work, which means they show their staffs that there are new ways to live.

If anything characterizes the DPRK today, it is a growing competition between Kim Jong Il, who seeks to reassert control after his government's failure during the 1990s, and ordinary citizens trying something new. The issue for Washington, therefore, is whether it should help the people by inundating their country with Peace Corps workers, diplomats, factory managers, and the most effective weapon of all, Britney Spears. North Koreans, when they are exposed to outsiders, will quickly figure out what they want. Why else would Kim Jong Il work so hard to isolate his subjects?

There are far more Americans than North Koreans. So far, Kim has used the disparity to attract sympathy, but Washington can turn the tables on him. Pyongyang's autocrat always says he wants better relations. Suppose Bush calls Kim's bluff and tells him he has just granted diplomatic recognition and put his ambassador on the plane. A regime built on intense antagonism toward America will face a critical problem. "North Korea wouldn't know what to do if there were peace," notes Columbia University's Charles Armstrong. "The government might collapse."

Washington's engagement of the DPRK would deny Kim Jong Il an enemy and hasten his end. So what are Americans waiting for?

Geopolitics Made Simple

If Washington is waiting for anything, it is for North Korea to concede. Seoul and Washington can agree on general goals such as the DPRK's disarmament, but they completely diverge on tactics. "The principal difference is that South Korea thinks the North can only change from within," notes Charles Armstrong. "The U.S., on the other hand, believes in pressure."

"Pressure and isolation have never been successful with communist countries, even during the Cold War," said Kim Dae Jung in the waning days of his presidency. Kim was a courageous dissident and successful politician but obviously never a political scientist or historian. Pressure, and even isolation, worked to defeat communism in the last century in the Soviet Union, Eastern Europe, and Mongolia. As we have seen, engagement can undermine a totalitarian regime. Will hard-line tactics work as well?

History, unfortunately, does not provide instruction manuals or even clear lessons. Ronald Reagan, who uncompromisingly fought Moscow—"My theory of the Cold War is that we win and they lose," he once remarked—also engaged the Soviet Union at crucial moments. Once he reduced the fears of Kremlin leaders, they accelerated domestic reform that led to the complete failure of their system. "The cold war ended in an act of faith and trust, not fear and trembling," writes John Patrick Diggins, the historian. If the historical record is unhelpful for today's crisis on the Korean peninsula, it's because the Gipper—and other American presidents both before and after him—used so many different tactics.

There was, however, one constant Reagan theme that survived the changes in his administration's Soviet policies. If he gets most of the credit for bringing on the downfall of Soviet Russia—and he should—it's largely because Reagan did not accept the right of totalitarianism to exist. "They say the world has become too complex for simple answers," he said in 1964. "They are wrong. There are no easy answers, but there are simple answers."

Reagan's simple answer was that free people always have to tell the truth. Yet recent South Korean presidents, in their desperation to avoid offending Pyongyang, have flinched in the face of apparent wickedness—and the unmistakable suffering of fellow Koreans. It is to their shame that it was a foreigner, George W. Bush, who was the one to use unambiguous language to describe the North Korean state. "I believe a president must speak with moral clarity," he said during his first term. "And one of the things I remember clearly about President Reagan, he didn't say, 'Well, Mr. Gorbachev, will you take the top three bricks off the wall?' He said, 'Tear it all down.'"

Bush was roundly criticized for criticizing the DPRK and thereby complicating already difficult negotiations over nuclear weapons. Yet plain speaking about tyranny, even at inopportune moments, is always in season. "If ideas are power, then words are weapons," writes Mark Palmer, a former American diplomat who believes the world can rid itself of every despot within two decades. "Dictators understand this. It is time for democrats to understand it too." Because we have lived in freedom for so long, we often forget that stirring words have significance in and of themselves. Andrei Zorin, a Soviet literary scholar, heard on the BBC World Service that Ronald Reagan called the USSR an "evil empire." The next thing he did was risk imprisonment by spreading the news. "I jumped out of my chair and started calling," he recalled. "Of course, to us it was no surprise that the Soviet Union was such an empire, but the idea that somebody would say it from the podium, out loud, was a revelation."

And an inspiration. We remember phrases like "evil empire" and "axis of evil" because they first tar despotic regimes and then set us in motion. They mark turning points, defining the times in which they are uttered. People do not forget the leaders who charge them with great responsibilities.

Unfortunately, none of those politicians runs the government in Seoul. It is ironic that it is not the freer and richer Korea that is trying to inspire and lead the other one to freedom and prosperity. South Koreans have, in their newfound wealth, lost their way. They criticize those who criticize Pyongyang because speaking the truth might dampen the South Korean economy. How callous is that? "In South Korea, poor people made some money, and they became blind," says Shin Sang-ok, the noted film director.

The failure of South Korea's eyesight started with Kim Dae Jung. The former president, who left office in 2003, is now known as "the Nelson

Mandela of Asia," but he didn't lead anyone to freedom from Kim Jong Il. On the contrary, D.J. solidified Kim's rule, perhaps extending its reach to future generations of North Koreans. He provided aid at a critical time and also legitimized the Pyongyang leadership by his warm physical embrace of its leader. He not only failed to speak the truth, he failed to speak at all: the former human rights activist said not one word to the North Korean Kim about human rights during his historic 2000 summit in Pyongyang. Unlike Ronald Reagan, he failed to understand that the grip of tyrants is always fragile and that legitimizing them weakens internal forces for change.

By failing to raise his voice, Kim Dae Jung highlighted the moral dilemma of all who deal with autocrats, despots, and other villains holding government office. How does one touch evil without becoming complicit? Of course, not all contact with a rancid regime is bad. As North Korean defector Hwang Jang Yop notes, "Even the best boxer can't hurt his opponent without getting close."

Kim Dae Jung argued that his dealings with the DPRK were beneficial for Koreans in the long run, but if historians treat him poorly, which is a rather safe bet, it will be because he compromised his own democracy. His payment to Kim Jong Il to facilitate the summit violated South Korean law, something D.J. later acknowledged after his cover-up failed. He tried to say the sum was just like a present for a close relative—"When a rich brother goes to visit a poorer brother, the rich brother should not go empty-handed," he explained—but when was the last time your sister gave you several hundred million to get together? There was absolutely no justification for undermining the rule of law. This was not some forgivable Clintonesque fib about fellatio—D.J.'s actions went straight to the heart of Korean democracy. When all else failed, he fell back on articulating the rationale for divine-right rule when he said his acts, although illegal, were nonetheless okay because *he* committed them.

Kim Dae Jung committed one other unforgivable sin during his term as president. In pursuing reconciliation with the North he failed to clearly state that his system ultimately had to prevail on the peninsula. Ronald Reagan's great contribution to the twentieth century was not that he saved D.J.'s life—something the South Korean thanked him for—but that he declared that freedom was going to triumph on every peninsula, island, and continent. Of course, Reagan was only joking when he said, "My fellow Americans, I'm pleased to tell you today that I've signed legislation that will outlaw Russia forever," but the sentiment was heartfelt—and repeated publicly many times though in more diplomatic ways.

We don't have to "begin bombing in five minutes"—the second part of Ronnie's joke about banning the Soviet Union—because "accommodation" is not a four-letter word. Yet engagement does not work when the accommodating party loses its will to prevail. Kim Dae Jung engaged the other Korea but ended up changing the South more than the North. He set the tone for today's society, which discourages North Korean refugees from entering for fear of riling Pyongyang and hounds human rights campaigners who criticize Kim Jong Il. After all, Norbert Vollertsen, the activist, was never physically abused in the DPRK but has been beaten in the South. Asia's Mandela risked his life to remove one authoritarian system only to lay the groundwork for a government that values conformity over freedom. In a hardening climate, Roh Moo-hyun's initiatives to legalize communist parties, abolish national security legislation directed against Pyongyang, and attack nongovernment media appear more like the enforcement of political uniformity than democratization.

First Kim Dae Jung and now Roh have embraced a dictator as vile as any who has roamed the earth this decade or last. If the South ultimately takes a wrong turn as a result of his diplomacy toward the North, we will then have the answer to the question often posed to the Bush administration: "Why is America afraid of engagement?"

Of course, engagement does not have to degenerate into a moral sinkhole. American policies, if they are to be sustainable, have to appeal to Americans' values as well as their generosity. They don't work when presidents and policymakers lose contact with their country's better instincts. As Jimmy Carter correctly says, Pyongyang is not entirely responsible for the collapse of the Agreed Framework. Washington did not keep its commitments made in that agreement largely because Americans would not accept a dramatic improvement in relations with a God-denying, famine-causing, drug-running hellhole.

In the future, therefore, Washington should make it clear that the ultimate goal of policy is to engage the North Korean people more than their government and that the policy rests on America's sense of morality. Lucifer, sometimes seen in the form of Henry Kissinger, disagrees. "Moral claims involve a quest for absolutes, a denial of nuance, a rejection of history," he wrote.

"In Texas, we don't do nuance," Dubya told CNN's Candy Crowley. And let's applaud President Bush's sentiment. On our seemingly complex planet, and especially in North Korea, clarity in Texas-sized doses helps us recognize that there are the oppressed and the oppressors and that we should do everything we can to help the former get rid of the latter. But that doesn't mean we can't employ a little nuance from time to time in the form of engagement.

Jimmy Carter's Solution

Jimmy Carter, who received most of the credit for solving 1994's North Korean nuclear crisis, has a fix for the current one as well. Carter, as many of us remember, said that we shouldn't have an "inordinate fear of communism which once led us to embrace any dictator who joined us in our fear." America, he now says, should embrace Kim Jong Il instead. Washington, the former president counsels, should lift all political and economic sanctions against North Korea and afford "the opportunity for that little country to become completely absorbed in world affairs on a normal basis."

Engagement, Carter says, is the route to ending the intractable standoff. His approach, unfortunately, suffers from one principal drawback. Engagement works, but, as Stapleton Roy notes, it transforms societies at grass-growing speeds. The tactic fosters change first in the lower rungs of the social order and eventually at the top in leadership councils. It is a process measured over the course of generations, not years. Small South Korea evolved into a democracy only after four decades of cajoling, encouragement, and engagement from the American superpower. China, after three decades of the world's engagement, still obstructs Washington's efforts to halt proliferation of nuclear weapons technology.

If the world needs a resolution to the North Korean crisis soon—and it does—then glacial progress will not do. Carter's proposal to absorb the DPRK is a worthy goal in and of itself, and the international community should undertake it by all means with aid, trade, and all other tools at its disposal. But let's not mistake engagement for a solution to the current nuclear standoff.

10

THE END OF AMERICAN PRIMACY

The Inevitable Consequences of
Irreversible Decline

If globalization really works, then what is the endgame?
—Kenneth Rogoff, American economist

"Not since Rome has one nation loomed so large above the others," Joseph Nye tells us. The Harvard academic uses an inadequate example as he tries to describe American might. Rome, as powerful as it was, extended its reach over only a small portion of the globe. The power of the United States, by contrast, is felt everywhere. Pundit Charles Krauthammer gets nearer to the truth: "America today is the closest the world has ever seen to God."

There is no more arms race or space race, and forget about America being on the wrong end of "the missile gap." Today, the United States is, as the French say, a "hyperpower," a country that has surpassed super status. There are other powers in the world, but none of them—not even any conceivable combination of them—can effectively challenge the United States across the globe. The world, for good or ill, lacks a counterweight to American ambition. At least for this moment, its rivals are far behind.

Yet for all its vaunted supremacy, America was far more powerful in the past—at least in relative terms. Much of the rest of the world—including all of the other great powers—had been devastated by the Second World War. U.S. armed forces were only blooded, not bloodied, by the conflict. Its industrial infrastructure was undamaged. America was the only nation that could project force anywhere on the globe and the only one with the atomic bomb. With the other powers in ruins, the United States was essentially invulnerable to harm.

It was also the world's economic colossus in the years immediately following the war. American output comprised more than half of the planet's total. The nation possessed almost two-thirds of global gold reserves, owned half the world's shipping, and accounted for more than half of its manufacturing. A third of mankind's exports left America's shores. The twentieth century, if it belonged to any nation, was America's.

Yet as the Chinese say, "No feast lasts forever." Wealth, power, and national strength constantly change, and for America at the end of the Second World War there was no place to go but down. Today, "declinists" argue with optimists, but there can be no question about the long-term trend of the United States. For all its immense power and prestige at this time, it is in a state of irreversible decline: America will never be as mighty as it was last century.

America Abolishes History

Decline does not necessarily prevent a second or even a third American century. The position of unquestionable dominance at the end of World War II was artificial, much like Britain's preeminence immediately after the defeat of Napoleon. Washington's relative influence and power, therefore, could not be maintained for long. And indeed America's position in the world has eroded; the United States has endured not only natural decline but also some especially dismal episodes of self-inflicted wounding— the Korean War, the war in Vietnam, and the loss of Iran, for example. Yet what goes down can come up as well. There has also been a remarkable renewal of American power since the Reagan presidency.

There has even been a period described as America's "unipolar moment," which began even before a dazed Gorbachev formally dissolved the Soviet Union on Christmas Day 1991. That "moment," however, has lasted longer than most everyone expected at the time: it still persists today. Predictions of ultimate Japanese and German dominance—some said they were the real winners of the Cold War—sound laughable now, although such pronouncements were widely accepted at the time. The one thing that distinguishes America from other nations is not so much its strength—although that is of course an important factor—but its unique ability to renew itself.

America is also unique in another sense: its power rests on an international system that has no historical antecedent. Washington's leading role is accepted by many nations, even some decidedly unfriendly toward the United States. Why? If Americans run an "empire," as many say, it is a "consensual" one.

The primary argument for the empire's durability is that most nations benefit from this global order in some fashion or another. It is stable simply because it more or less stands for things people want. "Nearly all countries perceive a clear stake in maintaining the international system, and in protecting their own umbilical cord to that system," writes Banning Garrett of the Washington, D.C.–based Atlantic Council. As American Express once put it, "Membership has its privileges."

America can continue to lead the system because, as Osama bin Laden has repeatedly said, people prefer strong horses to weak ones. Whatever one may think of the current American effort in Iraq, many members of the international community support it simply because Washington wants them to. The exercise of power tends to create even more of it. Power, if wielded well, can grow overnight.

And it can shrink just as fast. Great nations that flounder lose their following quickly. Even in the absence of debilitating mistakes, power naturally creates competitors, and sometimes adversaries, for those who hold it. Throughout the ages countries have tended to balance against the stronger members of the international order, and although there may be less of this phenomenon in a hegemonic system like the current one, the sentiment nonetheless persists. The United States may not now have a mortal enemy like Carthage was to Rome, but there will always be a little bit of France everywhere Americans look.

Today Parisian-type anti-Americanism is expressed all around the globe. Washington is estranged from its allies, and it would be comforting to describe the rift as merely temporary and attributable to Frenchie orneriness or envy. There is no more common Soviet enemy, and that doesn't help in maintaining unity, but the problem goes far deeper than that. Simply put, there is no common view of the troubling events of the day and there is no accepted approach to handling them. International harmony exists only when there is both a perceived commonality of interests—which generally exists—and agreement on how to further them—which does not.

The real "paradox of power" is that the most powerful often are the most insecure. And perhaps because Americans have the ability to change the world, they believe the world must be changed. As Uncle Ben said to a troubled Peter Parker, the alter ego of Spider-Man, "Remember, with great power comes great responsibility." Nations not so blessed with the ability to reorder the planet feel little responsibility to try and often do not sympathize with those who make the effort. They make a virtue out of necessity and ask, "Why can't we all just get along?"

Wouldn't it be nice if everyone could? The concept underlying the liberal world order led by the United States is that everyone will live, if not in harmony and friendship, then at least without major military conflict. Trade, the theory goes, leads to open economies, open economies to prosperity, prosperity to representative government, and representative government to peace. It's all very thrilling if you think about it: many of us believe that for the first time since leaving the Garden of Eden under less than favorable circumstances we know how to achieve a state of grace, at least in the geopolitical sense.

We have found our way back to peace because we had reached what appeared to be not just a historical transition but the ultimate destination. Karl Marx told us that history would end upon the attainment of communism, but Western analysts, optimists of a different sort, believe that the human story has already come to a close. History ended, Francis Fukuyama of Johns Hopkins argued in his landmark 1992 book, called, aptly, *The End of History and the Last Man*. Events continued to occur, he noted, but by the last days of the Cold War "the evolution of human societies through different forms of government had culminated in modern liberal democracy and market-oriented capitalism." There was no place else for humanity to go—we had finally reached the "end point of mankind's ideological evolution." In short, the victors of the twentieth century did not merely write history—they abolished it.

The death of history brought joy, relief, and the "debellicization" of the West. "Warlessness," academic Michael Mandelbaum notes, became for many people the only acceptable state of affairs. "The ideas that conquered the world"—his catchy description of capitalism, democracy, and all the other big concepts—led to the delegitimization of military force, even against tyrants, as reaction to the 2003 Iraq War later showed. Why should one go to all the trouble of inflicting death when the impersonal forces of history, relentlessly grinding forward, will finish off communists, autocrats, and bad actors of all stripes? An unintended by-product of the end of history is that loathsome leaders, such as Kim Jong Il, gained immunity from the international community.

What we wish to believe, however, may not exactly accord with reality. Although there was a swift advance of trade, capitalism, and democracy after the failure of the Soviet Union, the "victory" of these concepts, if we can call it that, has proven to be incomplete. Bad governance has been remarkably resilient during the last decade and a half: Russia is backsliding to authoritarianism, a quintet of communist nations remain committed to Leninist political institutions, and Africa and other large portions of the planet continue to be ravaged by failed leadership. George W. Bush named only three governments in his famous "axis of evil," but former American ambassador Mark Palmer said the president did not go nearly far enough. Palmer identified another forty-two regimes that free nations should replace by 2025.

Should we really be so ambitious? With just a few exceptions—China among them—most of the remaining rogue, failed, and disagreeable states are geopolitically irrelevant and economically unimportant. After all, who really cares if Myanmar's military insists on running the government? Wasn't Martin Luther King Jr. just engaging in rhetorical excess when he proclaimed, "Injustice anywhere is a threat to justice everywhere"? How can we be threatened by a country we can't even spell?

Former New York mayor Rudolph Giuliani has the reply. He adopted the controversial "broken windows" theory—which holds that it's important to fight petty infractions as a means of showing intolerance to more serious wrongdoing—in his successful bid to clean up Gotham. This tough but commonsense approach may or may not have been responsible for the large drop in the city's crime, but New Yorkers bought it, and the concept is equally applicable to the international scene.

We know that dictators, even faster than spouses and business partners, pounce at any sign of weakness or during a moment of inattention. North Korea's Kim Il Sung, for instance, invaded South Korea in June 1950 soon after Secretary of State Dean Acheson left it outside his announced security perimeter, and Saddam Hussein rolled his tanks into Kuwait days after American ambassador April Glaspie signaled, in her private meeting with him, Washington's indifference to intra-Arab conflicts.

What is surprising, and in its own way quite sad, is not that there are men with the proclivities of Kim Jong Il or Zimbabwe's Robert Mugabe but that democratic and prosperous states allow despots like them to do as they please. During the Cold War Americans perhaps had an excuse to excuse the bad behavior of anti-communist friends in the all-encompassing struggle against the Soviet Union.

Today, however, there are fewer plausible justifications for tolerance of this sort. Now, we need to be alive to the possibility that international misbehavior is contagious, spreading from insignificant countries to ones of more consequence—and from failed states to terrorist groups. That's the core of the broken-windows theory: if we don't fix windows right away, people will think that it's okay to break more of them.

History Abolishes America

"We stand tall," declared the rather stubby Madeleine Albright, "and we see further than other countries into the future, and we see the danger here to all of us." The truth is, for a farsighted people the Americans did not pick up the obvious clues of the last decade. The bombing of the World Trade Center, in which six people lost their lives in 1993, passed without much lasting impact on the collective American consciousness. Neither did the bombings of the U.S. military barracks in the King Abdul Aziz Air Base in

Saudi Arabia in 1996, the American embassies in Nairobi and Dar es Salaam in 1998, or the USS *Cole* in Yemen's port of Aden in 2000, to name just a few incidents that deserved more attention than they received. Americans were either "sleepwalking through history," to borrow columnist Haynes Johnson's phrase, or took a "holiday" from it, as Charles Krauthammer contended, but in either case they were truly oblivious.

They had ignored the obvious threats because they had not stopped congratulating themselves over the "victory" in the Cold War. If history hadn't actually ended, Americans at least felt that time had stopped so that they could enjoy the view. That, of course, was a mistake. "History knows no resting places and no plateaus," Henry Kissinger reminds all of us. And it knows no arbitrary divisions of the kind we assign for our own convenience like Middle Ages or Cold War: it just ploddingly moves forward "one damn fact after another."

As history moves from the welcome surprise of the fall of Soviet communism to tragic incidents, Americans should begin paying attention—and not because of Islamic attacks against the United States around the globe. As fearsome-looking as they are, terrorists are just bearded Luddites in robes. World politics may look as if it took a sharp turn on September 11, but bin Laden has not managed to derail modernity or even globalization. Unless they can get their hands on a nuclear weapon—and maybe not even then—terrorists will not be able to finish off present-day society.

What Washington *should* be concerned about is the continued success of the American-led liberal world order. As Karl Marx might have said, the United States planted the seeds of its own marginalization. Indeed, after the Second World War Harry Truman energetically went about rebuilding Western Europe and Japan and thereby hastened the erosion of his own country's relative standing. Postwar reconstruction ultimately led to globalization, the seemingly inexorable march of international capitalism. As the concept of free market economics continues to spread, other nations are becoming richer and stronger. And as a consequence, the United States is become relatively poorer and weaker. America, the most powerful force in the universe at this moment, is losing its primacy at an alarming rate. "If globalization really works, then what is the endgame?" asks Harvard's Kenneth Rogoff.

That's a troubling question for developed nations and especially their leaders. In 2004, Americans, who constituted 4.6 percent of the world's population, produced 21.2 percent of the world's gross domestic product. If future development is eventually to be shared equally, what will happen to the United States of America? For one thing, Rogoff predicts, the world's youth will grow up thinking that "Hollywood" is merely a wordplay on "Bollywood," the lively and productive Indian film industry, and McDonald's hamburgers are an example of a "minor ethnic cuisine." And something more important will occur: the U.S. dollar will become "a boutique currency" and the euro "a sideshow." Business will "clamor for Chinese yuan and Indian rupees."

Is it America's fate to be swamped? Yes is the obvious answer, at least in the long run. A nation with just 5 percent of the world's population will end up with around 5 percent of world economic output and so will be hard-pressed to maintain its leadership role. If bin Laden really wants to hurt America, he should be promoting even more economic integration. Zbigniew Brzezinski, best known as Jimmy Carter's national security adviser, turns common sense into a logical prediction when he says that America is the "first, only, and last truly global superpower." "In the long run," he writes, "global politics are bound to become increasingly uncongenial to the concentration of hegemonic power in the hands of a single state." Other nations, with newfound wealth, will at first want to have a say—and then a leading role—in global politics. Analysts argue about the relationship between economic and geopolitical influence, but the latter inevitably follows the former. In today's world of instant communication, perceptions change quicker than ever before. Tomorrow, changes in economic and political influence will tend to be even more tightly bound than they have been in the past.

Of today's economic powers, only Japan has been willing to remain a geopolitical midget—and that, for better or worse, is changing fast as the Japanese perceive China and North Korea to be threats to their security. Asia's other nations are less modest. The leaders in Beijing have put Americans, and everyone else, on notice that they intend to reduce Washington's influence and replace it with their own. Soon to become the most populous nation in the world, India is already beginning to demand influence appropriate to its size and strength. Its 1998 test of a nuclear weapon was meant to send a message. "This new world is too complex not to be multipolar," said France's defense minister, Michele Alliot-Marie, during a visit to Beijing. No surprise that China's leader, Hu Jintao, agrees: "The trend toward a multipolar world is irreversible and dominant."

The French and Chinese, who relish giving Americans bad news, haven't been specific about exactly when the world will end up multipolar. Harvard's Samuel Huntington, who at the end of the last century presciently predicted a "clash of civilizations," thinks that American dominance will end sometime early in this one. Bush administration officials privately talk of only two more decades of American primacy.

Whether quick or slow, the demise of American hegemony will surely be painful. "Americans, with their scant few centuries of history, have never experienced the shift from one major historical period to another," wrote Shintaro Ishihara, Tokyo's fiery governor. What Ishihara is really saying is that America has so far been spared the agony of watching its own decline.

Decline creates urgency. The world, at this moment, is not going the way Americans wish it to. History, inconveniently for them, has decided to continue. And in the event, none of capitalism, democracy, or peace has triumphed. At the moment they may be advancing, but that is because American might advances them. Whether Washington has a decade or a century left at the pinnacle of power, it can institutionalize its ideals only while it remains "the indispensable nation," as Madeleine Albright was so fond of saying.

America won—actually "survived" would be a better word—the Cold War because on some level its system was more attractive. Americans would like to think, as Francis Fukuyama suggests, that their ideas are alluring because they are universal. Perhaps they are, but no one should overestimate their inherent appeal. "No matter how compelling America's ideals, they still come wrapped in American power," Newsweek's Fareed Zakaria reminds readers. And we should also recall that economic success confers an aura of virtue. American ideals prevailed in part because the American economic system eventually proved to be more productive than the Soviet one. Until that became apparent, communism held great appeal because it was associated with the success of the Soviet economy.

When some other nation's system outperforms America's in the future, global attitudes and values will inevitably evolve again. Change is inevitable, but progress, at least as Washington defines it, is not. If, for example, the People's Republic of China should become the next global hegemon, Americans could find that another set of organizing principles, ones far less liberal than those they embrace, gains wide acceptance.

Asia, unfortunately, is ready for Chinese values, even the harsh ones of today. Economically successful Asians have been touting the superiority of their "Asian values" over "Western" ones for some time. Newly earned wealth has convinced them they possess virtue and so they have little need for representative government or even human rights, now portrayed as "foreign." "People here are talking of China and economics," says Tanun Anumanrajadhon of Thailand's Chiang Mai University. "People don't care about democracy now." And as time goes on, the attitudes have tended to become more extreme. Singapore's Lee Kuan Yew, perhaps the leading Asian values proponent, recently said that it would have been okay for China's Deng Xiaoping to have slaughtered 200,000 in Tiananmen Square in 1989.

What happens when authoritarian values are seen as virtuous? Everyone can only hope that Asia, as it becomes more modern, becomes less Asian, at least as Lee, the founder of modern Singapore, defines it. In the meantime, the West needs to plan for a world that is turning toward the East.

CIVILIZATION'S LAST WEAPON

Nuclear Arms Fragment Global Stability

More than any other time in history, mankind faces
a crossroads. One path leads to despair and utter
hopelessness. The other, to total extinction. Let us
pray we have the wisdom to choose correctly.
—Woody Allen

"The civilized world has spent more than a thousand years trying to limit
the destructiveness of war," wrote Colin Powell when he was secretary of
state. Humankind, however, has so little to show for centuries of effort. If
anything, we are backsliding. The end of the second millennium was
marked by devastation on an unprecedented scale.

In the first half of the last century, 15 million people lost their lives
during the First World War and 55 million more died in the Second. The
toll from the latter would have been higher but for two horrific explosions,

followed by waves of intense heat, pressure, and noise, that ended the fighting. America had manipulated the elemental building blocks of matter to devise weapons of previously unimagined power.

Then four years after the horror of Hiroshima and Nagasaki the Soviets tested their first atomic bomb. From the perspective of the middle of the twentieth century, the future of our species seemed grim. Two grand coalitions, both armed with the ultimate weapon, struggled for supremacy across continents. For four decades, the 1950s to the 1980s, everyone lived in fear of still another global battle, one that promised to be far more deadly than the preceding ones. Many thought that if it came, the next world war would put an end to history.

Now, as we enter the seventh decade of living with the possibility of instant extinction, we are hopeful. Turmoil still plagues the planet, yet we have somehow managed to avoid conflict on a cosmic scale. The period in which we live, for all its shortcomings, looks better, especially in comparison with what we had feared could happen. War could have consumed us all but didn't. How did we successfully escape the last century?

Plutonium Promotes Peace?

Some say we should thank nuclear arms for the peace we enjoy. Columbia University's Kenneth Waltz, a star of political science, believes more of these weapons would be better. The underlying logic of his theory is simple: nuclear war is so horrible and unpredictable that no leader would want to fight one. Countries may not even engage in conventional conflict if they think their adversaries might go ballistic—figuratively—and nuclear—literally. "Where nuclear weapons threaten to make the costs of wars immense, who will dare to start them?" he asks. So, according to Waltzian theory, the best possible result for humankind is the gradual spread of nuclear weapons, which is even preferable to no spread at all. Waltz, of course, is just applying the principle first enunciated by Frank Zappa: "There will never be a nuclear war; there's too much real estate involved."

The really good news, Waltz tells us, is that arsenals of destructive weaponry moderate the behavior of not only the big powers but the small ones as well. "Rulers want to have a country that they can continue to rule," he sensibly notes.

North Korean ruler Kim Jong Il is obviously obsessed with continuing his reign. In order to restrain his conduct, should we just let him keep his cache of bombs? Kim, an apparently uncontrollable tyrant, puts Waltz's thesis to the ultimate test.

Will we be safer when even despots have the power to trigger Armageddon? Unfortunately, there is less than meets the eye to the more-is-better argument. As an initial matter, advocates of nuclear proliferation are fond of noting that atomic war hasn't happened so it's unlikely to occur in the future. Although we shouldn't argue with history, the problem with this line of thinking is that the world order that existed for most of the period since 1945 no longer exists. In other words, we enjoyed relative peace largely because of the stability that was inherent in the bipolar Cold War system, not just because of the deterrent effect of nuclear arms.

During that period the two superpowers generally exercised restraint and kept their allies and cohorts in line. With only a few notable lapses— most of them, like the Korean War, occurring in the beginning stages of the Cold War—both major contestants acted with caution, as status quo powers have a tendency to do. The presence of the world's worst weapons reinforced a stability that already existed: both sides felt they had more to lose than gain from a fundamental realignment of geopolitical position.

Today, those who oppose the United States, the surviving Cold War contestant, have no leader to keep competition within understood bounds. In short, we live in a less predictable world where the least responsible actors, like Islamic fanatics, generally hold the initiative. Unfortunately, conflict in the first decade of the first century of the new millennium is, in every sense of the term, unsupervised.

Today's unsupervised challengers to world order know no fear. Analysts may argue that nuclear weapons terror creates peace, but the argument is plausible only if everyone is terrorized by nuclear weapons. We know that Soviet leaders were. They did not use their warheads against America because, in addition to other reasons, they knew America could make good on Barry Goldwater's infamous threat to lob a nuke into the men's room in the Kremlin—and a big one into just about every other lavatory and latrine in the USSR.

Osama bin Laden knows that the United States can also liquefy every cave in Afghanistan, but will that stop him from using the bomb against the West? Nuclear arms only keep the peace against adversaries who prefer to keep living. Terrorists may not be irrational or even evil, but they are hard to deter. As one al-Qaeda spokesman observed, "You love life, we love death." These particular death lovers, not surprisingly, want to inflict punishment in maximum dosages. Bin Laden buddy Sulaiman Abu Ghaith proclaimed that Muslims should avenge the loss of their own across the world: "We have the right to kill four million Americans—two million of them children—and to exile twice as many and wound and cripple hundreds of thousands."

In order to do that, al-Qaeda has been trying to become "the world's 10th nuclear power." Two Pakistani nuclear scientists who had ties with Dr. Abdul Qadeer Khan's infamous ring of black marketers met with al-Qaeda representatives in 2000 and 2001, and bin Laden has tried to buy South African uranium through Sudan and weapons-grade material in Central Asia. Yet far more disturbing is the rumor that won't go away: bin Laden bought suitcase nuclear weapons in 1998 and is storing them for just the right moment. American intelligence thinks the persistent reports are untrue, but even if Osama does not yet possess luggage of this sort, we don't have to guess how he plans to reach his goal of four million deaths. He can either hijack eight thousand 747s or create a massive explosion in four different American cities. Al-Qaeda's new project is to bring about an "American Hiroshima."

September 11, unfortunately, has raised the bar. Any future act of terrorism has to be far more deadly to have as massive an impact. So the best way to stop al-Qaeda is to keep horrific devices out of its hands, and the best way to do that is to slow, or even stop, proliferation. A world with more depots stocked with nuclear arms is a world with more guards to bribe and bombs to steal. Terrorists are the one group of actors on the international scene who disprove the argument that more is safer.

Moreover, the more-the-merrier line of reasoning doesn't take into account the randomness of error. Forces that in other contexts cause cars to go off roads and planes to fall from skies can, with the ultimate weapon, bring about the end of civilization. To borrow a phrase that we know is true, "Shit happens."

In other words, the more nations that have nuclear weapons, the more likely it is that one of those devices will go off by accident or mistake. The USSR and the United States would probably have destroyed a good portion of life on this planet on September 26, 1983, had it not been for one Lieutenant Colonel Stanislav Petrov, who happened to be the duty officer at the Serpukhov-15 early-warning center south of Moscow. During the first hours of that day Petrov had to decide what to do about successive alarms indicating that America had launched five Minuteman missiles from Montana toward Mother Russia. More than thirty reliability checks in Serpukhov-15 confirmed the attack was indeed taking place.

Petrov, however, trusted his intuition and ignored the warnings that the Apocalypse was approaching him at three miles a second. "I was drenched in sweat," the Soviet officer recalled. "People were shouting, the siren was blaring. But a feeling inside told me something was wrong." He guessed, correctly, that the Americans would not begin Armageddon in such a modest fashion. As it turned out, Soviet sensors aboard satellite Kosmos 1382 misinterpreted sunlight reflecting off the tops of clouds as incoming missiles. His co-workers congratulated him. An inquiry did not. Stanislav Petrov was disciplined for a technicality, and he left the military soon afterward.

The lieutenant colonel's caution buttresses the Waltzian notion that nuclear arms may never be used. Yet it's nonetheless troubling that the only thing that prevented mass annihilation was one soldier's instinct—what Petrov later called "a funny feeling in my gut." It was not actually Comrade Stanislav's turn to stand duty that day; he was sitting in for a friend. What would have happened if that other officer, perhaps one less experienced or more dutiful, was on watch?

The Petrov incident is the closest that the world has come to accidental nuclear war, but it is not the only time. In January 1995 Boris Yeltsin received his nuclear launch codes and had to decide whether to retaliate when America and Norway sent up a rocket to study the Northern Lights: a snafu in Moscow resulted in a failure to forward the advance notice of the weather rocket to the appropriate military command.

Americans, for their part, have put their strategic nuclear forces on highest alert after confusing migratory birds as incoming missiles, sent bombers halfway to the Soviet Union on false alarms, inadvertently run a test tape of a Soviet nuclear attack on Tampa and then confused the simulation as the real thing (during the Cuban Missile Crisis, no less), and accidentally launched a nuclear warhead when a maintenance worker dropped a tool inside a silo in Arkansas. The sad fact is that, whatever one may think about the rationality of states and statesmen, nuclear weapons are under the control of "imperfect humans inside imperfect organizations."

And some of those organizations are getting even less perfect. Soviet early-warning equipment has deteriorated over time, making Russia's system even more unreliable than it was in Petrov's era. About a third of the Russian horizon now lacks satellite coverage of missile launches, which leaves the country more vulnerable to false signals. Russia's nuclear missiles have become undependable due to many factors, including lack of maintenance. "We escaped disaster by the grace of God," said General George Lee Butler, commander of the Air Force's nuclear weapons before his retirement in 1994. And since then, the risk of unintended nuclear conflict has only increased.

"We know, with the certainty of statistical truth, that if enough of these weapons are made — by enough different states — some of them are going to blow up," said C. P. Snow in 1960. "Through accident, or folly, or madness — but the motives don't matter. What does matter is the nature of the statistical fact." The English novelist and physicist predicted that within a decade there would be a detonation of a nuclear device somewhere in the world. He was wrong about the timing, of course, but that doesn't necessarily discredit his underlying thesis. Even if new nuclear powers are more careful than the older ones — and how could they be any less? — the law of averages, and the law that made Murphy famous, do not leave room for optimism. In some fashion and at some time something is bound to go horribly wrong.

Unfortunately, things can go bad even if no spectacular explosions, accidental or otherwise, disrupt this planet. In the Cold War the two superpowers learned, albeit slowly, that nuclear arms were useful only for deterrence. Today, these "gizmos of mass destruction" hasten fragmentation of world order. Why did America attack Iraq in 2003 and leave a much larger danger in North Korea unattended? There were, as always, many reasons, but one of them was deterrence: Pyongyang was already a nuclear power and Baghdad was not. If Saddam Hussein had attacked Kuwait *after* he had built his first bomb, he might have been able to keep his conquest.

Some suggest he could have grabbed the Saudi oil fields as well. In any event, Washington would have been forced to try all other means, perhaps including a policy of engagement, to deal with him.

There is one essential rule for today's tyrants in training: "Don't fight the United States unless you have nuclear weapons." The corollary is even more important: "If you have nuclear weapons, the United States won't fight you." In other words, a bomb is the ultimate equalizer, or to borrow today's lingo, it's the last word in "force multipliers." It gives any miscreant in a leadership role at least an opportunity, and sometimes a free pass, to indulge unruly passions.

As tyrants, terrorists, and thugs get their hands on the ultimate weapon, when the malevolent can act with impunity, we can be sure that the world will be different, and, as unjust as it now is, it will undoubtedly be worse. Hence, all of us would be safer with fewer nuclear arms in the world. It may be our fate that more nations will possess them, but it's hard to see how we will be more secure if they do.

The Second Nuclear Age

Geopolitics abhors a monopoly. America's sole possession of nuclear weaponry lasted less than a half decade. Soon after the Soviet Union tested its atomic bomb in 1949 Britain followed suit in 1952. Then France and China joined the "nuclear club" in the first half of the 1960s.

Global anti-proliferation efforts apparently worked well from 1964, the year of China's first test, until almost the end of the last century. During this period the United States, in conjunction with others, stopped weapons programs in some countries, such as South Korea and Taiwan, and convinced the former Soviet republics of Ukraine, Belarus, and Kazakhstan to give up arsenals inherited on the breakup of the USSR. South Africa first built and then voluntarily dismantled six nuclear bombs. In 1960 John Kennedy said that by 1964 there could be as many as twenty nuclear states. That prediction, which seemed so reasonable at the time, proved far off the mark: by the middle of the 1960s there were only five nuclear powers.

If anything, we should feel relieved that the world has avoided the uncontrolled spread of the bomb. And perhaps we have shown that, despite pessimism surrounding the weaponization of the atom, the community of nations can collectively deal with its most important challenges. Stopping the spread of the ultimate instrument of destruction constitutes "the supreme test" of our age to come together and act in concert.

But let's hold our applause. Unless one subscribes to Kenneth Waltz's line of reasoning that "more is better," the future looks decidedly worse. Most of today's trends, unfortunately, promise to accelerate proliferation from this point forward.

During the "second nuclear age," as Yale's Paul Bracken calls the post–Cold War period, there is one fewer conservative superpower to prevent the spread of nukes, and Moscow has become one more source of arms technology and fissile material. At the same time, many smallish nations, fortified by newfound wealth generated by economic development, seek to establish their place in the world hierarchy after decades of suffering foreign rule or domination. A nuclear weapon is often seen as the best means of assuring national security—a device of this sort is the only way to counter the conventional arms superiority of Western nations. As Charles de Gaulle once said, "No country without an atom bomb could properly consider itself independent." And as important, a nuke permits the angry and the weak to assert national pride. It is, after all, the ultimate badge of "big guy" status in the world.

In 1974 India successfully earned its big-guy badge by testing a "peaceful nuclear explosive." Because the device was not called a "bomb," the rest of the world, apart from New Delhi's enemies Pakistan and China, pretended that the Indians had not in reality become a nuclear weapon state. Nonetheless, the test marked the beginning of "the Age of Proliferation." In that new age America and the West, navigating the tricky politics of the Cold War, had let other concerns come ahead of nuclear proliferation. Moreover, the United States and its allies demonstrated more than a touch of complacency.

In any event, Washington had no Cold War excuse in 1998 when, within weeks of each other, India and Pakistan tested nuclear weapons. New Delhi and Islamabad defied the world—and nothing happened. As in 1974, America appeared dazed by the news. The most serious challenge to global security went unanswered, as if the world's strongest powers were unable—or unwilling—to defend their most vital interests, not to mention the interests of all of humanity.

The failure had consequences. Pakistan sold its nuclear technology to

North Korea and the Arab world through the nuclear black market ring masterminded by Dr. A. Q. Khan. It was almost as if Islamabad was trying to disprove Kenneth Waltz's optimistic theory that nuclear weapons always make leaders cautious. We now know that possession of these arms does not necessarily make countries responsible; it just makes them more able to accomplish what they set out to do.

And thus more troublesome. Today, the biggest of the big guys has gone all out in trying to stop the spread of nuclear weaponry. The Iraq War was not just about Iraq. "Iraq was the first 'counterproliferation' war," writes Bill Keller of *The New York Times*. It was not so much a war as a beginning of a revolution—an abandonment of multilateralism and collective security, which had become the basis of the world's geopolitical religion. The failure so far to find Saddam's weapons of mass destruction is almost irrelevant because the conflict was intended to show the newfound resolve of the United States to stop the spread of atomic munitions.

As John Bolton, then the State Department's top arms control official, said, "We are hopeful that a number of regimes will draw the appropriate lesson from Iraq that the pursuit of weapons of mass destruction is not in their national interest." Those regimes, however, think that Bolton does not have their best interests at heart and that it *is* indeed to their advantage to possess nuclear arms. "The West promotes nonproliferation as reflecting the interests of all nations in international order and stability," writes Harvard's Samuel Huntington. "Other nations, however, see nonproliferation as serving the interests of Western hegemony."

Western hegemonists indeed benefited from the peace and stability of the Pax Americana of the post–Cold War period, but so has most everyone else. Third World nations might think they can better their lot if they acquire nuclear weapons and ballistic missiles—history since 1945 shows that countries covet these instruments of destruction—but everyone will ultimately lose when proliferation fragments global power. After all, the last century's two eras without a superpower produced two wars of unprecedented devastation.

Third World assertion, unfortunately, has prevented the world's only superpower from stopping the spread of the bomb. For all its strength the United States has had to move from nonproliferation to counterproliferation, as the Iraq War shows. America has even accommodated proliferation by remaining quiet about the Israeli bomb and meekly accepting Indian and Pakistani membership in the nuclear club. Finally, Washington, as a means of countering China's nuclear assistance to Pakistan and North Korea, is now agreeing to proliferate dual-use technologies to India. "The proliferation of nuclear and other weapons of mass destruction is a central phenomenon of the slow but ineluctable diffusion of power in a multicivilizational world," Huntington argues.

In our world with many civilizations, countries have nonetheless found common cause and joined hands. At last count there were 188 signatories to the Treaty on the Non-Proliferation of Nuclear Weapons, which went into force in 1970. That's all but four nations in existence today. Only India, Pakistan, and Israel are holdouts, and North Korea is the sole dropout. The pact's goal—the complete elimination of nuclear arms—is one of the most popular causes among the peoples of this planet.

The NPT is built on an unstable foundation, however. Its signatories are divided into two classes. Pursuant to the treaty, five nations—the United States, Russia, Britain, France, and China—are permitted to possess nuclear weapons. The rest do not have them—or at least are not supposed to. The first group, which coincidentally holds the five permanent seats on the U.N. Security Council, promised in Article VI of the treaty to work toward complete and final disarmament. In 1995 they reaffirmed that cosmetic—but nonetheless optically critical—pledge when the NPT, which first became effective for a term of twenty-five years, was extended indefinitely.

Since 1970 these five nuclear weapon states have shown little inclination to disarm. There have been reductions of stockpiles from Cold War levels, but the cutbacks would have occurred in any event due to the end of the superpower rivalry. The real test of the NPT is whether the five powers will honor their pledge to disarm.

From the perspective of today the prospects for disarmament do not look good. The United States, in particular, has shown a disregard, and sometimes even contempt, for its promise to give up its weapons. It was, for example, the only nation to vote against the Comprehensive Nuclear Test Ban Treaty in the U.N. and now is leading efforts to gut a treaty that would end the production of material for nuclear armaments. Worse, the Bush administration wants to develop a whole new generation of so-called usable nuclear weapons or "mini-nukes," such as "robust nuclear earth penetrators," or "bunker busters." The creation of these arms has triggered complaints of warmongering—"boutique bombs" lower the threshold for the use of nuclear weapons—as well as protests against American hypocrisy. Moreover, George Bush's Washington has threatened to use nukes against nonnuclear countries, a clear violation of America's 1995 global pledge. The United States specifically made that promise to nonnuke states to induce them to indefinitely extend the NPT.

In truth, the current Bush administration has never much liked treaties, which in its view are relics of an old era and have outlived their usefulness. It is better that America relies on its power to protect its security interests, or at least that's how current thinking goes. As policy wonks Ivo Daalder and James Lindsay have written, the American Gulliver is intent on shedding the restraints that he had helped the Lilliputians weave since the end of the Second World War.

So far, the members of the lower tier of the nonproliferation treaty's caste system have accepted their position largely because of their abhorrence of the bomb—the so-called nuclear taboo. There are, however, signs that "nuclear apartheid" won't last much longer. Kim Jong Il, by obtaining what he wants with nuke threats, is shredding the argument that atomic weapons have no value and reinforcing the notion that the NPT is disadvantageous for states without them. Moreover, there are just too many complaints from the have-nots to believe they will continue with an arrangement that leaves them on the wrong end of the great divide.

Countries are beginning to reframe the global discussion away from the aversion to these weapons, focusing instead on the discriminatory nature of the nonproliferation regime. When even more nations talk this way, the world's arms control structure, which already looks shaky, could disintegrate. The global nonproliferation treaty works only as long as nations believe in it. Once a few of them no longer do so, it will undoubtedly crumble. Countries now refrain from building nukes because they don't want them, not because they lack the ability. Unfortunately, the secrets of the atom have become, as the Iranians are fond of telling us, "a local technology." Mohamed ElBaradei, the head of the IAEA, estimates that forty nations or more could develop nuclear weapons within a few years' time.

Unfortunately, the disincentives for nuclearization are getting weaker—after all, the new nuclear states have escaped punishment—while the incentives are stronger as nations seek to defend themselves against the North Koreas of the world. Kim Jong Il's defiance of arms control norms, therefore, could move the international community to an age of rapid proliferation. We are, to borrow a phrase, approaching a nuclear tipping point.

At that point just one more country going nuclear would spell the end of the global pact. A collapse of the accord could be a problem, despite the Bush administration's instinctive disdain for treaties. An end to the NPT would obviously open the door to accelerated, and probably sustained, proliferation as some countries would realize their nuclear aspirations and others would rush to catch up with newly nuclearized neighbors.

Of course, even in the absence of a treaty, many countries would not bother to make bombs and some that would are not threats to world stability. So far, proliferation has taken place in slow motion over decades, giving the world time to accommodate new nuclear states. Apparently many think that a few more of them, even ones led by unpredictable leaders of dubious character, is not such a big deal. Call it complacency or fatalism, but the generally prevailing assumptions are that proliferation will be gradual and that the international system will not change much. After all, it is not foreordained that the worst possible outcome will actually occur.

Pessimists have been wrong before. Humanity has not yet, in Ronald Reagan's phrase, perished "in a hail of fiery atoms." But are we prepared to accept the consequences if the optimists are not correct this time? If we are entering a new global order, the West needs to be prepared for dozens of new nuclear powers, with some of them being hostile and unstable. In this dangerous environment, the American-led global order will undoubtedly disintegrate. Should that in fact happen, humankind will probably head into a period of prolonged conflict. We have to remember that in Aesop's fable the wolf does eventually show up. The bomb, in short, may be civilization's last weapon.

The Domino Duo

Syria, Egypt, Saudi Arabia, Algeria, and South Korea all appear to be pursuing nuclear weapons—albeit with varying degrees of rapidity and determination—and Brazil is laying the groundwork to restart its nuclear weapons program. Some of these countries have made sustained progress, but none of them is as close to actually weaponizing the atom as the unstable theocracy of Iran.

The mullahs say their efforts are peaceful, but it's hard to believe their assertions. In August 2003 the IAEA announced that its inspectors had found traces of highly enriched uranium at a newly constructed nuclear facility in Natanz, two hundred miles south of Tehran. Other Iranian plants were also found to be contaminated with bomb-grade uranium particles. The Iranians at first said that the traces came from imported components, but that explanation could not be squared with previous assertions that their program was entirely homegrown. Then they professed not to know where the contaminated equipment originally came from.

Iranian officials say they want more electric energy. Yet oil-rich Iran does not need uranium to generate power, its planned heavy water reactor that will produce plutonium is too small for economically making electricity and too large for conducting research, and its longest-range missiles are not suited for conventional warheads. In violation of their NPT obligations the Iranians hid whole facilities from IAEA inspectors and used the notorious A. Q. Khan black market ring to obtain all the technology needed for a bomb. They have stalled IAEA investigators, lied to them, and changed their story when it became clear they had fibbed. They told the truth about their nuclear program only when they had no alternative. In 2005 the Iranians admitted that their plans to enrich uranium were not commercially justifiable and turned down Europe's offer to provide a proliferation-resistant light water reactor if they would stop building one suitable for a weapons program. The country claims the right to possess nuclear arms to defend itself against Israel. There is only one explanation that fits known facts: for two decades Tehran has been trying to build the bomb.

There is, however, no consensus as to when the mullahs' technicians will be able to deliver a weapon. Some analysts believe the Iranians will not be able to do so until 2015—and others think it could happen as early as 2007 or 2008. The best assessments indicate that Tehran will join the nuclear club sometime at the end of this decade. In any event, it is evident that Iran has built the infrastructure necessary for bomb production. According to American intelligence reports, its technicians have only one more critical engineering problem to overcome: the rotors on their centrifuges come apart when spun at the high speeds necessary to enrich uranium. Once they find the solution, the "atomic ayatollahs" will be able to produce both lowly enriched uranium to turn the lights on and highly enriched uranium to permanently put them out.

Iran, therefore, is about to become the classic "bomb in the basement" country: a nation that has stopped just short of producing nuclear weapons but could deploy them in days or weeks once a decision is made. India and Pakistan, previous basement-bomb states, were never members of the global nonproliferation treaty. Iran, however, is. That pact, however, is as much of a help as a hindrance to Iran's weaponization. The NPT's basic bargain is assistance with peaceful applications of nuclear technology in return for promises not to militarize the atom. A determined government could take the help from the IAEA and develop a bomb out of the sight of the international community. That is, after all, what North Korea did until it dropped out of the NPT in 2003—by then it certainly had all it needed to produce an arsenal—and what Iran is now doing. Peaceful uranium-enrichment programs, unfortunately, are just a "couple turns of the screw" from covert ones that create warheads.

To no one's surprise, President Bush announced a plan to prevent the IAEA from being used as the help desk for weapons developers. In early 2004 he proposed closing what he termed a "loophole" by not permitting the export of nuclear fuel to states unless they renounced the right to enrich uranium and reprocess plutonium. He also wanted to prevent the export of enrichment and reprocessing equipment and technologies to nations that did not then have full-scale and functioning enrichment or reprocessing facilities. In short, Bush wanted to establish a fundamentally new arms control regime by taking away nuclear technology from non-nuclear states. In return, he offered them essentially nothing. Mohamed ElBaradei came up with a slightly more generous plan a little later, but it too was a dead-on-arrival idea.

We don't know what a new arms control regime will look like, but it is clear that the second-class citizens of the NPT are not going to accept a further erosion of their status. Iran has said that it will not do so, and neither will countries like Brazil, which want their own enrichment facilities. The desire to possess them is uneconomic—the world is awash in fissile material as it is—but the impulse is understandable. To many nations, the last half of the twentieth century was not defined by the Cold War but by the struggle to end the great European empires. Bush, who speaks so passionately about personal freedom, should understand the ardent desire for national self-sufficiency, which is considered akin to independence.

The West may be able, through one means or another, to slow down the proliferation of the world's most destructive weaponry, but it appears unable to stop it altogether. Yet it will have to do so if it wants to have a future. The control of nuclear arms and fissile material is the most important task facing the American-led world order. If Washington and its allies should fail in this grand endeavor, nothing else may matter. As Hassan Abassi, a senior member of Iran's increasingly influential Revolutionary Guards, said, "We have a strategy drawn up for the destruction of Anglo-Saxon civilization and for the uprooting of the Americans and the English."

Abassi's words sound like a hollow boast, but Tehran is nonetheless hostile to the West and undoubtedly has a strategy to win acceptance as the next nuclear power. Yet whether the unstable theocracy of Iran ultimately achieves that recognition may not be determined in the Middle East. Tehran has instructed its diplomats to find out what Washington will do about the events in Northeast Asia. The first question they ask is, "How will Washington handle North Korea?"

As the invasion of Iraq was not just about Iraq, American policy toward Korea is not just about Korea. Korea is also about Iran, Syria, Algeria, and every other state that wants an atomic arsenal. Never being NPT signatories, India, Pakistan, and Israel became nuclear powers outside the world's nonproliferation regime, but the DPRK is the first country to nuclearize inside it. The precedent could not be worse. Kim Jong Il's flouting of nonproliferation rules has shown that the world's greatest powers are helpless when it comes to dealing with the greatest threat to the world. An international system that cannot protect its most fundamental interest against one of its weakest members cannot last.

So what happens when despotic leaders possess humankind's most destructive weaponry? North Korea and Iran are situated in two of the three most dangerous geopolitical neighborhoods on the planet. History shows that once one nation goes nuclear, its enemies consider building bombs of their own. In a period when the world order is changing and the nonproliferation treaty is already weakened, the chain reaction of nuclearization promises to be quick. If Pyongyang is not disarmed, Japan probably will build its own arsenal. China, which perceives Japan as a rival, will react by adding to its own stockpile, and that will push India, China's adversary, to follow suit. Pakistan, India's enemy, then will have no choice but to match India's buildup. And worst of all, Tehran will see a green light for its own bomb-building program. "What is the problem with withdrawing from the Nuclear Nonproliferation Treaty?" asks Ayatollah Ahmad Jannati, the leader of Iran's powerful Guardian Council. "North Korea withdrew from the treaty."

So if the major powers cannot stop Pyongyang, there is probably little point in continuing the NPT, even if it can somehow be maintained. Therefore, the success or failure in creating a lasting geopolitical order for this century begins with the world's response to Kim's blatant challenge. Analysts tend to discuss North Korea as if this isolated nation were an isolated problem. Would that this were so. Unfortunately, North Korea is where the world's nonproliferation regime could finally collapse. "The 'domino theory' of the 21st century may well be nuclear," said George Tenet when he headed the CIA. "We have entered a new world of proliferation."

No responsible nation would ultimately benefit from fast proliferation and a consequent breakdown of global order. All countries have a stake in the outcome of the ongoing crisis on the Korean peninsula—and so does each failing state and terrorist group. Everything is on the line in North Korea. This is where the world writes its history for the next hundred years.

LAST EXIT BEFORE THE DARK AGES

What the World Should Do Now

We have it in our power to begin the world over again.
—Ronald Reagan

"I believe there is no problem that can't be solved through dialogue," said South Korea's Kim Dae Jung in the last days of his presidency. "If both sides are genuine and serious," proclaimed Kim Jong Il, "there is nothing we will not be able to do." With so much good will flowing on the Korean peninsula, why has there been no solution to the nuclear crisis?

In a perfect world all international disagreements, no matter how intractable, could be settled by discussion and debate. Yet for two decades North Korea's friends and adversaries have cajoled, threatened, and negotiated with Pyongyang over its atomic arms programs. Talks have been bilateral and multilateral, formal and informal. They have been conducted in Asia, Europe, and North America, in neutral settings and in the capitals of the participants. Every conceivable format has been tried at least once. Yet negotiations have not prevented the DPRK from acquiring the capability to manufacture nuclear weapons and the means to deliver them.

Perhaps the world has not tried hard enough to reach out to the North Koreans—or maybe it has tried too hard. Whichever is true, it is evident that no one has found the right formula to talk the Kimist regime out of its armaments.

Today, members of the international community—and especially the United States—have placed their hopes on the six-party negotiations in Beijing. These discussions, unfortunately, have resulted in no discernible progress toward disarming the regime.

The past may or may not provide lessons for the future, but it does show that some disputes are not resolved without death in great numbers. And the never-ending North Korean nuclear crisis is beginning to look like one of them. The Bush administration talks about a peaceful resolution but is rushing ahead with its costly missile defense system and is seeking authorization for a whole new generation of nukes. One interpretation of these events is that Bush is resigned to a nuclear North Korea. He is not, however, known for fatalism. So perhaps he is preparing for conflict. Is there anything the world can do to defang the DPRK short of the ultimate tragedy of war?

Extreme Dream

The world, if it wants, can disarm militant North Korea. If Kim Jong Il saw that every president and prime minister demanded the surrender of his weapons, he would have little choice but to comply. The international community might have to cut off aid, boycott his products, encourage the flight of North Koreans, and blockade the coasts. Nations might even have to threaten to use overwhelming force. In the face of a united world, Pyongyang would probably bend and voluntarily turn over its nuclear arms. It's unlikely that calculating Kim, intent on keeping power, would lash out in suicidal rage. North Korea, by one means or another, would eventually be disarmed. In short, unanimity would promote a stable peace.

The fact that Mr. Kim still brandishes his weapons means the world is not so single-minded. Nations, including the DPRK, may say they want to "denuclearize the Korean peninsula," but agreement stops there. Even among those who side with Washington, there is no shared sense of what to do and no common perception of urgency.

Moreover, many countries do not agree with American goals in the first place. The global nonproliferation treaty, which permits only a few states to have nukes, freezes the military advantage of a select group. Although the concept of controlling nuclear arms enjoys wide support around the world, the discriminatory nature of the arms control regime does not. When Kim Jong Il proposes to turn the six-party negotiations in Beijing into mutual "disarmament talks" he is undoubtedly insincere, but he is nonetheless allying himself with a generally popular cause. By saying it is unfair for the United States to develop nuclear weapons for offensive purposes and not permit its adversaries to possess them for defense, he is tapping into an argument that resonates in most quarters of the planet, especially after the politicization of the ongoing conflict in Iraq. Today, it's clear that most nations do not like America's counterproliferation initiatives.

Despite the apparent unpopularity of their methods, some Americans say that the 2003 Iraq invasion serves as a model for future disarmament efforts. It is true that Baghdad will not be a nuclear threat for a long time — and neither will Tripoli. The Iraq War undoubtedly had a large role in convincing Colonel Mohammar Qaddafi to drop his atomic arms program. Yet his decision was due as much to long-standing multilateral sanctions and international diplomacy as muscular American policy. Moreover, the disarming of Libya was partially the result of the mercurial nature of Qaddafi, who can change his mind as fast as he switches costumes and eyewear. Leaders of other nations that seek the bomb appear much more determined than Tripoli's strange strongman.

Like Kim Jong Il, for instance. The United States now has the raw power to take away his weapons but for various reasons will not use force. Even if there is a military solution in this case — and most analysts think none of them is practical — Americans cannot forcibly disarm every nation that wants a doomsday arsenal. The continual waging of war will first isolate and then exhaust America and would not be acceptable to the rest of the world in any event. Furthermore, the ability of the United States to resort to military solutions will erode over time, especially as the rest of the world catches up with it.

The eventual decrease in American power means that Washington should be looking for solutions that do not involve force. While it still can, the United States needs to build an international system where other nations *want* to help—as opposed to being *coerced* into doing so or refusing altogether. "We are in a race between cooperation and catastrophe," said former Senator Sam Nunn. "To win this race, we have to achieve cooperation on a scale we've never seen or attempted before."

So how does America create cooperation of that magnitude? Let's start with what won't work. Efforts like the current ones are obviously not the answer, as the successive nuclearization of India, Pakistan, and North Korea demonstrates. Flat-out telling other countries that they can't have nuclear weapons only increases the desire for them. President Bush's latest proposal to enlist others against the spread of crucial nuclear technologies is in fact going nowhere. Countries won't support a plan that asks them to give up a lot for nothing in return. Oft-heard suggestions—cracking down on nuclear black market rings, stepping up IAEA inspections, enacting laws to criminalize proliferation—are only recipes for postponing failure rather than achieving success. They can slow the spread of armaments during uneventful times but cannot stop the rapid disintegration of the nonproliferation regime during a transition to a fundamentally different era as far as nuclear weapons are concerned—in other words, when the world is on the verge of crisis.

To avoid crisis during a period of transition, America may have to employ "transformational diplomacy," to borrow Condoleezza Rice's buzz phrase. What would completely turn the tables on the North Koreans and all the others who want to wield the ultimate weapon? In a contest decided by legitimacy and credibility as much as power, the United States may have to take a giant first step and honor the obligations it undertook in the nonproliferation treaty to seek the elimination of nuclear weapons—*its own* as well as others'.

For many, disarmament is simply not possible because nuclear weapons cannot be "uninvented" and we cannot repeal $E = mc^2$. Yet these indisputable assertions do not mean these arms can't be scrapped if abolition found a powerful sponsor. At least at this moment, what Washington says matters. In a world of wants, there is a lot it can give—or take away—to bring about the end of nuclear terror. Moreover, the task is not impossible. The world, after all, came close to destroying its nukes even during the

Cold War: Ronald Reagan almost clinched a complete disarmament deal with Gorbachev at their summit in Reykjavík in 1986.

But why would the United States, which possesses the most robust nuclear arsenal today, ever want to get rid of its weapons? Simply because no country would benefit more from worldwide disarmament than the American colossus. America may be the strongest nation in history, but neither size nor strength matters that much in a nuclear weapons world. Any country with just one bomb can indefinitely stalemate a superpower. Any terrorist with uranium can incinerate America's cities, destroy its economy, paralyze society, kill millions. And, of course, end Washington's role atop the world order for generations. Why would America not do everything it can to eliminate the only threat to its existence? Today there is no conceivable combination of foreign conventional forces that matches the Pentagon's, so the United States would essentially be unchallengeable and invulnerable in a no-nuke world. By giving up their most destructive weapon, Americans would, paradoxically, become even more powerful.

Of course, disarmament is not possible in George W. Bush's Washington. The current administration is, as noted, generally hostile to arms control treaties and wants to develop a new generation of tactical nukes. Yet by hoping to build even more of them, Bush bolsters the legitimacy of using the only class of weapons that poses an existential threat to the United States. This appears to be just one more illustration of state-sponsored folly. "A phenomenon noticeable throughout history regardless of place or period is the pursuit by governments of policies contrary to their own interests," wrote Barbara Tuchman. Americans, even after Bush's term, may never entertain disarmament—at least until they lose a city to nuclear terrorism.

Or to a North Korean warhead. Kim Jong Il will soon be able to land a nuke anywhere in America. To stop him, the superpower will need the help of its foes as well as its friends. Elimination of nuclear stockpiles around the world would not persuade Kim to give up his small arsenal—he would undoubtedly like to be the only leader with his finger on a button—but it would create the desire, and even the urgency, on the part of other nations to disarm him. Who, after all, would want to leave Chairman Kim in charge of humanity? With global momentum against him and without external support, the North Korean would have little alternative but to allow weapons inspectors to tread where even food monitors cannot now go. Except during the Korean War, the DPRK has never been more dependent on outsiders than it is today. That provides a historic opportunity to overwhelm North Korea.

The United States does not need to achieve complete abolition—or even arrive at an agreement with others to do so—to build worldwide momentum against North Korea's nuclear program. It may be sufficient if America unilaterally scraps a large portion of its own weapons.

The counterintuitive aspect of this tactic—creating a global wave against North Korea—is that it carries virtually no cost for the United States. American planners want to reduce the size of the nation's strategic nuclear force anyway, as it is far larger than necessary to counter existing threats. The Pentagon's stockpile is so big and well protected that elimination of most of its nukes would have no discernible effect on either the nation's security or its ability to protect allies. The arsenal, even after a substantial reduction, could still survive a first strike by another nation, for instance. More than half of America's warheads are carried on ballistic missile submarines, which are undetectable when submerged. Each "boomer"—the United States Navy has about nine of them on patrol at any one time and fourteen altogether—is permitted under existing arms control rules to carry the destructive power of 1,536 Hiroshimas. Just one of a sub's twenty-four missiles can make Central America uninhabitable for 150 years. The American president can give the order to eliminate all human life on this planet several times over. If he decides to reduce his arsenal so that he can kill everyone only once, are his constituents any less safe?

Yet they will certainly be in greater danger if proliferation continues. Over time, every nation that wants the bomb will get the bomb. Eventually, terrorists will get their hands on a nuclear device. Straight-line extrapolations are often wrong, but these are so compelling. As even Henry Kissinger admitted about proliferation at the end of 2004, "Now we are in a world in which there is no end-game."

Our world is on the brink of an age more perilous than any other period in history, including the first two decades of the Cold War. It is comforting to think that we will be able to meet tomorrow's challenges with yesterday's approaches, but too much has changed since the end of the superpower rivalry. Conventional diplomacy got us into this tight spot, so it's unlikely that conventional thinking will save us. "There are times in history when the middle way does not work any more," says a Bush administration official concerned about the lack of options regarding North Korea's nukes. "We have worked our way into that."

To obtain security in a far less structured environment, the existing nuclear powers will probably have to cooperate with one another and give something up. Disarmament may seem like an extreme dream, but there is no known alternative that is assured of preventing dozens of new nuclear states, some of them with links to terrorists, and the almost certain disintegration of global order. We have a good idea what the world will look like if nothing new is done.

As insurance giant AIG says, "The greatest risk is not taking one." At no time has humankind taken a risk and surrendered its most powerful weapons. For many, it is hard to believe that nations will ever consider giving up their nukes. Americans in particular may reject disarmament, but then they must be prepared to live in the most dangerous world imaginable. They can have nuclear weapons or New York. In the long run, it's unlikely they will be able to keep both.

The Land of Lousy Options

In the short term, we all hope the world unites to peacefully disarm the DPRK. The United States, however, does not need to build a grand coalition or even cooperate with any other nation in order to stop Kim Jong Il. It has, at least at this moment, the military power to end the North Korean state. It would not be as much a policy of regime change as regime obliteration. "We don't negotiate with evil," said Vice President Dick Cheney, "we defeat it." Destroying evil, despite what pacifists and pragmatists may say, is always a defensible moral choice.

And no country today presents a more compelling case for "humanitarian intervention"—a polite term for the use of force—than the Democratic People's Republic of Korea. Our "duty to protect" North Koreans is derived not so much from Pyongyang's butchery and torture of them as from government policies that condemn large numbers to death. Any regime that intentionally lets hundreds of thousands and perhaps millions perish when it has the means to save them should not be allowed to exist. Kim Jong Il does not exterminate great numbers in gas chambers, but his policies, both during the famine of the 1990s and today, have resulted and continue to result in mass loss of life. Kim exhibits less organization and efficiency than the leaders of the Third Reich, but those deficiencies seem of no moral consequence in comparing their respective crimes.

If nations have a moral obligation to intervene to relieve the suffering of the North Korean people, how can we legitimize the source of their misery? By merely talking to his agents we tend to bolster Kim Jong Il's rule, as much as we would like to think that we do not. The world has yet to hear, whether from diplomat or aid worker, a convincing justification, on moral grounds, for cooperation with the DPRK.

Take Madeleine Albright, for instance. She has said it was acceptable for her to converse with Kim Jong Il in 2000 because America had talked to Stalin. That is, however, not much of a defense. One is tempted to reply that America made a mistake before and she merely committed another one—with hers being worse because she had the benefit of hindsight.

Yet mistake or not, America is again negotiating with evil, or at least the most hideous, barbaric, and dictatorial regime in existence today. Bush, understandably, shows little enthusiasm for these discussions, but he has no attractive alternative. As Washington defense analyst Kurt Campbell notes, "Korea is the land of lousy options."

Or no options other than China's. In September 2005 the Bush administration did something it said it would never do: it accepted the possibility of a nuclear energy program for North Korea. Such a program was the linchpin of a Beijing-sponsored joint statement, which set out a road map for the continuation of the six-party talks. The United States approved the statement because it essentially had no choice. Chinese negotiators presented their plan on a take-it-or-leave-it basis and told their American counterparts that they would publicly blame them if they rejected the deal. Having prevailed once, Beijing will, in all probability, again employ these strong-arm tactics—usual for negotiations of this sort—against Washington. The question for the Bush administration is how it can regain the initiative in the six-party deliberations.

The answer: America will have to become more ambitious. To keep the North Koreans off balance—Bush's impressive achievement so far—Washington should put all issues on the table such as the return of the Japanese and South Korean abductees, improvement of the human rights of the North Korean people, China's forced repatriation of Korean refugees, Pyongyang's continuing detention of prisoners from the Korean War, the DPRK's drug running and counterfeiting, its possession of chemical and biological weapons, its missile testing and sales, and the deployment of the North's armed forces near the DMZ. Raising these issues puts Pyongyang on the defensive.

And shames its supporters in Beijing, Moscow, and Seoul. Although adding new problems will initially complicate the talks, this maneuver, by highlighting indefensible North Korean conduct, may ultimately hasten a solution by weakening the support that other governments can extend to the Kim regime. Moreover, Chinese and North Korean diplomats say they want a comprehensive settlement, so raising all outstanding issues, even at this late date in the talks, is an appropriate thing to do. The DPRK poses many challenges to world order, and it's unlikely that any of them will be solved if the West flinches by pursuing piecemeal solutions.

It may not matter what approach the West takes, however, because the North Koreans might reject all reasonable proposals at the six-party talks. The Kims, as misguided as they have been on strategic issues, are not dullards on the tactical ones and have avoided deals that are bad for their longevity. The family regime, over more than a half century, has staked out many extreme positions. To compromise on the most important of them would be self-delegitimizing. Therefore, the current Kim is not about to sign on to a plan that might, in the words of analyst Michael O'Hanlon, be "a form of assisted suicide."

If Kim continues to refuse to disarm, he will make it clear that he's the one at fault for the current deadlock in the six-party talks. Among other things, the North Korean has not agreed to rigorous inspections, the condition America insists on. In the early 1990s Kim the Elder had to trigger a crisis to prevent discoveries of undeclared plutonium, and Kim the Younger was forced to do the same thing in 2002 to avoid inspections pursuant to the existing safeguards agreement, as required by the much maligned Agreed Framework. The demand for the strictest inspections regime in history is reasonable in light of Pyongyang's past cheating, and Lil' Kim now looks insincere when he says that he cannot tolerate inspectors in his country.

Now that Washington is offering real incentives to Pyongyang to disarm, the North Korean leader will have to make a historic decision. If he makes the wrong one, Americans will need to be realistic about what they can accomplish in any further negotiations. Since 2002 no amount of bad-boy behavior in Pyongyang has persuaded China to sign on to a policy of sanctions or tough measures. An increasingly assertive Beijing under leader Hu Jintao has been consistently supportive of the DPRK despite the strains in their bilateral relationship.

The Chinese leader has been able to protect Kim Jong Il because South Korean president Roh Moo-hyun, nominally America's ally, wants to do the same thing. As a result, the Chinese pay almost no price for backing the DPRK. So while everyone says that China is the key to a negotiated deal, the key to China is South Korea. Stripping Seoul from the Beijing-Pyongyang axis should be Washington's most immediate tactical goal in the six-party talks.

And the key to doing that is influencing the badly divided public in the lower half of the Korean peninsula. The election to pick Roh's successor is scheduled for December 2007. At present, the Grand National Party's Park Geun Hye, the politically savvy daughter of former strongman Park Chung Hee, can win that race. Given the growing numbers of younger voters, 2007 will undoubtedly be the last election in the next two decades where a conservative can take over the Blue House. The White House between now and then can help Park's party by making Kim Jong Il look bad, thereby discrediting the "progressive" forces in the South. And America can do that best by making even more attractive proposals to solve the nuclear crisis and having Kim turn them down.

If Washington can help South Korea reverse course, the Chinese will be alone in their support of Pyongyang and will, therefore, have to take a clear stand. They will have to choose between their future, cooperation with the United States, and their past, the alliance with the DPRK.

America can help Beijing make the correct choice, but there are limits on what it should do. To begin with, America cannot agree to abandon Taiwan if China gives up North Korea, as the Chinese have repeatedly suggested. That deal, which envisions the destruction of an emerging democracy, is too cynical to contemplate. Furthermore, Washington should not threaten to encourage Taiwan and Japan to nuclearize and thereby play upon Beijing's fears of encirclement by hostile nuclear powers. That course of action, although it might be effective, is simply too irresponsible for a superpower to take.

If Washington wants Beijing to rein in Pyongyang—or, for that matter, Tehran—it will have to specify the price for not doing so. Because nuclear proliferation constitutes the gravest threat to global security, the penalty for noncooperation should be set exceedingly high. The West and Japan have patiently engaged China for decades, and now is the time to expect Beijing to act responsibly in return. Moreover, there is a lot the Chinese still need, especially access to foreign markets and forbearance of their blatant trade violations. So Washington, preferably in conjunction with Tokyo and Brussels, should tell Beijing that if it wants, for instance, the free ride on trade to continue, it is going to have to help on proliferation matters of critical importance. If the Chinese are not willing to do so, then relations with China should be downgraded immediately. What's the point of trying to integrate China into a world order that it's working to undermine?

Unless America makes help on proliferation a litmus test, it cannot blame the Chinese for not leaning on the difficult North Koreans. The Bush administration is trying to make sure that if negotiations fail, they fail with Beijing on Washington's side. If America doesn't do something dramatic, however, China will certainly remain on North Korea's.

The Ultimate Responsibility

In China's view, the six-party talks should continue for as long as it takes and need never end. In fact, that is Beijing's publicly stated position. As Liu Jianchao, a government spokesman, said, "It's China's hope that the process of the six-party talks can go on and on." Of course, there's plenty to discuss at the drawn-out negotiations in the Chinese capital. The North Koreans, Seoul's Kim Dae Jung once complained, "keep making the same mistakes over and over again."

There is no end in sight to Pyongyang's ability to make the wrong choices. But why should Kim Jong Il ever change his reckless ways? With material support from neighboring governments high and the threat from the American military low, Kim has little motivation to stop his atomic antics. The current situation works for him. Why should he ruin a good thing by agreeing to a peace that could lead to the end of his regime?

Suppose the world offers Kim Jong Il development aid, diplomatic

recognition, a peace treaty, security guarantees, and all the other induce-
ments suitable for a reforming tyrant. And suppose he refuses to return the
favor by agreeing to disarm in a verifiable manner. Then what?

The world has to be prepared for the possibility that the six-party negotiations—or talks in any other format—will not result in agreement. Today,
there are few shared assumptions, the goals of the two main protagonists
are diametrically opposed, and North Korea views compromise as internally threatening. Moreover, the consequences of failure for each side
could not be greater. Global politics has never been played at a higher
level. "As a former negotiator, I like to think of all positions as negotiable,"
said Robert Gallucci of Agreed Framework fame. Yet as we have learned
throughout history, that is often not the case.

And often, the past shows, adversaries cannot avoid coming to blows.
"There will be no war on the Korean Peninsula as long as we do not want
a war," said Roh Moo-hyun, displaying his trademark optimism. Yet Seoul's
passionate efforts to avoid conflict have helped make Kim Jong Il the threat
he is today, not only to Roh's South Korea but to the rest of the world.
"Whenever peace—conceived as the avoidance of war—has been the primary objective of a power or a group of powers, the international system has
been at the mercy of the most ruthless member of the international community," wrote Henry Kissinger, long before the emergence of Kim Jong Il.
"Whenever the international order has acknowledged that certain principles could not be compromised even for the sake of peace, stability based
on an equilibrium of forces was at least conceivable." In other words, the
most reliable way to become engaged in a war is to desperately try to avoid
one.

And being willing to fight can mean avoiding the necessity for doing so,
as the last century—and the ones before it—demonstrate. It seems that
every generation has to learn for itself elemental lessons such as these.
What will be our price for rediscovering geopolitical truth? There have
been many opportunities for America to get rid of the Kim regime since the
Korean War. Each time Washington took the easy way out and let the situation slide. Some problems solve themselves, and others run out of control.
Korea, we know by now, belongs to the latter category. Today's potential
cost of getting rid of the DPRK has reached tremendous proportions.

Has the cost of fighting become too great? The Allies were not willing
to pay any price to confront Hitler when he remilitarized the Rhineland,

absorbed Austria, or took the Sudetenland. Stopping him could have cost lives, and that was considered unacceptable at those moments. Later, the price of a solution proved to be far higher. History records that tens of millions died during the effort to end the Third Reich.

Today, we similarly recoil when we are told that war on the Korean peninsula could kill hundreds of thousands or even millions. Of course, any toll, even a significantly smaller one, should strike us as horrible, but we should keep in mind tomorrow's cost for ending the existential threat posed by Kim Jong Il. It would be nice to believe that the danger will disappear on its own, but by now, after more than a half century, that is surely wishful thinking. If America had destroyed the regime at the time his father snatched the *Pueblo*, the cost would have been high, but nothing like today's probable toll. Today's price, however high, would probably be small compared to tomorrow's. There are patterns in the past that are hard to ignore. The cost of inaction will continue to go up as North Korea's military capabilities increase. Virtually every analyst criticizes Bush's belief that regime change is possible at this time. If the critics are right and the government is stable enough to survive, then what's the endgame for the world?

At this moment the North Korean leader cannot put nuclear warheads on his missiles, even the short-range ones. Moreover, it's unlikely he has miniaturized nukes to make them suitable for terrorist applications. So the time to stop him is before he masters either of these tasks—and before he can preposition his bombs in the cities of his adversaries. Today, he can target Japan with conventional explosives and probably chemical and biological warheads, but Japan is also defended by American anti-missile systems as well as the Pentagon's superb forces in the air and on the sea. It is improbable that Kim's air force or navy could cross what he calls the East Sea to land a gravity-delivered nuke to Japanese soil. He can, however, kill millions of fellow Koreans in the South with the greatest of ease. This threat is the main deterrent to action that exists at this time.

The loss of any South Korean diminishes the world, of course. But should it deter America? Of course it should when Seoul stands with Washington in trying to contain Pyongyang, but the South has declared itself to be Korean first and world citizen second. Roh Moo-hyun, by word and deed, is dedicated to supporting Kim Jong Il and his system and does virtually nothing to help disarm the North. So far, there has been no North Korean threat, boast, or act that has prevented the South from providing

material and other assistance to the DPRK. Short of an invasion of its territory, it is unlikely that Seoul under its current set of leaders will ever break
with Pyongyang.

South Korea's support of the North is understandable in the context of
the peninsula's history and within its right as a sovereign nation. Yet it is
also America's obligation, as the defender of last resort of global order, to
deal with existential threats to the international community. Washington
should be patient and explore every avenue to strike a deal with the DPRK,
yet if a negotiated solution is not possible, America needs to know where
South Korea stands. Washington can defer asking that critical question
until after the 2007 election, but not much beyond that pivotal contest. If
the new government in Seoul ultimately chooses Pyongyang, Washington
will have to proceed without South Korea in disarming the DPRK.

It will be a major defeat for American diplomacy if Washington and
Seoul part company, but it will be a setback necessary to meet the challenge of the times. American Secretary of Defense Donald Rumsfeld
sounds arrogant when he says that "the mission determines the coalition,
and we don't allow coalitions to determine the mission," but he's right insofar as some tasks are critical and must be accomplished regardless of external support. Stephen Bosworth, a former American ambassador to
Seoul, says that an American unilateral attack on North Korea would be
"one of the most immoral acts conceivable," yet eliminating the primary
threat to the survival of humanity is not such a bad idea. "If you fight a war
to preserve the NPT, it's like burning the village in Vietnam to save it," says
Donald Gregg, the former spy and diplomat. But if there ever were a reason to go to war, it is to save the nonproliferation treaty and the global arms
control regime. No other justification for conflict comes close.

As Henry Kissinger implied, those prepared to fight a war often don't
have to. If China believed that America was about to resort to force, it
would do most anything to prevent regional conflict, perhaps even apply
real pressure on Pyongyang—as it did in 1994 when Clinton was about to
attack. South Korea, for its part, would have to begin making realistic assessments about the North Korean threat to its own security. And in these
circumstances Kim Jong Il would probably begin negotiating in good faith
at the six-party talks, especially if he thought Bush was unconcerned about
South Korea's fate. Kim might even honor his many pledges to denu-

clearize. In the face of overwhelming power arrayed against him, that would certainly be the rational course to take.

Yet the world has to be prepared in case "the ultimate rogue" makes the wrong choice. After all, Kim has been an aggressor as well as a tyrant. High-ranking defector Hwang Jang Yop has said, "He really intends to start a war." We do not know Kim's real intentions—and maybe even he's not sure what he eventually will do—so it's best to assume he's armed and danger-ous. As former State Department official Jack Pritchard says, "When your opponent has an established pattern of violent behavior, it is imprudent to assume his next assertion of impending disaster is only rhetorical flourish."

If there is even a possibility that Kim Jong Il will fight, we should not permit him to choose the time and place. That's what the world let Hitler do. Western leaders were obsessed by his motives when they should have been concentrating on the increases in German military might. In hind-sight, it's clear that was a mistake of the highest order. So far, the world has allowed Kim Jong Il to dictate events as we ponder what he intends to do. Now, we are letting him build his arsenal so he can wage war when he has a larger number of nuclear weapons and better means to deliver them.

Recent developments mean there should be a limit to the patience of the most powerful Texan in history. "Well, I don't think you give timelines to dictators and tyrants," Bush said in 2004, one year after delivering a fa-mous ultimatum to Saddam of Iraq. Maybe passiveness made sense at that moment, but there will soon come a point when time is of the essence. Kim may or may not be manageable now, but he certainly will be less so in the future.

So there must be a solution. It need not be American, unilateral, or mil-itary, but it needs to be near at hand. We can avoid the horror of armed struggle, but only if the world shows determination. And we have to con-front reality. The old diplomatic stratagems no longer work. We cannot endlessly repeat them and expect a different result. Now, more than at any other time in history, we have to steel ourselves for war if we don't take great risks for peace.

"We have it in our power to begin the world over again," Ronald Reagan once said. Now we not only have the power—we have the responsibility.

Epilogue

Plutonium Pâté

The North Korean nuclear problem is more predictable and is better managed than any other dispute in the world.
—Roh Moo-hyun, South Korean president

"What North Korea wants most is oddly to be left alone, to run this rather odd country, a throwback to Stalinism," notes Ashton Carter of Harvard. If he is right, should America try to contain Pyongyang instead of disarming it? Even as they continue to engage in the six-party negotiations, Bush administration officials privately talk about having to live with the DPRK nuclear program. Maybe they're on to something.

Time, as we know, is the enemy of autocratic governments. The world's largest arsenal of nuclear weapons did not save the Soviet regime. How can a handful of bombs stop the disintegration of the far weaker Kimist state? As years pass the North Korean people, already in motion, will fundamentally change their society. As they do so, their leaders should become more benign, moving from the bizarre Kims to "a better brand of dictators" and eventually to representatives in the liberal democratic tradition.

The hope is that during this transformation from dictatorship to democracy the nuclear crisis will eventually take care of itself. When North Korea adopts representative government Americans probably won't worry about its armaments. After all, they are not now concerned about Britain's.

So what could possibly be wrong with long-term containment of the DPRK? Well, to start with, such a policy assumes it is possible to control events over the course of years, not to mention decades. That, unfortunately, cannot be done, especially by democracies, which are not particularly good at either keeping focus or maintaining consistent foreign policies.

Moreover, maintaining control, even for a short period, is exceedingly unlikely in Northeast Asia, an exceptionally volatile region where rivalries are intense. Few agree with Roh Moo-hyun when he says that the North Korean nuclear crisis is well managed today—a view that is empirically false—and it is inconceivable that a badly divided international community can keep that impasse under control indefinitely.

For one thing, Kim Jong Il is not about to let the world alone, even if, as Ashton Carter suggests, he wants us to stay out of his affairs. His economic system cannot sustain itself without substantial foreign assistance because he eschews structural economic and political reform. Therefore, he has little choice but to cause geopolitical turmoil—or to export strategic insecurity, as one analyst termed it—to ensure inflows of aid into his country's coffers. Moreover, Kim creates a sense of continual emergency to maintain control over society. Even assuming the nuclear threat were not imminent today—and it is—his "attack diplomacy" would make it imminent tomorrow. He and his father, in short, have been able to do something that other communist leaders have not: institutionalize crisis for decades.

As he goes about his daily routine of destabilizing world order, Kim Jong Il can now employ his arsenal of weapons and advanced delivery systems. Although North Korea has made President Bush's missile defense plan seem prudent in retrospect, it is folly to think that the Americans or Japanese can rely on it indefinitely while their governments try to contain the DPRK. Centuries of warfare demonstrate that offensive weapons eventually overwhelm defensive measures. Washington can spend a trillion dollars on missile defense—a current estimate—yet in all probability Kim will still retain the capability to make plutonium pâté out of Tokyo or the American city of his choice.

Most analysts argue he won't try to do that, however. After all, they say, America and its allies have deterred the Kims, father and son, from starting another major conflict on the Korean peninsula, so deterrence will prevent Pyongyang from a truly horrendous act in the future. Yet that's just applying non-Korean logic, which is dangerous because the one thing we know about North Korea is that we don't know much about North Korea.

The concept of deterrence in a nuclear age rests upon the belief that an adversary will not launch missiles because he will not risk retaliation that could bring about casualties in the millions. Yet should we still make that assumption with regard to Kim Jong Il? He not only let hundreds of thousands—and perhaps millions—of his citizens die during the famine of the 1990s, he pursued policies that could have no other result. Therefore, he has shown an indifference to death that calls into question the applicability of the concept at the heart of nuclear deterrence, Mutual Assured Destruction. As long as he thinks he will personally survive, he might just decide to take the biggest gamble in history and risk the lives of fellow Koreans. It is imprudent to underestimate any adversary, and especially one who relishes provocative acts.

Once he can mate warheads to missiles, there is little to prevent him from taking out Tokyo or a lesser Japanese city. And he might believe he could get away with it, especially if he thinks the United States would not come to the aid of Japan for fear of a North Korean attack on, say, Los Angeles. When they wanted to change the status quo in the 1970s and 1980s, Kim and his father authorized a series of terrorist assaults against South Korea and American forces stationed on the peninsula. Who is to say he has given up on this general tactic today? Of course, we cannot definitely state he is willing to use nuclear weapons, yet we know he is not restrained by the inhibitions affecting the leaders of other nuclear states. Time will eventually kill off Kim, but in the meantime it will give him a larger and more destructive arsenal.

And an opportunity to sell fissile material. Kim Jong Il has a history of merchandising everything he has been able to produce, from designer drugs to processed uranium. A policy of containment also assumes that America and the West will be able to prevent North Korea from selling fissile material and intercept all shipments of it—for decades if that is what it takes.

That is a hopelessly unrealistic assumption. The Bush administration announced its Proliferation Security Initiative in May 2003. Today more than sixty nations have joined this attempt to interdict weapons of mass destruction and fissile material in transit on the high seas or in international airspace. That's quite an accomplishment, but it's not nearly good enough. For one thing, neither China nor South Korea is a part of this effort, and Russia, the third nation sharing a land border with North Korea, is an uncertain participant. But even if Moscow, Beijing, and Seoul were enthusiastic partners in PSI, they could not intercept every shipment from North Korea.

And neither can America. As columnist George Will notes, every day drug runners smuggle 21,000 pounds of cocaine and marijuana into the United States. There are 30,000 trucks, 6,500 rail cars, 50,000 cargo containers, and 324,000 cars arriving daily. Furthermore, every twenty-four hours about 14,500 people illegally walk, run, swim, and scamper over— and sometimes under—mostly unguarded borders. How are customs agents going to find a softball of uranium or an orange of plutonium in all that traffic? American border guards may catch a shipment now and then, but to be successful they have to find *every single one.* The odds say that sometime they will miss something, and all it takes is one failure to change the course of history. Entertainer Tiny Tim said he believed everything in the supermarket tabloids because eventually it would all happen. Unfortunately, he may have been right.

And perhaps we will see it all sooner than we think. "Today, the modern era is in its terminal phase," writes Shintaro Ishihara, the Japanese politician. In times of geopolitical transition—and the world is still adjusting to the momentous change following the Cold War—we always witness turbulence. This may not be humankind's "final century," as Cambridge University's Martin Rees suggests, but we are entering a period more dangerous than the one we somehow managed to survive and more perilous than any other in history. Today, in the words of *Washington Post* journalist David Von Drehle, "some very different sort of world is roaring up at us." As it does, the system of global security is trying to adjust but no longer functions as it should.

North Korea is emblematic of the challenges that the great powers face as the international order transitions to something new. If we choose to ignore Kim Jong Il today, we will only have to confront another militant despot with a nuclear arsenal, probably when the world is less stable than it is now. Therefore, we can all guess what is at stake in the crisis Kim has caused: civilization or at least our version of it. Maybe our struggle with him is not the clash of good and evil, as some would have it, but it is at the very least a fight to preserve the liberal international system that has been responsible for so much global progress.

In the past, America and her allies recovered from devastating military attacks to ultimately prevail. Therefore, we think our societies capable of doing so again. In our nuclear age, however, that confidence is misplaced. Moreover, we have come to see ourselves as deserving and strong, the ultimate victors of history. But of course we are not. The course of human events continues, and we now face a challenge we are only beginning to understand.

So this is the showdown of the century. North Korea is taking on the world, and we have no choice but to respond.

Acknowledgments

It takes a medium-sized village to write a book.
I don't live in one so I have to rely on my friends.
—Anonymous

First, I express my appreciation to the despot who rules the Democratic People's Republic of Korea. Of course, "The Lodestar of the 21st Century" provided wonderful material—what other aging male threatens humanity with extinction while wearing curlers at home and four-inch heels in public?—but, more important, he closed off his society. I had planned to write an anecdotal account but, despite extraordinary effort, couldn't gain entry into Kim Jong Il's bizarrist state.

So I had to change the focus of this book to look at North Korea from a broader perspective, global as well as regional. This is what I should have tried to do in the first place. So thanks a million, Chairman Kim.

Others provided more traditional assistance. I begin with Jim Seymour, who sparked my interest in the Korean peninsula. Richard Fisher and James Swanson, two Washington defense specialists, read portions of the manuscript and made valuable suggestions. London journalist Lynne O'Donnell provided numerous leads and anecdotes about North Korea. Author Bill Triplett supplied interesting facts about Beijing's relationship with Pyongyang and North Korea's missile program. Friend David Welker introduced me to Carolyn Bartholomew, who put me in touch with the U.N.'s Randy Rydell, who has influenced my thinking on nuclear weapons more than any other person. Academic Ruediger Frank provided insights on North Korean domestic politics, as did Charles Armstrong on culture. Both could have viewed me as an annoyance but didn't. Buzzmeister Chris Nelson offered Washington gossip and introductions to his circle of friends, which seems to include the entire foreign policy establishment in the United States. Stanson Yeung gave me good advice and encouragement along the way, and so did Eric Heginbotham. Ambassador Stapleton Roy was most generous with his time. Arthur Waldron is for me the guiding light.

Other folks who helped during this long journey include Joyce Yen, Rino Balatbat, James Tam, Tina Mosetis, Sun Bae Kim, Walter LaFeber, Andrew Meier, Roger Robinson, Tion Kwa, Norbert Vollertsen, Peter Koh, Oh Kilnam, Matt Miller, Peter Gordon, Elaine Leung, Sohn Jie-Ae, B. J. Lee, Don and Rosanna Hall, Kongdan Oh, Steve Munson, Susan and George Saridakis, Evan Stewart, Jay Branegan, Keith Luse, Michael "Shanghai" Shelley, Kathy Michels, Clare Smith, Tim Tenne, the hardworking staff at the Clarence Dillon Public Library in my hometown of Bedminster, and Queen Bee Dimon Liu.

In Tokyo, where I otherwise would have been lost without translation, Atsuko Masuda and Hiroko Kuroda from publisher Soshisha were pathfinders. Both devoted so much of their time to arranging interviews and accompanying me through the wondrous maze that is the capital of Japan. Yoshiro Kamijima of *Seiron Magazine* was also generous with his time and commentary. And then there is Yuichi Yamamoto of Yokohama, the TokyoFreePress blogger who over the course of years has stripped away myth and misunderstanding so that I could see Japan in sharper perspective.

In Seoul, Usung Chung of the EyesonKorea blog spent a week opening up the South Korean capital, and one very remote village, to me. I cannot thank him enough for his assistance and insights. Before he moved from Seoul to Seattle, friend Chris Tibbs explained South Korea, put me in touch with one of the most interesting observers of the two Koreas, and took care of my wife and me. Journalist Duck-hwa Hong was a gracious host and wonderful guide. I have enjoyed his friendship for many years. Many thanks go to Chung Jae Ho and Jung-Hoon Lee for their penetrating analyses, which have shaped this book.

Folks from my old—and new—hometown of Hong Kong also helped. Willy Lam, the prominent China watcher, passed along hot information on Beijing as well as provided perceptive commentary. How could I go wrong with his help? New friend Kathi Zellweger assisted, as did Brian Bridges. They both changed my views.

Elizabeth Economy helped in so many ways and on so many occasions. Among other things, she arranged for Ambassador Donald Gregg, Jerry Cohen, and Jason Shaplen to read manuscripts. I express my appreciation to them.

I thank research assistants Winnie Chang, Neil Chisholm, Seo Jin Kim, Sung Shin Kim, Suh-Young Shin, Amy Wong, Wang Ting, and David Yang. Hansol Seo got me through Seoul. Sonja Sray got me through geopolitics, disarmament, and international relations. She also read this book in its early versions and provided needed repairs.

My editor, Susanna Porter, carried this book from inception to release. There would be no *Nuclear Showdown* without her. Steve Messina, bless his heart, never once grimaced when I repeatedly updated these pages. And thanks to other Random House folks who helped, Johanna Bowman, Benjamin Dreyer, Tom Perry, London King, Dana Leigh Blanchette, T. J. Mancini, Rose Ann Ferrick, Laura Starrett, Elizabeth Kellogg, and Fred Chase. I am also grateful for the support and assistance of my Random U.K. editor, Tiffany Stansfield.

If I live to be a hundred—I'm working on it—I will not have enough time to tell the world how much I owe to my agent, Rosalie Siegel, and her assistant, Denise Lager.

Winnie Chang let her father write this book, and I appreciate her patience. My father provided meals and traditional parental assistance whenever needed.

And now there is just one more person to thank. This book is dedicated to her.

Notes

Foreword: *North Korea Takes the World Backward*

xix   "If we lose": Bradley K. Martin, *Under the Loving Care of the Fatherly Leader: North Korea and the Kim Dynasty* (New York: St. Martin's Press, Thomas Dunne Books, 2004), p. 491. Kim reportedly made this statement in response to a question from his father, Kim Il Sung.

xx   assembly-line basis: See Timothy J. Burger and Perry Bacon Jr., "A New Eye on North Korea," *Time*, June 2, 2003, p. 19.

xx   "nuclear Kmart": "The Many Faces of Kim Jong Il," cnn.com, April 19, 2004, http://edition.cnn.com/2004/WORLD/americas/04/16/kim.

xx   sold processed uranium: North Korea either sold uranium tetrafluoride to Pakistan, which then processed it into uranium hexafluoride and sold it to Libya, or sold uranium hexafluoride to Libya through a Pakistani broker. David E. Sanger and William J. Broad, "Using Clues from Libya to Study a Nuclear Mystery," *New York Times*, March 31, 2005, p. A12. North Korea denies the sale, calling the allegation part of a "smear campaign." See "North Korea Denies It Provided Libya with Uranium," Dow Jones

Newswires, May 29, 2004. Tehran's new airport reportedly was closed within hours of its opening in 2004 because of a spill of weapons-grade uranium from North Korea. See Con Coughlin, "Iran 'Covered Up Nuclear Spill,' " *Sunday Telegraph* (London), June 27, 2004, p. 24.

xx   pickup truck: See "Korea Society Chairman Donald Gregg on the North/South Korea Summit," Council of Foreign Relations online interview, June 15, 2000, http://www.cfr.org/.

xx   withdraw from the nuclear nonproliferation treaty: The United Nations maintains that North Korea is still a signatory to the nuclear nonproliferation treaty because it failed to adhere to the formalities required for withdrawal. Although the U.N. argument has technical merit, North Korea is generally viewed as having withdrawn from the treaty.

xxi   "beyond evil": Radek Sikorski, "Into Korea's Fantasy Land," wsj.com, January 16, 2003, http://wsj.com/.

xxi   million casualties: Doug Struck and Bradley Graham, "U.S., Asian Allies Face Tough Choices," *Washington Post*, April 25, 2003, p. A18.

xxi   "range from the deeply unsatisfying": David E. Sanger, "U.S. Sees Quick Start of North Korea Nuclear Site," *New York Times*, March 1, 2003, p. A1.

xxii "It may be too late": Peter Slevin and Walter Pincus, "U.S. Will Refer N. Korea Nuclear Effort to U.N.," *Washington Post*, December 28, 2002, p. A1.

Chapter 1: KU KLUX KOREA

4   worst country in the world: See, e.g., *The Worst of the Worst: The World's Most Repressive Societies 2005*, Freedom House, 2005 (report to the United Nations Commission on Human Rights).

4   "repellent": Bruce Cumings, *North Korea: Another Country* (New York: New Press, 2004), p. ix.

4   "Orwellian": Selig S. Harrison, *Korean Endgame: A Strategy for Reunification and U.S. Disengagement* (Princeton: Princeton University Press, 2002), p. xvi.

4   "a pretty crazy place": Noam Chomsky, interview by John Junkerman, Cambridge, Massachusetts, July 22, 2003, http://www.cine.co.jp/chomsky9.11/interview.html.

4   nine hundred invasions: Don Oberdorfer, *The Two Koreas: A Contemporary History* (New York: Basic Books, 2001), p. 3.

6   the tsar's old claim: Ibid., p. 6.

6   no justification: Bruce Cumings, *Korea's Place in the Sun: A Modern History* (New York: W. W. Norton, 1997), p. 186.

7   "to use armed force": David McCullough, *Truman* (New York: Simon & Schuster, 1992), p. 781.

7   During the conflict: There is little agreement on the number of deaths during the Korean War. Apart from the figures for the U.N. forces, almost all casualty statistics are imprecise estimates.

8   "stockings, cigarettes": Michael Mandelbaum, *The Ideas That Conquered the World: Peace, Democracy, and Free Markets in the Twenty-first Century* (New York: PublicAffairs, 2002), p. 15.

9   *Time* picked: See "80 Days That Changed the World," *Time*, March 31, 2003, p. A1.

9   "Are you familiar": "Kim Jong Il," *Biography*, A&E, September 4, 2003.

9   the longest engagement: Japanese leaders at the time considered the war in the Pacific to have begun in 1931 in Manchuria. The battle for control of that area continued to the end of the hostilities in 1945. See Saburo Ienaga, *The Pacific War: World War II and the Japanese, 1931–1945*, trans. Frank Baldwin (New York: Pantheon Books, 1978), pp. 247–48.

10   appropriated elements: Charles K. Armstrong, *The North Korean Revolution, 1945–1950* (Ithaca: Cornell University Press, 2003), p. 223.

10   stunned to learn: See T. R. Reid, "Which Kim Will U.S. Deal With?" *Washington Post*, October 22, 1994, p. A26.

10   both time and space: Kongdan Oh and Ralph C. Hassig, *North Korea Through the Looking Glass* (Washington, D.C.: Brookings Institution Press, 2000), p. 4.

10   "We were told": *Nuclear Nightmare: Understanding North Korea*, Discovery Channel, August 6, 2003.

11   no one else ever had exercised: See Nicholas Eberstadt, *The End of North Korea* (Washington, D.C.: AEI Press, 1999), p. 3.

11   fifty-one categories: The number of categories is subject to some dispute. Compare Jae-Jean Suh, "North Korea's Social System," in *Prospects for Change in North Korea*, ed. Tae Hwan Ok and Hong Yung Lee, pp. 209–65 (Berkeley: Institute of East Asian Studies, 1994), with Andrei Lankov, "Social Strata," *Korea Times* (Seoul), April 4, 2005, http://times.hankooki.com/lpage/opinion/200504/kt2005040419495654140.htm.

11   every Korean: Christopher Hitchens, "Why North Korea Is Number One," *Newsweek* (international edition), July 9, 2001, p. 44.

11   no place for the individual: "Kim Il Sung is said to have boasted that a thousand North Koreans asked the same question would all give the same answer." Norman D. Levin, "What If North Korea Survives?" *Survival*, Winter 1997/98, p. 156.

11   "an astonishing capacity": Marcus Noland, *Korea After Kim Jong-il* (Washington, D.C.: Institute for International Economics, 2004), p. 18.

11   "People asked me": Parris Chang, interview by author, Taipei, October 30, 2003. Chang was chairman of the Foreign Relations Committee of Taiwan's national legislature.

11   "I didn't know anything": *Nuclear Nightmare: Understanding North Korea*, Discovery Channel, August 6, 2003.

12   "a garrison state": Cumings, *North Korea*, p. 2.

12   "truly terrible destruction": Ibid., p. xi.

12   *Juche:* See Oh and Hassig, *North Korea Through the Looking Glass*, pp. 15–19.

13   Asia's Talleyrand: Oberdorfer, *The Two Koreas*, p. 19.

14   "a better way to be Korean": Michael Breen, *Kim Jong-il: North Korea's Dear Leader* (Singapore: John Wiley & Sons, 2004), p. xiii.

14   large-denomination American currency: North Korea makes the "Super K" notes, which are so good that bank equipment cannot distinguish them from real ones. William C. Triplett II, *Rogue State: How a Nuclear North Korea Threatens America* (Washington, D.C.: Regnery, 2004), pp. 101–02.

14   Joseph Mobutu: Charles Armstrong, interview by author, New York City, September 30, 2002.

14   "dictator groupie": Claudia Rosett, "Is Bush Selling Out?" OpinionJournal, December 3, 2003, http://www.opinionjournal.com/.

14   "Light of Human Genius": Kang Chol-hwan and Pierre Rigoulot, *The Aquariums of Pyongyang: Ten Years in a North Korean Gulag*, trans. Yair Reiner (New York: Basic Books, 2001), p. 3.

14   "Kim Il Sung was God": Joohee Cho and Doug Struck, " 'Dear Leader' Feted in N. Korea," *Washington Post*, February 17, 2003 p. A21.

14   "Because someone is dead": Halle Berry's *Gothika*, directed by Mathieu Kassovitz, Warner Bros., 2003.

15   "bigger than Buckingham Palace": Brian Barron, "Britain Moves into Kim's Secret State," BBC News, August 29, 2001, http://news.bbc.co.uk/1/hi/world/asia-pacific/1514253.stm.

15   is still alive: "Many countries have presidents for life, but only North Korea has one who is dead." Nicholas D. Kristof, "The Hermit Nuclear Kingdom," review of *Under the Loving Care of the Fatherly Leader: North Korea and the Kim Dynasty*, by Bradley K. Martin, and *Nuclear North Korea: A Debate on Engagement Strategies*, by Victor D. Cha and David C. Kang, *New York Review of Books*, February 10, 2005, p. 25.

15   Famine: The number who perished is still unknown. Some say 3.5 million died, but the better estimates indicate a much lower toll of around 600,000. North Korea has essentially admitted that about 220,000 died.

15   it was tragic: *Nuclear Nightmare: Understanding North Korea*, Documentary Screening and Discussion, Asia Society, New York City, August 5, 2003.

15   Some argue: See, e.g., Oberdorfer, *The Two Koreas*, p. 340.

16   "contemporary god": Noland, *Korea After Kim Jong-il*, p. 17.

16   gift of the heavens: Oh and Hassig, *North Korea Through the Looking Glass*, p. 120.

16   "general who will rule": Peter Carlson, "Sins of the Son," *Washington Post*, May 11, 2003, p. D1.

16   "three generals": Oh and Hassig, *North Korea Through the Looking Glass*, p. 120.

16   "great ideological and theoretical exploits": "Kim Jong Il Authors 1,400-Odd Works During University Days," Korean Central News Agency, March 18, 2004.

16   ten bull's-eyes: Triplett, *Rogue State*, p. 128.

16   Golfer Tiger Kim: See Charles McGrath, "Teeing Off with the 'Dear Duffer,'" *New York Times*, Week in Review, July 4, 2004, p. 5; "Move Over Tiger: N. Korea's Kim Shot 38 Under Par His 1st Time Out," worldtribune .com, June 16, 2004, http://216.26.163.62/2004/ea_nkorea_06_16 .html; and Paul Eckert, "N. Korea's Kim Turns 62 as World Wans [sic] Nuclear Solution," Reuters, February 15, 2004.

17   "A totalitarian dynasty": *Nuclear Nightmare: Understanding North Korea*, Documentary Screening and Discussion, Asia Society, New York City, August 5, 2003 (comments of Kenneth Levis).

18   "behind-the-scenes operator": Oh and Hassig, *North Korea Through the Looking Glass*, p. 97.

18   "least typical citizen": Madeleine Albright with Bill Woodward, *Madam Secretary* (New York: Miramax Books, 2003), p. 468.

18   NBA cheerleaders: Thomas L. Friedman, *The Lexus and the Olive Tree* (New York: Anchor Books, 2000), p. 312.

18   S&M videos: Nicholas D. Kristof, "Tunneling Toward Disaster," *New York Times*, January 21, 2003, p. A23.

18   stashed seventy children: Triplett, *Rogue State*, p. 131. There are differing counts of the women considered his wives because of the impossibility of verifying official marriages.

18   music boxes: Cumings, *North Korea*, pp. 163–64.

18 Daffy Duck cartoons: Robert Windrem, "Death, Terror in N. Korea Gulag," msnbc.com, January 15, 2003, http://msnbc.msn.com/id/3071466. Kim Jong Il has 15,000 movies on videotape. Donald MacIntyre and Massimo Calabresi, "Star of His Own Show," *Time*, January 13, 2003, p. 10.

18 garage mechanic: "Kim Jong Il," *Biography*, A&E, September 4, 2003.

18 four-inch platform shoes: Kim's shoes have earned him the nickname "Altitude." Oh and Hassig, *North Korea Through the Looking Glass*, p. 94.

18 may have carried out: Ibid., p. 93.

18 notion of evil: Cumings, *North Korea*, p. 206.

18 mausoleum for his preserved remains: After renovating his father's office to serve as his mausoleum, Kim Jong Il ordered several other monumental showcase projects. See Samuel S. Kim, "Introduction: A Systems Approach," in *The North Korean System in the Post–Cold War Era*, ed. Samuel S. Kim, pp. 1–37 (New York: Palgrave, 2001).

18 "Is he insane": *Fox on the Record*, Fox News Channel, January 15, 2003.

19 "the Lodestar": Sang-Hun Choe, "North Korean Leader Has Many Titles," Associated Press, March 8, 2004.

19 "Guardian of Our Planet": Anthony Faiola, "No Questions? Good. Now Enjoy Your Stay," *Washington Post*, December 2, 2003, p. C1.

19 absolutely brilliant: Bill Gertz, "Kim Wants to Rule All Korea, Defector Warns," *Washington Times*, November 4, 2003, p. A1.

19 more than two thousand titles: Anthony Faiola and Sachiko Sakamaki, "Missing Homages Spur Rumors on N. Korean," *Washington Post*, November 19, 2004, p. A15.

19 "The Illustrious General": Choe, "North Korean Leader Has Many Titles."

20 "From east to west": Mike Chinoy, "North Korea's Surreality TV," cnn.com, February 24, 2004, http://edition.cnn.com/2004/WORLD/asiapcf/02/24/nkorea.tv.

20 "odiocracy": Breen, *Kim Jong-il*, p. xiii.

20 the North Koreans beat: See, e.g., "USS *Pueblo* Commander Bucher Has Died," cnn.com, January 29, 2004, http://edition.cnn.com/2004/US/West/01/29/obit.bucher.ap.

20 largest loss of U.S. servicemen: Doug Struck, " 'With Circumspection,' U.S. Planes to Resume Spy Flights off N. Korea," *Washington Post*, March 13, 2003, p. A1.

20 "will suffer no penalty": Henry Kissinger, *White House Years* (Boston: Little, Brown, 1979), p. 315.

21 "weak, indecisive, and disorganized": Ibid., p. 321.

21   "I believe": Ibid.

21   "I always had this philosophy": *I'll Be Your Mirror: The Selected Andy Warhol Interviews, 1962–1987*, ed. Kenneth Goldsmith (New York: Carroll & Graf, 2004), p. 90.

Chapter 2: AN ARSENAL OF AMBITIONS

22   "manufactured nukes": "DPRK FM on Its Stand to Suspend Its Participation in Six-Party Talks for Indefinite Period," Korean Central News Agency, February 10, 2005.

22   "number of proven weapons": Peter James Spielmann, "Reports on N. Korea Nukes May Lack Proof," Associated Press, October 1, 2004.

22   "the longest-running intelligence failure": "Kim's Nuclear Gamble," *Frontline*, PBS, February 20, 2003.

23   just hot air: "Russian Official: N Korea Has No Nuclear Weapons — Report," Dow Jones Newswires, March 10, 2005.

23   despite recent assertions: See "DPRK FM on Its Stand to Suspend Its Participation in Six-Party Talks for Indefinite Period."

23   Pyongyang sent scientists to China: Alexandre Y. Mansourov, "The Origins, Evolution, and Current Politics of the North Korean Nuclear Program," *Nonproliferation Review*, Spring/Summer 1995, p. 25.

24   "We need the atom bomb": Don Oberdorfer, *The Two Koreas: A Contemporary History* (New York: Basic Books, 2001), p. 253. This is not the first time North Korea pestered East Germany for nuclear weapons technology; the requests go back to at least 1963. See Murray Hiebert, "Pyongyang Long Sought Atomic Bomb," *Wall Street Journal*, May 18, 2005, p. A13. In 1972 Kim Il Sung suggested to South Korea in secret talks that the two Koreas jointly develop nuclear weapons. See Bruce Cumings, *Korea's Place in the Sun: A Modern History* (New York: W. W. Norton, 1997), p. 467.

24   may not have understood: Oberdorfer, *The Two Koreas*, pp. 254–55.

25   negative guarantee: The United States stated that it would not use nuclear weapons against a nonnuclear state unless it attacked the U.S. or one of its allies with the support of a nuclear power.

25   landmark agreement: The Joint Declaration of the Denuclearization of the Korean Peninsula was actually signed on January 20, 1992. It entered into force on February 19, 1992.

25   "We have no nuclear reprocessing facilities!": Oberdorfer, *The Two Koreas*, p. 264.

25   over a hundred buildings: Yongbyon is "a city unto itself." Senate Committee on Foreign Relations, *North Korea: Status Report on Nuclear Program*,

Humanitarian Issues, and Economic Reforms, 108th Cong., 2nd Sess., 2004, S. Prt. 108–40, p. 2.

25   inevitable conclusion: Oberdorfer, *The Two Koreas,* p. 270.

26   DPRK delegates: See ibid., p. 277; and James Traub, "The Netherworld of Nonproliferation," *New York Times Magazine,* June 13, 2004, p. 48.

26   "a question of civilization": Oberdorfer, *The Two Koreas,* p. 249.

27   contingency plans for air strikes: Ronald Fogleman, interview by author, Vancouver, July 26, 2003. Fogleman was the general in charge of American air forces in Korea at the time and is now a member of the Pentagon's Defense Policy Board.

27   Selig Harrison's suggestion: See Selig S. Harrison, *Korean Endgame: A Strategy for Reunification and U.S. Disengagement* (Princeton: Princeton University Press, 2002), p. 217.

28   "a miracle": Jimmy Carter, interview by Judy Woodruff, CNN, June 22, 1994.

29   Pyongyang blames: See, e.g., "KCNA Terms U.S. Violator of AF," Korean Central News Agency, October 21, 2004.

29   no-nuclear-attack pledge: The closest Washington ever got to issuing a pledge was its signing of the October 2000 U.S.-DPRK Joint Communiqué, which states that "neither government would have hostile intent toward the other."

30   "There is blame on both sides": Jimmy Carter, interview by Jonathan Mann, *Prize for Peace: Nobel 2002,* CNN International, December 11, 2002.

30   one of the most brazen betrayals: See Jim Hoagland, "Talk Plus Muscle on North Korea," *Washington Post,* May 25, 2003, p. B7.

30   The DPRK probably began: See Daniel A. Pinkston and Stephanie Lieggi, "North Korea's Nuclear Program: Key Concerns," Monterey Institute of International Studies, January 17, 2003, http://cns.miis.edu/research/korea/keycon.htm#fn5. Pakistan's Dr. Abdul Qadeer Khan preliminarily talked to the North Koreans about a uranium-based program in the late 1980s. See, e.g., David E. Sanger, "Pakistani Says He Saw North Korean Nuclear Devices," *New York Times,* April 13, 2004, p. A12.

30   gone beyond the planning stage: Pyongyang has steadfastly refused to make a public admission of the existence of its uranium-based weapons program. Nonetheless, Selig Harrison announced in 2005 that the North told him it maintains a laboratory studying lightly enriched uranium for civilian purposes. See Burt Herman, "S.Korea: North's Nuke Plans Not an Issue," Associated Press, September 1, 2005. The lab's work undoubtedly has weapons applications because once a country can enrich uranium, it has acquired most of the technology needed for a bomb.

30   began working with North Korea: Carol Giacomo, "N.Korea Nuclear Program Older Than First Believed," Reuters, March 12, 2004.

30   the middle of 2002: See David Rohde, "Pakistani Finger-Pointing and Denials Spread in the Furor Over Nuclear Transfers Abroad," *New York Times*, February 4, 2004, p. A11. Pakistani military flights to North Korea continued until as late as the middle of 2002, indicating that the trade between the two countries in missiles and nuclear technology continued at least until then. See Burt Herman, "Pakistan Denies Sending Nuclear Technology to North Korea on Military Flight; Says Pardon for Khan 'Conditional,' " Associated Press, February 9, 2004.

30   "whopping lie": "KCNA Blasts U.S. Smear Campaign against DPRK," Korean Central News Agency, February 21, 2004.

30   numerous sightings: Khan traveled to North Korea somewhere between twelve to nineteen times. Compare Paul Eckert, "North Korea Says Pakistan Nuclear Confession a Lie," Reuters, February 10, 2004 (twelve trips), with Irfan Husain, "Pakistan's Rogue Scientists," *Asian Wall Street Journal* (Hong Kong), February 6, 2004, p. A9 (nineteen trips).

30   satellite photos: See Carol Giacomo, "Pakistan Crackdown Expected to Hurt Nuclear Bazaar," Reuters, February 4, 2004; and William J. Broad, David Rohde, and David E. Sanger, "Inquiry Suggests Pakistanis Sold Nuclear Secrets," *New York Times*, December 22, 2003, p. A1.

30   aluminum tubes: See David E. Sanger and William J. Broad, "From Rogue Nuclear Programs, Web of Trails Leads to Pakistan," *New York Times*, January 4, 2004, p. 1; and Barbara Slavin and John Diamond, "N. Korean Nuclear Efforts Looking Less Threatening," *USA Today*, November 5, 2003, p. 18A. North Korean diplomats have been making purchases for Pyongyang's nuclear programs. See William C. Triplett II, *Rogue State: How a Nuclear North Korea Threatens America* (Washington, D.C.: Regnery, 2004), p. 158.

31   Pakistan's help: See David Isenberg, "Nukes: Is Pandora Chinese?" Asia Times Online, June 25, 2004, http://www.atimes.com/atimes/China/FF23Ad02.html.

31   Pyongyang boasted: Edith M. Lederer, "North Korea Warns of War on Peninsula," Associated Press, September 27, 2004.

31   six to eight bombs: Estimates of the size of North Korea's store of plutonium vary widely. See David Albright and Kimberly Kramer, "Stockpiles Still Growing," *Bulletin of the Atomic Scientists*, November/December 2004, p. 14. North Korea may have one fewer bomb if, as some suspect, the Pakistanis in 1998 detonated a plutonium device for North Korea when they tested their first weapons.

31   doubts the weaponization boast: Carol Giacomo, "Chinese Minister Doubtful on N.Korea Nuclear Claim," Reuters, September 28, 2004.

31   "we take all their claims seriously": U.S. Department of State, Daily Press Briefing, September 28, 2004.

31   restarting Yongbyon: The Yongbyon five-megawatt reactor was restarted in 2003 after IAEA inspectors were ejected. North Korea shut down the reactor in April 2005, presumably to harvest plutonium.

31   thirty bombs a year: Gallucci noted that the Agreed Framework froze construction of two reactors that could produce plutonium in such quantities. See Steven Greenhouse, "Senators Cool to Pact with Koreans," *New York Times*, December 2, 1994, p. A6. Some believe the reactors could produce plutonium for as many as fifty-five bombs a year. See "N.Korea Noisily Resumes Reactor Construction," *Chosun Ilbo* (Seoul), June 30, 2005, http://english.chosun.com/w21data/html/news/200506/200506300039.html. For a more probable estimate, see Glenn Kessler, "N. Korea Nuclear Estimate to Rise," *Washington Post*, April 28, 2004, p. A1.

31   bought plutonium from Russian sources: "Flurry of Diplomacy with N. Korea," Nelson Report, October 12, 2004.

31   characteristic mark: John Loftus, interview by Eric Shawn, "Inside Scoop," *Fox News Live Weekend*, Fox News Channel, September 12, 2004. North Korea has conducted high-explosive tests to validate their designs since the 1980s. See John J. Lumpkin, "CIA: North Korea Verifies Nuclear Designs," Associated Press, November 9, 2003.

31   had probably mastered: See David E. Sanger, "North Korea's Bomb: Untested but Ready, C.I.A. Concludes," *New York Times*, November 9, 2003, p. 8. Private analysts concur. See Nicholas Kralev, "N. Korea Atomic Bomb in Doubt," *Washington Times*, January 22, 2004, p. A1.

31   Pakistan taught: Seymour M. Hersh, "The Cold Test," *New Yorker*, January 27, 2003, p. 42.

31   these experiments cannot provide: See Jon Herskovitz, "N.Korea Nuclear Test Could Change Dynamics in Asia," Reuters, May 1, 2005.

32   North Korea reportedly told China: Stephanie Hoo, "U.S., N. Korean Envoys Hold Third Meeting," Associated Press, July 28, 2005.

32   as one recent defector claimed: Song Seung-Ho, "A Representative of North Korea's Supreme People's Assembly Defects to South Korea and Gives Grave Testimony About the North's Nuclear Development," *Chosun Monthly*, August 2005, p. 8.

32   Dr. Khan says: Sanger, "Pakistani Says He Saw North Korean Nuclear Devices," p. A12. If Khan saw three nuclear weapons, then the North Koreans were more efficient in the use of plutonium than previously thought. Kessler, "N. Korea Nuclear Estimate to Rise," p. A1.

32   might not have known enough: Peter Slevin, "3 Nuclear Devices Cited in N. Korea," *Washington Post*, April 14, 2004, p. A22.

32   Washington generally believes: See Adam Entous and Brian Rhoads, "Cheney Presses China on N.Korea, Gets Pressed on Taiwan," Reuters, April 14, 2004.

32   as some suspect: See David E. Sanger and William J. Broad, "Pakistan May Have Aided North Korea A-Test," *New York Times*, February 27, 2004, p. A10.

32   Khan's operation delivered: There is disagreement as to what the Khan ring provided. Compare Barton Gellman and Dafna Linzer, "Unprecedented Peril Forces Tough Calls," *Washington Post*, October 26, 2004, p. A1 (Khan delivered "tens of thousands of gas centrifuge parts that brought North Korea to the threshold of unlimited bomb production"), with Slavin and Diamond, "N. Korean Nuclear Efforts Looking Less Threatening," p. 18A (North Korea obtained a "starter kit" for uranium enrichment but no technical expertise). In mid-2005, Pakistani leader Pervez Musharraf confirmed that Khan had transferred complete centrifuges and centrifuge parts and designs to North Korea. See "Musharraf Says Khan Offered Centrifuges, Designs to N. Korea," Kyodo News Service, August 24, 2005. Musharraf, however, said that there was no evidence that Khan had transferred a Chinese design for a nuclear weapon to the North Koreans. See David E. Sanger, "Pakistan Leader Confirms Nuclear Exports," *New York Times*, September 13, 2005, p. A10.

32   full-scale uranium production: Giacomo, "N.Korea Nuclear Program Older Than First Believed." Some doubt that North Korea has the industrial infrastructure to build uranium weapons. See, e.g., Selig S. Harrison, "Did North Korea Cheat?" *Foreign Affairs*, January/February 2005, p. 99.

32   at least three years: Gellman and Linzer, "Unprecedented Peril Forces Tough Calls," p. A1.

32   "production-scale" centrifuge facility: Ibid.

32   skeptical of that assessment: Kessler, "N. Korea Nuclear Estimate to Rise," p. A1.

33   "unlimited" bomb production: Gellman and Linzer, "Unprecedented Peril Forces Tough Calls," p. A1.

33   based on South Korean intelligence: Sanger and Broad, "From Rogue Nuclear Programs, Web of Trails Leads to Pakistan," p. 1.

33   soundest view: See Sang-Hun Choe, "Nations to Hold Talks on N. Korean Nukes," Associated Press, April 29, 2004; and Kessler, "N. Korea Nuclear Estimate to Rise," p. A1.

33   undoubtedly has a weapon: Some think that North Korea already has produced uranium bombs. See "Nuclear Weapons Program," GlobalSecurity .org, April 2, 2005, http://www.globalsecurity.org/wmd/world/dprk/nuke.htm.

33   no longer a matter of science: Mitchell B. Reiss, "The Nuclear Tipping

Point: Prospects for a World of Many Nuclear Weapons States," in *The Nuclear Tipping Point: Why States Reconsider Their Nuclear Choices*, ed. Kurt M. Campbell, Robert J. Einhorn, and Mitchell B. Reiss, pp. 3–17 (Washington, D.C.: Brookings Institution Press, 2004).

33   a set of designs: Khan may have peddled weapon designs to many countries. See William J. Broad, "Libya's Crude Bomb Design Eases Western Experts' Fear," *New York Times*, February 9, 2004, p. A7.

33   ready-to-use device: There are reports that North Korea may have purchased a completed nuclear weapon from Pakistan or a former Soviet republic. See "N.Korea Has Bought Complete Nuclear Bomb—Report," Reuters, January 27, 2005.

33   but not about the direction: David E. Sanger, "About-Face on North Korea: Allies Helped," *New York Times*, June 24, 2004, p. A12.

33   "It's one thing to make": Timothy J. Burger and Perry Bacon Jr., "A New Eye on North Korea," *Time*, June 2, 2003, p. 19. Some believe that North Korea could have as many as a hundred weapons by the end of this decade.

33   "It's one thing to be able": *The Meaning of the Bomb*, Discovery Times Channel, August 19, 2003.

33   "remarkable breakthroughs": Linda Sieg, "Signs N.Korea Preparing a Missile Test a Worry—U.S.," Reuters, September 26, 2004.

33   "North Korean missiles": Ryan Nakashima, "North Korea's Aim Is Reunification, Not Aid, 'Unofficial Spokesman' Says," Agence France-Presse, March 7, 2003.

34   "a whopping lie": "U.S. Escalated Moves to Establish MD Under Fire," Korean Central News Agency, March 30, 2004.

34   a National Intelligence Estimate: See DCI National Intelligence Estimate, "Emerging Missile Threats to North America During the Next 15 Years," November 1995.

34   suggested that Washington: "Report of the Commission to Assess the Ballistic Missile Threat to the United States," July 15, 1998.

34   misfired or failed to ignite: For weeks the Pentagon and the American intelligence community were not sure what had happened. See Lim Yun-Suk, "N. Korea Boasts of Satellite Launch After US Admits It Was Wrong," Agence France-Presse, September 15, 1998.

34   debris landed: Most reports say debris landed in the Pacific Ocean, but some remnants actually fell in Alaska. William C. Triplett II, e-mails to author, November 3, 2004. Triplett worked for the Senate Defense Appropriations Subcommittee at the time.

34   "If you're going to try": Scott Conwell, interview by author, Annapolis, Maryland, November 5, 2003.

35   "We don't know": Ibid.

35   may be in the process of deploying: North Korea may be deploying two bal-
      listic missile systems. One is land-based with a range of 1,500–2,500 miles,
      and the second is ship- or submarine-launched with a range of at least 1,500
      miles. Both are of Soviet design. Joseph S. Bermudez, "North Korea Deploy
      New Missiles," *Jane's Defence Weekly*, August 2, 2004, http://www.janes
      .com/defence/news/jdw/jdw040802_1_n.shtml; and Yu Yong-won, "North
      Deploys New 4,000Km Range Missiles," *Chosun Ilbo* (Seoul), May 4, 2004,
      http://english.chosun.com/w21data/html/news/200405/200405040031.html.

35   power to put plutonium: Jack Kim, "N.Korea Remembers Founder Kim Il-
      Sung, Warns U.S.," Reuters, July 8, 2004.

35   strike the American mainland: Tenet made his assessment public on Febru-
      ary 12, 2003, in a hearing before the Senate Armed Services Committee.

35   a new version: The Taepodong-2, which has not yet been deployed, can
      deliver a heavy warhead to Alaska or Hawaii and a lighter one to the West
      Coast of the United States. See Christopher Torchia, "North Korea
      Believed to Be Working on Missile Capable of Reaching Parts of the United
      States," Associated Press, January 11, 2003. It is believed that a more
      advanced version of this missile can reach anywhere in the United States.
      See John J. Lumpkin, "Agencies: N. Korea Missile Can Reach U.S.," Asso-
      ciated Press, February 12, 2003.

35   not reliably accurate: Victor D. Cha and David C. Kang, "The Korea Cri-
      sis," *Foreign Policy*, May/June 2003, p. 20.

35   fired from merchant ships: Richard Fisher Jr., "North Korea's New Mis-
      siles," strategycenter.net, September 20, 2004, http://www.strategycenter.net/
      research/pubID.3/pub_detail.asp.

35   troubling rumors: Some say North Korea has actually purchased at least one
      sub. See "North Korean Missile Story . . . ," Nelson Report, September 12,
      2003. It is unlikely that Russia would sell North Korea such sophisticated
      hardware. It is, however, possible that Pyongyang obtained Soviet missile-
      launching technology in the mid-1990s when a North Korean shipyard
      scrapped Soviet Golf-class submarines. There are plausible reports that the
      North kept the subs' launch tubes intact. See Fisher, "North Korea's New
      Missiles."

35   Pyongyang implies that its technicians: See Burt Herman, "North Korea
      Boasts It Has More Bombs," Associated Press, June 9, 2005. In testimony
      before the Senate Armed Services Committee in April 2005, Vice Admiral
      Lowell Jacoby, the director of the Defense Intelligence Agency, said North
      Korea could put nuclear weapons on missiles that can hit the United States.
      David Morgan, "U.S. Agency Says N.Korea Can Mount Warhead on Mis-
      sile," Reuters, April 28, 2005. Defense analysts and officials, however, dis-
      agreed, saying Jacoby misspoke. See, e.g., U.S. Department of Defense,

Defense Department Regular Briefing, April 29, 2005. It appears that, so far, the best the North Koreans have managed is a one-ton gravity bomb, as a recent defector claimed. See Song, "A Representative of North Korea's Supreme People's Assembly Defects to South Korea and Gives Grave Testimony About the North's Nuclear Development," p. 8.

36   "Technology and time": White House Office of the Press Secretary, "Press Briefing by Ari Fleischer," February 12, 2003.

36   "is of purely": "Japan Urged to Stop Acting Rashly," Korean Central News Agency, March 19, 2003.

36   "Why are Americans": Song Young Gil, interview by author, Seoul, May 6, 2004. Song is a leading Uri Party legislator.

36   "I have always believed": "Korea Society Chairman Donald Gregg on the North/South Korea Summit," Council on Foreign Relations online interview, June 15, 2000, http://www.cfr.org/.

36   "deterrence works": David Kang, "Threatening, but Deterrence Works," in Victor D. Cha and David C. Kang, *Nuclear North Korea: A Debate on Engagement Strategies*, pp. 41–69 (New York: Columbia University Press, 2003).

36   "the little madman": Mary McGrory, "Fuzzy-Headed on North Korea," *Washington Post*, February 9, 2003, p. B7.

37   Selig Harrison thinks: See Selig Harrison, interview by Erich Weingartner, "Selig Harrison Reflects on His Latest Trip to DPRK," Canada-Korea Electronic Information Service, May 28, 2004, http://www.cankor.ligi.ubc.ca/issues/167.htm#INTERVIEW; and Selig Harrison, interview by Rebecca MacKinnon, "Harrison: 'Time for Fresh Start on NK,' " nkzone, May 4, 2004, http://nkzone.typepad.com/nkzone/2004/05/harrison_time_f.html.

37   "Unless we become friends": "Correction from Selig Harrison," nkzone, May 21, 2004, http://nkzone.typepad.com/nkzone/2004/05/correction_from.html.

37   "The only reason": Selig Harrison, "Inside North Korea: Leaders Open to Ending Nuclear Crisis," *Financial Times*, May 4, 2004, p. 9.

37   "Why would we need": Selig S. Harrison, "The North Korean Conundrum," *Nation*, June 7, 2004, p. 23.

37   Eisenhower hinted: Oberdorfer, *The Two Koreas*, p. 252. President Truman, at a news conference held on November 30, 1950, had also threatened to use nuclear weapons in the conflict. General Douglas MacArthur actually proposed dropping between thirty and fifty atomic bombs "strung across the neck of Manchuria" to seal off Korea from China. Nonetheless, Pyongyang goes too far when it claims that America was preparing to use atomic weapons during the Korean War. See "Rodong Sinmun on U.S. Attempted

Use of Nuclear Weapons During Korean War," Korean Central News Agency, June 27, 2004.

39   still harbored notions: According to Moscow's intelligence services, Kim Il Sung went to Mao Zedong in Spring 1975 to seek Chinese help for a second Korean War. William C. Triplett II, e-mail to author, October 26, 2004.

39   "When the American President": Thomas L. Friedman, *The Lexus and the Olive Tree* (New York: Anchor Books, 2000), p. 467.

39   Jimmy Carter told us: Jim Abrams, "Carter Says He Believes Nuclear Crisis in Korea Is Over," Associated Press, June 19, 1994.

39   "We both implemented": Glenn Kessler, "North Korea's Moves Appear Familiar," *Washington Post*, January 19, 2003, p. A19.

40   serious diplomacy: James Mann, *Rise of the Vulcans: The History of Bush's War Cabinet* (New York: Viking, 2004), p. 277.

40   thorough review of policy: White House Office of the Press Secretary, "Statement by the President," June 13, 2001.

40   "grim": Hugo Restall, "Last Gasp of Pyongyang's Appeasers," *Asian Wall Street Journal* (Hong Kong), July 25, 2003, p. A7.

41   Iraqi nuclear program: See Mahdi Obeidi and Kurt Pitzer, *The Bomb in My Garden: The Secrets of Saddam's Nuclear Mastermind* (Hoboken, New Jersey: John Wiley & Sons, 2004), pp. 6–7.

41   "We're not going": George W. Bush, interview by Tom Brokaw, *Nightly News*, NBC, April 24, 2003.

41   test, export, or use: George Gedda, "North Korea Warns U.S. It Has Nuclear Weapons and May Use Them," Associated Press, April 24, 2003. The circumstances surrounding the North Korean threat are in dispute. For more on the incident, see Frank Ching, "Sowing Confusion," *South China Morning Post* (Hong Kong), June 5, 2003, p. A14.

42   "Smith & Wesson": Arthur Waldron, interview by author, Bryn Mawr, Pennsylvania, July 9, 2001. Waldron is the Lauder Professor of International Relations at the University of Pennsylvania.

42   "rather shocked": Gareth Evans, interview by Nayan Chanda, YaleGlobal Online, September 26, 2003, http://yaleglobal.yale.edu/about/evans.jsp.

42   "a common understanding": Mitchell B. Reiss, "North Korea's Legacy of Missed Opportunities" (remarks, Heritage Foundation, Washington, D.C., March 12, 2004).

42   "No longer can the North": Ibid.

42   fatalistic approach: See Robert J. Einhorn, "Talk Therapy," *New York Times*, February 12, 2003, p. A37.

42   "no carrots": Graham Allison, "'94 Deal with North Korea Holds Lessons for Today," review of *Going Critical: The First North Korean Nuclear Crisis*, by Joel S. Wit, Daniel B. Poneman, and Robert L. Gallucci, *New York Times*, July 20, 2004, p. E6.

43   "Confusion, Vacillation": "North Korea Policy . . . Moving, or Captive?" Nelson Report, March 25, 2004.

43   outraged by being neglected: Bill Richardson, "The Santa Fe Trail," *Wall Street Journal*, January 24, 2003, p. A12.

43   "breakthrough": Kim Kwang, "Agreement Reached at Six-Way Talks on N. Korean Nuke Issue," Yonhap News Agency, September 19, 2005. South Korean president Roh Moo-hyun called the joint statement "epoch-making." Byun Duk, "Roh Welcomes 'Epoch-Making' Nuke Agreement," Yonhap News Agency, September 19, 2005.

43   statement of principles: See "Text of Joint Statement from Nuclear Talks," Associated Press, September 19, 2005.

44   his Foreign Ministry told: "Spokesman for DPRK Foreign Ministry on Six-Party Talks," Korean Central News Agency, September 20, 2005.

44   nuclear war with the United States: "Vigilance Against U.S. Attempt for Pre-emptive Nuclear Attack Called For," Korean Central News Agency, September 21, 2005.

44   "Framework Two": "Iran Take Note . . . US Agrees to DPRK Right to Peaceful Nuclear Program If Under the IAEA," Nelson Report, September 19, 2005.

44   strengthened North Korea: See James Sterngold, "South Korea President Lashes Out at U.S.," *New York Times*, October 8, 1994, p. 3.

45   "We cannot create ambiguities": Elaine Kurtenbach, "Nations Extend North Korea Nuclear Talks," Associated Press, September 17, 2005.

45   America accepted an arrangement: One conservative nonetheless hailed the joint statement. See Balbina Y. Hwang, "Nuclear Agreement Marks a Victory for the U.S.," *Asian Wall Street Journal* (Hong Kong), September 21, 2005, p. A13.

45   "We will not tolerate": White House Office of the Press Secretary, "President Bush Meets with Japanese Prime Minister Koizumi," May 23, 2003.

46   "taking off one's pants": The Korean Central Satellite TV broadcast this statement on April 11, 2003.

46   "They absolutely simply": Selig Harrison, interview by MacKinnon.

46   "aura of invulnerability": Jim Hoagland, "Nearing a Nuclear Jungle," *Washington Post*, January 9, 2003, p. A25.

46   "ultimate weapon of survival": Parris Chang, interview by author, Taipei, October 30, 2003.

47   generals' loyalty: See C. Kenneth Quinones, "North Korea Nuclear Talks: The View from Pyongyang," *Arms Control Today*, September 2004, http://www.armscontrol.org/act/2004_09/Quinones.asp.

47   the only unqualified success: See Sang-Hun Choe, "With Outside Pressure Building Up, North Korean Leader Relies on Military," Associated Press, June 4, 2003.

47   "radioactive lunatic": Mary McGrory, "Bush's Moonshine Policy," *Washington Post*, December 29, 2002, p. B7.

47   "They have had these": Colin Powell, interview by Tim Russert, *Meet the Press*, NBC, December 29, 2002.

47   "If you have only one or two": Michael R. Gordon, "In North Korea, Every New Bomb Is a Greater Peril," *New York Times*, Week in Review, January 5, 2003, p. 1.

48   fiercest game of chicken: See Peter S. Goodman and Akiko Kashiwagi, "Surveillance Gear Removed, N. Korea Admits," *Washington Post*, December 23, 2002, p. A12.

Chapter 3: THE PYGMALION OF PYONGYANG

49   "dance in step": Madeleine Albright with Bill Woodward, *Madam Secretary* (New York: Miramax Books, 2003), p. 464.

51   "The concept of dictatorship": Jean-Pierre Lehmann, e-mail to author, December 9, 2003.

52   enemy of later success: See Kongdan Oh and Ralph C. Hassig, *North Korea Through the Looking Glass* (Washington, D.C.: Brookings Institution Press, 2000), p. 187.

53   oversized monuments: Bruce Cumings, *North Korea: Another Country* (New York: New Press, 2004), pp. 134–35. There were no fewer than 34,000 monuments to Kim Il Sung in North Korea in the late 1980s. Don Oberdorfer, *The Two Koreas: A Contemporary History* (New York: Basic Books, 2001), p. 20. Surprisingly, there are no statues of Kim Jong Il. Andrei Lankov, "Written in Stone," *Korea Times* (Seoul), May 2, 2005, http://times .hankooki.com/1page/opnion/200505/kt2005050216325454140.htm.

53   first communist state: Marcus Noland, *Korea After Kim Jong-il* (Washington, D.C.: Institute for International Economics, 2004), p. 25. It's not clear that Kim ever intended to repay in the first place. See Nicholas Eberstadt, *The End of North Korea* (Washington, D.C.: AEI Press, 1999), p. 101.

53   even more beholden: See Marcus Noland, "North Korea's External Economic Relations: Globalization in 'Our Own Style,' " in *North Korea and Northeast Asia*, ed. Samuel S. Kim and Tai Hwan Lee, pp. 165–93 (Lanham, Maryland: Rowman & Littlefield, 2002).

54   communist cousins: "I do not think Kim Jong Il went to China and saw the future," says Balbina Hwang of the Heritage Foundation about the North Korean's 2001 trip. Instead, Kim saw that China was an open society and Communist Party leaders were sitting in a walled compound. "I think Kim Jong Il said that this is *exactly* where I don't want to go." Balbina Hwang, interview by author, Washington, D.C., September 10, 2003.

54   *Juche* Master: "North Korea . . . Something's Happening, but What??" Nelson Report, August 26, 2004.

54   ran on charcoal: See Andrei Lankov, "A Fleeting Industry," *Korea Times* (Seoul), April 27, 2005, http://times.hankooki.com/1page/opinion/200504/kt2005042716245454140.htm.

55   "a planned economy without planning": Nicholas Eberstadt, "The Persistence of North Korea," *Policy Review*, October/November 2004, p. 23.

55   "controlled, centralized, collectivized": Pierre Rigoulot, introduction to Kang Chol-hwan and Pierre Rigoulot, *The Aquariums of Pyongyang: Ten Years in a North Korean Gulag*, trans. Yair Reiner (New York: Basic Books, 2001), p. xiv.

55   "relentless enforcement": Eberstadt, *The End of North Korea*, p. 10.

55   even more orthodox: Oh and Hassig, *North Korea Through the Looking Glass*, pp. 9–10.

56   probably *growing*: The military's share of the economy grew because the civilian one shrank considerably. By the mid-1990s virtually the only factories still operating at capacity were military ones. Ibid., p. 105. See also Eberstadt, *The End of North Korea*, p. 122.

56   never met: Oh and Hassig, *North Korea Through the Looking Glass*, p. 84.

56   world's three Sinic cultures: See Samuel P. Huntington, *The Clash of Civilizations and the Remaking of World Order* (London: Simon & Schuster, Touchstone Books, 1998), p. 45.

57   "the Sun of the 21st Century": " 'Period of Celebrating the Sun of the 21st Century' Set in Denmark," Korean Central News Agency, February 13, 2004.

57   said to lack empathy: See Peter Carlson, "Sins of the Son," *Washington Post*, May 11, 2003, p. D1.

57   Kongdan Oh identifies: Kongdan Oh, interview by Jim Clancy, "N. Korea Nuclear Row," *Your World Today*, CNN International, January 14, 2003. In her writings Oh identifies four separate economies. See Kongdan Oh and Ralph Hassig, "North Korea Between Collapse and Reform," *Asian Survey*, March/April 1999, p. 287.

58   "inner reserves": Oh and Hassig, *North Korea Through the Looking Glass*, p. 52.

58   "speed battles": Ibid., p. 50.

58   concentrate on heavy industry: Ibid., p. 8.

58   "poverty trap": Deok Ryong Yoon and Bradley O. Babson, "Understanding North Korea's Economic Crisis," *Asian Economic Papers*, Summer 2002, p. 69.

59   dismantled and carted: See Bertil Lintner, "Shop Till You Drop," *Far Eastern Economic Review*, May 13, 2004, p. 14. See also James Brooke, "Trial Runs of a Free Market in North Korea," *New York Times*, March 11, 2003, p. C1.

59   South Korea's assistance: From 1998 the South Korean government annually provided about $200 million to permit the jump-starting of economic growth. Deok Ryong Yoon, interview by author, Seoul, April 30, 2004. Yoon is a South Korean economist. Kim Young Sam, Kim Dae Jung's predecessor as president, also provided assistance to Pyongyang, but only as a gesture.

59   "Expect no change": Oh and Hassig, *North Korea Through the Looking Glass*, p. 103.

60   no inkling: Brian Bridges, interview by author, Hong Kong, October 24, 2003.

60   package of economic measures: See e.g., Andrei Lankov, "North Korea's Antique Food Rationing," Asia Times Online, January 15, 2005, http://www.atimes.com/atimes/Korea/GA15Dg01.html; Noland, *Korea After Kim Jong-il*, pp. 46–52; "N. Korea Introduces Individual Farming System," *Korea Times* (Seoul), August 22, 2002, http://search.hankooki.com/times/times_view.php?term=individual+farming+system++&path=hankooki1/kt_nation/200208/t2002082219003041110.htm&media=kt; and "NK Needs to Open Door Wider: BOK," *Korea Times* (Seoul), August 22, 2002, http://search.hankooki.com/times/times_view.php?term=door+wider++&path=hankooki1/times/200208/t2002082217200140110.htm&media=kt.

60   the won was devalued: Doug Struck, "A Taste of Capitalism in N. Korea," *Washington Post*, September 13, 2002, p. A1. The won was devalued again in October 2003. "North Korea Sharply Devalued Currency: Report," Agence France-Presse, October 4, 2003.

60   made responsible for their own costs: The July 2002 measures did not include bankruptcy procedures. This means that Pyongyang may keep some enterprises alive through hidden subsidies, such as loans from banks on terms determined by the state. See Noland, *Korea After Kim Jong-il*, p. 47.

60   a severe downturn: Lim Changwon, "Grim Reality Behind North Korean Growth Drive: Report," Agence France-Presse, July 6, 2005.

60   headed to the countryside: See, e.g., Tim Judah, "First Tremor in the Last Outpost," *Guardian Weekend* (London), May 29, 2004, p. 28.

61   better to die at home: See John Larkin, "Why Refugees Flee," *Far Eastern Economic Review*, March 6, 2003, p. 14.

61   need even more time: Ruediger Frank, an academic from Germany, estimates Pyongyang needs about ten years before economic restructuring increases farm productivity. Ruediger Frank, interview by author, New York City, June 23, 2003.

61   for the first time: Struck, "A Taste of Capitalism in N. Korea," p. A1.

61   wanted a diplomatic triumph: Koizumi told Washington about the proposed summit only three weeks beforehand and presented the upcoming visit as a fait accompli. Koizumi refused to call off the trip despite Washington's concerns. See, e.g., Tetsuya Harada, "Pressure on North Korea to Change," *Yomiuri Shimbun* (Tokyo), August 31, 2002, p. 1. For background information, see Selig S. Harrison, "Did North Korea Cheat?" *Foreign Affairs*, January/February 2005, p. 99; and Cumings, *North Korea*, pp. 88–89.

61    $10 billion: See Takuji Kawata and Michio Hayashi, "U.S. Keeps Careful Watch over 'Security' Issue," *Yomiuri Shimbun* (Tokyo), September 1, 2002, p. 2.

62   "Now what are you": "N. Korea 'Admits Having Nukes,' " cnn.com, April 25, 2003, http://edition.cnn.com/2003/WORLD/asiapcf/east/04/24/nkorea.us.

62   "Kim expected": Larkin, "Why Refugees Flee," p. 14.

63   people who do not understand: Noland, *Korea After Kim Jong-il*, p. 54.

64   Kim's floating prices allowed: Pyongyang thought that it could use the market without having the market take over all pricing decisions. Ruediger Frank, interview.

64   had long ago appropriated: See, e.g., Kang and Rigoulot, *The Aquariums of Pyongyang*, p. 175.

64   "desperate measures": Balbina Hwang, interview.

64   people got won back instead: Noland, *Korea After Kim Jong-il*, p. 52; and Danny Gittings, "Kim Can't Kill the Free Market," *Asian Wall Street Journal* (Hong Kong), May 30, 2003, p. A9.

64   an expropriation of hard currency: The government also expropriated money by other means. See Howard W. French, "North Korea Experiments, with China as Its Model," *New York Times*, March 28, 2005, p. A6.

64   People's Life Bonds: Noland, *Korea After Kim Jong-il*, p. 52.

64   worst bargain: Gittings, "Kim Can't Kill the Free Market," p. A9.

65   many workers were forced: Workers were forced to take the bonds in lieu of salary. See Moon Ihlwan, "Open for Business—a Bit," *BusinessWeek* (international edition), July 26, 2004, p. 23; and "North Korea Eyes Economic

Rescue with Diplomacy Shift," *South China Morning Post* (Hong Kong), April 14, 2003, http://www.scmp.com/. In an era of high inflation, the bonds are almost worthless.

65   government was not resorting: Ruediger Frank, "North Korea: 'Gigantic Change' and a Gigantic Chance," Nautilus Institute Policy Forum Online, May 9, 2003, http://www.nautilus.org/fora/security/0031_Frank.html.

65   30 to 50 percent: American General Leon LaPorte estimates that the army's share of the economy may be as much as half. See *Nuclear Nightmare: Understanding North Korea*, Discovery Channel, August 6, 2003.

65   Pyongyang suspended: See Seung-Ryun Kim, "North Korea Suspends Market Economy Reforms," *Dong-A Ilbo* (Seoul), August 19, 2004, http://english.donga.com/srv/service.php3?bicode=060000&biid=2004082099388.

66   In their minds: Ruediger Frank, interview.

66   it is free: Eric Heginbotham, interview by author, Washington, D.C., November 19, 2003. Heginbotham is a senior fellow at the Council on Foreign Relations.

66   "world's last truly command economy": Kay Seok, "Speak Out About Human Rights in North Korea," *Asian Wall Street Journal* (Hong Kong), April 16, 2004, p. A7.

66   the private sector: See Park Suhk-sam, "Measuring and Assessing Economic Activity in North Korea," in *Korea's Economy in 2002*, pp. 76–83 (Washington, D.C.: Korea Economic Institute, 2002).

66   About twice as much money: Gittings, "Kim Can't Kill the Free Market," p. A9. The private economy accounts for a disproportionately large share of circulating cash because many of the transactions occurring within the military and palace economies take place offshore. Moreover, the military relies heavily on unpaid labor in prison camps.

66   the most eligible husbands: Joo Sang-min, "N. K. Preoccupied with Controlling Regime: Experts," *Korea Herald* (Seoul), November 18, 2004, http://www.koreaherald.co.kr/SITE/data/html_dir/2004/11/18/200411180005.asp.

66   size of their presents: Kang Chol Hwan, "Weddings Devoid of Honeymoons," *Chosun Ilbo* (Seoul), July 8, 2001, http://english.chosun.com/w21data/html/news/200107/200107080124.html.

67   "I can do": Kathi Zellweger, interview by author, Hong Kong, April 22, 2004.

67   trinkets by the roadside: See, e.g., Anthony Faiola, "A Crack in the Door in N. Korea," *Washington Post*, November 24, 2003, p. A10.

67   markets have spread: There are three hundred markets nationwide and forty in Pyongyang. Choi Kyong-ae, "NK Marks 2nd Year of Market Reform," *Korea Times* (Seoul), June 30, 2004, http://times.hankooki.com/1page/nation/200406/kt2004063017551911990.htm.

67   entrepreneurs develop: See Rebecca MacKinnon, "Letter from a Recent NK Visitor," nkzone, August 22, 2004, http://www.nkzone.org/nkzone/entry/2004/08/letter_from_a_r.php.

67   now beyond the control: North Korea, as a practical matter, cannot go back to the old system. People have now learned to live in a new system even though it is not perfectly institutionalized. The July 2002 reforms, which acknowledged what had already happened in the economy, have reinforced customs that had developed. Deok Ryong Yoon, interview. "The North Koreans are now going to play this game until the end," says German academic Ruediger Frank. They "are doomed to be successful in their economic reforms." Ruediger Frank, interview. As one visitor in 2004 noted, "More has changed in North Korea over the past year than in the 50 years before that." Andrew Ward, "N Korea Seeks to Boost Trade with Outside World," *Financial Times*, March 29, 2004, p. 9.

67   "future Rotterdam": "Free-Trade Zone Touted for Tumen," *People's Daily* (Beijing), July 9, 2004, http://english.people.com.cn/200407/09/eng20040709_149034.html.

68   "the delivery room": Kim Mi Young, "North Korea's Border Cities See Bleak Future," nk.chosun.com, January 4, 2004, http://nk.chosun.com/english/news/news.html?ACT=detail&cat=10&res_id=4960.

68   independent country: See Mark O'Neill, "From a Great Height," *South China Morning Post* (Hong Kong), May 18, 2004, p. A16; Mark O'Neill, "Grand Plans for the SAR That Never Was," *South China Morning Post* (Hong Kong), May 18, 2004, http://www.scmp.com/; Harpal Sandhu, "A Doomed Reform," *Harvard International Review*, Spring 2003, p. 36; and Jay Solomon and Charles Hutzler, "North Korea Flirts with Capitalism — As Best It Can," *Wall Street Journal*, October 3, 2002, p. A1.

68   a woman from California's Orange County: Mark O'Neill, "Kim Eyes New Chief Executive," *South China Morning Post* (Hong Kong), September 10, 2004, p. A20.

68   "Let's consider": Oh and Hassig, *North Korea Through the Looking Glass*, p. 182.

68   Beijing's style of market reforms: Albright, *Madam Secretary*, p. 466.

68   "Swedish model": Kim Jong Il is attracted to the socialist aspects of Sweden's system. Ibid.

Chapter 4: COLLAPSE PERHAPS?

70   "half-life": David E. Sanger, "Next Question: How to Stop Nuclear Blackmail," *New York Times*, Week in Review, March 9, 2003, p 1.

70   only months to live: American intelligence briefings on North Korea's sta-

bility were deeply flawed. Assessments, which were wrong year after year, never changed. Briefers merely said that North Korea was going to collapse because North Koreans were starving and the Soviet Union collapsed before it. Scott Conwell, interview by author, Annapolis, Maryland, November 5, 2003.

70   "Don't wait": "Update: N Korea Finds Nuclear Impasse Beneficial — Expert," Dow Jones Newswires, January 15, 2004.

71   hidden resilience: Even Pyongyang's insiders do not understand North Korea's internal strength. See "North Korean Regime Not Close to Collapse: Defector," Agence France-Presse, November 1, 2003.

71   did not have the strength: The destitute, who have the most to gain from destruction of an existing social order, are not generally revolutionary. See Eric Hoffer, *The True Believer: Thoughts on the Nature of Mass Movements* (New York: Harper & Row, 1951), pp. 7–8.

71   "Western history": Michael Breen, *The Koreans: Who They Are, What They Want, Where Their Future Lies* (New York: St. Martin's Press, Thomas Dunne Books, 2004), p. 38.

72   "Korean heroes": Ibid.

72   "If you know": *Children of the Secret State*, narr. Joe Layburn, Discovery Times Channel, August 19, 2003.

73   "we only need one party": Alfonso Chardy, "Castro Wants No Talk of *Glasnost* in Cuba," *Miami Herald*, July 28, 1988, p. 1A.

73   "the most successful totalitarian regime": *Nuclear Nightmare: Understanding North Korea*, Discovery Channel, August 6, 2003.

73   "My power comes from": Samuel S. Kim, "Introduction: A Systems Approach" in *The North Korean System in the Post–Cold War Era*, ed. Samuel S. Kim, pp. 1–37 (New York: Palgrave, 2001).

73   5 million reservists: There is no consensus on the number of reservists. For a high estimate, see Kongdan Oh and Ralph C. Hassig, "North Korea: The Hardest Nut," *Foreign Policy*, November/December 2003, p. 44 (6 million reservists).

73   handpicked about a thousand: "North Korea Collapse Unlikely, Unwelcome in South," *South China Morning Post* (Hong Kong), January 30, 2003, http://www.scmp.com/.

73   lavishes senior officers: See Don Oberdorfer, *The Two Koreas: A Contemporary History* (New York: Basic Books, 2001), p. 415.

73   command-and-control authority: David Reese, *The Prospects for North Korea's Survival* (New York: Oxford University Press, 1998), p. 19.

73   only one constituency: Kim Jong Il's reliance on the military was high-

lighted in 1998 when he ran for a seat in the Tenth Supreme People's Assembly, a rubber-stamp legislature. Kim was recommended as a candidate in all 687 districts across the country, but he chose the district numbered 666, composed entirely of soldiers. He chose another military constituency in 2003. See "Kim Jong Il Nominated as Candidate for Deputy to 11th SPA," Korean Central News Agency, July 1, 2003; and "Korean Voters Participate in SPA Election," Korean Central News Agency, July 27, 1998.

73   the most solid state of all: Eric Heginbotham, interview by author, Washington, D.C., November 19, 2003.

73   no nation has matched: See Marcus Noland, *Korea After Kim Jong-il* (Washington, D.C.: Institute for International Economics, 2004), p. 25.

74   greatest potential enemy: See Samuel P. Huntington, *Political Order in Changing Societies* (New Haven: Yale University Press, 1968), p. 289.

74   loosening of social controls: Jae-Jean Suh, "North Korea's Social System," in *Prospects for Change in North Korea*, ed. Tae Hwan Ok and Hong Yung Lee, pp. 209–65 (Berkeley: Institute of East Asian Studies, 1994).

74   are still leaving: Kim Jong Il's position ironically has been bolstered by the sheer desperation of his citizens. Although the stream of refugees is deeply embarrassing to Pyongyang, the outflow has relieved pressure on the regime by draining the country of its discontents. The same thing happened in both communist Cuba and Vietnam.

74   wives build capitalism: Andrei Lankov, "North Korea: Market Forces Have Female Faces," Asia Times Online, April 6, 2005, http://www.atimes.com/ atimes/Korea/GD06Dg01.html.

75   Foreign analysts don't know: See Tim Judah, "First Tremor in the Last Outpost," *Guardian Weekend* (London), May 29, 2004, p. 28; and "Through a Glass, Darkly," *Economist*, March 13, 2004, p. 41. Although there is real evidence of an uptick, some of the consumerism is staged for foreigners. See James Robbins, "North Korea: On the Face of It," BBC News World Edition, September 18, 2004, http://news.bbc.co.uk/2/hi/programmes/ from_our_own_correspondent/3666676.stm.

75   own foodie guide: *Eating Out in Pyongyang: The Restaurant Guide for Pyongyang, Democratic People's Republic Korea*, was compiled by three international aid workers. The guide lists and rates more than fifty of the 350 restaurants in the North Korean capital.

75   the young Moonwalk: Norbert Vollertsen, interview by author, Seoul, May 7, 2004.

75   clutching the Gucci bags: Norbert Vollertsen, then an aid worker, was walking in the huge Beijing airport looking for an Air Koryo flight to North Korea a few years ago. He asked directions from a bystander, who told him

the secret for getting to the right gate in the busy terminal: "Oh, quite simple. Follow those guys with Kim Jong Il badges or follow the Gucci bags,"
the man said. "Those are the guys who are going to Pyongyang." Ibid.

75   "fiber of self-reliance": Lee Dung Ki, who claims credit for developing
     vinalon, is also considered the "godfather" of the North Korean nuclear
     weapons program. Oberdorfer, *The Two Koreas*, p. 253.

75   Baseball caps: Bertil Lintner, "Shop Till You Drop," *Far Eastern Economic
     Review*, May 13, 2004, p. 14.

75   the black leather jacket: Norbert Vollertsen, interview.

75   social changes taking place: One sign of increasing official concern about
     social change is the recent campaign against long hair. See "North Korea
     Magazine Introduces Hairstyle to Conform to 'Military First Era,' " *Chosun
     Ilbo* (Seoul), March 16, 2005, http://chinese.chosun.com/site/data/html
     _dir/2005/03/16/20050316000001.html (women); and "N Korea Wages War
     on Long Hair," BBC News World Edition, January 8, 2005, http://news.bbc
     .co.uk/2/hi/asia-pacific/4157121.stm (men).

75   "breeds a sense of entitlement": Ben Dolven, "A Home Revolt at Ground
     Level," *Far Eastern Economic Review*, October 23, 2003, p. 35. For one of
     the best explanations why ownership breeds entitlement, see Alexis de
     Tocqueville, *The Old Regime and the French Revolution* (New York: Dou-
     bleday, 1983), pp. 30–31.

77   "I believe that the ideals": *Cold War: Conclusions, 1989–1991*, narr. Ken-
     neth Branagh, CNN, July 2, 2000.

77   "In North Korea": Ruediger Frank, interview by author, New York City,
     June 23, 2003.

77   "If rain falls": Kongdan Oh, "North Korea Braves a New World," in *Korea
     Briefing, 1992*, ed. Donald N. Clarke, pp. 27–49 (Boulder: Westview Press,
     1992).

77   "practical socialism": See Young Chul Chung, "North Korean Reform and
     Opening: Dual Strategy and 'Silli (Practical) Socialism,' " *Pacific Affairs*,
     Summer 2004, p. 283.

78   now keep the legacy alive: See Bruce Cumings, *North Korea: Another
     Country* (New York: New Press, 2004), p. 170; and Charles K. Armstrong,
     The North Korean Revolution, 1945–1950 (Ithaca: Cornell University Press,
     2003), p. 27.

78   "from poetry to potato farming": Kongdan Oh and Ralph C. Hassig, *North
     Korea Through the Looking Glass* (Washington, D.C.: Brookings Institution
     Press, 2000), p. 13.

78   to the letter: "Rodong Sinmun Calls for Implementing Kim Il Sung's Last
     Instructions to Letter," Korean Central News Agency, July 6, 2004.

79   method of implementing change: Ruediger Frank, interview.

79   "modernization": See Andrew Ward, "N Korea Seeks to Boost Trade with
       Outside World," *Financial Times*, March 29, 2004, p. 9. The word "reform"
       is still not used. See Jack Kim, "Profit Is Good, N.Korea's Kim Tells Factory
       Workers," Reuters, June 2, 2004.

79   "perfection": See "N. Koreans Say Reforms Are Perfection of Communism,"
       South China Morning Post (Hong Kong), August 22, 2002, http://www.scmp
       .com/.

79   impeding change: See, e.g., Oh and Hassig, *North Korea Through the Look-
       ing Glass*, p. 13.

80   no longer following orders: Economic shocks have degraded discipline in
       the bureaucracy since the middle of the 1990s. See, e.g., Jay Solomon and
       Carla Anne Robbins, "Amid Nuclear Standoff, Food Aid Shrinks for Hun-
       gry North Korea," *Wall Street Journal*, May 15, 2003, p. A1. This trend has
       resulted in Pyongyang's loss of control over the provinces, which some mis-
       take for a gradual liberalization. Tim Peters, interview by author, Seoul,
       May 7, 2004. Peters is a Seoul-based refugee activist. Local governors now
       have more autonomy, and this is a "profound change." Balbina Hwang,
       interview by author, Washington, D.C., September 10, 2003.

80   at will: The travel permit system broke down after 1995 as the government
       allowed people to roam the country for food. Officials tightened travel
       restrictions as the famine subsided, but these rules are not strictly enforced
       today except around Pyongyang and sensitive sites elsewhere.

80   past military guards: See Scott Snyder, "Lessons of the NGO Experience in
       North Korea," in *Paved with Good Intentions: The NGO Experience in
       North Korea*, ed. L. Gordon Flake and Scott Snyder, pp. 111–22 (Westport,
       Connecticut: Praeger, 2003); and Kang Chol-hwan and Pierre Rigoulot,
       The Aquariums of Pyongyang: Ten Years in a North Korean Gulag, trans. Yair
       Reiner (New York: Basic Books, 2001), p. 197.

80   "As a matter of practice": Kang and Rigoulot, *The Aquariums of Pyongyang*,
       p. 176. It is even possible to spring people from North Korean prisons with
       payoffs. Tim Peters, interview.

80   "The regime": Kang and Rigoulot, *The Aquariums of Pyongyang*, p. 170.

80   looting property: See Solomon and Robbins, "Amid Nuclear Standoff, Food
       Aid Shrinks for Hungry North Korea," p. A1. North Korea also is developing
       "apparatchik capitalism." Marcus Noland, "North Korea's External Eco-
       nomic Relations: Globalization in 'Our Own Style,'" in *North Korea and
       Northeast Asia*, ed. Samuel S. Kim and Tai Hwan Lee, pp. 165–93 (Lan-
       ham, Maryland: Rowman & Littlefield, 2002).

80   "bulging envelopes": Kang and Rigoulot, *The Aquariums of Pyongyang*,
       p. 191.

80   "hush money": Ibid., p. 185.

81   its security apparatus: State security officials "are forming the basis of a new class of legal and illegal economic operators." Hazel Smith, "Brownback Bill Will Not Solve North Korea's Problems," *Jane's Intelligence Review*, February 2004, p. 42.

81   "We'll do anything": Cindy Sui, "No Turning Back for North Korea's Economic Reforms: UN Official," Agence France-Presse, August 18, 2004. See also Burt Herman, "Cautious Development Looms in North Korea," Associated Press, January 2, 2005.

81   land grabs: Kang and Rigoulot, *The Aquariums of Pyongyang*, p. 175.

81   "failure in socialization": Suh, "North Korea's Social System," pp. 209–65.

81   "Our younger generation": "Our People's Army Is an Army of the Working Class, an Army of the Revolution; Class and Political Education Should Be Continuously Strengthened," speech, February 8, 1963, in *Kim Il Sung: Selected Works*, vol. III (Pyongyang: Foreign Languages Publishing House, 1971), pp. 465–525.

82   were executed: Bradley K. Martin, *Under the Loving Care of the Fatherly Leader: North Korea and the Kim Dynasty* (New York: St. Martin's Press, Thomas Dunne Books, 2004), pp. 548–49.

82   "continuous revolution": Pyongyang continued to talk about "continuous revolution" after Kim Il Sung's death. See, e.g., "Historic Work Ushering in Revolutionary Upswing in Socialist Construction," Korean Central News Agency, December 13, 1996.

82   "catacomb church": Religion, and especially Christianity, is spreading and undermining Kim's position. See Andrei Lankov, "North Korea's Missionary Position," Asia Times Online, March 16, 2005, http://www.atimes.com/atimes/Korea/GC16Dg03.html.

83   is beginning to admit: See Ruediger Frank, "North Korea: 'Gigantic Change' and a Gigantic Chance," Nautilus Institute Policy Forum Online, May 9, 2003, http://www.nautilus.org/fora/security/0031_Frank.html.

84   longevity is both: See Huntington, *Political Order in Changing Societies*, p. 13.

84   There must exist: See Martin King Whyte, "Chinese Social Trends: Stability or Chaos?" in *Is China Unstable?: Assessing the Factors*, ed. David Shambaugh, pp. 143–63 (Armonk, New York: M. E. Sharpe, 2000).

84   "Many great things": Anita Snow, "Castro Blasts EU as Trojan Horse for U.S.," Associated Press, July 27, 2003.

85   "Patiently endured": Tocqueville, *The Old Regime and the French Revolution*, p. 177.

85   Nobody likes: See W. E. Mosse, *Alexander II and the Modernization of Russia* (New York: Collier Books, 1962), p. 149.

85   "Things can happen": Malcolm Gladwell, "What Is the Tipping Point?" gladwell.com, http://gladwell.com/tippingpoint/index.html.

85   "I recall that my friends": Vaclav Havel, "The Soul of a Nation," *Washington Post*, October 12, 2003, p. B7.

85   no opposition: Andrew Meier, interview by author, Washington, D.C., May 14, 2003. Meier was a *Time* correspondent assigned to the Soviet Union.

86   perhaps three hundred citizens: See Carol Giacomo, "Defector Said to Call North Korea Rulers Unstable," Reuters, October 30, 2003.

86   only one fat man: Michael Breen, *Kim Jong-il: North Korea's Dear Leader* (Singapore: John Wiley & Sons, 2004), pp. xii and 147. Tours to Mount Kumgang, which is just above the DMZ, were temporarily halted when a South Korean woman asked a North Korean why Kim Jong Il was the only fat man in the country. See Steven Knipp, "Moving Mountains," *South China Morning Post* (Hong Kong), October 28, 2004, p. A16.

86   One-man dictatorships: Huntington, *Political Order in Changing Societies*, p. 18.

86   "As we all know": Norbert Vollertsen, interview.

86   "My guess": Tim Peters, interview.

86   "Ten years ago": Erica Kang, interview by author, Seoul, April 30, 2004.

87   elite to mass politics: Noland, *Korea After Kim Jong-il*, p. 51.

87   "cannot reverse": Roh Moo-hyun, address, World Affairs Council, Los Angeles, November 12, 2004.

87   consistent application of coercion: See Ekkart Zimmermann, *Political Violence, Crises, and Revolutions: Theories and Research* (Cambridge, Massachusetts: Schenkman, 1983), pp. 82–83.

87   plots and protests: See, e.g., Jasper Becker, *Rogue Regime: Kim Jong Il and the Looming Threat of North Korea* (New York: Oxford University Press, 2005), pp. 197–99, 201; Martin, *Under the Loving Care*, pp. 441–42, 547–48; Andreas Lorenz, "Joyful Dancing," *Der Spiegel*, October 30, 2004, http://www.spiegel.de/spiegel/english/0,1518,325971,00.html; and Suh, "North Korea's Social System," pp. 209–65.

87   involving the military: There have been numerous reports of military coups, especially in 1991, 1992, and 1995. See, e.g., Lorenz, "Joyful Dancing"; Danny Gittings, "China Props Up an Evil Regime," *Asian Wall Street Journal* (Hong Kong), January 17, 2003, p. A7; and Oh and Hassig, *North Korea Through the Looking Glass*, pp. 119–20. At the end of the 1990s generals who had plotted to kill Kim Jong Il were doused with gasoline and set alight

in Pyongyang's May Day Stadium. Sergey Soukhorukov, "Train Blast Was 'a Plot to Kill North Korea's Leader,' " *Sunday Telegraph* (London), June 13, 2004, p. 27. In addition to the rumors of military coups, there are stories of army discontent. See, e.g., James Brooke, "Japanese Official Warns of Fissures in North Korea," *New York Times*, November 22, 2004, p. A3 (130 generals defected to China); and Won-Jae Park, "Strange Atmosphere Along Border Between North Korea and China," *Dong-A-Ilbo* (Seoul), October 10, 2004, http://english.donga.com/srv/service.php3?bicode=060000&biid =2004101179748 (North Korean troops defecting across Chinese border in groups).

87   new reports suggesting trouble: See, e.g., "North Korean Leader's Son Survives Assassination Twice: Report," Agence France-Presse, March 14, 2005 (two attempts on life of Kim Jong Nam); Jong-Heon Lee, "N. Korea Launches Harsh Crackdown," United Press International, March 11, 2005 (public executions to stem tide of unrest); Michael Sheridan, "Chairman Kim's Dissolving Kingdom," *Sunday Times* (London), January 30, 2005, p. 27 (security clampdown on foreign aid workers and shootout inside a Kim family palace); Jack Kim, "Activist: Video Shows Dissent in Communist N.Korea," Reuters, January 17, 2005 (defaced Kim Jong Il portrait); Khang Hyun-sung, "Kim Badges May Be the Latest Clue to Waning Power," *South China Morning Post* (Hong Kong), November 26, 2004, p. A10 (people no longer wearing Kim Jong Il badges); "N.Korea Reports Kim Troop Trip After Portraits Flap," Reuters, November 16, 2004 (portraits of Kim Jong Il removed from public places); and Michael Sheridan, "Power Battle as Kim Grieves for Mistress," *Sunday Times* (London), November 14, 2004, p. 31 (influential North Koreans shipping out money and assets to China).

87   as the economy failed: See Andrei Lankov, "Cracks in North Korean 'Stalinism,' " Asia Times Online, December 7, 2004, http://atimes.com/atimes/ Korea/FL07Dg01.html.

87   Kim Jong Il has tightened: See "North Korea Introduces Real Economic Reform—Seoul Officials," Agence France-Presse, December 8, 2003.

87   the cost of monitoring: See Kang Chol-hwan, "Cell Phones Spark 'Communication Revolution' in N.K.," *Chosun Ilbo* (Seoul), December 3, 2004, p. A3.

87   infrastructure of fear: "In the long run, the real limits to dictatorship are chiefly economic: the ability of a government to continue to harness resources sufficient to maintain military control at home or to satisfy ambitions abroad." Bill Emmott, *20:21 Vision: Twentieth-Century Lessons for the Twenty-first Century* (New York: Farrar, Straus and Giroux, 2003), p. 15. Since the early 1990s, control measures in North Korea have been relaxed. The change is not the result of policy liberalization but of Pyongyang's lack of resources.

87   for every fifty citizens: Andrei Lankov, "A Spyhole into North Korea," *Korea*

Times (Seoul), September 17, 2004, http://times.hankooki.com/1page/special/200409/kt2004091717303527130.htm.

87   to remove the taint: North Korean concentration camps contain, among others, many children of high-ranking government officials, especially diplomats. The children had a hard time acclimating to North Korea. Ahn Hyeok, interview by Maiken Baird, Seoul, April 15, 2003. Ahn Hyeok is a former political prisoner held in North Korea. North Korea indoctrinates not only people who have come back but also people who go. See Kang Chol-hwan, "Children of Displaced Families Favored as Spouse Candidates," *Chosun Ilbo* (Seoul), November 6, 2002, p. A13.

88   talk to relatives: See Rebecca MacKinnon, "Chinese Cell Phone Breaches North Korean Hermit Kingdom," YaleGlobal Online, January 17, 2005, http://yaleglobal.yale.edu/display.article?id=5145. As ordinary North Koreans chat with outsiders on cell phones, Pyongyang is blocking almost all international calls. See Brent Choi and Brian Lee, "North Is Said to Cut Back Phone Use," *JoongAng Daily* (Seoul), June 8, 2005, http://joongangdaily.joins.com/200506/07/200506070003592109900090309031.html.

88   foreign radio programs: For the effect of foreign radio, see Kang and Rigoulot, *The Aquariums of Pyongyang*, p. 186.

88   videocassettes and DVDs: See, e.g., "Winds of Change in North Korea Evident in Chinese Border City," Yonhap News Agency, December 12, 2004.

88   "I don't like them": Norbert Vollertsen, interview.

88   now live abroad: Kim Jong Nam, Kim Jong Il's eldest son, lived in Beijing but may have moved back to Pyongyang. Kim Jong Il's adopted daughter, Ri Nam Ok, lives in Switzerland.

88   it just happens: See Michael Mandelbaum, *The Ideas That Conquered the World: Peace, Democracy, and Free Markets in the Twenty-first Century* (New York: PublicAffairs, 2002), p. 381.

88   None of the great reformers: Fred Coleman, *The Decline and Fall of the Soviet Empire: Forty Years That Shook the World, from Stalin to Yeltsin* (New York: St. Martin's Griffin, 1996), p. 225.

Chapter 5: HOUSEWIVES FOR NUCLEAR TERROR

89   "Don't worry too much": *BizAsia*, narr. Sohn Jie-Ae, CNN International, January 21, 2003.

90   "Koreans are very cocky": Usung Chung, interview by author, Seoul, April 28, 2004.

90   "The North Korean nuclear issue": Roh Moo-hyun, address, World Affairs Council, Los Angeles, November 12, 2004.

90   "Korean Civil War": Song Young Gil, interview by author, Seoul, May 6, 2004.

90   America did not intend: Bruce Cumings, *Korea's Place in the Sun: A Modern History* (New York: W. W. Norton, 1997), p. 209.

91   who could be excused: See ibid., p. 347.

92   the detention and execution: Don Oberdorfer, *The Two Koreas: A Contemporary History* (New York: Basic Books, 2001), p. 10.

92   a century's worth of progress: See ibid., p. 37.

93   "Korean-style democracy": See Cumings, *Korea's Place in the Sun*, p. 359.

93   "a policy of disassociation": See Oberdorfer, *The Two Koreas*, p. 40.

93   "internal affairs": Ibid., p. 41.

93   "Korean barbecue": Ibid.

94   evidently came to believe: See ibid., pp. 114–15.

94   "at a loss": Henry Scott Stokes, "Korean General Filling Key Posts with His Men to Bolster Power," *New York Times*, December 15, 1979, p. 1.

94   too preoccupied: See Oberdorfer, *The Two Koreas*, p. 123.

95   "Democracy requires blood": Song Young Gil, interview.

95   more than the official toll: There are various official tolls, which now vary from 191 to 240.

95   "democratic moment": Tony Michell, interview by author, Seoul, May 7, 2004.

96   simply failed to say no: See Michael Breen, *The Koreans: Who They Are, What They Want, Where Their Future Lies* (New York: St. Martin's Press, Thomas Dunne Books, 2004), pp. 210–11. See also Oberdorfer, *The Two Koreas*, pp. 129–30.

96   "The Americans knew": Jung Sunghwan, interview by author, Seoul, May 3, 2004.

96   Zbigniew Brzezinski: Oberdorfer, *The Two Koreas*, p. 129.

96   "cool and aloof": Ibid., pp. 130–31.

97   the price America paid: Washington saved Kim Dae Jung's life during the Park era as well.

97   Moments before seeing Reagan: Breen, *The Koreans*, p. 211.

98   public displays of disaffection: South Korean disaffection has not gotten any better since 1988. Vendors in Seoul were selling the flags of all countries participating in the 2002 World Cup except for the American one. See Susan Oak, "Anti-Americanism in Korea," *Korea Herald* (Seoul), June 9, 2004, http://www.koreaherald.co.kr/.

98   "Anti-Americanism emerged": Breen, *The Koreans*, p. 212.

99   "deliberate plot": Ibid., p. 18.

99   A fundamental aspect: Cumings, *Korea's Place in the Sun*, p. 489.

100   was not coincidental: Selig S. Harrison, *Korean Endgame: A Strategy for Reunification and U.S. Disengagement* (Princeton: Princeton University Press, 2002), p. 78.

101   Roh's idea: For other confederation ideas, see ibid., pp. 74–101.

101   National Security Law: "Security Law Revision," *Korea Herald* (Seoul), May 8, 2004, http://www.koreaherald.co.kr/.

101   removing American troops: Americans are beating the South Koreans to the punch. See Sang-Hun Choe, "South Korea Says Washington Will Delay Troop Redeployment," Associated Press, October 6, 2004.

101   "foreign interference": See David Scofield, "Seoul Rows Against the US Tide," Asia Times Online, November 24, 2004, http://www.atimes.com/atimes/Korea/FK24Dg03.html.

102   "horse trading": Brad Glosserman, "For the Sunshine Policy to Work, South Korea Must Learn to Be Tough," *South China Morning Post* (Hong Kong), February 20, 2003, p. A15.

102   "appeasement": Hugo Restall, "Peculiar Pyschologies in the Hermit Kingdom," *Asian Wall Street Journal* (Hong Kong), December 20, 2002, p. A11.

102   infiltrations and incursions: Moreover, at that time North Korea moved its forces to areas near the DMZ. William C. Triplett II, *Rogue State: How a Nuclear North Korea Threatens America* (Washington, D.C.: Regnery, 2004), p. 70.

102   an end in itself: See Glosserman, "For the Sunshine Policy to Work, South Korea Must Learn to Be Tough," p. A15.

102   created a desert: Norbert Vollertsen, interview by author, Seoul, May 7, 2004.

102   "sun burnt": Park Jin, interview by author, Seoul, May 6, 2004.

103   the Koreans themselves: Breen, *The Koreans*, pp. 244–45.

103   $600 billion: See Gordon Fairclough, "South Korean Aid to North Increases Tensions with U.S.," *Wall Street Journal*, March 11, 2005, p. A1. There are also a few estimates that are extremely low, but they are out of the range of mainstream opinion.

103   $1.8 trillion: "No Aid to North Korea Until Nuclear Crisis Ends: Roh," Reuters, April 13, 2005.

103   "our people do not want": Don Oberdorfer, "Koreans 'Cautious' on Unification After Germany," *Washington Post*, July 4, 1991, p. A17.

103   was skeptical: In April 1998, just a few months after Kim Dae Jung's inaugu-
      ration, Seoul's new unification minister, Jeong Se-hyun, went to the DPRK
      to talk about its request for fertilizer. During a break in the contentious talks
      a North Korean negotiator came up to Jeong and asked, "What is the real
      intention of the so-called Sunshine Policy?" "My president stated that we
      will not seek unification by absorption, didn't he?" Jeong replied. "Why are
      you concerned?" "Is the real intention perhaps to melt and consume the
      North?" the North Korean suggested. Jeong says it was natural for his North
      Korean interlocutor to be suspicious in view of the preceding half century of
      war and confrontation. Jeong Se-hyun, interview by author, Seoul, April 29,
      2004. Jeong served as unification minister until June 2004.

103   "more dangerous": Harrison, *Korean Endgame*, p. 83.

104   "We're simply going": Tim Peters, interview by author, Seoul, May 7, 2004.

104   "is *systematically incapable*": Nicholas Eberstadt, *The End of North Korea*
      (Washington, D.C.: AEI Press, 1999), p. 4 (emphasis in original).

104   "For South Koreans": Erica Kang, interview by author, Seoul, April 30,
      2004.

104   "It was like a cartoon shaking hands": Hansol Seo, interview by author,
      Seoul, April 30, 2004.

105   no longer a perpetrator: Jung-Hoon Lee, interview by author, Seoul, May 3,
      2004. Lee is a professor of international relations at Seoul's Yonsei Univer-
      sity.

105   considered deliberate: See, e.g., Sang-Hun Choe, "Koreans March with
      Candles amid Spreading Anti-US Sentiment," Associated Press, December
      7, 2002.

105   no large-scale expressions of outrage: The biggest demonstration was a
      protest on July 4, 2002, of about three thousand veterans. Jae-Suk Yoo,
      "South Korean Veterans March, Burn Kim Jong Il's Effigies," Associated
      Press, July 4, 2002.

105   "Fucking USA": Breen, *The Koreans*, p. 253.

105   "Anti-Americanism": Peter S. Goodman and Joohee Cho, "Anti-U.S. Senti-
      ment Deepens in S. Korea," *Washington Post*, January 9, 2003, p. A1.

105   no particular love: The 386ers are probably more leftist than anti-American.
      For a discussion of the attitudes of this generation, see Andrei Lankov,
      "Body Snatching, North Korean Style," Asia Times Online, February 26,
      2005, http://www.atimes.com/atimes/Korea/GB26Dg01.html.

106   "several decades": Kim Yong-bom, "Kim Calls for Stronger ROK-US Secu-
      rity Cooperation," *Korea Times* (Seoul), October 1, 2000, http://search
      .hankooki.com/times/times_view.php?term=kim+calls+for+stronger++&
      path=hankooki1/times/200010/t2000100116501340112.htm&media=kt.

107   incompatible with democracy: The Newspaper Law and the Press Arbitration Law, which both went into effect in July 2005, may be unique, at least in countries with firmly established democratic institutions, with regard to government involvement in newspaper matters. See "Newspaper Indus Still Vital, So Is Press Freedom—Assoc," Dow Jones Newswires, May 30, 2005.

107   Roh Moo-hyun's public embrace: See Gordon Fairclough, "Spy Case Reflects Political Divide in South Korea," *Wall Street Journal*, March 29, 2004, p. A16.

107   "Permitting a communist party": Choi Hoon, "Roh Says He Would Meet Japan Red Boss in Korea," *JoongAng Daily* (Seoul), June 11, 2003, http://joongangdaily.joins.com/.

107   "The only thing left": Lee Do-hyung, interview by author, Seoul, May 1, 2004.

107   "unification under the red flag": Song Young Gil, interview.

107   more than three times larger: Hong Young Lim, "2004 Poll on the People's Opinions," *Chosun Ilbo* (Seoul), May 3, 2004, p. A5.

108   "Basically we expect Vietcongs": Usung Chung, interview.

108   "This is not a country": Ibid.

108   a late-day surge: "Roh's Online Supporters Behind Victory," *Korea Times* (Seoul), December 24, 2002, http://search.hankooki.com/times/times_view .php?terms=body%3A+internet+code%3A=kt&path=hankooki3%2Ftimes% 2F1page%2Ftech%2F200212%2Fkt2002122317284612350.htm&kw =internet.

108   "2030 Generation": Chang Se-moon, "Young Generation Shapes New ROK-US Alliance," *Korea Times* (Seoul), May 9, 2003, http://times .hankooki.com/cgi-bin/hkiprn.cgi?pa=/1page/special/200305/ kt2003050919092811440.htm&ur=times.hankooki.com&fo=print_kt.htm.

108   after a fistfight: See Chang Jae-soon, "Parliament Passes Impeachment Motion, President Roh Suspended," Yonhap News Agency, March 12, 2004.

108   less than six months: The Uri Party was formed in November 2003 when it split from Roh Moo-hyun's Millennium Democratic Party.

108   a "generation" is only three years: Tony Michell, interview.

108   "We have hope": Park Jin, interview.

109   "Roh the idiot": Jae-Suk Yoo, "Impeachment Vote Unravels Success of Roh," Associated Press, March 12, 2004.

109   "Captain Roh": Sang-Hun Choe, "South Korean President, Facing Impeachment Verdict, Has History as Survivor," Associated Press, May 13, 2004.

109   to refuse to have: "SKorean President's Loyalists Launch New Party,"
Agence France-Presse, November 11, 2003.

109   "our" in Korean: The name is sometimes translated as "Our Open Party."

109   "patiently": Park Jin, interview.

109   "the momentum of generational change": Ibid.

109   "political core": Song Young Gil, interview.

109   came from nowhere: This party was formed in January 2000.

109   newest subgroup: Park Jin calls people in their early twenties an "emerging
new conservative generation in Korea." Park Jin, interview. This group,
however, appears to be less political than their elders. Chang-Gi Kim, interview by author, Seoul, May 3, 2004. Kim is a deputy managing editor of the
conservative newspaper *Chosun Ilbo* in Seoul.

110   "New Right" movement: See Dongjin Park, "South Korea's 'New Right'
Party Sprouts from Left," *Wall Street Journal*, August 24, 2005, p. A9.

110   "too noisy": Cumings, *Korea's Place in the Sun*, p. 333.

110   "a land of extremes": Sohn Jie-Ae, interview by author, Seoul, May 7, 2004.
Sohn is CNN's Seoul bureau chief.

110   "I want North Koreans": Doug Struck, "N. Korea's Neighbors Unmoved by
Threats," *Washington Post*, February 11, 2003, p. A13.

111   "never accept": Jong-Heon Lee, "S. Korea's Roh Says No to N. Korean
Nuke," United Press International, June 2, 2003. Roh administration offi-
cials have not been so emphatic in private, however. See Charles Roh,
"Does S Korea Sunshine Policy Seek to Avert North's Fall?" Dow Jones
Newswires, March 3, 2003.

111   "panic gap": See, e.g., James Fallows, "The Panic Gap: Reactions to North
Korea's Bomb," *National Interest*, Winter 1994/95, p. 40.

111   want their country to side: See Martin Nesirky, "U.S. Needs to Offer More
to N.Korea—Security Report," Reuters, November 15, 2004.

111   "I believe the danger of war": Joohee Cho and Doug Struck, "Seoul Plays
Down N. Korea Threat on Armistice," *Washington Post*, February 19, 2003,
p. A17.

111   "We will lose everything": Roh Moo-hyun, interview by Gordon Fairclough,
Peter Kann, and Karen Elliott House, "The President Counsels Patience,"
Far Eastern Economic Review, May 22, 2003, p. 16.

111   "It is my firm determination": "North Korea Accuses U.S. of Stoking War
Jitters," Associated Press, March 21, 2003.

112   "guarantee the security and survival": Bruce Cumings, "Rising Danger in
Korea," *Nation*, March 24, 2003, p. 5.

112   "should stand together": Lee Jung-min and Choi Hoon, "Roh Blasts 'Boss-
      ing' from U.S.," *JoongAng Daily* (Seoul), February 14, 2003, http://
      joongangdaily.joins.com/200302/14/200302140153306439900090309031
      .html. Taking Roh's advice to heart, two-thirds of South Koreans of military
      age say they would side with the North against the United States in the
      event of war. See "Poll Finds Pragmatic Patriotism Among the Young,"
      Chosun Ilbo (Seoul), August 14, 2005, http://english.chosun.com/w21data/
      html/news/200508/200508140019.html.

112   Seoul's officials: See, e.g., Park Song-wu and Reuben Staines, "Seoul Clos-
      ing Door on Mass Defections," *Korea Times* (Seoul), January 5, 2005,
      http://times.hankooki.com/1page/nation/200501/kt2005010417081510510
      .htm. Seoul's refugee policies have gone so far that they may be unconstitu-
      tional. See "Minister Chung, Call Your Lawyer: South Korea's New Anti-
      Refugee Policy May Violate International Law and the South Korean
      Constitution," nkzone, January 10, 2005, http://www.nkzone.org/nkzone/
      entry/2005/01/minister_chung.php#more.

112   about 540: See "North, South Korea Red Crosses Meet," Associated Press,
      August 23, 2005. More than thirty South Korean POWs have escaped the
      North since 1994. POWs have been able to do so because of the relaxation
      of social controls. See Sang-Hun Choe, "South Korean POW Discharged
      from Army," Associated Press, January 19, 2004. For perhaps the most strik-
      ing POW story, see "POW's Daughter Flees North Korea with Her Father's
      Remains," Agence France-Presse, February 9, 2004.

112   486 South Koreans: See, e.g., Lankov, "Body Snatching, North Korean
      Style." Seoul has done little to get back abducted South Koreans. See
      Anthony Faiola, "Abducted South Koreans' Kin Fault Seoul for Failure to
      Act," *Washington Post*, September 21, 2004, p. A15.

112   "mediate": "Seoul Should Reconcile North Korea-US Standoff," *Korea
      Times* (Seoul), December 19, 2002, http://times.hankooki.com/1page/
      nation/200212/kt2002121918231912010.htm. Roh Moo-hyun has contin-
      ued to stress South Korea's mediation role. See Ji-Soo Kim, "Roh Urges
      Seoul's Mediation in Nuke Talks," Associated Press, August 10, 2005.

112   "balancing role": Roh Moo-hyun, "Address at the 40th Commencement
      and Commissioning Ceremony of the Korea Third Military Academy,"
      March 22, 2005. About 75 percent of South Korea backs Roh's concept of
      balancing. See Lee Joo-hee, "Majority of Public Back Korea 'Balancer'
      Role," *Korea Herald* (Seoul), April 11, 2005, http://www.koreaherald.co
      .kr/SITE/data/html_dir/2005/04/11/200504110004.asp. Implementing Roh's
      concept of "balancing," South Korea's Defense Ministry is taking steps to
      upgrade military cooperation with China and Russia.

112   "Success or failure": Sang-Hun Choe, "South Korea's President-Elect Ques-
      tions U.S. Plan to Pressure North Korea," Associated Press, December 31,
      2002.

113   "South Korea is not": Scofield, "Seoul Rows Against the US Tide."

113   "I think in some respects": "New S Korean Pres Faces Tricky Path in Relations with US," Dow Jones Newswires, February 21, 2003.

113   almost as out of favor: Tom Plate, "A Rift of Olympian Proportions," *South China Morning Post* (Hong Kong), September 1, 2004, p. A13.

113   "defunct": Robyn Lim, "Japan as the 'New South Korea'?" (lecture, Japan Center for Global Partnership, Tokyo, March 5, 2003). Seoul has contributed 3,600 troops to the Coalition effort in Iraq, and this contribution shows that there is still some life left to South Korea's military alliance with the United States.

113   "reasonable," "honorable": Roh Moo-hyun made these comments in a question-and-answer session after his controversial speech before the World Affairs Council in Los Angeles on November 12, 2004.

113   "good": "S.Korea's Roh Sees Slow Progress in 6-Party Talks," Reuters, September 5, 2004.

113   American troop withdrawals: In Pentagonese, the withdrawals are a "forcing function" with regard to South Korean military modernization. Ronald Fogleman, interview by author, Vancouver, July 26, 2003.

113   is closer to Beijing: See An Yong-kyoon, "China or the US: Realistically, Korea Should Side with China, but It Could Be a Big Mistake," *Chosun Ilbo* (Seoul), April 29, 2004, p. A5.

114   "Appeasement of tyrants": Mary Anastasia O'Grady, "Friends Don't Let Friends Fight Terror Alone," *Wall Street Journal*, March 21, 2003, p. A15.

114   appeasing an appeaser: See Nicholas Eberstadt, "Tear Down This Tyranny," *Weekly Standard*, November 29, 2004, p. 19.

114   or is it neutrality?: See James Brooke, "2 Koreas Sidestep U.S. to Forge Pragmatic Links," *New York Times*, June 26, 2004, p. A1.

Chapter 6: SYMPATHY FROM THE DEVIL

116   "the most important power": Eliot A. Cohen, "Isolate or Liberate?" *Wall Street Journal*, October 4, 2004, p. A16.

116   BYD Company: Ted C. Fishman, "The Chinese Century," *New York Times Magazine*, July 4, 2004, p. 24.

116   a third of the world's socks: David Barboza, "In Roaring China, Sweaters Are West of Socks City," *New York Times*, December 24, 2004, p. A1.

116   world's top consumer: Lester R. Brown, "China Replacing the United States as World's Leading Consumer," Earth Policy Institute, February 16, 2005, http://www.earth-policy.org/Updates/Update45.htm.

117   218 billion text messages: "Last Year Cell Phone Short Messages Reached 217.7 Billion," *People's Daily* (Beijing), January 21, 2005, http://it.people .com.cn/GB/1068/42899/3136578.html.

117   166 cities: Some analysts put the number at over 200. See Lyric Hughes Hale, "It's a Juggernaut . . . Not!" *Los Angeles Times*, May 22, 2005, p. M1.

117   undercounted in their census: Fishman, "The Chinese Century," p. 24.

117   1.5 billion: Beijing says China has slightly more than 1.3 billion people, but most analysts believe official numbers grossly understate the population.

117   "is the biggest player": Han Fook Kwang, "SM Calls for New Security Arrangement," *Straits Times* (Singapore), May 19, 1993, p. 1.

117   by 2039: See Dominic Wilson and Roopa Purushothaman, "Dreaming with BRICs: The Path to 2050," Goldman Sachs Global Economic Paper No. 99, October 1, 2003.

117   "I believe that we are": "China to Drive Global Economy in 21st Century: Economist," Agence France-Presse, November 27, 2002.

118   "China is the most successful development story": Fareed Zakaria, "The Big Story Everyone Missed," *Newsweek*, December 30, 2002, p. 52.

118   "The sleeping dragon": Nury Vittachi, "Changing at Blinding Speed," *Far Eastern Economic Review*, October 4, 2001, http://www.feer.com/.

119   almost recalled: See Yu Kai, "Diplomat's Rich Life Revealed," *China Daily* (Beijing), September 17, 2003, p. 9.

120   will never seek hegemony: See "Peacefully Walk the Development Road and Seek Mutual Prosperity in the Asia Pacific Region," *People's Daily* (Beijing), April 27, 2004, p. 3.

120   "We are trying": People's Republic of China, Ministry of Foreign Affairs, "Press Conference by Minister of Foreign Affairs Li Zhaoxing during the Second Session of the Tenth National People's Congress," March 6, 2004.

120   "a thing of beauty": Robert Keatley, "Beautiful Diplomacy," *South China Morning Post* (Hong Kong), December 11, 2003, p. A19.

120   "China is not America's ally": Leslie Fong, "China's US Ties: Tricky Road Ahead," *Straits Times* (Singapore), May 24, 2003, http://straitstimes.asia1 .com.sg/.

121   "China is the only large power": Robert Sutter, "China's Rise in Asia: Bumps in the Road and Unanswered Questions," *PacNet*, March 17, 2005, http://www.csis.org/pacfor/pac0512.pdf.

121   *Bowditch*: Chinese media reported that a Chinese vessel intentionally rammed the USNS *Bowditch*, an unarmed U.S. Navy oceanographic vessel, in September 2002 in the Yellow Sea, to disable its sonar. The ramming

claims were apparently untrue, but it is clear that Chinese planes buzzed the ship and China filed a diplomatic protest. The incident took place in waters recognized as international by every nation but China. See Robert Burns, "U.S. Says Chinese Vessels Harassed Navy Oceanographic Research Ship in Yellow Sea," Associated Press, September 27, 2002.

121   "discreet": Eric Teo, "Asian Security and the Reemergence of China's Tributary System," China Brief, September 16, 2004, http://www.jamestown .org/publications_details.php?volume_id=395&issue_id=3073&article _id=2368520.

121   are equal: See, e.g., "Strengthen Traditional Friendship and Deepen Comprehensive Cooperation Between China and Africa," *People's Daily* (Beijing), February 4, 2004, p. 1.

121   "democratization of international relations": Hu Jintao, "Speech at the Commemoration of the 100th Birthday of Comrade Deng Xiaoping," *People's Daily* (Beijing), August 23, 2004, p. 3.

121   "common cultural identity": Yu Zheng, Li Lei, and Zhou Zhengping, "Boao Forum Annual Meeting Complete," *People's Daily* (Beijing), April 26, 2004, p. 1.

121   Beijing is still angry: For a discussion of Beijing's unhappiness with Singapore, see Eric Teo, "A Counter to the US Tilt," *South China Morning Post* (Hong Kong), October 11, 2004, p. A17.

121   Beijing continually advocates: A prime example of such a grouping is the Shanghai Cooperation Organization, which includes China, Russia, and four Central Asian republics: Kazakhstan, Kyrgyzstan, Tajikistan, and Uzbekistan. Beijing organized the SCO to cement its relations with Moscow and extend influence beyond its western border. In July 2005 China persuaded the SCO to call upon the United States to give up its military bases in Central Asia. A few weeks later Uzbekistan ordered America to leave an important air base on its soil.

121   China complains: For a typical complaint, see "Cold War Senior Brains Got Frustrated Again: Comment," *People's Daily* (Beijing), November 25, 2003, http://english.people.com.cn/200311/25/eng20031125_128964.shtml. Beijing, for all its commitment to modernity, does not want modern societies on its borders, especially societies allied with the West.

122   East Asian Community: See, e.g., "Establishing East Asian Community Becomes Common Understanding: Interview," *People's Daily* (Beijing), October 14, 2004, http://english.people.com.cn/2004/10/14/eng20041014 _160226.html.

122   "unprecedented grand endeavor": Ma Xiao Ning, "Deepen Strategic Partnership and Promote Comprehensive Cooperation," *People's Daily* (Beijing), November 30, 2004, p. 1.

122 largest free trade area: "Asian Summit Moves to Create Single Market, Inks Historic Deal with China," Agence France-Presse, November 29, 2004.

122 "relic of the Cold War": People's Republic of China, Ministry of Foreign Affairs, "Foreign Ministry Spokesperson's Press Conference," February 12, 2004.

122 "that 1989 affair": Audra Ang, "China Leader Speaks Out on 1989 Protests," Associated Press, March 14, 2004.

122 "A liberal internationalist": Minxin Pei, "Beijing's Closed Politics Hinders 'New Diplomacy,' " *Financial Times*, September 13, 2004, p. 21.

122 How can a country: See Willy Wo-Lap Lam, "China Aiming for 'Peaceful Rise,' " cnn.com, February 6, 2004, http://edition.cnn.com/2004/WORLD/ asiapcf/02/02/willy.column/index.html.

123 outsized claims: In 1992 China's legislature codified the claim to all of the South China Sea, and since then the country has continued to reinforce its outposts in the Spratley Islands. Beijing agreed in November 2002 to a nonbinding code of foreign conduct for the settlement of South China Sea claims and signed a declaration covering such claims in November 2004.

123 imperial tributary system: See Teo, "Asian Security and the Reemergence of China's Tributary System."

123 "It is an irreversible trend": "Create a Peaceful and Prosperous Beautiful Tomorrow for the World," *People's Daily* (Beijing), January 1, 2004, p. 1.

123 That's a line: China's leaders are using their enormous buying power to make surrounding economies dependent on the Chinese miracle. The country runs a large trade deficit with Asia. Beijing is popular also because it can offer more than Washington: the U.S. market is already open so it has relatively little to hand out. Robert Broadfoot, interview by author, Hong Kong, October 28, 2003. Broadfoot is a business risk consultant in Hong Kong.

123 "once again standing up for something": Laurence Brahm, "Siding with the Little Guys," *South China Morning Post* (Hong Kong), September 22, 2003, p. A13.

123 As wrongheaded as it was: See Gerald Segal, "Does China Matter?" *Foreign Affairs*, September/October 1999, p. 24.

124 where it really counts: *Newsweek*'s Fareed Zakaria compares today's Americans to the English during the waning days of the British Empire. Then, the English worried about inconsequential places while unwatched America rose. Fareed Zakaria, "America's Big Challenge: Asia," *Washington Post*, October 19, 2004, p. A23. The consequence of American inattention is great. "We're in a tectonic situation," says Charlene Barshefsky, former U.S. trade representative, speaking of recent changes in Asia. "The plates are moving." Charlene Barshefsky, e-mail to author, April 2, 2004.

124   "has always adopted": Hu Xiaodi, speech, 1st Session of the Preparatory Committee for the 2005 NPT Review Conference, New York City, April 8, 2002.

124   "The just struggle": Oran R. Young, "Chinese Views on the Spread of Nuclear Weapons," *China Quarterly*, April/June 1966, p. 136.

124   "elated": Jonathan D. Pollack, "Chinese Attitudes Towards Nuclear Weapons, 1964–9," *China Quarterly*, April/June 1972, p. 244.

124   Kenneth Waltz: See Kenneth N. Waltz, "More May Be Better," in Scott D. Sagan and Kenneth N. Waltz, *The Spread of Nuclear Weapons: A Debate Renewed*, pp. 3–45 (New York: W. W. Norton, 2003). Despite Waltz's theory, China conducted the most extraordinary test of a nuclear weapon in history. In October 1966 the nation launched a DF-2 missile five hundred miles across its territory with a uranium-based weapon. Fortunately, the missile hit its target in western Xinjiang province.

125   as it is so proud of saying: See Information Office of the State Council, "China's Endeavors for Arms Control, Disarmament, and Non-Proliferation," reprinted in *People's Daily* (Beijing), September 2, 2005, p. 7; "China Makes Consistent Efforts in Arms Control," *People's Daily* (Beijing), January 4, 2005, http://english.peopledaily.com.cn/200501/04/eng20050104_169569.html; and "China Established Legal System for Non-Proliferation Export Control: White Paper," *People's Daily* (Beijing), December 27, 2004, http://english .peopledaily.com.cn/200412/27/eng20041227_168794.html.

125   "minimum deterrence": China maintains the world's third largest nuclear arsenal of over four hundred weapons. Its arsenal is outdated and considered vulnerable. See, e.g., Jing-dong Yuan, "Beijing's Hour of Nuclear Judgment," *South China Morning Post* (Hong Kong), October 19, 2004, p. A13.

125   "China consistently advocates": Hu Xiaodi, speech, 1st Session of the Preparatory Committee for the 2005 NPT Review Conference, New York City, April 8, 2002.

125   "China is really located": *Inside Asia*, narr. Jaime Florcruz, CNN International, December 8, 2002.

125   "There is a circle": Richard Fisher Jr., telephone interview by author, September 18, 2003.

125   If Pandora carries: See David Isenberg, "Nukes: Is Pandora Chinese?" Asia Times Online, June 23, 2004, http://www.atimes.com/atimes/China/ FF23Ad02.html.

126   Beijing began helping: William C. Triplett II, *Rogue State: How a Nuclear North Korea Threatens America* (Washington, D.C.: Regnery, 2004), p. 156. For background information, see Siobhan McDonough, "Documents Show U.S. Unease over Pakistan-China Security Cooperation," Associated Press, March 5, 2004.

126 "crude technology": Johanna McGeary, "Inside the A-Bomb Bazaar," *Time*, January 19, 2004, p. 40.

126 Beijing transferred to Islamabad: See Isenberg, "Nukes: Is Pandora Chinese?" For background information, see Mohan Malik, "A. Q. Khan's China Connection," China Brief, April 29, 2004, http://www.jamestown.org/publications_details.php?volume_id=395&issue_id=2939&article_id=236639.

126 five thousand ring magnets: See, e.g., Bill Gertz, "China Nuclear Transfer Exposed," *Washington Times*, February 5, 1996, p. A1.

126 nuclear test data: Ashok Kapur, "The New Indian Factor in China's Proliferation Policy," China Brief, March 19, 2004, http://www.jamestown.org/publications_details.php?volume_id=395&issue_id=2923&article_id=23621.

126 modern warhead designs: Malik, "A. Q. Khan's China Connection."

126 plutonium technology: China also provided uranium enrichment tech and plutonium production tech to Pakistan and reached a cooperative agreement in 2003 to build a nuclear-power-generating plant in Chashma. See Kensuke Ebata, "Chinese Shadows Flickering Behind Downfall of Dr. Khan," *Sekai Shuho*, March 9, 2004, p. 38.

126 "is much diminished": "China Helps to Stem N.Korea Proliferation, U.S. Says," Reuters, June 2, 2004.

126 might be correct: The CIA, however, says it cannot rule out continuing assistance. See Central Intelligence Agency, "Unclassified Report to Congress on the Acquisition of Technology Relating to Weapons of Mass Destruction and Advanced Conventional Munitions, 1 January through 30 June 2003."

126 answering the phone: James Swanson, interview by author, Washington, D.C., November 20, 2003. Swanson is a defense analyst in Washington.

126 "If you subtract": Triplett, *Rogue State*, p. 156.

126 "managed proliferation": John J. Mearsheimer, "Why We Will Soon Miss the Cold War," *Atlantic Monthly*, August 1990, p. 35.

127 China traded technology: John Loftus, interview by Eric Shawn, "Inside Scoop," *Fox News Live Weekend*, Fox News Channel, September 19, 2004.

127 Khan confessed: See, e.g., George Jahn, "AP: Nuclear Black Market Is Small, Covert," Associated Press, February 2, 2004.

127 adorned with Chinese characters: The design was for the weapon China tested on October 27, 1966. For more on the Chinese plans, see Joby Warrick and Peter Slevin, "Libyan Arms Designs Traced Back to China," *Washington Post*, February 15, 2004, p. A1.

127   Beijing supported: See Malik, "A. Q. Khan's China Connection"; and
      David Rohde, "Nuclear Expert Receives Pardon from Musharraf," *New York
      Times,* February 6, 2004, p. A1.

127   to build relationships: China used Pakistan as a front for dispersing nuclear
      technology, and, according to various analysts, Saudi money financed
      much of this proliferation. See, e.g., Thomas Woodrow, "The Sino-Saudi
      Connection," China Brief, October 24, 2002, http://www.jamestown.org/
      publications_details.php?volume_id=18&issue_id=661&article_id=4680.
      For additional information, see "Iran Smuggling from China for Nuclear
      Program—Opposition," Dow Jones Newswires, September 13, 2005 (Iran);
      Carol Giacomo, "China Helping Iran, North Korea on Weapons—Panel,"
      Reuters, June 15, 2004 (Iran); and George Jahn, "AP: Pakistan Knew of Nuclear
      Black Market," Associated Press, March 7, 2004 (Syria). China sold nuclear-
      capable missiles to Saudi Arabia in the 1980s. The sale raises the troubling pos-
      sibility that Riyadh was also trying to acquire warheads for these missiles. See
      Richard L. Russell, "A Saudi Nuclear Option?" *Survival,* Summer 2001, p. 69.

128   President Bush's agreement: See, e.g., Steven R. Weisman, "U.S. to
      Broaden India's Access to Nuclear-Power Technology," *New York Times,* July
      19, 2005, p. A1.

128   the best explanation: See M. D. Nalapat, "North Korea: A 'Proxy' Nuclear
      State?" China Brief, March 25, 2003, http://www.jamestown.org/
      publications_details.php?volume_id=19&issue_id=671&article_id=4720.

128   a long-term master plan: John Loftus, telephone interview by author, Febru-
      ary 18, 2004.

129   reportedly ordered: Ibid.

129   "completely in the dark": White House Office of the Press Secretary, "Presi-
      dent Bush, Chinese President Jiang Zemin Discuss Iraq, N. Korea," Octo-
      ber 25, 2002.

129   "a real signal of partnership": John Loftus, telephone interview by author.

129   yet at the same time it blocked: China agreed to have the IAEA refer the
      matter to the U.N. Security Council but then blocked any action at the
      U.N. See "China Says No Flip-Flop in North Korea Policy," Dow Jones
      Newswires, February 13, 2003.

129   its other nuclear client: See Ali Akbar Dareini, "China Seeks to Avoid Iran
      Nuclear Issue," Associated Press, November 6, 2004.

129   First come: William Reinsch, interview by author, Washington D.C.,
      November 19, 2003. Reinsch was under secretary for export administration
      in the Commerce Department.

130   could not bring himself: Barry Schweid, "U.S. Opts Against Punishing
      China for Technology Sale to Pakistan," Associated Press, May 10, 1996.

130 "Chinese officials can find": James Swanson, interview.

130 "unacceptable": Colin L. Powell, "A Strategy of Partnerships," *Foreign Affairs*, January/February 2004, p. 22.

130 giving the Russians the idea: See Nalapat, "North Korea: A 'Proxy' Nuclear State?"

130 "killing with a borrowed knife": See Triplett, *Rogue State*, p. 9.

130 "If there is one": "Chinese Foreign Min Calls for Talks Between US, N Korea," Dow Jones Newswires, June 27, 2003.

131 Shi Yinhong: John Pomfret, "As Talks Begin, China Views N. Korea as Risk," *Washington Post*, August 27, 2003, p. A19.

131 fall into China's lap: Some say that the Chinese government has been preparing for this possibility by claiming that the ancient Koguryo kingdom, which occupied what is now North Korea and the adjoining parts of China, was in reality a Chinese state. Koreans, both north and south of the DMZ, are upset at what they perceive to be an attempt by Beijing to hijack their history. The dispute over history has strained ties between the two Koreas and China.

131 "knows the Chinese": Evan Thomas, "Women, Wine and Weapons," *Newsweek* (international edition), January 13, 2003, p. 16.

132 "If you want to be": Tai Ming Cheung, interview by author, Washington, D.C., November 20, 2003.

132 cold hard cash: China agreed to pay North Korea $50 million to attend the February 2004 round of the six-party talks. See Edward Cody and Anthony Faiola, "N. Korea's Kim Reportedly in China for Talks," *Washington Post*, April 20, 2004, p. A13.

132 "China will never allow": Glenn Kessler and John Pomfret, "North Korea's Threats a Dilemma for China," *Washington Post*, April 26, 2003, p. A1.

132 "I believe you can never": Terence Hunt, "Bush Aims to Push N. Korea on Nuke Talks," Associated Press, November 19, 2004.

132 "as close as lips and teeth": The closeness of Beijing's relationship with Pyongyang became evident in September 2005, when American law enforcement officials disclosed China's interlocking financial links to North Korea's global criminal activities. See Glenn R. Simpson, Gordon Fairclough, and Jay Solomon, "U.S. Probes Banks' North Korea Ties," *Wall Street Journal*, September 8, 2005, p. A3.

132 still felt an emotional attachment: Willy Wo-Lap Lam, interview by author, Hong Kong, April 22, 2004. Lam is a commentator and journalist covering China.

133 the two of them: See Benjamin Kang Lim and John Ruwitch, "N.Korea's Kim Says to Be Patient, Flexible in Talks," Reuters, April 21, 2004.

133   just a tool: Willy Wo-Lap Lam, interview.

133   make Kim nervous: "China and Russia Lack Clout to Dictate to North
      Korea," *South China Morning Post* (Hong Kong), January 17, 2003,
      http://www.scmp.com/.

133   started purposively removing: Yu Bin, "China Maneuvers to Bring a Soft-
      Landing to the Korean Crisis," YaleGlobal Online, February 11, 2003,
      http://yaleglobal.yale.edu/display.article?id=952.

133   people who know much less: Tai Ming Cheung, interview.

134   "could neither bark nor bite": James Yang, "China Must Dump North
      Korea," *Asian Wall Street Journal* (Hong Kong), April 9, 2003, p. A9.

134   "We have some influence": Philip P. Pan, "China Treads Carefully Around
      North Korea," *Washington Post*, January 10, 2003, p. A14.

135   will pay back: Chung Jae Ho, interview by author, Seoul, May 4, 2004.

135   China might adhere: Shi Jun Yu, "Situation on the Korean Peninsula
      Tenses Up Again," *Ta Kung Pao* (Hong Kong), June 3, 1994, p. 4.

135   cut off oil: Gady A. Epstein, "From Beijing, Stern Words for an Uneasy
      Ally," *Sun* (Baltimore), March 28, 2003, p. 12A. China has suspended
      flights to Pyongyang, cut off commercial lines of credit, closed border cross-
      ings, and restricted the number of train cars going to North Korea. See
      Jasper Becker, "China's Waning Influence on North Korea," *San Francisco
      Chronicle*, January 9, 2003, p. A10.

135   "Pyongyang and Beijing have operated": Triplett, *Rogue State*, p. 10.

135   "The truth is": John Tkacik, "Sanctions Against North Korea," *Asian Wall
      Street Journal* (Hong Kong), January 13, 2003, p. A9.

136   "in a common purpose": White House Office of the Press Secretary, "Press
      Briefing by Ari Fleischer," January 10, 2003.

136   "package deal": See, e.g., Guo Shiping, "Cheney in for Some Straight Talk
      in Beijing," *Straits Times* (Singapore), April 13, 2004, http://straitstimes
      .asia1.com.sg/.

136   threatened to halt cooperation: See Glenn Kessler, "China Warns U.S. on
      Policies," *Washington Post*, July 14, 2004, p. A13.

136   "But what we are saying": John Pomfret, "Beijing Is Cool to Powell's Pleas,"
      Washington Post, February 25, 2003, p. A19.

Chapter 7: TOKYO, TARGET FOR TERMINATION

137   "an act beyond comprehension": Sakie Yokota, *My Daughter, Mother Will
      Come and Find You* [in Japanese] (Tokyo: Soshisha, 1999), p. 11.

137   into a car: Megumi's mother, Sakie, believes North Korean agents forced her daughter into a car because a police search dog lost her scent at a particular spot on a roadway. Sakie Yokota, interview by author, Tokyo, April 25, 2004. North Korean agent An Myung Jin, in a secondhand account, implies two North Korean agents carried her to the beach. See An Myung Jin, *North Korean Abduction Agents* [in Japanese] (Tokyo: Tokuma-shoten, 2000), pp. 149–50.

138   She was then driven: There is speculation that North Korean agents took Megumi to a ferry shuttling between Japan and North Korea instead of a spy ship. See William C. Triplett II, *Rogue State: How a Nuclear North Korea Threatens America* (Washington, D.C.: Regnery, 2004), pp. 116, 119.

138   covered in blood: See An, *North Korean Abduction Agents*, p. 151.

138   she happened to see: Although facts about the kidnapping remain in dispute, there is general agreement about the reason for the crime.

138   suffered a mental breakdown: See Yokota, *My Daughter, Mother Will Come and Find You*, p. 109.

139   taken her own life: There is some dispute as to the year she is said to have committed suicide. See "List of 10 Japanese Abductees," Kyodo News Service, December 24, 2004.

139   could not locate her remains: See "List of Abducted Japanese," Kyodo News Service, October 2, 2002. Pyongyang said that the remains of most of the others were washed away either by heavy rains or floods.

139   "I know that everything": Joseph Coleman, "Photos of Japanese Kidnapping Victim Intensify Outrage," Associated Press, November 17, 2004.

139   they know too much: See Shinichi Nishiwaki and Tetsushi Teruyama, "Put in Charge of Training of Agents?" *Mainichi Shimbun* (Tokyo), December 12, 2004, p. 31; and "Missing Japanese Abductees Taught North Korean Spy Who Blew Up Airliner," *Mainichi Daily* (Tokyo), December 9, 2004, p. 8.

139   one poor soul: Mrs. Yokota is actually trying to rescue two poor souls. Megumi gave birth to a daughter, Kim Hye Gyong.

140   the medically incredible claim: In another coincidence, both abductees who died of heart problems, Rumiko Masumoto and Shuichi Ichikawa, were married to each other. The two were married after they were abducted.

140   "blindly motivated patriotism": "Pursue Dialogue to Spur Change in North Korea," Asahi News Service, September 19, 2002.

140   political leaders: One explanation for an otherwise inexplicable lack of reaction was corruption. Kim Il Sung reportedly handed prominent Japanese politician Shin Kanemaru gold bars.

140   actually in the hundreds: There could be as many as four hundred Japanese
      abductees in North Korea. See Julian Ryall, "Japanese See Double Stan-
      dards on Hostages," *South China Morning Post* (Hong Kong), May 28,
      2004, p. A10. Governor Shintaro Ishihara of Tokyo believes there are
      around 150. Shintaro Ishihara, interview by author, Tokyo, April 27, 2004.

140   Hyomoto ran across: See Yokota, *My Daughter, Mother Will Come and
      Find You*, pp. 104–8.

141   "The primary duty": Shintaro Ishihara, interview.

141   "stop dilly-dallying around": John Nathan, *Japan Unbound: A Volatile
      Nation's Quest for Pride and Purpose* (Boston: Houghton Mifflin, 2004), pp.
      196–97.

141   "unpardonable country": "Koizumi Says N. Korea Abducts, Kills Japanese,"
      Kyodo News Service, October 14, 2002.

141   "We must normalize": Eric Talmadge, "N. Korea to Release Japanese Rela-
      tives," Associated Press, May 22, 2004.

141   secured the release: See Eric Talmadge, "Koizumi Faces Criticism After
      Summit," Associated Press, May 23, 2004.

141   "hostage negotiator": Peter Kammerer, "Bring Your Own Rice," *South
      China Morning Post* (Hong Kong), May 21, 2004, p. A17.

142   "It's the responsibility": James Brooke, "North Korea and Japan Sign a Deal
      on Abductions," *New York Times*, May 23, 2004, p. 11.

142   He cut off aid deliveries: "Calls Grow for DPRK Sanctions," *Daily Yomiuri*
      (Tokyo), December 10, 2004, p. 3.

142   testing later showed: "Japan Brought Second Set of Ashes from N. Korea,"
      Kyodo News Service, November 17, 2004.

142   "evidence": "Family Members: 'Will Persist in Fighting,' " *Asahi Shimbun*
      (Tokyo), November 16, 2004, p. 35. Five of the seven containers were
      empty and the remaining two had little according to various reports.

142   dug up her ashes: See "Remains Received from N. Korea Not Those of
      Megumi Yokota," *Mainichi Shimbun* (Tokyo), December 8, 2004,
      http://mdn.mainichi.co.jp/news/20041208p2a00m0dm013000c.html; and
      "50-Hour Battle Still Leaves Questions," *Asahi Shimbun* (Tokyo), Novem-
      ber 16, 2004, p. 2.

142   DNA testing in Japan: See Kento Hayakawa, "Megumi's 'Remains' Turn
      Out to Be Someone Else's," *Mainichi Shimbun* (Tokyo), December 9,
      2004, p. 1; and "Evidence from N. Korea on Abductees Insufficient,
      Hosoda Says," Kyodo News Service, December 9, 2004.

142   "This case clearly shows": "DNA in Remains Not Yokota's," *Daily Yomiuri*
      (Tokyo), December 9, 2004, p. 1.

142 "When I think of Ms. Yokota": "Japan's Koizumi Considering Sanctions on N Korea—Aide," Dow Jones Newswires, December 11, 2004.

142 "We will have to see": "Japan to Delay Imposing Economic Sanctions on N Korea," Dow Jones Newswires, December 17, 2004.

142 Koizumi keeps on trying: In September 2005 Japan and North Korea, conferring on the sidelines of the six-party negotiations in Beijing, agreed to resume normalization talks. See "Japan, North Korea Agree to Resume Talks," *Yomiuri Shimbun* (Tokyo), September 21, 2005, p. 1.

142 the problem with Japan: The relatives of the abductees have savaged Koizumi more than Kim Jong Il. See, e.g., "Japan–North Korea Summit Talks," *Sankei Shimbun* (Tokyo), May 23, 2004, p. 30.

143 "They have learned": Yuichi Yamamoto, e-mail to author, May 23, 2004.

143 "the honorable Mr. Watchdog": Shintaro Ishihara, *The Japan That Can Say No*, trans. Frank Baldwin (New York: Simon & Schuster, 1991), p. 32.

144 ice cubes from Antarctica: Sonja Sray, e-mail to author, January 22, 2005. Sray, who lived in Japan in the 1990s, was told by her Japanese friends that Antarctica ice had different qualities from other ice.

144 "Japanese Century": "Japan's Struggle to Cope with Plenty," *Time*, August 1, 1969, p. 69B.

144 largest asset deflation: Nathan, *Japan Unbound*, p. 19.

145 "missing": See ibid., pp. 19–20.

145 "As you know": Song Young Gil, interview by author, Seoul, May 6, 2004.

146 "Speaking of kidnappings": Sohn Jangnai, interview by author, Seoul, April 29, 2004.

146 has taken Pyongyang's side: See Roh Moo-hyun, Address on the 86th March First Independence Movement Day, March 1, 2005.

146 "tough diplomatic war": Roh Moo-hyun, "An Open Letter to the Nation Concerning Korea-Japan Relations," March 23, 2005.

146 generally recognized: See, e.g., Eugene A. Matthews, "Japan's New Nationalism," *Foreign Affairs*, November/December 2003, p. 74.

146 aviation maps: In addition to aviation maps, a Chinese map from 1958 shows the islands as Japanese. See Katsushi Okazaki, "China's Seaward Adventurism and the Japan-US Alliance," 1997, GlobalSecurity.org, http://www.globalsecurity.org/military/library/report/1997/Okazaki.htm#_edn34.

147 Exclusive Economic Zones: The U.N. Convention on the Law of the Sea, signed by both Beijing and Tokyo, permits a country to claim an Exclusive Economic Zone that extends two hundred nautical miles from its shore.

China and Japan have not settled where their Exclusive Economic Zones meet. Japan's claim is based on its southernmost territory, the Okinotori Islands. Beijing disputes the boundary, saying that the Okinotori outcroppings do not provide a legal basis for extending Tokyo's zone. Japan's Okinotori-based claim permits it to draw a zone that is larger than Japan's landmass.

147 raising the stakes: To enforce its claims, China sent a fleet of five warships near the disputed area in September 2005. See "Japan Spots Chinese Warships Near Disputed Gas Field," Agence France-Presse, September 9, 2005. The arrival of the warships was soon followed by the beginning of Chinese drilling in the area. Japan claims that Chinese wells may actually be extracting Japanese gas. See Sebastian Moffett, "China, Japan Bicker Over Gas Extraction," *Asian Wall Street Journal* (Hong Kong), September 21, 2005, p. A1. The Japanese have begun to abandon their admirable restraint by preparing for drilling in the disputed area. See "Japan Petroleum Exploration Co. and Teikoku Oil Co. to Explore Natural Resources in East China Sea," *Nihon Keizai Shimbun* (Tokyo), January 16, 2005, p. 1.

147 entered Japan's territorial waters: See Martin Fackler, "Japanese Pursuit of Chinese Sub Raises Tensions," *Wall Street Journal*, November 15, 2004, p. A20.

147 a deep level: "China Shift," *Asahi Shimbun* (Tokyo), December 18, 2004, p. 1.

147 repeatedly refusing to promise: See, e.g., William Foreman, "Japanese, Chinese Leaders Refuse to Give In on Demands About Shrine Visits, Submarine Incursion," Associated Press, November 30, 2004.

147 mutually dependent: Japan is the largest foreign investor in China, which is now Japan's largest trading partner. Japan has been China's top trading partner for more than a decade. Japan is the largest donor of assistance to China. Japan's exports to China are crucial to the recovery of the Japanese economy.

147 as if they were news: Actually, it is news. The Chinese government keeps increasing its official death toll in the Second World War. See Mark O'Neill, "State of Recrimination," *South China Morning Post* (Hong Kong), June 15, 2004, p. A14.

147 as being anti-Japanese: See Jim Frederick, "Respect and Resentment," *Time* (Asia edition), November 29, 2004, p. 21.

147 after inflaming public opinion: Beijing apparently instigated anti-Japan protests in April 2005 in a few cities along its coast, but they spread across the country and ultimately proved difficult for the central government to control. Japan protested the disturbances, many of which ended in violence.

147 "We should teach the Japanese": David J. Lynch, "Animosity Toward Japan Is Again the Rage in China," *USA Today*, February 24, 2005, p. 8A.

148 "Unless we have the will": Nathan, *Japan Unbound*, pp. 192–93.

148 "from scratch": Shintaro Ishihara, interview.

148 no person in Japan: Nathan, *Japan Unbound*, pp. 13–14. There is little support in the Diet for retaining Article 9. See Linda Sieg, "Push to Revise Japan Pacifist Constitution Growing," Reuters, September 14, 2005.

148 fourth largest military budget: Japan's defense budget is often listed as third in size, but it would be recognized as fourth largest if China issued accurate figures.

148 "collective self-defense": Not everyone agrees that collective self-defense is prohibited. See, e.g., Teruaki Ueno, "Japan Foreign Minister Favors Constitution Change," Reuters, September 28, 2004.

149 assigned to guard: See, e.g., Izumi Ogura, "Australian Troops Arrive in Samawah," *Asahi Shimbun* (Tokyo), April 25, 2005, p. 2.

149 are not even allowed: See "Koizumi to Meet China's Hu This Weekend to Mend Ties (Update2)," Bloomberg, November 19, 2004. Moreover, the troops are under extremely stringent rules as to when they can defend themselves. See "Focus: Doubts Remain over GSDF Troops' Use of Weapons in Iraq," Kyodo News Service, February 9, 2004.

149 the important thing: America severely chastised Tokyo for not sending a single soldier to fight in the 1991 Gulf War, when Japan opted instead to pay money, about $17 billion. International criticism resulted. The Japanese were stunned by the reaction because America wrote their constitution forbidding involvement in war.

149 the first time: It is often said that Japanese troops entered a war zone for the first time when they arrived in Iraq, but they were also sent to Afghanistan in 2001.

149 1992 mission in Cambodia: The Cambodia mission is the first time Japan's Self-Defense Forces had been deployed abroad.

149 "We follow too easily": Anthony Faiola, "Japan's Military Sculpts New Image in Iraqi Sand," *Washington Post*, February 10, 2004, p. A1.

149 "giving liqueur chocolates": Michael Richardson, "But Many in the Region Are Uneasy, Lee Says," *International Herald Tribune*, May 4, 1991, p. 1.

149 "I feel that the state": Nathan, *Japan Unbound*, p. 198.

150 "Sun King": Ibid., p. 169.

150 its principal tormentors: See "Japan New Defense Outline Names China, N. Korea as Concerns," Kyodo News Service, December 10, 2004.

150 inert presence: As powerful as Russia still is, the country has not had much influence on the six-party talks. Russian negotiators participated so little in the fourth round of the discussions in mid-2005 that analysts began openly

to question Moscow's participation in the process. Russia seems much more interested in North Korea as an economic opportunity than as a security threat.

151   Tokyo's circumstances: See Jack Kim and Masayuki Kitano, "Japan, S.Korea to Aid N.Korea After Nuclear Resolution," Reuters, July 21, 2004.

151   "alliance management": "N.K. Talks . . . Progress & Alliance Management," Nelson Report, June 24, 2004.

151   proposed benefits for Pyongyang: Joe McDonald, "N. Korea Reportedly Requests Energy Aid," Associated Press, June 24, 2004.

151   has initially gone along: See "Japan Downplays N Korean Criticism on Ashes Dispute—Kyodo," Dow Jones Newswires, December 15, 2004.

151   that is not how: Tokyo has no power to solve the nuclear issue so it has concentrated on domestic issues, such as the fate of the abductees. See Joseph Coleman, "Japanese Kidnap Victims Take Center Stage," Associated Press, January 29, 2004.

151   "There is not a shred": George Nishiyama, "Japan Protests to N.Korea Over Fake Evidence," Reuters, December 8, 2004.

152   maritime insurance regulations: See George Nishiyama, "Japan Ship Law to Close Ports to Most N.Korea Vessels," Reuters, February 28, 2005.

152   has threatened to pull out: "DPRK Stand on Japanese Ultra Right Forces—Proposed Sanctions Against DPRK Clarified," Korean Central News Agency, December 14, 2004.

152   demanded that the Japanese leave: "Imprudent Moves of Japan Under Fire," Korean Central News Agency, April 2, 2005.

152   "kowtow diplomacy": Ishihara, The Japan That Can Say No, p. 113.

153   right of preemption: See "Japan Threatens Force against N Korea," BBC, February 14, 2003, http://news.bbc.co.uk/2/hi/asia-pacific/2757923.stm.

153   "mystery ship": For a description of the events surrounding the sinking, see "Mystery Vessel Likely Multipurpose N. Korean Spy Ship: Agency," Kyodo News Service, December 28, 2001.

153   "The chances of North Korea": Elaine Lies, "Hiroshima Laments Nuclear Trend on Anniversary," Reuters, August 5, 2003.

153   incineration of Tokyo: One of the most popular novels in South Korean history is The Rose of Sharon Has Blossomed, which involves a South Korean nuclear attack on Japan.

153   unexpected violence: See Victor D. Cha, "Weak but Still Threatening," in Victor D. Cha and David C. Kang, Nuclear North Korea: A Debate on Engagement Strategies, pp. 13–40 (New York: Columbia University Press, 2003).

153   Mr. Kim's primary launch vehicle: Pyongyang has warned Japan that it is within the range of its missiles. See "KCNA Urges Japan to Behave with Discretion," Korean Central News Agency, April 9, 2003.

153   might remain neutral: Howard W. French, "Seoul May Loosen Its Ties to the U.S.," New York Times, December 20, 2002, p. A1.

153   "advance base": "U.S. Ambition to Dominate Asia Under Fire," Korean Central News Agency, September 23, 2004. If North Korea were to attack Japan, it would be in the early stages of a conflict to prevent Tokyo from aiding America. Hisahiko Okazaki, interview by author, Tokyo, April 27, 2004. Okazaki is a former Japanese diplomat who runs a Tokyo think tank bearing his name.

154   "the sworn enemy": "S. Korean Authorities Hit for Pro-Japanese Toadyism," Korean Central News Agency, February 7, 2005.

154   North Korean diplomats privately say: Alexandre Y. Mansourov, "The Origins, Evolution, and Current Politics of the North Korean Nuclear Program," Nonproliferation Review, Spring/Summer 1995, p. 25.

154   take the Japanese hostage: North Korea's general strategy, according to Hwang, is to attack South Korea and then prevent American intervention by threatening the annihilation of Japan. See Hwang Jang Yop, " 'South Korea's Attempt to Uproot North Korea's Underground Methods Will Be Difficult,' " Chosun Ilbo (Seoul), April 22, 1997, p. 4.

154   "Of course, both": Tony Mitchell, interview by author, Seoul, May 7, 2004.

154   "won't be satisfied": Doug Struck, "N. Korea's Neighbors Unmoved by Threats," Washington Post, February 11, 2003, p. A13.

154   "used its men": Norimitsu Onishi, "Japan Heads to Iraq, Haunted by Taboo Bred in Another War," New York Times, November 19, 2003, p. A1.

154   "a pacifist military": Faiola, "Japan's Military Sculpts New Image in Iraqi Sand," p. A1.

154   safer than joining the police: Sebastian Moffett and Martin Fackler, "Cautiously, Japan Returns to Combat, in Southern Iraq," Wall Street Journal, January 2, 2004, p. A1.

154   "a bewildered giant": Nathan, Japan Unbound, p. 23.

Chapter 8: AID CHARADE

155   "I can still hear": "Eunju," interview by author, Magpie Village, South Korea, May 8, 2004. "Eunju" is the name she used in China.

155   denied food: Even members of military and party elites were dying of hunger. Jasper Becker, "The Son Also Falls," Asian Wall Street Journal (Hong Kong), November 24, 2004, p. A11.

156   "Anyone who has stood": Kang Chol-hwan and Pierre Rigoulot, *The Aquari-ums of Pyongyang: Ten Years in a North Korea Gulag*, trans. Yair Reiner (New York: Basic Books, 2001), p. 235.

156   "You cannot make": "U.N. Envoy Says North Korea Is Short of Food," *New York Times*, January 19, 2003, p. A14.

157   surreptitious shipments: See Don Oberdorfer, *The Two Koreas: A Contem-porary History* (New York: Basic Books, 2001), p. 372; and Kongdan Oh and Ralph C. Hassig, *North Korea Through the Looking Glass* (Washington, D.C.: Brookings Institution Press, 2000), p. 208.

157   North Korea responded: See Scott Snyder, "The NGO Experience in North Korea," in *Paved with Good Intentions: The NGO Experience in North Korea*, ed. L. Gordon Flake and Scott Snyder, pp. 1–13 (Westport, Con-necticut: Praeger, 2003).

157   declared off-limits: See Senate Committee on Foreign Relations, *North Korea: Status Report on Nuclear Program, Humanitarian Issues, and Eco-nomic Reforms*, 108th Cong., 2nd Sess., 2004, S. Prt. 108–40, p. 6.

157   In other areas: See, e.g., Jay Solomon and Carla Anne Robbins, "Amid Nuclear Standoff, Food Aid Shrinks for Hungry North Korea," *Wall Street Journal*, May 15, 2003, p. A1. Aid organizations "have no idea how their stuff is being used or where it's going." Gordon Flake, interview by Chris Nelson, Nelson Report, September 9, 2003.

157   even more intransigent: See Snyder, "The NGO Experience in North Korea," pp. 1–13.

157   America had stopped aid: See Tyler Marshall, "Nuclear Plans May Put Food Aid for N. Korea at Risk," *Los Angeles Times*, December 17, 2002, p. A10.

157   threatened to stop assistance: See U.S. Agency for International Develop-ment, Statement by Andrew S. Natsios, June 7, 2002.

157   "We want to be generous": Irwin Arieff, "US Interrupts North Korea Food Aid," Reuters, January 13, 2003.

157   The regime directed aid: See Amnesty International, "Starved of Rights: Human Rights and the Food Crisis in the Democratic People's Republic of Korea (North Korea)," January 17, 2004.

158   fed the armed forces: See Jim Mann, "U.S., China Are Awkward Aid Part-ners for N. Korea," *Los Angeles Times*, September 10, 1997, p. A5.

158   first cut of the home harvest: See Masood Hyder, "In North Korea: First, Save Lives," *Washington Post*, January 4, 2004, p. B7.

158   were malnourished: Soldiers were malnourished as late as early 2000. Erica Kang, interview by author, Seoul, April 30, 2004.

158   did not tolerate elsewhere: See Solomon and Robbins, "Amid Nuclear Standoff, Food Aid Shrinks for Hungry North Korea," p. A1.

158 the only group: Oh and Hassig, *North Korea Through the Looking Glass*, p. 115.

158 whenever food inspectors: William C. Triplett II, *Rogue State: How a Nuclear North Korea Threatens America* (Washington, D.C.: Regnery, 2004), p. 142.

158 "North Korea is based": Ibid.

158 at gunpoint: See Ichiro Ue, "Military 'Snatched Away' Food Aid," *Yomiuri Shimbun* (Tokyo), June 1, 1997, p. 2.

158 Canned food: Triplett, *Rogue State*, pp. 139–40.

158 "We don't want to feed": Sonya Ross, "N. Korea Accused of Playing Aid Games," Associated Press, February 25, 2003.

158 "is not a professional army": Kang and Rigoulot, *The Aquariums of Pyongyang*, p. 236.

158 "When you have": Erica Kang, interview.

159 allow Mr. Kim to shift: In 2005 North Korea said it developed nukes with its own resources, thereby rejecting speculation that it used surreptitious cash payments from Seoul. "North Korea Says It Developed Nuclear Weapons with Its Own Money," Associated Press, March 30, 2005.

159 "No North Korean child": "US's Powell: North Koreans Can't Eat Enriched Uranium," Dow Jones Newswires, October 29, 2002.

159 "If India builds": Steve Weissman and Herbert Krosney, *The Islamic Bomb: The Nuclear Threat to Israel and the Middle East* (New York: Times Books, 1981), p. 161.

159 "The best way": James Brooke, "Defectors Want to Pry Open North Korea," *New York Times*, January 9, 2003, p. A12.

159 "We will not use food": Ross, "N. Korea Accused of Playing Aid Games."

159 "mendicant diplomacy": Samuel S. Kim, "North Korea and Northeast Asia in World Politics," in *North Korea and Northeast Asia*, ed. Samuel S. Kim and Tai Hwan Lee, pp. 3–58 (Lanham, Maryland: Rowman & Littlefield, 2002).

159 "the tactics of tears": Charles Hutzler and Gordon Fairclough, "Great Wall Splits China, North Korea," *Wall Street Journal*, July 31, 2003, p. A14.

159 "If I'm very frustrated": Kathi Zellweger, interview by author, Hong Kong, April 22, 2004.

160 "Marxist economies": Dennis Hays, interview by author, Washington, D.C., September 25, 2002.

160 North Korean agriculture: See "US Citizen Living in N Korea Struggles to Feed the Needy," Dow Jones Newswires, August 11, 2005. Even the DPRK's

best harvests are not enough to feed its population. See Joe McDonald, "Amid Korean Nuclear Tensions, WFP Appeals for More Food Aid for Hungry North," Associated Press, October 30, 2003. North Korea, absent structural reform, appears to be at the limit of its capacity to grow food. See "North Korean Agriculture Peaking Out: UN Expert," Agence France-Presse, January 21, 2005. Instead of reforming agriculture, Pyongyang is trying to solve problems with additional manpower. See James Brooke, "North Korea, Facing Food Shortages, Mobilizes Millions from the Cities to Help Rice Farmers," *New York Times*, June 1, 2005, p. A8.

160 why should Kim Jong Il: See Marcus Noland, "North Korea's External Economic Relations: Globalization in 'Our Own Style,'" in *North Korea and Northeast Asia*, pp. 165–93.

160 probably saved that regime: See Robert W. McElroy, *Morality and American Foreign Policy: The Role of Ethics in International Affairs* (Princeton: Princeton University Press, 1992), pp. 57–58.

161 Kim Young Sam publicly warned: See James Sterngold, "South Korea President Lashes Out at U.S.," *New York Times*, October 8, 1994, p. 3.

161 During this dire period: See Norman D. Levin, "What If North Korea Survives?" *Survival*, Winter 1997/98, p. 156.

161 made it acceptable: See Oberdorfer, *The Two Koreas*, p. 374. Aid not only saved the regime but made Kim Jong Il confident. See Bradley K. Martin, *Under the Loving Care of the Fatherly Leader: North Korea and the Kim Dynasty* (New York: St. Martin's Press, Thomas Dunne Books, 2004), p. 518.

161 Seoul provided $200 million: Deok Ryong Yoon, interview by author, Seoul, April 30, 2004.

161 aid has generally gone up: For a detailed estimate of Seoul's aid to Pyongyang, see Mark E. Manyin, "Foreign Assistance to North Korea," May 26, 2005 (Congressional Research Service Report for Congress).

161 $942 million: See "Hyundai to Invest $397 Mil. in Mt. Kumgang," *Korea Times* (Seoul), January 15, 1999, http://search.hankooki.com/times_view .php?terms=Mt.+Kumgang+code%3A+kt&path=hankooki2%2F14 _3%2F199901%2Ft4351190.htm&kw+mt.%20Kumgang.

162 sum for the summit: Kim Dae Jung admitted that $100 million went to the North in connection with the summit. Kim also admitted to $500 million in illegal transfers. "Repeat&Correct: Convictions Upheld in Inter-Korean Scandal," Dow Jones Newswires, November 28, 2003. Some speculate that such payments in fact total as much as $1 billion. See Lee Dong-bok, "Sunset for Kim Dae Jung," *Asian Wall Street Journal* (Hong Kong), February 13, 2003, p. A7.

162 thought to have been included: See Barbara Demick, "8 Indicted in South Korea Probe," *Los Angeles Times*, June 26, 2003, p. A3. The facts may never

be revealed because in 2003 the head of Hyundai Asan, Chung Mong Hun, either was murdered or, much less probably, committed suicide.

162 eventually scaled back: Anthony Faiola, "A Crack in the Door in N. Korea," *Washington Post*, November 24, 2003, p. A10. In 2001 Hyundai Asan had defaulted on its payments to North Korea. See Yoo Cheong-mo, "Hyundai Merchant Marine Set to Quit Money-Losing N.K. Tourism Business," *Korea Herald* (Seoul), May 1, 2001, http://www.nexis.com/.

162 provided cash subsidies: See Park Chan-Kyong, "Cross-Border Tour to North Korea Endangered by Nuclear Crisis," Agence France-Presse, January 4, 2004.

162 crude oil: See, e.g., Michael Richardson, "China—North Korea's Wary Protector," *South China Morning Post* (Hong Kong), January 16, 2004, p. A13.

162 almost half its food: See Elaine Kurtenbach, "Nuke Negotiators Try to Avoid '94 Repeat," Associated Press, February 28, 2004.

162 No one, however, expects: North Korea's accumulated trade deficit with China is a good measure of aid. Nicholas Eberstadt, "The Persistence of North Korea," *Policy Review*, October/November 2004, p. 23.

162 "If those people die": Bruce W. Nelan, "The Politics of Famine," *Time*, August 25, 1997, p. 50.

162 "It is morally wrong": Kathi Zellweger, "The Humanitarian Situation in North Korea and the Caritas Engagement" (paper, Lingnan University, Hong Kong, April 23, 2004).

163 "Food, medicine": Norbert Vollertsen, interview by author, Seoul, May 7, 2004.

163 in a more favorable light: Eunju, the North Korean defector, notes that the authorities in North Korea said that food that came from abroad was from China and "came in because we are strong." Eunju, interview.

164 virtual monopoly: See Andrei Lankov, "North Korea's Antique Food Rationing," Asia Times Online, January 15, 2005, http://www.atimes .com/atimes/Korea/GA15Dg01.html.

164 is trying to reassert: See Scott Snyder, "Lessons of the NGO Experience in North Korea," in *Paved with Good Intentions*, pp. 111–22.

164 "The purpose of humanitarian aid": Fiona Terry, "The Deadly Secrets of North Korea," Doctors Without Borders, August 2001, http://www .doctorswithoutborders.org/publications/other/deadly_2001.shtml.

164 "morally repugnant": "A Dialogue with Evil," editorial, *Washington Post*, January 9, 2003, p. A24.

164 "As we entered": Lynne O'Donnell, e-mails to author, January 30, 2004, February 3, 2004, and February 25, 2004. North Korea used to repackage

aid from the United States so that the populace would not know its origin, but the government stopped that practice at the end of the 1990s. Erica Kang, interview.

164   they're afraid: The World Food Programme has even gone so far as to defend North Korea from charges of misuse of aid. See, e.g., Cho Mee-young and Jack Kim, "North Korea Sells Food Aid on Local Market—South," Reuters, October 22, 2004. For a particularly egregious example of the World Food Programme turning a blind eye, see "UN Tells Japan N Korea Probably Didn't Divert Food Aid," Dow Jones Newswires, June 22, 2005.

165   "Anybody, a twelve-year-old": Tim Peters, interview by author, Seoul, May 7, 2004.

165   began distributing aid directly: See "Fertilizer to North Korea," Summer 2000, Events in the Tzu Chi World, http://taipei.tzuchi.org.tw/tzquart/ 2000su/qs18.htm.

165   reshipped to Africa: See Triplett, *Rogue State*, p. 142. The North has sold food aid. See Cho and Kim, "North Korea Sells Food Aid on Local Market—South."

165   thought she was Chinese: Kathi Zellweger, interview.

166   traveled inside: See Snyder, "Lessons of the NGO Experience in North Korea," pp. 111–22.

166   it didn't want: "N. Korea Declines U.N. Humanitarian Aid in 2005, Later," Kyodo News Service, August 14, 2004. Pyongyang was not serious because it accepted food from the United Nations in 2005, but in August of that year it informed the World Food Programme that it was putting the agency's activities in North Korea under review. One report, denied by the WFP, said that the regime had ordered the United Nations to stop food assistance and close its Pyongyang office. See "N.Korea Rejected Further UN Food Aid," *Chosun Ilbo* (Seoul), September 8, 2005, http://english.chosun.com/ w21data/html/news/200509/200509080015.html. In any event, the North Korean government may have taken a tougher line with the U.N. because China and South Korea were providing sufficient food and fertilizer with no or virtually no monitoring.

166   needed food: Joe McDonald, "U.N. Agencies Say Millions in North Korea Still Need Food Aid," Associated Press, November 23, 2004.

166   open the windows: Lin Chiou-Shan, interview by author, Taipei, October 31, 2003. Lin is a member of the Control Yuan, a branch of the Taiwan government.

166   "I have said publicly": Ibid.

166   Development assistance: In mid-2005 Pyongyang finally began to consider accepting development aid. See Jae-Soon Chang, "North Korea Says It

Prefers Development Assistance Over Emergency Food Aid," Associated Press, September 9, 2005.

166 "We want to find out": Stephanie Hoo, "China Expresses Support for U.S.–North Korea Dialogue," Associated Press, January 14, 2003.

167 another famine: See "New Famine Feared as Food Crisis Grips North Korea," Agence France-Presse, May 27, 2005. North Koreans have become increasingly desperate. See Alexa Olesen, "U.N.: N. Koreans Scavenging for Food," Associated Press, July 26, 2005.

Chapter 9: FLIRTING WITH UNSPEAKABLE EVIL

168 "No one has found": Stapleton Roy, interview by author, New York City, February 25, 2004.

169 "Why are we afraid": David Kang, "Why Are We Afraid of Engagement?" in Victor D. Cha and David C. Kang, *Nuclear North Korea: A Debate on Engagement Strategies*, pp. 101–27 (New York: Columbia University Press, 2003).

170 North Korean tanks: Sang-Hun Choe, "Ten Million South Koreans Live in Their Capital, Within Range of North Korean Artillery," Associated Press, March 5, 2003.

170 "red unification": Martin Nesirky, "U.S. Needs to Offer More to N.Korea— Security Report," Reuters, November 15, 2004.

170 will even bite a cat: See Ronald Brownstein, "For Wary U.S. and Asia, North Korea Is 'Land of Lousy Options,' " *Los Angeles Times*, November 10, 2003, p. A10.

170 "First we need": Jeong Se-hyun, "The Future of Inter-Korean Relations: The Current Standoff and Roadmap for Peace and Prosperity," address, Columbia Law School and Weatherhead East Asian Institute, New York City, September 29, 2003.

171 kitchenware: See Khang Hyun-sung, "Disunity Still Simmers, but Pots Hint at a Shinier Future," *South China Morning Post* (Hong Kong), December 16, 2004, p. A9.

171 "It's easy to prove": Stapleton Roy, interview.

171 John Patrick Diggins notes: John Patrick Diggins, "How Reagan Beat the Neocons," *New York Times*, June 11, 2004, p. A27.

171 "an unappeasable state": Nicholas Eberstadt, *The End of North Korea* (Washington, D.C.: AEI Press, 1999), p. 22.

172 "If they try to change": Eric Heginbotham, interview by author, Washington, D.C., November 19, 2003.

172   "theology": Charles K. Armstrong, "Apocalypse Postponed? Pyongyang, Inter-Korean Relations, and the Politics of Survival" (paper presented at conference on Inter-Korean Relations, Columbia University, May 2002).

172   "culture of hatred": Rick Chu, e-mail to author, December 1, 2003. Chu is the editor of the *Taipei Times*.

172   "single-hearted unity": "Rodong Sinmun on Kim Jong Il's Exploits in Party Building," Korean Central News Agency, October 2, 2003.

172   "These buttons": Emily Zhang, interview by Lydia Chang, Madison, New Jersey, October 11, 2003.

172   "The leader puts": Jianying Zha, "Saddam Hussein As Surrogate Dictator," *New York Times*, April 8, 2003, p. A23.

173   "all talented and good people": Philip Gourevitch, "Alone in the Dark," *New Yorker*, September 8, 2003, p. 54.

173   "Not everyone here": David Zweig, interview by author, Hong Kong, October 27, 2003.

173   "There is no greater subversive": Nicholas D. Kristof, "North Korea's Secret," *New York Times*, January 14, 2003, p. A27.

173   fresh notions: See Burt Herman, "Cautious Development Looms in North Korea," Associated Press, January 2, 2005. I have personally seen the transformation of employees working for foreign businesses in communist states. From 1996 to 1998 I spent substantial time working in the Shanghai branch of Citibank as outside counsel. During this period there was a noticeable change in the attitudes of local employees, even Communist Party members, as they learned international business practices.

173   the most effective weapon: See Nicholas D. Kristof, "The Tiananmen Victory," *New York Times*, June 2, 2004, p. A19.

173   will quickly figure out: See Bradley K. Martin, *Under the Loving Care of the Fatherly Leader: North Korea and the Kim Dynasty* (New York: St. Martin's Press, Thomas Dunne Books, 2004), p. 457.

173   Suppose Bush calls Kim's bluff: See Joe Klein, "Why Not Kill Dictators with Kindness?" *Time*, March 10, 2003, p. 21.

173   "North Korea wouldn't know": Charles Armstrong, interview by author, New York City, September 4, 2003.

174   "The principal difference": Charles Armstrong, e-mail to author, October 2, 2003.

174   "Pressure and isolation": Jay Solomon and David S. Cloud, "A Split with Seoul Complicates Crisis Over North Korea," *Wall Street Journal*, January 2, 2003, p. A1.

174 "My theory of the Cold War": Peter Robinson, " 'Morning Again in America,' " *Wall Street Journal,* June 7, 2004, p. A20.

174 "The cold war ended": Diggins, "How Reagan Beat the Neocons," p. A27.

174 "They say the world": Ronald Reagan, "A Time for Choosing," speech, San Francisco, October 27, 1964.

175 "I believe a president": *Ronald Reagan: A Legacy Remembered,* History Channel, June 5, 2004.

175 "If ideas are power": Mark Palmer, *Breaking the Real Axis of Evil: How to Oust the World's Last Dictators by 2025* (Lanham, Maryland: Rowman & Littlefield, 2003), p. 33.

175 "I jumped out of my chair": Susan B. Glasser, "Ambivalence in Former 'Evil Empire,' " *Washington Post,* June 7, 2004, p. A1.

175 might dampen: See Khang Hyun-sung, "US Push on Human Rights Divides Parties," *South China Morning Post* (Hong Kong), October 1, 2004, p. A8.

175 "In South Korea": Gourevitch, "Alone in the Dark," p. 54.

176 said not one word: Thomas Omestad, "Gulag Nation," *U.S. News & World Report,* June 23, 2003, p. 12.

176 weakens internal forces for change: See Michael Horowitz, "Callousness in Seoul," *Asian Wall Street Journal* (Hong Kong), January 30, 2003, p. A7.

176 "Even the best boxer": "Notable N Korea Defector Slams Anti-US Sentiment in South," Dow Jones Newswires, July 4, 2003.

176 "When a rich brother": Andrew Ward, "Shadow Across the Sunshine," *FT Magazine,* June 19, 2004, p. 14.

176 were nonetheless okay: See Doug Struck, "Alleged Payoff to North Tarnishes S. Korea's Kim," *Washington Post,* February 10, 2003, p. A12.

177 discourages North Korean refugees: Park Song-wu and Reuben Staines, "Seoul Closing Door on Mass Defections," *Korea Times* (Seoul), January 5, 2005, http://times.hankooki.com/lpage/nation/200501/ kt2005010417081510510.htm.

177 As Jimmy Carter: See James Brooke, "North Korean Standoff Poses 'Greatest Threat,' Carter Says," *New York Times,* September 6, 2003, p. A4.

177 hellhole: Some stories about torture in North Korea are so horrific that it is difficult to believe they are true. Nonetheless, it is clear by now that the state employs torture widely. Perhaps Mun Guk-hwan, the secretary general of the International Coalition for North Korean Human Rights, put it best: "North Korea is a place where mankind is obliterated." Chu Yong-Jung, "National Assembly's First North Korean Holocaust Exhibit Opens," *Chosun Ilbo* (Seoul), November 9, 2004, p. A6.

177 "Moral claims": Henry A. Kissinger, *A World Restored: Metternich, Castlereagh and the Problems of Peace, 1812–22* (Boston: Houghton Mifflin, 1957), p. 316.

178 "In Texas, we don't do nuance": George W. Bush, interview by Candy Crowley, *CNN Live Today*, CNN, April 25, 2001.

178 "inordinate fear of communism": Jimmy Carter, address, Notre Dame University, South Bend, Indiana, May 22, 1977.

178 "the opportunity": Brooke, "North Korean Standoff Poses 'Greatest Threat,' Carter Says," p. A4.

Chapter 10: THE END OF AMERICAN PRIMACY

179 "Not since Rome": Joseph S. Nye, "Ill-Suited for Empire," *Washington Post*, May 25, 2003, p. B7.

179 "America today": Charles Krauthammer, "Help Wanted," *Time*, September 1, 2003, p. 72.

180 world's economic colossus: See Paul Kennedy, *The Rise and Fall of the Great Powers: Economic Change and Military Conflict from 1500 to 2000* (New York: Random House, Vintage Books, 1989), p. 358.

180 much like Britain's preeminence: Ibid., p. 357.

181 "unipolar moment": Samuel P. Huntington, "The Lonely Superpower," *Foreign Affairs*, March/April 1999, p. 35.

181 the real winners: Paul Tsongas in 1992 famously said, "The Cold War is over. Japan won. Germany won."

181 "consensual": See G. John Ikenberry, "Illusions of Empire: Defining the New American Order," *Foreign Affairs*, March/April 2004, p. 144.

181 "Nearly all countries perceive": Banning Garrett, "The Strategic Straitjacket of Globalization," YaleGlobal Online, February 11, 2004, http://yaleglobal .yale.edu/display.article?id=3311&page=1.

182 the most powerful: See John J. Mearsheimer, *The Tragedy of Great Power Politics* (New York: W. W. Norton, 2001), pp. 2–3.

182 "Remember, with great power": *Spider-Man*, directed by Sam Raimi, Columbia Pictures, 2002.

182 "Why can't we": This famous question has been attributed to Rodney King, the motorist whose beating set the stage for the 1992 riots in Los Angeles.

183 "the evolution of": Francis Fukuyama, "History and September 11," in *Worlds in Collision: Terror and the Future of Global Order*, ed. Ken Booth and Tim Dunne, pp. 27–36 (Basingstoke, England: Palgrave Macmillan, 2002).

183   "end point": Francis Fukuyama, "The End of History?" *National Interest*, Summer 1989, p. 3.

183   only acceptable state: See Michael Mandelbaum, *The Ideas That Conquered the World: Peace, Democracy, and Free Markets in the Twenty-first Century* (New York: PublicAffairs, 2002), pp. 121–28. Spanish officials are even considering abolishing their government's power to declare war. See "No More . . . Bad Hair Days," editorial, *Wall Street Journal Europe* (Brussels), June 29, 2005, p. A6.

183   "The ideas that conquered": This phrase comes from the title of Mandelbaum's 2002 book.

183   Palmer identified: See Mark Palmer, *Breaking the Real Axis of Evil: How to Oust the World's Last Dictators by 2025* (Lanham, Maryland: Rowman & Littlefield, 2003), pp. 18–19.

184   "We stand tall": Madeleine Albright, interview by Matt Lauer, *Today*, NBC, February 19, 1998.

185   "sleepwalking through history": Haynes Johnson, *Sleepwalking Through History: America in the Reagan Years* (New York: W. W. Norton, 1991).

185   "holiday": Charles Krauthammer, "Holiday from History," *Washington Post*, February 14, 2003, p. A31.

185   "History knows": Henry Kissinger, *White House Years* (Boston: Little, Brown, 1979), p. 55.

185   "one damn fact": Jared Diamond, *Guns, Germs, and Steel: The Fates of Human Societies* (New York: W. W. Norton, 1999), p. 421.

185   seemingly inexorable march: See, e.g., Bill Emmott, *20:21 Vision: Twentieth-Century Lessons for the Twenty-first Century* (New York: Farrar, Straus and Giroux, 2003), p. 25.

185   "If globalization": Kenneth Rogoff, "A Development Nightmare," *Foreign Policy*, January/February 2004, p. 64.

186   Rogoff predicts: Ibid.

186   "first, only, and last": Zbigniew Brzezinski, *The Grand Chessboard: American Primacy and Its Geostrategic Imperatives* (New York: Basic Books, 1997), p. 215.

186   "In the long run": Ibid., p. 209.

186   "This new world": "French Defence Minister Defends Multipolarism," Agence France-Presse, July 1, 2003.

187   "The trend toward": Vladimir Isachenkov, "China, Russia Issue Multipolar World Call," Associated Press, May 28, 2003.

187   will end sometime early: See Huntington, "The Lonely Superpower."

187   two more decades: See, e.g., Frederick Kempe, " 'A New Wind' Out of Washington," *Wall Street Journal Europe* (Brussels), January 26, 2005, p. A8. See also Timothy Garton Ash, *Free World: America, Europe, and the Surprising Future of the West* (New York: Random House, 2004), p. 176.

187   "Americans, with their": Shintaro Ishihara, *The Japan That Can Say No*, trans. Frank Baldwin (New York: Simon & Schuster, 1991), p. 30.

187   "indispensable nation": Madeleine Albright with Bill Woodward, *Madam Secretary* (New York: Miramax Books, 2003), p. 506. The phrase originally comes from Bill Clinton's second inaugural address in 1997.

187   "No matter how compelling": Fareed Zakaria, "The Previous Superpower," review of A *History of Britain: The Fate of Empire, 1776–2000*, by Simon Schama, *New York Times Book Review*, July 27, 2003, p. 11.

187   held great appeal: See Thomas L. Friedman, *The Lexus and the Olive Tree* (New York: Anchor Books, 2000), pp. 464–65; and Samuel P. Huntington, *The Clash of Civilizations and the Remaking of World Order* (London: Simon & Schuster, Touchstone Books, 1998), p. 92.

187   Change is inevitable: Huntington, *The Clash of Civilizations*, p. 31.

188   another set of organizing principles: America has its free market "Washington Consensus," but China has countered with a "Beijing Consensus." See " 'Beijing Consensus,' a China Model," *People's Daily* (Beijing), May 26, 2004, http://english.people.com.cn/200405/26/eng20040526_144393 .html.

188   "People here are talking": Jane Perlez, "Chinese Move to Eclipse U.S. Appeal in South Asia," *New York Times*, November 18, 2004, p. A1.

188   would have been okay: "Report: Singapore's Elder Statesman Says China Wouldn't Have Been as Successful if Tiananmen Protestors Had Been Victorious," Associated Press, August 16, 2004.

Chapter 11: CIVILIZATION'S LAST WEAPON

189   "The civilized world": Colin L. Powell, "A Strategy of Partnerships," *Foreign Affairs*, January/February 2004, p. 22.

190   "Where nuclear weapons threaten": Kenneth N. Waltz, "More May Be Better," in Scott D. Sagan and Kenneth N. Waltz, *The Spread of Nuclear Weapons: A Debate Renewed*, pp. 3–45 (New York: W. W. Norton, 2003).

190   gradual spread: Ibid.

191   "Rulers want": Ibid.

192   "You love life": Josef Joffe, "The Meaning of Spain," *Time*, March 29, 2004, p. 31.

192 "We have the right": There are various formulations of this quotation. The earliest English-language version appears in *Special Dispatch*, Middle East Media Research Institute, June 12, 2002, http://memri.org/bin/articles .cgi?Page=archives&Area=sd&ID=SP38802.

192 "world's 10th nuclear power": Sam Nunn and Michele Flournoy, "A Test of Leadership on Sea Island," *Washington Post*, June 8, 2004, p. A23.

192 met with al-Qaeda representatives: One of the scientists is reported to have met bin Laden himself. See, e.g., Kathy Gannon, "Bin Laden and the Pakistani Scientist: Al-Qaida Leader Said to Have Sought Help on Nuclear Bomb," Associated Press, December 29, 2002.

192 has tried to buy: Nicholas D. Kristof, "An American Hiroshima," *New York Times*, August 11, 2004, p. A19.

192 suitcase nuclear weapons: See, e.g., "Al-Qaida's No. 2 Claims to Have Nukes," Associated Press, March 21, 2004. Both Russia and Ukraine predictably denied the story, but former Russian national security adviser Alexander Lebed said as many as one hundred suitcase-sized bombs went missing after the fall of the Soviet Union. Alexander Lebed, interview by Steve Kroft, "The Perfect Terrorist Weapon," *60 Minutes*, CBS, September 7, 1997. In 2002 Ukraine Communist Party leader Petro Symonenko maintained that in 1992 Russia took possession of only 2,200 of 2,400 nuclear devices and that the remaining 200 weapons are missing. Taras Kuzio, "Loose Nukes and al-Qaeda," Terrorism Monitor, March 25, 2004, http://www.jamestown.org/terrorism/news/article.php?articleid=23647.

192 American intelligence thinks: "Al-Qaida's No. 2 Claims to Have Nukes." Israeli intelligence thinks that Osama bin Laden paid more than £2 million to a Kazakhstan broker for a stolen nuclear warhead but may not have actually obtained it. Barton Gellman and Dafna Linzer, "Unprecedented Peril Forces Tough Calls," *Washington Post*, October 26, 2004, p. A1.

192 "American Hiroshima": Kristof, "An American Hiroshima," p. A19.

193 Apocalypse was approaching: "Red Army Man Who Kept Calm and Saved the World," *Daily Mail* (London), September 24, 1998, p. 14.

193 "I was drenched": Tom Parfitt, "No Hollywood Ending for the Man Who Saved the World," *South China Morning Post* (Hong Kong), July 24, 2004, p. A14.

193 "a funny feeling": David Hoffman, " 'I Had a Funny Feeling in My Gut,' " *Washington Post*, February 10, 1999, p. A19.

193 closest that the world: See Parfitt, "No Hollywood Ending for the Man Who Saved the World," p. A14.

193 a snafu in Moscow: Tim Zimmermann, "Take Nuclear Arsenals Off Hair-Trigger Alert," *U.S. News & World Report*, December 29, 1997, p. 71.

194 dropped a tool: See Art Harris and George C. Wilson, "Blast Kills 1, Injures 21 at Missile Silo," *Washington Post*, September 20, 1980, p. A1. For more on these American mistakes, see Anna Libak, "Nuclear War: Minuteman," Weekendavisen, April 2, 2004, http://www.brightstarsound.com/world_hero/ weekendavisen.html; and Scott D. Sagan, "More Will Be Worse," in Sagan and Waltz, *The Spread of Nuclear Weapons*, pp. 46–87.

194 "imperfect humans": Scott D. Sagan and Kenneth N. Waltz, "Indian and Pakistani Nuclear Weapons: For Better or Worse?" in Sagan and Waltz, *The Spread of Nuclear Weapons*, pp. 88–124.

194 vulnerable to false signals: See Parfitt, "No Hollywood Ending for the Man Who Saved the World," p. A14.

194 have become undependable: See Peter Baker, "Russian Missile Launch Flops," *Washington Post*, February 18, 2004, p. A14; and "Russian Missile Self-Destructs After Launch," Reuters, February 18, 2004.

194 "We escaped disaster": James Carroll, "War Inside the Pentagon," *New Yorker*, August 18, 1997, p. 52.

194 "We know": See Kenneth N. Waltz, "Waltz Responds to Sagan," in Sagan and Waltz, *The Spread of Nuclear Weapons*, pp. 125–55.

194 "gizmos of mass destruction": Laura Miller, "Smiley's People," review of *The Great Game: The Myth and Reality of Espionage*, by Frederick P. Hitz, *New York Times Book Review*, June 6, 2004, p. 39.

195 Some suggest: See, e.g., Kenneth M. Pollack, *The Threatening Storm: The Case for Invading Iraq* (New York: Random House, 2002), p. 187.

195 "Don't fight the United States": Samuel P. Huntington, *The Clash of Civilizations and the Remaking of World Order* (London: Simon & Schuster, Touchstone Books, 1998), p. 187.

195 twenty nuclear states: Kennedy said this during the third presidential debate in 1960. As president, he changed his assessment to twenty-five nuclear states by the end of the 1970s. See President John F. Kennedy, Press Conference, Washington, D.C., March 21, 1963.

196 "the supreme test": James Traub, "The Netherworld of Nonproliferation," *New York Times Magazine*, June 13, 2004, p. 49.

196 "second nuclear age": Paul Bracken, "The Second Nuclear Age," *Foreign Affairs*, January/February 2000, p. 146.

196 "No country without": "The Thoughts of Charles De Gaulle," *New York Times Magazine*, May 12, 1968, p. 102.

196 ultimate badge: See Gareth Evans, interview by Nayan Chanda, YaleGlobal Online, September 26, 2003, http://yaleglobal.yale.edu/ about/evans.jsp.

196   "the Age of Proliferation": Steve Weissman and Herbert Krosney, *The Islamic Bomb: The Nuclear Threat to Israel and the Middle East* (New York: Times Books, 1981), p. 129.

197   not just about Iraq: David E. Sanger, "Viewing the War as a Lesson to the World," *New York Times*, April 6, 2003, p. B1.

197   "Iraq was the first 'counterproliferation' war": Bill Keller, "The Thinkable," *New York Times Magazine*, May 4, 2003, p. 48.

197   "We are hopeful": Carla Anne Robbins and Neil King Jr., "After War, America Must Decide What Kind of Power to Be," *Wall Street Journal*, April 10, 2003, p. A1.

197   "The West promotes": Huntington, *The Clash of Civilizations*, p. 191.

198   "The proliferation": Ibid., p. 192.

198   reductions of stockpiles: See Robert S. Norris and Hans M. Kristensen, "Russian Nuclear Forces, 2005," *Bulletin of the Atomic Scientists*, March/April 2005, p. 70; Robert S. Norris and Hans M. Kristensen, "U.S. Nuclear Forces, 2005," *Bulletin of the Atomic Scientists*, January/February 2005, p. 73; and Robert S. Norris and Hans M. Kristensen, "U.S. Nuclear Reductions," *Bulletin of the Atomic Scientists*, September/October 2004, p. 70.

198   only nation to vote against: See United Nations General Assembly Resolution 58/71, December 8, 2003. Despite withdrawing its support for the treaty, the United States has not detonated a nuclear device since 1992.

198   leading efforts to gut a treaty: The United States is trying to remove from the Fissile Materials Cut-Off Treaty provisions requiring inspections or verification. See Dafna Linzer, "U.S. Shifts Stance on Nuclear Treaty," *Washington Post*, July 31, 2004, p. A1.

199   lower the threshold: See, e.g., Theresa Hitchens, "Slipping Down the Nuclear Slope: Bush Administration Nuclear Policy Lowers Bar Against Usage" (address, Center for Defense Information, Washington, D.C., February 26, 2003). Of course, some analysts disagree. See, e.g., William J. Broad, "Facing a Second Nuclear Age," *New York Times*, Week in Review, August 3, 2003, p. 1. Nonetheless, the Pentagon's planning for countering rogue states with offensive strikes blurs the distinction between conventional and nuclear armaments. See William Arkin, "Not Just a Last Resort?" *Washington Post*, May 15, 2005, p. B1.

199   has threatened to use nukes: See Department of Defense, "Nuclear Posture Review," January 8, 2002. In September 2005 the Defense Department revealed a draft of its revised nuclear weapons doctrine, entitled "Doctrine for Joint Nuclear Operations." See "Pentagon Document Would Alter Nuclear Weapons Plan," Reuters, September 10, 2005.

199   America's 1995 global pledge: See Harold A. Feiveson, ed., *The Nuclear*

Turning Point: A Blueprint for Deep Cuts and De-alerting of Nuclear Weapons (Washington, D.C.: Brookings Institution Press, 1999), p. 34. The United States made similar pledges in 1978 and 1991. See C. S. Eliot Kang, "North Korea's Security Policy: Swords into Plowshares?" in *North Korea and Northeast Asia*, ed. Samuel S. Kim and Tai Hwan Lee, pp. 195–215 (Lanham, Maryland: Rowman & Littlefield, 2002); and George Bunn, "The Legal Status of U.S. Negative Security Assurances to Non-Nuclear Weapons States," *Nonproliferation Review*, Spring/Summer 1997, p. 1.

199   never much liked treaties: The Bush administration has rejected the test ban treaty, withdrawn from the anti-ballistic-missile treaty, and is trying to undermine a fissile materials treaty by objecting to verification. The administration in 2002 did sign the Treaty of Moscow. Pursuant to this agreement, both the United States and Russia will reduce operationally deployed strategic nuclear weapons to 2,200 by the last day of 2012. Neither country agreed to destroy any such weapon, however, or permit verification. The treaty, such as it is, will no longer be in force on January 1, 2013.

199   is intent on shedding: See Ivo H. Daalder and James M. Lindsay, *America Unbound: The Bush Revolution in Foreign Policy* (Washington, D.C.: Brookings Institution Press, 2003), p. 13.

199   too many complaints: The failure of the U.N.'s 2005 NPT Review Conference indicates that the have-nots are not happy with the discriminatory nature of the global arms-control regime. See, e.g., Louis Charbonneau, "Nuclear Arms Conference Collapses Without Deal," Reuters, May 27, 2005.

199   "a local technology": William J. Kole, "European Powers to Offer Iran Incentives," Associated Press, October 20, 2004.

199   within a few years' time: See George Jahn, "U.N. Official: 40 Nations Can Make Nukes," Associated Press, September 20, 2004.

199   have escaped punishment: Failing to impose meaningful punishment set a terrible precedent, but rewarding the new nuclear states for bad behavior was even worse. See William J. Broad and David E. Sanger, "As Nuclear Secrets Emerge, More Are Suspected," *New York Times*, December 26, 2004, p. 1.

200   nuclear tipping point: See Mitchell B. Reiss, "The Nuclear Tipping Point: Prospects for a World of Many Nuclear Weapons States," in *The Nuclear Tipping Point: Why States Reconsider Their Nuclear Choices*, ed. Kurt M. Campbell, Robert J. Einhorn, and Mitchell B. Reiss, pp. 3–17 (Washington, D.C.: Brookings Institution Press, 2004). The Bush administration says its efforts to develop new nuclear weapons do not affect what other nations say or do and so denies the charge that it is moving the world to a tipping point. See Walter Pincus, "$27 Million Sought for Nuclear Arms Study," *Washington Post*, March 20, 2004, p. A4.

200   "in a hail of fiery atoms": This phrase is from his famous Westminster speech of June 8, 1982.

200   the wolf does: See Madeleine Albright with Bill Woodward, *Madam Secretary* (New York: Miramax Books, 2003), p. 323.

200   Syria: See George Jahn, "More Than 20 Firms Supplied Nuclear Arms," Associated Press, July 9, 2004. Syria may even be operating centrifuges. John Loftus, interview by Gregg Jarrett, "Fox Files," *Fox News Live Sunday*, Fox News Channel, December 12, 2004.

200   Egypt: See George Jahn, "IAEA Finds Egypt Secret Nuclear Program," Associated Press, January 4, 2005.

200   Saudi Arabia: Saudi Arabia has probably financed nuclear weapons research in various Islamic countries. See Gopalaswami Parthasarathy, "Pakistan Plays Nuclear Footsie; Does Anyone Care?" *Wall Street Journal*, January 2, 2004, p. A8. Furthermore, Saudi Arabia has wanted to lease nuclear weapons from China or Pakistan. Henry Sokolski, "Iran on the Brink," YaleGlobal Online, September 22, 2004, http://yaleglobal.yale.edu/ display.article?id=4557.

200   Algeria: Algeria has raised suspicions by covertly building a large research reactor at Ain Oussera and then protecting it with air defense missiles. See Henry Sokolski, "The Qaddafi Precedent," *Weekly Standard*, January 26, 2004, p. 12. For additional information on Algeria's program, see David Albright and Corey Hinderstein, "Algeria: Big Deal in the Desert?" *Bulletin of the Atomic Scientists*, May/June 2001, p. 45.

200   South Korea: In 2004 South Korea admitted enriching uranium and extracting plutonium—violations of the NPT—after the IAEA started asking pointed questions. Its uranium-enrichment experiments have only military applications. See Sang-Hun Choe, "South Korea Extracted Plutonium in 1982," Associated Press, September 9, 2004; Jack Kim and Louis Charbonneau, "S.Korea Says It Has No Nuclear Weapons Plans," Reuters, September 3, 2004; and David E. Sanger and William J. Broad, "South Korea Says Secret Program Refined Uranium," *New York Times*, September 3, 2004, p. A1.

200   Brazil: Brazil, which once maintained secret nuclear weapons programs, has a history of resisting IAEA inspections of its enrichment facilities and exerts its right from time to time to possess the ultimate weapon. See Mike Esterl, "U.S.-Latin American Relations Hit Heavy Turbulence," Dow Jones Newswires, January 13, 2003.

201   nuclear facility in Natanz: Natanz contains a huge underground facility, which was built to enrich uranium. See, e.g., Carla Anne Robbins, "As Evidence Grows of Iran's Program, U.S. Hits Quandary," *Wall Street Journal*, March 18, 2005, p. A1. Inspectors found traces of uranium enriched to 90 percent purity—bomb grade—at this previously secret location. Craig S.

Smith, "Iran Postpones a Visit by U.N. Nuclear Inspectors Until April," *New York Times*, March 13, 2004, p. A3.

201   found to be contaminated: See Louis Charbonneau, "More Bomb-Grade Uranium Found in Iran—Diplomats," Reuters, April 2, 2004.

201   previous assertions: See, e.g., Carla Anne Robbins, "An Atomic Bargain Hampers the Hunt for Illicit Weapons," *Wall Street Journal*, April 8, 2004, p. A1.

201   professed not to know: See George Jahn, "Iran Turns Over Documents It Says Fully Explain Its Nuclear Program," Associated Press, October 23, 2003.

201   too large for conducting research: William J. Broad and Elaine Sciolino, "Iranians Retain Plutonium Plan in Nuclear Deal," *New York Times*, November 25, 2004, p. A1.

201   not suited for conventional warheads: Iranian specifications for its warheads are almost certainly nuclear weapons. Robbins, "As Evidence Grows of Iran's Program, U.S. Hits Quandary," p. A1.

201   hid whole facilities: Iran hid its massive enrichment facility at Natanz and a heavy water plant at Arak, but it may have hundreds of other sites as well, some of them intended to serve as decoys. See Louis Charbonneau, "Diplomats: New Data Suggests Secret Iran Atomic Plan," Reuters, March 31, 2004; and "Exiles: Iran Fooled U.N. Inspectors with Decoy Site," Reuters, November 19, 2003.

201   to obtain all the technology: George Jahn, "Iran Said to Acquire Knowledge on Weapons," Associated Press, February 26, 2005.

201   when it became clear: Iran has not only lied about its nuclear program, it has lied about lying. See, e.g., "Iran Dials Back Nuclear Declaration," Reuters, March 8, 2004.

201   no alternative: See Louis Charbonneau and Francois Murphy, "U.S. Says Iran Deceiving UN Over Nuclear Work," Reuters, June 16, 2005; and David E. Sanger, "In Face of Report, Iran Acknowledges Buying Nuclear Components," *New York Times*, February 23, 2004, p. A11.

201   not commercially justifiable: Iran admitted the lack of commercial justification in negotiations with Britain, France, and Germany. Tehran had no choice but to make the admission: it is seeking to enrich uranium for nuclear power plants it does not possess and is not now building. See Leonard S. Spector, "How to Be Weapon-Ready NPT Members," Yale-Global Online, August 16, 2005, http://yaleglobal.yale.edu/display.article?id=6153.

201   turned down Europe's offer: See Ali Akbar Dareini, "Iran Rejects Demand on Nuclear Reactor," Associated Press, February 13, 2005. Europe's offer to provide the light water reactors was on terms extremely favorable to Tehran.

201   claims the right: See Karl Vick, "Iranians Assert Right to Nuclear Weapons," *Washington Post*, March 11, 2003, p. A16.

201   only one explanation: There is evidence of procurement of dual-use items, procurement patterns that are not consistent with official explanations, military involvement in supposedly civilian energy programs, and suspicious behavior. One unnamed diplomat put it best: "Usually the IAEA doesn't judge intentions but perhaps in this case it should." Louis Charbonneau, "U.N.: Iran Must Be More Open on Atomic Program," Reuters, February 28, 2005.

201   until 2015: See Dafna Linzer, "Iran Is Judged 10 Years from Nuclear Bomb," *Washington Post*, August 2, 2005, p. A1.

201   as early as 2007 or 2008: See Louis Charbonneau, "Diplomats: Iran Not Yet Capable of Building Nuke Bomb," Reuters, March 1, 2005. See also George Jahn, "Experts: Iran Able to Make Nuclear Bomb," Associated Press, September 11, 2004. There are persistent rumors that Tehran has either bought or is in the market for a nuclear weapon. See, e.g., Kerstin Gehmlich, "Exiles: Iran Seeks to Obtain Nuclear Warheads," Reuters, March 31, 2005.

201   their centrifuges come apart: John Loftus, e-mail to author, June 6, 2005.

202   in days or weeks: The critical issue is not whether a nation has the bomb but how long it will be before it no longer needs outside help. Iran, by all accounts, does not need much time for that purpose and is close to the point when it will acquire "surge capacity," the ability to build a nuclear arsenal in a short period. In short, Iran is close to possessing a "virtual bomb."

202   India and Pakistan: India had the bomb at least as early as 1974, and Pakistan has had the capability to build one since the late 1980s. Both countries tested their nuclear weapons in 1998.

202   "couple turns of the screw": Gordon Fairclough, "Nuclear Testing Triggers Calls for More Control," *Wall Street Journal*, September 16, 2004, p. A15.

202   In early 2004 he proposed: See "President Announces New Measures to Counter the Threat of WMD," remarks by George W. Bush, National Defense University, Washington, D.C., February 11, 2004. In a sign that the president was not serious about his initiative, the White House did not consult IAEA head Mohamed ElBaradei about the speech and informed him of the contents just a few hours beforehand.

202   offered them essentially nothing: The Bush administration, in trying to create a new arms control regime, may end up weakening the global nonproliferation treaty. See "Iran Criticizes Proposed UN Limits on Nuclear Tech Access," Dow Jones Newswires, April 7, 2005.

202   slightly more generous plan: See Mohamed ElBaradei, "Saving Ourselves from Self-Destruction," *New York Times*, February 12, 2004, p. A37.

202 a dead-on-arrival idea: Bush's approach, like ElBaradei's, is not especially attractive to states without enrichment and reprocessing capabilities. See, e.g., David E. Sanger, "Reshaping Nuclear Rules," *New York Times*, March 15, 2005, p. A1.

202 the struggle to end: See Bracken, "The Second Nuclear Age," p. 146.

203 "We have a strategy": *Special Dispatch*, Middle East Media Research Institute, May 28, 2004, http://memri.org/bin/articles.cgi?Page=archives&Area=sd&ID=SP72304.

203 "How will Washington": See Henry Sokolski, "Axis of Proliferation," *Wall Street Journal*, August 19, 2003, p. A8. Iran is already taking lessons from North Korea. There are reports that Iranians traveled to North Korea three times in 2003 to learn how to handle the IAEA's nuclear weapons inspectors. See "Iranian Nuclear Experts' Visits to North Korea," *Sankei Shimbun* (Tokyo), June 11, 2003, p. 1.

204 "What is the problem": Nazila Fathi, "Iran Cleric Suggests Nation Quit Nuclear Nonproliferation Treaty," *New York Times*, September 20, 2003, p. A2. Since this statement, Iran has threatened on several occasions to withdraw from the NPT and, contrary to earlier promises, to not follow the Additional Protocol on inspections.

204 " 'domino theory' ": George Tenet, testimony to the Senate Select Committee on Intelligence, *Current and Projected National Security Threats to the United States*, February 11, 2003.

Chapter 12: LAST EXIT BEFORE THE DARK AGES

205 "I believe there is no": "U.S. Still Keen for North Korea Talks, Energy Aid," *South China Morning Post* (Hong Kong), January 13, 2003, http://www.scmp.com/.

205 "If both sides are genuine": Madeleine Albright with Bill Woodward, *Madam Secretary* (New York: Miramax Books, 2003), p. 463.

207 "disarmament talks": Jon Herskovitz and Jack Kim, "Report: North Korea Wants Comprehensive Arms Talks," Reuters, March 31, 2005. Moreover, during the fourth round of the six-party talks, held in the middle of 2005, North Korean negotiators complained about America's nuclear threat to the DPRK. They at first wanted the removal of American nuclear weapons from South Korea (Washington says it no longer has nukes there). Next, they wanted American nuclear weapons out of Japan. Because American warheads based in, say, South Dakota, threaten North Korea, Pyongyang is laying the groundwork for arguing that the United States should also disarm.

207 saying it is unfair: See, e.g., "U.S. Moves to Develop Smaller Nukes Assailed," Korean Central News Agency, December 20, 2003.

207   appear much more determined: North Korea, for example, rejects Washington's suggestion that it follow the Libyan model of disarmament. See Khang Hyun-sung, "North Korea Rejects Libya Model in Nuclear Row," *South China Morning Post* (Hong Kong), January 21, 2005, p. A12.

207   continual waging of war: See Henry Kissinger, "The War Option," *San Diego Union Tribune*, August 11, 2002, p. G1.

208   "We are in a race": Paul Ames, "Simulation Gives Glimpse of Nuke Terror," Associated Press, May 4, 2004.

208   Oft-heard suggestions: In April 2004, the United Nations Security Council unanimously adopted Resolution 1540 requiring all 191 member states to criminalize nuclear proliferation by passing laws intended to keep weapons of mass destruction from terrorists and black market operators. The resolution was an important step forward, but China essentially gutted the measure before passage. See William R. Hawkins, "Chinese Realpolitik and the Proliferation Security Initiative," China Brief, February 1, 2005, http://www.jamestown.org/publications_details.php?volume_id=408&issue_id=3217&article_id=2369183. The Bush administration has, to its credit, placed great emphasis on using law-enforcement tools to attack global black market rings. See, e.g., White House Office of the Press Secretary, "Executive Order: Blocking Property of Weapons of Mass Destruction Proliferators and Their Supporters," June 29, 2005.

208   "transformational diplomacy": Neil King Jr., "Rice Vows to Mend Alliances, Defends Bush's Policy in Iraq," *Wall Street Journal*, January 19, 2005, p. A4.

208   legitimacy and credibility: See Joseph S. Nye, "Selling America," Project Syndicate, January 2005, http://www.project-syndicate.org/commentary/nye17.

208   cannot repeal $E = mc^2$: "Doomsday Mission," *Centennial of Flight*, Discovery Wings Channel, September 24, 2003 (comments of William Perry).

209   just one bomb: A country does not even have to possess a proven capability to deter other nations. The prime example, of course, is North Korea.

209   even more powerful: The other nuclear powers would have their own reasons to support abolition. India, Israel, and China would increase their regional dominance by eliminating the power of weaker rivals. Russia and Pakistan, however, would have much to lose by denuclearization, and the United States and others would probably have to guarantee their borders and provide other benefits to convince them to give up their arsenals.

209   "A phenomenon noticeable": Barbara W. Tuchman, *The March of Folly: From Troy to Vietnam* (New York: Alfred A. Knopf, 1984), p. 4.

210   if America unilaterally scraps: Many analysts persuasively argue that countries do not directly take into account the size of the American nuclear arsenal in making decisions about whether to build nukes of their own. Their

primary consideration is their own security needs. North Korea, however, has already made that decision, and the task for Washington is obtaining the cooperation of other nations to roll back Pyongyang's nuclear weapons program. In any event, the Bush administration, using traditional tools, has failed so far to obtain sufficient assistance from other nations.

210 far larger than necessary: In 2004 the United States announced that it would reduce its arsenal of nuclear weapons by about half. The cuts go beyond its obligations contained in 2002's Treaty of Moscow, which does not require the destruction of any weapons. See Matthew L. Wald, "U.S. to Make Deep Cuts in Stockpile of A-Arms," *New York Times*, June 4, 2004, p. A17; and John J. Fialka, "U.S. Nuclear-Weapons Stockpile to Be Cut Nearly in Half by 2012," *Wall Street Journal*, June 4, 2004, p. A8.

210 ability to protect allies: America's "nuclear shield" for its nonnuclear allies has been widely credited with convincing many of them not to build nukes of their own. Nonetheless, the United States can still protect its allies with a smaller arsenal, especially if other nuclear powers reduce their stockpiles in a coordinated fashion.

210 1,536 Hiroshimas: Each boat could carry the destructive power of 2,304 Hiroshimas, but the number of warheads is limited by treaty obligations to Russia.

210 make Central America uninhabitable: *Submarine: Life on a Boomer*, Military Channel, April 20, 2005. Each missile on a boomer carries more explosive power, including the two atomic bombs dropped on Japan, than that detonated by all combatants in World War II. Each boomer has more explosive power than has been detonated in all human history and is the third most powerful country in the world by itself. Ibid.

210 "Now we are in a world": Nirmala George, "U.S. Should Resume Lead in Arms Control; Sign Treaty, Says Hans Blix," Associated Press, November 6, 2004.

210 "There are times": Nayan Chanda, "China's Mediation Backfires on North Korea," YaleGlobal Online, April 28, 2003, http://yaleglobal.yale.edu/display.article?id=1501.

211 At no time: Mohamed ElBaradei, interview, "A Nuclear War Is Drawing Closer," *Der Spiegel*, January 26, 2004, http://service.spiegel.de/cache/international/spiegel/0,1518,283229,00.html.

211 "We don't negotiate": Warren P. Strobel, "Vice President's Objections Blocked Planned North Korean Nuclear Talks," Knight Ridder, December 20, 2003.

211 gas chambers: Defectors have claimed that the DPRK conducts human experiments in a gas chamber. See, e.g., Peter Apps, "N.Korea Tests Weapons on People, Gases Inmates—BBC," Reuters, January 31, 2004. The reports remain unconfirmed and have been subject to much criticism.

212   acceptable for her to converse: "I do not think that dialogue is appeasement and that it is absolutely essential to talk to someone or a leader that you want something from. We talked to Stalin. We talked to Mao Zedong." "N. Korea Nuclear Row," *Your World Today*, narr. Lisa Rose Weaver, CNN International, January 16, 2003.

212   "Korea is the land of lousy options": Ronald Brownstein, "For Wary U.S. and Asia, North Korea Is 'Land of Lousy Options,' " *Los Angeles Times*, November 10, 2003, p. A10.

212   Chinese negotiators presented: Joseph Kahn and David E. Sanger, "U.S.-Korean Deal on Arms Leaves Key Points Open," *New York Times*, September 20, 2005, p. A1.

213   are not dullards: See Kongdan Oh and Ralph C. Hassig, "North Korea's Nuclear Politics," *Current History*, September 2004, p. 273.

213   "a form of assisted suicide": Michael O'Hanlon, "Think Bigger on North Korea," *Washington Post*, September 17, 2003, p. A27.

213   to avoid inspections: See, e.g., Victor Gilinsky and Henry Sokolski, "North Korea Is an International Problem," *Asian Wall Street Journal* (Hong Kong), January 15, 2003, p. A7.

214   should not threaten: It appears that Washington has already been threatening Beijing with proliferation. See, e.g., Walter Russell Mead, "Should Nukes Bloom in Asia?" Nautilus Institute Policy Forum Online, June 23, 2005, http://www.nautilus.org/fora/security/0552Mead.html.

215   on Washington's side: See David E. Sanger and William J. Broad, "U.S. Asking China to Increase Pressure on North Korea to End Its Nuclear Program," *New York Times*, February 9, 2005, p. A8.

215   "It's China's hope": Audra Ang, "N. Korea Nuke Talks May Continue in April," Associated Press, February 27, 2004.

215   "keep making the same mistakes": Albright, *Madam Secretary*, p. 472.

216   internally threatening: Kim Jong Il compromised when he agreed to the Agreed Framework, but he was carrying out his father's wishes at that time. It is not clear that *he* is willing to compromise today, especially because he has staked his regime on the military. See Jon Herskovitz, "North Korea Seeks Hefty Price for Giving Up Nukes," Reuters, February 27, 2005.

216   at a higher level: See Jim Hoagland, "Nearing a Nuclear Jungle," *Washington Post*, January 9, 2003, p. A25.

216   "As a former negotiator": Robert L. Gallucci, interview by Bernard Gwertzman, "Gallucci: Questions Remain on U.S. Nuclear Offer and North Korea's Ambiguous Response," Council on Foreign Relations, June 30, 2004, http://www.cfr.org/publication.php?id=7159.

216   "There will be no war": Vincent Yu, "North Korea Calls Off U.N. Meet-ing," Associated Press, March 26, 2003.

216   "Whenever peace": Henry A. Kissinger, *A World Restored: Metternich, Castlereagh and the Problems of Peace, 1812–22* (Boston: Houghton Mif-flin, 1957), p. 1.

217   even a significantly smaller one: U.S. Air Force officers express confidence that the death toll would not be as high as many fear. Analysts, often noting that Pyongyang can bombard the South with up to 500,000 artillery shells in the first hour of a war, focus on the damage that North Korea can inflict. See, e.g., Thomas Omestad, "Squeezing North Korea," *U.S. News & World Report*, June 23, 2003, p. 18. Yet these estimates do not take into account expected American and South Korean defensive measures. Most of North Korea's artillery is housed in caves, for example, and the Air Force believes it knows the location of virtually all of them and can seal them quickly. Moreover, both the United States and South Korea operate sophisticated radar, which can pinpoint enemy artillery positions and immediately direct counterbattery fire. Furthermore, North Korean forces are particularly vul-nerable to strikes from American warplanes, which could reach their targets in minutes due to Korea's small size and proximity to water. As a result, the United States could fly five times more missions in Korea than in Iraq with the same number of planes. Tom McInerney, interview by Tony Snow, *Weekend Live*, Fox News Channel, August 31, 2003.

217   American anti-missile systems: Japan is also cooperating with America in building a stronger missile shield. See "Japan, U.S. to Jointly Assess Missile Performance," Kyodo News Service, December 14, 2004. In late 2004 the U.S. Navy started to patrol the Sea of Japan, thereby providing the first ele-ment of Japan's missile shield. See Eric Talmadge, "U.S. Navy Ship to Keep Eye on N. Korea," Associated Press, October 1, 2004.

218   "the mission determines": Donald H. Rumsfeld, interview by Bob Schieffer, *Face the Nation*, CBS, September 24, 2001.

218   "one of the most immoral acts conceivable": Nicholas D. Kristof, " 'Empire of a Devil,' " *New York Times*, April 29, 2003, p. A29.

218   "If you fight a war": Donald Gregg, speech, "Threats and Opportunities on the Korean Peninsula," Korean Information Center, Washington, D.C., July 20, 1994.

218   begin making realistic assessments: America made the Sunshine Policy pos-sible by guaranteeing South Korea's security. Without that backstop, South Korean options vis-à-vis the North become limited. Chang-Gi Kim, inter-view by author, Seoul, May 3, 2004.

219   "the ultimate rogue": Gerhard Spoerl, Wieland Wagner, Georg Mascolo, and Erich Follath, "The Tyrant and the Bomb," *Der Spiegel*, February 14, 2005, http://service.spiegel.de/cache/international/spiegel/0,1518,341804,00.html.

219 "He really intends": Pauline Jelinek, "Defector Tells AP World Must
Oppose Kim," Associated Press, October 31, 2003.

219 "When your opponent": Charles L. Pritchard, "North Korean Nuclear
Brinkmanship: Testing the Nuclear Nonproliferation Regime" (paper pre-
sented at the Monterey Nonproliferation Strategy Group Conference,
Carmel, California, November 16, 2003).

219 "Well, I don't think": George W. Bush, interview by Elisabeth Bumiller and
David E. Sanger, "Excerpts of an Interview with President Bush," New York
Times, August 27, 2004, http://www.nytimes.com/2004/08/27/politics/
campaign/bush_excerpts.html.

219 "We have it in our power": Ronald Reagan, address, "Time to Recapture
Our Destiny," Republican National Convention, Detroit, Michigan, July
17, 1980. Reagan was quoting the American revolutionary Tom Paine.

Epilogue: *Plutonium Pâté*

221 "What North Korea wants": Ashton Carter, interview by Zain Verjee, Q&A,
CNN International, January 14, 2003.

221 officials privately talk: See, e.g., Doug Struck and Glenn Kessler, "Foes
Giving In to N. Korea's Nuclear Aims," Washington Post, March 5, 2003,
p. A1. The Bush administration disputes the reports. See "White House
Denies It's Resigned to a Nuclear N Korea," Dow Jones Newswires,
March 5, 2003.

222 "a better brand of dictators": Carol Giacomo, "Bush Administration Divide
Re-Emerges Over N. Korea," Reuters, November 10, 2004.

222 are not particularly good: America's relations with Pakistan prove that cooperating with a troubled regime on proliferation can be risky. For two
decades, American diplomacy, designed to quiet various foreign policy
crises, made things worse on proliferation matters. As a result, Washington
obtained immediate solutions for small problems at the expense of creating
potential catastrophes of global significance. Today, despite American
assurances, Pakistan is still an irresponsible nuclear power.

222 nuclear crisis is well managed: "S Korean Pres: Nuclear Issue Will Be
Resolved Peacefully," Dow Jones Newswires, November 3, 2004.

222 export strategic insecurity: Nicholas Eberstadt, "The Persistence of North
Korea," Policy Review, October/November 2004, p. 23.

222 "attack diplomacy": B. R. Myers, "Stranger than Fiction," New York Times,
Week in Review, February 13, 2005, p. 15.

222 institutionalize crisis: See Charles K. Armstrong, The North Korean Revolution, 1945–1950 (Ithaca: Cornell University Press, 2003), p. 225.

223   a trillion dollars: See Liz Sidoti, "U.S. Congress Weighs Money for Missile Defense Despite Series of Setbacks," Associated Press, April 4, 2005.

224   prevent North Korea from selling fissile material: The Bush administration has not formally set a "red line" for North Korea; in other words, it has not specifically said what conduct would trigger an American military response. It is often said that Washington has privately told Pyongyang that the sale of fissile material would cross the line, and there are a few public comments to this effect, especially from Colin Powell when he was secretary of state. Yet Powell also noted in late 2004 that there were no such red lines. See Colin L. Powell, interview by Mike Chinoy, Beijing, October 25, 2004, http://www.state.gov/secretary/former/powell/remarks/37366.htm.

224   Proliferation Security Initiative: President Bush's Proliferation Security Initiative scored a big success in fall 2003 when Americans, Germans, and Italians seized centrifuge parts on their way from the A. Q. Khan network to Libya. See, e.g., Carla Anne Robbins, "Cargo Seizure Fueled Libya Arms Shift," *Wall Street Journal*, December 31, 2003, p. A4. The United States leads a related effort called the Illicit Activities Initiative, which is intended to cut off North Korea's earnings from selling illegal drugs and counterfeiting currency and consumer products. See Jay Solomon and Gordon Fairclough, "North Korea's Counterfeit Goods Targeted," *Wall Street Journal*, June 1, 2005, p. A4.

224   drug runners smuggle: George F. Will, "Holocaust in a Suitcase," *Washington Post*, August 29, 2004, p. B7.

224   "Today, the modern era": Shintaro Ishihara, *The Japan That Can Say No*, trans. Frank Baldwin (New York: Simon & Schuster, 1991), p. 29.

224   "final century": Martin Rees, *Our Final Century: A Scientist's Warning: How Terror, Error, and Environmental Disaster Threaten Humankind's Future in This Century—on Earth and Beyond* (London: William Heinemann, 2003).

224   "some very different sort": David Von Drehle, "The Yikes Years," *Washington Post Magazine*, November 21, 2004, p. 16.

225   no longer functions: See Alan Crosby, "ElBaradei Sees No Military Link in Iran Atom Plans," Reuters, June 1, 2004.

225   emblematic of the challenges: See Leon V. Sigal, *Disarming Strangers: Nuclear Diplomacy with North Korea* (Princeton: Princeton University Press, 1998), p. 5.

INDEX

ABOUT THE AUTHOR

GORDON G. CHANG lived and worked in China and Hong Kong for almost two decades, most recently in Shanghai, as counsel to the American law firm Paul, Weiss. His writings on China and North Korea have appeared in *The New York Times*, *The Wall Street Journal*, the *Far Eastern Economic Review*, the *International Herald Tribune*, *The Weekly Standard*, and the *South China Morning Post*. He has spoken at Columbia, Cornell, Georgetown, Princeton, and other universities, and at the Heritage Foundation, the Cato Institute, RAND, the American Enterprise Institute, the Council on Foreign Relations, and other institutions. He has given briefings at the National Intelligence Council, the Central Intelligence Agency, the State Department, and the Pentagon. Chang has appeared before the U.S.-China Economic and Security Review Commission and has delivered to the commission a report on the future of China's economy. He has appeared on CNN, CNBC, and Bloomberg Television.

He has spoken in Beijing, Shanghai, Hong Kong, Seoul, Singapore, Tokyo, The Hague, Vancouver, and Taipei. He has served two terms as a trustee of Cornell University.

ABOUT THE TYPE

This book was set in Electra, a typeface designed for Linotype by W. A. Dwiggins, the renowned type designer (1880–1956). Electra is a fluid typeface, avoiding the contrasts of thick and thin strokes that are prevalent in most modern typefaces.